D1238686

Britain and Biological Warfare

Britain and Biological Warfare

Expert Advice and Science Policy, 1930–65

Brian Balmer
Senior Lecturer
Department of Science and Technology Studies
University College London

palgrave

First published 2001 by
PALGRAVE
Houndmills, Basingstoke, Hampshire RG21 6XS and
175 Fifth Avenue, New York, N. Y. 10010
Companies and representatives throughout the world

PALGRAVE is the new global academic imprint of
St. Martin's Press LLC Scholarly and Reference Division and
Palgrave Publishers Ltd (formerly Macmillan Press Ltd).

ISBN 0–333–75430–1

This book is printed on paper suitable for recycling and made from fully managed and sustained forest sources.

A catalogue record for this book is available from the British Library.

Library of Congress Cataloging-in-Publication Data
Balmer, Brian, 1965–
    Britain and biological warfare : expert advice and science policy, 1930–65 / Brian Balmer.
      p. cm.
    Includes bibliographical references and index.
    ISBN 0–333–75430–1
    1. Biological warfare—Great Britain. 2. Great Britain––Military policy. I. Title.
    UG447.8 .B324 2001
    358'.35'0941—dc21

2001021741

10   9   8   7   6   5   4   3   2   1
10 09 08 07 06 05 04 03 02 01

Printed and bound in Great Britain by
Antony Rowe Ltd, Chippenham, Wiltshire

Contents

List of Tables and Diagram   viii

Acknowledgements   ix

List of Abbreviations   x

1 **Biological Warfare and Scientific Expertise**   1
  What are biological weapons?   3
  Secrecy   5
  The politics of expertise   6
  Threat assessments and the sociology of risk   7
  Before biological warfare   8
  The invisible enemy   9

2 **Bacteriological Warfare as a Public Health Threat**   14
  The 'datum line' on biological warfare   16
  Formalizing advice   19
  Emergency response becomes the Public Health
     Laboratory Service   22
  Intelligence and bacteriological possibilities   25
  Secrecy   27
  Responding to different bacteriological warfares   28

3 **Hankey's 'Step Further'**   29
  Reorganization and policy revision   29
  Porton Down   36
  Gruinard Island   41
  Special Operations   42
  The American programme   46
  Ordering anthrax   47
  Bombs and committees   52
  The legacy of world war   53

4 **The Growth of Biological Warfare Research**   55
  Handing over   55
  Organizing biological warfare policy   59
  Biological warfare takes top priority   61
  Mass destruction   62
  Promises   65
  Offence or defence?   67

Imagining the threat   68
The place of civil defence   72
Recruitment   74
Biological weapons ascend   77

5 Project Red Admiral   **79**
Negotiating Red Admiral   79
Biological and atomic bombs   85
Tripartite collaboration and the biological bomb   87
Killing the bomb   89
Experimental Plant No. 2   91

6 Trials for Biological Warfare   **104**
Operation Harness   104
Operation Cauldron   110
Operation Hesperus   116
Virology   119
Return to the Bahamas: Operation Ozone   120
The last trial: Negation   124
Sea trials sink   125

7 The Drift of Biological Weapons Policy   **128**
Some doubts   128
Divergence and change   134
Directives   139
Further divergence from the United States   142
More atomic weapons   143
Defending biological warfare   147
Sabotage   151
Losing the BW Subcommittee   154

8 A New Threat   **157**
Abandoning offensive chemical warfare   158
New trials, new danger   159
Zinc cadmium sulphide   161
Strategic insignificance   162
Change and anxiety   167
More trials   170
From inert to living simulants   172
Large Area Concept, early warning, defence and renewed
    interest   175
Sea trials with simulants   179
Test tube   180
Surviving and redefining policy   182

9 **Making Threats** **184**

**Appendix 1   Organization of Advice on Biological
     Warfare (1947)** **188**

Outline Chronology 189

Notes 193

Bibliography 233

Index 238

List of Tables and Diagram

Box 4.1   Future directions for biological warfare research in
                the UK (1946)   62
Box 5.1   Top Secret Air Staff Requirement for a biological
                bomb (1946)   81
Appendix 1 Organization of Advice on Biological
                Warfare (1947)   188

Acknowledgements

There are a number of people I want to thank for their help and support in the writing of this book. Julian Perry Robinson at the University of Sussex deserves a particular mention for introducing me to the whole area of biological warfare, for his constant encouragement and detailed comments on previous drafts of the manuscript. Thanks also to Julian for his occasional reminders that a history of biological warfare might make some contribution to contemporary debates on arms control issues. Current and former staff in the Department of Science and Technology Studies at University College London – Joe Cain, Hasok Chang, Jane Gregory, Andrew Gregory, Rebecca Hurst, Steve Miller, Arthur Miller, Norma Morris, Piyo Rattansi, Chris Stokes and Jon Turney – have either commented on drafts or provided encouragement and intellectual stimulation. Beyond the department, this book has benefited directly from discussions with Jon Agar, Robert Bud, Gradon Carter, David Edgerton, Rob Evans, Philip Gummett, Anne Hardy, Melissa Hersh, Kathryn McLaughlin, Caitriona McLeish, Dean Sivell, Stephen Twigge, John Walker, Henrietta Wilson and Sally Wyatt. Thank you. Needless to say, any errors and disagreeable interpretations still in the book are my own and not the responsibility of any one mentioned here.

Michael Brown provided essential research assistance towards the closing stages of writing and his employment was generously supported by a grant from the British Academy. The work also benefited from the support of the Harvard–Sussex Program at the Science Policy Research Unit, University of Sussex. Sections of Chapters 7 and 8 were previously published as 'The Drift of Biological Weapons Policy, 1945–65' in the *Journal of Strategic Studies* 20 (4), 115–45. I am grateful to Frank Cass Publishers for their permission to reproduce sections of the paper in this monograph.

Dedicating a book on the grisly topic of germ warfare to anyone would not be fitting, so my parents and family – Leslie and Eileen Balmer, Kim and Peter Rowe, Richard Balmer and Louise Coole – will have to make do with a general thank you here for their support. And my good friends Kevin Hannigan, Mary Tighe and Helen Tighe will have to do likewise.

List of Abbreviations

BRAB	Biological Research Advisory Board
BW	biological warfare
CAMR	Centre for Applied Microbiology and Research
CBW	chemical and biological warfare
CDEE	Chemical Defence Experimental Establishment
CW	chemical warfare
DRPC	Defence Research Policy Committee
DRPS	Defence Research Policy Staff
FRS	Fellow of the Royal Society
ISSBW	Inter-Services Subcommittee on Biological Warfare
JIC	Joint Intelligence Committee
LAC	Large Area Concept
MOS	Ministry of Supply
MRC	Medical Research Council
MRD	Microbiological Research Department
MRE	Microbiological Research Establishment
N	anthrax (code name)
R&D	research and development
RAF	Royal Air Force
SAC	Scientific Advisory Council
SOE	Special Operations Executive
UK	United Kingdom
UN	United Nations
US	United States
USAF	United States Air Force
USSR	Union of Soviet Socialist Republics
VEE	Venezuelan equine encephalitis
X	Botulinum toxin (code name)

1
Biological Warfare and Scientific Expertise

> The doctor was still looking out of the window. Beyond it lay the tranquil radiance of a cool spring sky; inside the room a word was echoing still, the word 'plague'. A word that conjured up in the doctor's mind not only what science chose to put into it, but a whole series of fantastic possibilities. . . .
>
> Albert Camus, *The Plague*

> Chemical warfare, in its modern form, and Biological Warfare are untried weapons. It has yet to be proved to what extent they can be relied on and effectively used in twentieth century war. At the moment their efficacy is largely a matter of conjecture; this is especially so in the case of Biological Warfare. In these circumstances our only safe course is to assume that they are dangerous forms of warfare and make every effort to render attacks as ineffective as possible.[1]
>
> *Chiefs of Staff Report, 1952*

A history of germ warfare is a history of uncertainty and a sociology of secret fears. Compared with other weapons, disease has rarely been used in military combat and the 'fantastic possibilities' marked out by science and plagues remain elusive. Other weapons possess symbolic markers that signal their destructive capabilities. The mushroom cloud has become an icon of the horrors of nuclear weapons, the gas mask has assumed a similar role for the chemical weapons of the First World War.[2] In contrast, there is nothing much we can attach to biological warfare except by analogy with naturally occurring epidemics and plagues. At best, these connections are diffuse, a point exemplified by the doctor in Camus' novel *The Plague*. After diagnosing the first case of plague to strike his small town, the doctor contemplated the scale of the oncoming epidemic and was forced to admit that any casualties, any figure such as 10 000 dead, lay beyond his everyday experience. Such devastation was unimaginable. In vain, the doctor attempted to picture his fear, forcing himself to think of the audience from five large

1

cinemas lying dead in the local town square. But this scene was so conjectural and his imagined dead so anonymous that it merely reinforced his sense of dread.

The consequences of biological warfare are equally difficult to picture as the weapons have been much researched and little used. So, what practical advice have experts provided when faced with uncertainties about the nature or extent of threat? What aspects of their own work have they judged to be relevant and what have they dismissed as irrelevant? This book is about how scientists called upon by the British Government to provide advice on biological warfare attempted to cope with such challenges. It traces the history of biological warfare policy in Britain, and the role of expert advisors in shaping that policy.

The account covers a period from the 1930s, when the Government first sought formal advice from the scientific community on the threat of biological warfare, to the mid-1960s when the open literature closes. Much current concern about germ warfare focuses on the Middle East and also the threat of bioterrorism, so it is easy to ignore the largely untold history of biological weapons research and policy in the UK. Along with the US, Canada, France, Japan and the former Soviet Union, the British programme ranks as one of the most significant efforts, in scale and scope, to develop knowledge about biological warfare in the twentieth century.[3] The extreme secrecy surrounding the UK programme means that there have only been partial accounts published of Britain's involvement in germ warfare. What exists concentrates narrowly on activities at the Porton Down research establishment in Wiltshire.[4] There has been no attempt to relate this activity to the broad development of secret Government policy towards biological warfare in the context of the Second World War and Cold War.

Most of the sources in this account have only been released in the past few years and extremely little has been written about this material. In this opening chapter I want to provide some basics for navigating this history. In particular, to describe some of the diseases that feature later in the narrative and outline what social scientists have written about the nature of scientific expertise and the nature of risk. The historical narrative in the body of the book can be read as a straightforward description without recourse to these more theoretical sections, but I would argue that reading the history through the insights from recent academic literature provides a far more nuanced and thought-provoking account of how scientists played a key role in the development of biological warfare policy. What follows is a preliminary overview of the scope of biological warfare and descriptions of the main diseases that have been researched as potential weapons of war in the period covered in this history. I have written these descriptions from a contemporary scientific, rather than historical, perspective so that readers can orientate themselves around the repertoire of diseases mentioned in later chapters.[5]

What are biological weapons?

A working definition of biological warfare, or more colloquially germ warfare, is the deliberate use of disease to harm humans, other animals and plants. This broad definition highlights the main feature of this type of warfare, that it involves living organisms. These micro-organisms include bacteria, viruses and, to a lesser extent in biological warfare, fungi.[6] Although there are a vast number of species of these micro-organisms, it is only *pathogenic* organisms, those capable of causing disease, which are potential agents for biological warfare.[7] In contemporary discussions, non-living but potent chemical toxins extracted from living organisms also fall within the rubric of biological weapons. While this addition tends to blur the boundary around this class of weapons, in general the working definition helps to differentiate biological from chemical warfare.[8]

The military advantages that have, at various times, been attributed to biological weapons include their insidious nature and the small doses required.[9] Yet, even among the vast array of known pathogenic organisms, various military considerations limit the choice of possible agents. Their ease and safety of production, storage, handling and dissemination have all been taken into consideration at various times by researchers in biological warfare. While military scientists have attempted to exploit the deadly nature of some pathogens, they have also selected other diseases on the grounds of their severe incapacitating effects. The military appeal of such incapacitating agents might be their potential use in conditions where a high number of civilians were present. A different feature of pathogens, one that has played a significant role in the history of biological warfare research, is the degree to which they are readily transmissible between hosts. Whereas most popular depictions of germ warfare draw on images of outbreaks reaching epidemic and pandemic proportions, many agents selected by scientists for biological warfare research are far less contagious.

The 'classic' biological warfare agent is the bacterium *Bacillus anthracis*, responsible for the disease anthrax.[10] Although it infects mainly herbivores, sheep and cattle in particular, the bacteria can infect humans although it is rarely, if ever, passed between humans. The bacteria form extremely tough spores which enable them to survive outside of a host and contact with the skin, ingestion or inhalation can all result in different manifestations of anthrax.[11] All forms of the disease are dangerous, but when the spores reach the lungs the resultant pulmonary anthrax is almost invariably lethal. Breathing in large numbers of the bacterial spores results in an incubation period, which may be as short as a few days, before the disease manifests itself as an exhausting fever and cough. The victim may appear to recover over the next few days but as the bacteria multiply and exude toxins, they eventually enter the bloodstream resulting in septicaemia (blood poisoning), with death following within 24–36 hours.[12]

Another organism which came under scrutiny early in the British programme was the bacterium *Clostridium botulinum*, responsible for botulism food poisoning. The bacterium itself has been of less interest to researchers than the potent toxins it produces. Indeed, these botulinum toxins remain the most poisonous substances known to science. They fall into the class of neurotoxins, chemicals which block the transmission of nerve impulses to muscles. When this interruption happens, botulinum poisoning progresses rapidly to paralysis, respiratory failure and death.

Continuing the litany of possible agents, Black Death or bubonic plague is strongly associated in popular imagination with widespread epidemic destruction.[13] The bacterium responsible for the disease, *Yersinia pestis*, prior to 1970 dubbed *Pasteurella pestis*, is transmitted from rodents to humans via fleas. It is also passed from rodents to humans, and between humans, in respiratory droplets. While bubonic plague, with its associated fever and dark swollen lymph nodes, is the commonest form of the disease, a biological warfare attack would more likely target the lungs and result in cases of pneumonic plague. In such cases, the bacteria incubate for two or three days before victims begin to suffer from fever and start coughing up bloody sputum. Without treatment, this form of plague is nearly always fatal.

I mentioned earlier that widespread fatalities may not be the only aim of a putative germ warfare attack and some diseases have featured in biological warfare research programmes on the grounds that they rarely kill their host. Brucellosis is a prime example. It normally infects domestic animals but can be passed to humans. The bacteria responsible for brucellosis in humans are *Brucella melitensis* which generally infect goats, *B. suis* usually infect pigs, *B. abortus* tends to be a disease of cattle, while *B. canis* generally infect dogs. In humans, the disease is severely incapacitating, inducing a whole gamut of non-specific symptoms but marked by severe bouts of so-called undulant fever which can reoccur for periods of about a month. Another potential incapacitant researched in the British biological warfare programme was the bacterium *Francisella tularensis* (previously dubbed *Bacterium tularense*). This micro-organism is responsible for tularemia, a disease that usually manifests itself as a severe fever lasting up to a month and with debilitating effects persisting for several more months. For the early biological warfare investigators these diseases offered the potential to immobilize but not kill an enemy.

These are not the only diseases to have attracted attention from scientists who advised on or were engaged in biological warfare research. In 1971, the Stockholm Institute for Peace Research listed 48 anti-personnel, anti-animal and anti-plant agents that had been researched in various countries as potential biological warfare agents.[14] Some of these were relatively minor historical players compared with the diseases and bacteria described here, all of which featured heavily in the early British research programme. The macabre nature of the diseases under consideration coupled with the military intentions of the research ensured that much of the work was performed under strict secrecy. Documents dealing with biological warfare research and policy were frequently classified as 'top secret' and this has affected their release into the public domain and the availability of an oral history.[15] In this context, it is worth saying a little more about the nature of these sources and how I have treated them.

Secrecy

The most detailed sources for narrating a history of British germ warfare are the minutes and documents of the various secret Government committees concerned with defence policy and research. A large number, but by no means all, of these papers are now open at the Public Record Office, Kew, and there are sufficient documents released to piece together an outline history. A far smaller body of correspondence associated with these committees has also been declassified in recent years. Many key documents have not been released and my account inevitably reflects the nature of the evidence – minutes, notes, memoranda – which can hardly be taken as verbatim or even contextualized accounts. Indeed, the documents make extremely little reference to national and international events except in the most veiled terms. The record of biological warfare, in this respect, is hermetically sealed. It is nonetheless the best (or only) source of material and there is enough to present a coherent interpretation of events.[16] While it must always be borne in mind that the bulk of these materials are official records, there is nevertheless a remarkable amount of detail in the minutes of many meetings. Enough disagreement and discussion has been recorded to provide some insight into what options were considered as alternatives to decisions and recommendations on germ warfare. Without details of these deliberations, such decisions might otherwise appear, in retrospect, inevitable.

Furthermore, these debates are frequently spread across meetings, memos, drafts and redrafts while, in contrast, decisions or recommendations are usually recorded as having been made at one point, at a single meeting or in a report. This presentation reinforces the commonsensical idea that decisions are *taken*. But because the documents frequently record much negotiation and dispute both before and after the 'official' decisions or recommendations are made, this process can usefully be regarded as a *flow* of decision-making, rather than thinking of decisions as being made at a particular instance in time. This, in turn, focuses our analytical attention on both the decisions and the process by which those decisions ossify. Nonetheless, the written accounts do still serve as fixed points of reference for civil servants, politicians, advisors and commentators such as myself. Phrases used in reports and correspondence frequently surface again verbatim during the course of any discussion and are often used in finalized recommendations and policies or in their justification. At later dates, especially when personnel have changed or committees been abolished, these fixed points are often used by officials to reconstruct events. So, although the documents may need to be treated cautiously because of their 'official' status, they should also be seen as a rich component of the Government's institutional memory, not least because the official version of history sometimes feeds back into the policy process and helps shape the course of events.

In making this point, it is important to emphasize that prior statements of policy, terms of reference for committees, their recommendations or decisions do not constrain the future actions and decisions of advisors and policy-makers in any straightforward manner. They are far more flexible resources. At times they are invoked in order to constrain action or promote new activities, for example an advisor may try to persuade colleagues that existing policy dictates a certain course of action, or the terms of reference of a committee may be called upon to bring a discussion to a close. At other times, prior decisions and policies are ignored by expert advisors or invoked simply in order to be broken. In the latter case, the prior policy or decision may be used as a reference point that is depicted as ripe for reinterpretation or plain abolition in the light of new developments or options.

The politics of expertise

Documents perform a further practical role. They link discussion and activity in Whitehall with the military and with research and development (R&D). Effectively, they bring the laboratory into the committee room.[17] This seemingly mundane observation highlights the idea that any weapons research programme can be usefully viewed as extending far beyond the laboratory. It reminds us that the success or failure of a military research programme is affected by more than just the narrowly defined technical success or failure of an innovative new weapon. To take matters further, what *counts* as success or failure in any case may be negotiated and decided upon at a site far distant from the laboratory.[18] Crudely put, a weapon that 'works' so far as scientists are concerned may not serve the purposes of politicians or military planners and vice versa. And, less crudely, for any weapons programme to succeed there may have to be a complex negotiation settled between these actors' differing requirements.[19] MacKenzie has argued that the weapons development process can fruitfully be regarded in this respect as an instance of *heterogeneous engineering*, where participants are constantly striving to build a functioning network of 'things and people'. He claims that:

> A successful weapons programme can indeed plausibly be seen as a network linking physical artefacts and human beings. Weapons system developers have often to spend as much time constructing and maintaining their relationship to human actors (politicians, industrialists, senior officers,

the multifarious forms of 'bureaucratic politics') as they do forging physical artefacts.[20]

Part of that bureaucratic politics involves providing advice, and advice is as much a 'product' of scientific and technological research as the more obvious products of new knowledge and artefacts.[21] Expert advisors in the biological warfare programme were called on to guide research, but equally the scientific findings emerging from research entered into deliberations over the future of policy and the nature of the threat. In this respect, scientific advisors cannot be regarded as standing outside of the policy process and injecting a measure of objectivity into the proceedings.[22]

Advisors are frequently called on to make normative judgements such as how *acceptable* a risk may be, to provide practical options in the face of uncertainty and unresolved controversy, to pose particular questions and ignore others, to prioritize some types of evidence or studies over others and so on.[23] Detailed case studies of the role of experts frequently demonstrate that scientific advisors do not merely present the facts, and the facts by no means speak for themselves. All of the recommendations that any useful scientific advisor is called on to make will blur the boundary between technical and policy advice despite this remaining a convenient distinction in everyday political life. Indeed, much can be at stake in the way in which the boundary is rhetorically constructed by advisors and officials, and much can be made of contrasting the convenient image of two distinct domains (science and policy) with the 'revelation' that this is not actually the case.[24] A normative policy decision can be reinforced if advisors present it as inevitable in virtue of the authority of science. Alternatively, a seemingly incontestable scientific decision on policy matters can be reduced to the apparent tatters of its social, political and psychological components by reversing the rhetorical strategy.

Threat assessments and the sociology of risk

One of the crucial discussions in which policy-makers expected scientific experts to make an authoritative contribution was over the nature of the threat from biological warfare. Subsumed under this question is a multitude of other questions. What exactly constitutes a working biological weapon? What effects can they achieve in practice? What defences are available? Can we extrapolate from experimental to military situations? Do our own capabilities reflect our enemy's capabilities? A raft of such questions adds up to an assessment of the opportunities afforded and hazards posed by biological warfare.

Following the anthropology of Mary Douglas, I use hazard, threat, danger and risk interchangeably in my account.[25] This moves away from a view that all the questions posed above can be captured neatly in a straightforward 'risk assessment'. In line with much recent thinking on the sociology of risk, I argue that risk can be regarded as a social construct.[26] This is not an argument, as some contend, that hazards and our knowledge of hazards are somehow conjured out of thin air or made up as stories without any bearing on the material world.[27] It does, however, recognize that there is more to risk assessment than simply weighing up the frequency with which events occur and assuming that an assessment can be treated independently of the priorities and requirements of those producing and using any risk assessment.[28] So, for example, even if an imaginary spy in the 1950s gained access to the entire Soviet biological warfare programme, wandered around, copied documents and inspected equipment, she would *still* need to weigh up and assess the significance of her findings before passing a report on. Once inside an organizational machinery geared to interpreting this report, the advisors would need to discuss what they found significant in her report and policy-makers would provide still further interpretation of these findings in relation to such matters as national defence policy.

All of this seems somewhat obvious when we consider that, for the most part, the British advisors and policy-makers were quite aware that they had no incontestable answer as to what even *their own* achievements amounted to at any particular point.[29] Nonetheless, because risk is frequently written about as if it exists in a social vacuum, my hypothetical example is intended to illustrate how the *sense* that some threats are more imminent or hazardous than others is built up.[30] Likewise, *ascribing* properties to risky objects may usefully be construed as a social process, where knowledge about the nature of a hazard may frequently be contested by various groups.[31] With these insights on board, the history of advice on the nature of biological warfare can be read as a narrative of changing conceptions of the threat in a shifting political, scientific and institutional context.

Before biological warfare

The history of biological warfare, broadly conceived, predates expert advice on the subject. Corpses and other decaying matter have been used to poison water sources since ancient times and most histories of biological warfare pinpoint the siege of Kaffa, in what is now the Ukraine, in the fourteenth century as the first recorded use of this means of destruction. In the course of the siege the invading Tatar force hurled the cadavers of their plague victims over the city walls with catapults. The resulting epidemic spread across the city, forcing its defenders to evacuate.[32] Another, much cited, use of biological warfare before the twentieth century involved British troops passing smallpox-infected blankets and a handkerchief to Native Americans during an uprising in 1763.[33]

These sporadic uses of biological warfare differ markedly from the efforts to create biological weapons in the twentieth century. More recent endeavours were underpinned by and aimed to contribute to systematic scientific knowledge. The 'germ theory' of disease, developed in the work of early bacteriologists such as Pasteur and Koch, gradually took hold of scientific and medical thinking in the late nineteenth century. Germ theory espoused the idea of specific aetiology, that diseases were caused by specific micro-organisms, and scientists, on the back of this notion, elaborated the list of microbes linked to specific diseases at a tremendous rate into the early twentieth century.[34] This reduction of disease to a simple causal narrative would most likely have lent plausibility to the idea of germ warfare. If a single causative organism could be tamed and controlled to effect a cure, why not so for more malign purposes? Such a shift in the conception of disease would have been necessary but not sufficient for modern biological warfare to be seriously entertained.[35]

Ideas also require institutions to sustain and embody them. Increasingly in the twentieth century, scientists, science and science-based technologies have been appropriated by the military.[36] During the First World War, British defence research expanded beyond the province of the Navy and into the ambit of the other Armed Forces.[37] These links between military and scientific institutions cannot be envisaged as an invasion of science by the military, the full co-operation of both parties was apparent even into peacetime.[38] So, by the time that biological warfare was first contemplated in earnest in the 1930s, the institutional connections made between science and the military were no longer a novelty, indeed they were fast becoming a matter of routine.

The invisible enemy

Biological warfare policy in the UK passed through a number of phases between the early 1930s and mid-1960s. My main argument in this book is that policy shifted along with the dominant conceptions of the threat in the scientific and policy arena. Neither remained static. An overtly defensive stance in the 1930s was linked with an extremely broad definition of biological warfare as *any* threat to public health caused by conventional war. During and after the Second World War the specific characteristics of an offensive regime were bound up with the goal to obtain a working biological bomb before the enemy deployed a similar weapon. Then, as biological warfare moved down the policy agenda and Britain once again adopted a defensive stance in the mid-1950s, scientists began to agitate about the horrible possibilities of biological agents spread as an aerosol across large tracts of land. As I have suggested already in more theoretical terms, the processes by which these changes occurred do not resemble one-way causal traffic between policy and science. The answers to the 'scientific' question 'what is the nature of biological warfare?' were inextricably bound up with the answers to the 'policy' question 'what shall we do with biological warfare?'[39] The precise ways in which these answers were woven together is the subject of my detailed historical narrative.

Before outlining this narrative, it is worth identifying a number of areas into which I do not delve in this book. The sources concentrate on the work of advisory and policy-making committees and, despite the subject being swathed in secrecy, these documents have provided fairly rich pickings for a history of policy and the role of advisors. But this book is not a comprehensive history of research at Porton Down. I have become obsessed with some of the things which obsessed the military and scientific advisors and write about these at length; the scope of biological warfare research at Porton was undoubtedly broader, although this is not reflected in the coverage of the open documents.[40] A second, more deliberate, omission is the considerable debate and discussion of anti-crop and anti-livestock biological warfare. These forms of biological warfare, which were intended to create economic disruption, should not be underestimated and there is some good historical work being undertaken on these topics.[41] Simply in order to scale down my own project, I have largely sidestepped these weapons except where they impinged directly on deliberations about anti-personnel measures. Finally, I make no apology for writing a history that focuses on the British research programme. International matters, particularly the supposed intentions of Germany and the Soviet Union, and the state of alliances with the United States and Canada, were extremely important in shaping policy. I have dealt with biological warfare activities in these countries only in so far as they were seen through the records of the various committees to which I now turn.

The origins of formal scientific advice on biological warfare can be found in the inter-war period when the Committee of Imperial Defence's Subcommittee on Bacteriological Warfare was established. The British Government, at this time, had not instituted a programme of biological warfare research and the predominant role of this committee was to discuss defensive possibilities. In Chapter 2, I discuss how the Subcommittee on Bacteriological Warfare drew its advice from the expertise of a small band of scientists associated with the Medical Research Council (MRC). These advisors dismissed the likelihood that biological agents might be employed deliberately to engineer an outbreak of disease. Instead, they advocated a position which I dub the 'public health' definition of biological warfare. To these advisors, the real threat of bacteriological warfare was already present. A conventional bombing raid, they argued, would be sufficient to disrupt water supplies and other sanitary provisions. The result would be the spread of diseases such as typhoid without recourse to designed biological weapons. Having provided such a definition, the advisors successfully proposed, by way of response to their problem, the strengthening of public health provisions throughout the country. Such advice, in the context of the growing threat of war, led to the founding in 1939 of the Emergency Public Health Laboratory Service covering England and Wales.

Just over a year into the Second World War, the British biological warfare programme was launched. At Porton Down in Wiltshire, the bacteriologist Paul Fildes and a team of other scientists began top secret work on retaliatory measures that could be employed at short notice if Britain was subjected to a germ warfare attack. By 1943, their work had produced concrete results, a stockpile of cattle cakes contaminated with anthrax, ready for waging economic warfare, and a prototype anthrax bomb for use against humans. Chapter 3 explores how this research was precipitated by a change in scientific thought from the 'public health' definition of biological warfare to one dominated by the quest for a bomb. The shift was somewhat fragmented as the main expert advisory committee, which espoused both the 'public health' view together with overt scepticism about the possibilities of deliberate biological warfare, was prevented the opportunity to exercise its scepticism. This Biological Warfare Committee was never confronted with a proposal to change direction and sanction offensive research at Porton. Neither was the War Cabinet. Instead, the Minister without Portfolio, Sir Maurice Hankey, navigated around these committees in order to take what he labelled his 'next step' to enable retaliation in kind if Germany resorted to biological weapons. Such measures, ostensibly part of Prime Minister Chamberlain's instruction to seek a means of protection under a defensive regime, resulted in actions which are more readily construed as 'offence for defence'.

This 'offence for defence' stance continued after the war as the biological research programme received an unprecedented injection of resources. In parallel, a web of new advisory and policy-making committees with varying responsibilities for biological warfare was formed in Whitehall. By 1947, the Chiefs of Staff had elevated research into biological weapons to the highest priority, in the same category as the atomic bomb. In the wake of this promotion, three research goals were set: a biological weapon for strategic use; a means for mass production of pathogens; and defensive measures against biological warfare agents. The 'offence for defence' regime which fuelled these developments, while superficially resembling a continuation of policy from the Second World War, cannot be regarded as a static extension of that policy. Military and scientific beliefs about the nature and role of biological warfare were under continual examination and in Chapter 4 I argue that the regime, orientated around a bomb as the principal goal *and* threat, was sustained through these ongoing debates about the relationship of biological weapons to atomic weapons, together with expert assessments of the threat derived chiefly from research at Porton rather than intelligence information.

The material result of the high priority accorded to biological warfare was an injection of funds into the post-war research programme. The bomb project, largely carried out at the Chemical Defence Experimental Establishment at Porton, continued in earnest. A pilot production plant for non-pathogenic organisms was built rapidly and plans to spend around £1m. on a similar plant for pathogens, Experimental Plant No. 2, were tabled. In addition to the basic microbiological research carried out at Porton, an ambitious series of open air sea trials with pathogens was planned by scientists and their advisors. Five secret sea trials involving pathogens took place in the Bahamas and off the coast of Scotland between 1948 and 1955. Chapters 5 and 6 explore these developments in some detail.

Despite the favourable policy environment and the general momentum with which the post-war biological warfare research programme began, it was not long before the first signs appeared that this research would not always remain a high priority. The experimental plant for mass production of pathogens suffered several reversed decisions over its future and eventually was shelved. At the same time, the Royal Air Force cancelled their request for a biological bomb. In Chapter 7, I chart how open statements on policy drifted in an ambiguous and ambivalent manner throughout the early 1950s. The drift, nonetheless, was in the direction of defensive in preference to offensive priorities. With biological weapons labelled as weapons of mass destruction their fate had become tied to the fortunes of nuclear weaponry. As such, it is impossible to understand changes to the biological warfare programme in isolation from increasing enchantment in some quarters, particularly among the Air Staff, with nuclear deterrence. Despite these concerns and growing economic pressures on the national defence budget, there is no evidence that a Cabinet-level decision was ever taken to abandon offensive biological warfare. I argue instead that the move to a defensive regime was effectively a decision taken by proxy.

The decline of biological warfare on the policy agenda nearly meant closure for the research programme at Porton. The idea was tabled in policy circles in the mid-1950s but the view prevailed that some minimal expenditure on both chemical and biological warfare research was a necessary cheap insurance. In parallel, the wavering influence of expert advice was marked by the dissolution of the Chiefs of Staff's Biological Warfare Subcommittee, the key interface between biowarfare scientists and policy-makers. Yet, as I argue in Chapter 8, biological research at Porton not only endured these threats, but also rejuvenated itself as scientists deployed a measure of conceptual opportunism. From 1956 onwards a new dominant theme emerged in scientific advisory discussions. Superseding the risk from biological bombs, came the threat from widespread dissemination of biological agents, the so-called Large Area Concept (LAC). In the LAC scenario, an enemy plane would spray a deadly bacterial cloud capable of spreading over several hundred square miles. Within the new defensive policy regime, the threat of large area coverage led to a variety of outdoor trials to assess the danger and provided a new rationale for research on microbial detection methods to provide early warning. The overall level of concern expressed by scientific advisors about large area attack eventually found its way into higher-level policy deliberations. By 1963, Cabinet had approved a modest expansion of research on offensive *aspects* of biological warfare. Although an offensive *capability* was still not a goal of the UK research programme, the Cabinet's approval set in train a new series of large-scale outdoor tests with inert and living agents and, more broadly, injected renewed vigour into the biological warfare research programme in Britain. Expert advice had prevailed and biological warfare research had survived.

2
Bacteriological Warfare as a Public Health Threat

Some years before Britain launched its biological warfare research programme, independent scientists had already been enrolled as advisors on the nature of the threat. Need arose as rumours of germ warfare activities in other countries grew persistently throughout the 1920s and 1930s. Previously, and in contrast to chemical agents such as chlorine and mustard gas – agents which had been used with deadly effects as a new form of weaponry during the First World War – germ warfare was far more shadowy, appearing primarily in intelligence reports. German plans to use anthrax, cholera and glanders in various sabotage attempts on livestock in neutral countries were known to British intelligence.[1] These plans were carried to fruition in Romania, the USA, Norway, Argentina and possibly Spain, although it is unlikely that these activities were known about in the UK.[2]

Chemical warfare in the trenches left an institutional legacy, an active research programme in Britain at Porton Down, Wiltshire, and a corresponding advisory structure in Government. Biological weapons had not been utilized in any overt fashion and the threat remained vague and poorly defined, so no immediate attempt was made within Government to seek further advice. Further afield, at the international level, attempts were made to deal with the future threat from both chemical and biological warfare. A significant result of these efforts was the 1925 'Geneva Protocol for the Prohibition of the Use of Gas and of Bacteriological Methods of Warfare' that acted, essentially, as a 'no first use' agreement between state signatories. Yet, even at the diplomatic level, bacteriological warfare remained a poorly articulated notion. Germ warfare had been added, almost as an afterthought, to the final draft of the agreement at the behest of the Polish. This last minute addition did little to shift the primary focus of the protocol from the control of chemical warfare.[3]

In Britain, almost a decade after the advent of the protocol, a resurgence of rumours concerning bacteriological warfare was to prompt a more local response from Government than that provided by international law. Public anxiety centred on a report published in July 1934 by the journalist, and former *Times* editor, Henry Wickham Steed.[4] Steed, a well-respected writer, claimed in *The Nineteenth Century and After* that German spies had been testing biological warfare agents on the London Underground and Paris Metro.[5] Steed, some months before these allegations had been made public, passed the documents on which he based his story to Sir Maurice Hankey, a senior civil servant and secretary of the Committee of Imperial Defence.[6] Hankey, after discussion with the Chiefs of Staff, took the matter outside Government and solicited the views of the Medical Research Council (MRC).[7]

The allegations were discussed by a trio of scientists, Professor John Ledingham, Director of the Lister Institute; the epidemiologist and bacteriologist Professor William Topley who was at the London School of Hygiene and Tropical Medicine; and Captain Stewart Ranken Douglas, Deputy Director of the National Institute for Medical Research.[8] By April, the three scientists had provided the Committee of Imperial Defence with a general memorandum on bacteriological warfare and later, after publication of Steed's article, with a shorter comment specifically on the story.

In both cases their response was guarded. The commentary on *The Nineteenth Century* article displayed some ambivalence about the veracity of the claims made by Wickham Steed. By way of endorsement, the authors remarked that:

> In support of their authenticity we would, as bacteriologists, merely remark that if *ad hoc* experiments were to be undertaken by any Power as a guide to contemplated offensive action involving the distribution of bacteria discharged directly from aircraft, from explosive bombs, dropped glass containers or from spray machines in the hands of enemy agents, they would take very much the form and method of those detailed in Wickham Steed's secret documents.[9]

Yet, despite this defence, the authors noted reservations about the bacteria allegedly used in the tests, *Bacillus prodigiosus*.[10] The species was known for the coloured growths it made on nutrient media plates and this property was significant because it had been exploited in research investigating patterns of discharged droplets. Ledingham and his colleagues, as a consequence, were 'strongly inclined to suspect, in fact, that the main problem in the minds of the experimenters is really the distribution of discharged gases under varying wind conditions and not that of bacteria'. Following this qualification, the authors added their own general assessment of the feasibility of a biological attack on the Underground. In their opinion, a limited number of people might be infected by these methods but the initiation of an epidemic, the very characteristic they proposed to be the main advantage of a biological attack, was deemed most unlikely.

The 'datum line' on biological warfare

The cautious position adopted by Ledingham, Topley and Douglas in their comment on the Wickham Steed affair had already been signalled in their initial memorandum to the Chiefs of Staff. This memo was to assume considerable importance in future deliberations on defence policy, to the extent that a year and a half after being written it was described by Hankey as the 'datum line' for discussion on bacteriological warfare.[11] Because of its significance in framing debate and assessment of the threat from bacteriological warfare, I will discuss the contents of the memorandum in some detail.

There is no doubt that Douglas, Ledingham and Topley regarded their position on germ warfare as grounded in their knowledge of science. The memo opened by contrasting their position with the non-scientific perspective, and also by hinting at their dismissal of the threat:

> The average layman's attitude to bacteria as potential sources of danger to human, animal and vegetable life is notoriously one of mingled dread and scorn, both alike the fruit of ignorance. As a preliminary, therefore, to any dispassionate discussion of the possibilities of bacteriological warfare from the points of view of user and intended victim, we think it necessary to set forth certain elemental considerations which must influence, and, in the main, limit the issue of any deliberate attempt to produce death and disease by the bacterial weapon.[12]

Next, they registered a series of factors that would set these limits. Natural or induced immunity, the route of entrance, and the effectiveness of bacteria in different host species were listed as the key barriers to any workable biological weapon. The authors also noted that the spread of any disease to epidemic proportions would be dependent on a wide range of environmental factors. They summarized by emphasizing their doubts:

> issue of any form of bacteriological warfare will, therefore, always be uncertain owing to the multiplicity of factors concerned and can never have the decisiveness associated with the chemical weapon. On the other hand, it must be acknowledged that the mysteriousness of the bacterial agent, the uncertainty of the weapon and the fear engendered by such uncertainty may be powerful in destroying mental and physical morale in time of war.[13]

In further support of their case, Ledingham, Topley and Douglas cited various published opinions on germ warfare, including, and at length, a *Report to the League of Nations of the Temporary Mixed Commission for the Reduction of Arms*. A prior statement by four scientific experts, named as Pfeiffer, Bordet, Madsen and Cannon, had informed this report.[14] This statement, Ledingham and his colleagues confessed, was 'admittedly in the direction of minimising, even discounting the possibilities of serious danger'.

Ledingham, Topley and Douglas built on this scepticism in their ensuing discussion concerning the delivery of any putative biological agent. Shock from explosive devices would, they argued, kill most bacteria. Dropping 'glass globes filled with germs' from aeroplanes would only be effective in a restricted and crowded area where contaminated glass splinters might injure people. With regard to spraying, they thought that 'it does not seem likely that any method of spraying from aeroplanes would give rise to a concentration in the air at ordinary breathing levels, sufficient to cause any considerable number of infections'. Even the possibility of an epidemic resulting from direct sabotage attack on a reservoir with cholera or typhoid was treated with some incredulity. The advisors conceded the possibility with the qualification that:

> it is probable that the infection would have to be really massive for this result to be achieved. The successful carrying out of such a plan would depend on the deposition of the bacteria at the correct spot at the correct time e.g. in a reservoir designed for immediate distribution without storage or filtration.

Finally, towards the end of their report, the authors noted that the possibility of infecting herds and crops was 'rather more dubious'.

Despite this tone of rejection towards the threat, the memorandum did suggest situations where biological weapons might be successfully employed. In so doing, it also began to establish a definition of biological warfare that appears quite alien from a contemporary perspective. At several points in their memorandum, the scientists drew attention to the unusual public health conditions that would prevail in times of war. This situation, they contended, would render the population vulnerable to disease. In the context of their opening discussion they raised this vulnerability in connection with just one exception in their list of limitations on bacterial weapons:

> if the natural immunity is small or entirely lacking owing to the debilitating conditions of war and if no active immunity has been conferred by specific vaccination against the microbe in question, the chances of initiating infection and perhaps of its subsequent propagation by personal and other forms of contact may be considerable.

The scientists returned to this theme again in their memorandum, but in order to highlight a different feature of wartime conditions. Mass epidemics and wound infections, they argued, should be regarded as a form of bacteriological warfare which was 'an inevitable accompaniment of all wars'. Moreover, these types of bacteriological warfare would 'probably exceed anything that can be brought about by calculated and deliberate distribution of infective bacteria'. Later on in the memorandum, this new definition of biological warfare became explicitly linked to practical issues when the authors contended that: 'A disorganised public health service may play into the enemy's hands, while a defectively nourished and mentally distressed population may undoubtedly have its resisting powers so weakened as to fall ready victims to infections not previously encountered'.

One further point was made about the situations in which bacteriological warfare might be employed. Here, the authors offered judgement not about the technical but the ethical feasibility of waging germ warfare:

> only opinions, usually exaggerated and ill-informed ones, have been expressed as to its probable employment in future wars...we take the opinion that this weapon cannot be ignored as a weapon of offence and that its 'ethical' standing is neither lower nor higher than that of the bayonet, the shell and the chemical arm. Indeed if its 'ethical' standing as a deliberate instrument of warfare is to be judged by the 'fighting chance' it gives its victim, it would in our opinion take a higher place than any of these three recognised instruments.

The observation that some people were able to survive infection better than others was taken as a positive, almost Darwinian, justification of bacteriological warfare. Such an explicit defence of biological weapons is extremely rare in the minutes and papers that are open on the topic. At the outset, these scientists were prepared to provide a moral diagnosis of offensive germ warfare. In their opinion, the infectious nature of pathogens, one of the very features which has placed biological weapons apart from other forms of warfare in other debates, was to be counted as a virtue.

The overall dismissal of the direct threat from bacteriological warfare was consonant with more general views emerging in epidemiology at the time. Topley himself had played a key role in initiating experimental epidemics in laboratory animals and had concluded that the causes of epidemics were many and complex. The historian of medicine, J. Andrew Mendelsohn, has noted a more general shift in epidemiological thinking in the early years of the twentieth century.[15] Epidemic disease was being construed less and less as the invasion of a population from outside by micro-organisms, and with it the idea of the epidemiologist's role as 'chasing' the responsible germ was becoming unfashionable. Instead, epidemics were viewed in more ecological terms as a disturbance of the equilibrium between a human population and an already present microbial population. Within this emerging paradigm, the suggestion that epidemics could be deliberately engineered – possibly together with the metaphors evoked by notions of invasion – would likely have run counter to the trends in epidemiological thinking which, at that time, had only recently become established.

In summary then, this memorandum set out a position in which the threat of biological warfare was posed not so much in terms of a direct attack with explosives, bombs or sabotage. Instead the whole definition of bacteriological warfare was linked to problems of maintaining public health during times of war. This frame for biological warfare would be developed further once the Committee of Imperial Defence instituted its own bureaucratic structure to oversee this novel area of warfare.

Formalizing advice

After the Wickham Steed affair concern about bacteriological warfare did not disappear. The same three authors from the MRC submitted a further memorandum to the Chiefs of Staff in April 1935 regarding defence measures against biological weapons. It dealt with the possibilities of defending against anthrax, botulism, typhoid and paratyphoid fevers. The memo also made reference to a need for tetanus antitoxins, 'in view of the almost certain occurrence of wounds involving tetanus risks whether such wounds are produced by glass or metal fragments contaminated with tetanus spores discharged from air bombs or by similar fragments contaminated by soil'.[16] Again, bacteriological warfare was being linked to the health risks associated with both deliberate employment of agents and also with a conventional weapon attack.

A year later the Committee of Imperial Defence's Subcommittee on Bacteriological Warfare was formed with Hankey as the chairman. The subcommittee consisted of bacteriologists, representatives of the Armed Forces, the Air Raid Precautions Department of the Home Office, the Treasury, the Chemical Defence Research Department at Porton Down and the MRC.[17] The initial membership of ten included Sir Edward Mellanby, secretary of the MRC, together with Ledingham and Topley.[18] Another two members also had institutional affiliations beyond Government. The new and secret subcommittee's terms of reference were: 'to report on the practicability of the introduction of bacteriological warfare and to make recommendations as to the counter measures which should be taken to deal with such an eventuality'.[19] Hankey put this remit into his own words at the opening of the first meeting in November 1936. He commented that there were signs of German interest in bacteriological warfare and stated that the UK needed to take this into account when addressing its own defence preparations. With respect to a general policy: 'He pointed out that we were, of course, considering the problem from the defensive aspect; it was unthinkable that we should contemplate the adoption of bacteriological warfare offensively.'[20]

During the course of the inaugural meeting, the 'datum line' memo by Ledingham, Topley and Douglas, the latter now deceased, was discussed and accepted by the subcommittee 'as representing the present position on the question'. Ledingham commented that since it had been written the views of the authors had not altered, even though 'in the interval the subject of bacteriological warfare had been dealt with in numerous papers, both in the lay and medical press'. Both the surviving authors felt that tetanus was the most imminent danger, which Topley connected to his more general definition of bacteriological warfare by commenting that 'he could not help feeling that the greatest danger, particularly in relation to tetanus, was from the accidental infection of wounds caused by explosive bombs, or in other ways, rather than from any dropping of infective material by enemy aircraft'.

The discussion then moved on to countermeasures. Hankey pointed out that it was necessary to stockpile sera and anti-toxins, and to ascertain national requirements for these defensive precautions. In this respect, the Admiralty, Air Ministry and Air Raid Precautions Department were to be approached and asked for a possible week-by-week estimate of their require-ments for tetanus antitoxin, gas gangrene antitoxin and anthrax serum during the first three months of a war. Ledingham noted that 'there was the possibility, though not a very likely one, of distribution of anthrax bacteria by air', so it could be useful to hold a reserve of anthrax serum. At the close of the meeting yet another potentiality was raised. Dudley, the Medical Director-General of the Navy, 'pointed out that as a result of air raids there might be serious dislocation in the country's water supplies and in sanitary arrangements'. If this breakdown might result in an outbreak of typhoid, he argued, then the subcommittee should also arrange for some means of protection. So the advisors entertained a number of scenarios requiring defence against direct and incidental bacteriological warfare.

Although these measures for defence were to take up much of the future discussion of the subcommittee, the nature and extent of the threat from germ weapons were also revisited at several points. Again, the original memorandum by Ledingham, Topley and Douglas acted as the benchmark for debate. At the third meeting in January 1937, Hankey reiterated the contents of this memo in some detail for the benefit of the subcommittee and then drew his own conclusion: 'it was justified to deduce the view that, whilst bacteriological warfare was sufficiently possible and sufficiently dan-gerous to demand careful watching, it was not so serious a menace as chem-ical warfare and it was not likely to be resorted to by an enemy'.[21] In reply, Topley yet again put across the public health definition of bacteriological warfare as a mixture of deliberate use of bacteria with secondary effects from conventional bombing:

> He felt that a severe attack on this country by air might seriously upset normal sanitary conditions. The extensive migration of the civil popu-lation would cause a dislocation in normal sanitary arrangements, and there was therefore a risk of intestinal infections. Then, in his view, was the time when bacteriological warfare might be deliberately introduced, but he felt that it would be a case of what might be termed 'bacteriological

sabotage'. He put forward the view that some form of civilian bacteriological service should be organised. At present there was nothing.

Topley's particular definition of the threat now explicitly separated indirect biological warfare from purposive sabotage. The response to this particular construal of the danger, a civilian bacteriological service, was in terms of public health. The suggestion appears to have received quite an immediate and favourable reception from Topley's fellow advisors. Discussion picked up on the idea of a bacteriological service and eventually the subcommittee decided to recommend that the MRC be asked about establishing a skeleton organization.

One month later and the public health definition of bacteriological warfare was clearly articulated in scientific terms. A 'technical memo' by Ledingham, Topley and F. Griffiths, of the Ministry of Health, provided a twofold definition of bacteriological warfare:

> a) as attempt, by any means, to induce the occurrence and spread of infective disease among armies of an enemy country or among its civilian population or b) in a narrower sense as the attempt to procure the same and deliberate dissemination of bacteria or viruses with the aid of aeroplanes, bombs or other less obvious channels.[22]

After offering these definitions of bacteriological warfare, the authors noted that the narrower sense was the one that was generally understood and was so used in their report. Then they proceeded to qualify their position, stating that 'the narrower and the wider definitions cannot be sharply differentiated, because the effect of introducing any bacterial culture or virus will be largely determined by environmental factors and these in turn will be modified by war'. By erecting this rather shaky boundary, the rhetoric of the memo could be adjusted to accommodate the earlier, and broader, definition of bacteriological warfare favoured by Topley and Ledingham.

The technical memo maintained the cautious stance of earlier reports, pointing out the threat of use of biological warfare was attenuated by the possibility of infecting friendly troops. This, of course, would not be a consideration where bacteria were employed against a civilian population, thus making the island of Great Britain particularly susceptible to such an attack. From these premises, the memo continued by diverting emphasis to the public health aspects of a putative attack. The authors repeated their view that it was improbable to initiate an epidemic by dropping biological agents from planes. A greater possibility, in their opinion, was from sabotage, although this could be countered by adequate sanitary control. Yet the most important peril, in their view, remained the vulnerable position of a wartime population to bacterial attack:

> under war conditions, especially under the stress of severe and continuous bombardment from the air, a sanitary situation might well arise in which

the risk of infection, and particularly of various types of intestinal infection, would be far higher than at present. Under such conditions bacterial sabotage might be a serious added danger.

By the end of the report this 'serious added danger' was all but dispensed with and the authors maintained that 'much more urgent and important, we think, are the probable or possible bacteriological consequences of modern war, apart altogether from any attempt to disseminate bacterial cultures or viruses'. Preventative and therapeutic measures, they argued, should be concerned with those wounded during aerial bombardment and the epidemics that would be expected from 'any temporary breakdown in sanitary control, apart altogether from bacteriological sabotage'. The report closed by re-emphasizing how a 'disorganised public health service' could play into the enemy's hands.

By now certain phrases were surfacing and resurfacing in the various minutes and reports issued by the subcommittee. Each repetition of key terms and phrases appears to have sedimented into an overall view, that the threat from biological warfare was rooted in danger to public health. Although this hazard was linked to deliberate use of bacterial agents, it was also bound up with the consequences of conventional warfare. By April 1938, this view had become paramount in defining the scope of the subcommittee's activities, as they reported back to the Committee of Imperial Defence that:

> Comparatively early in our investigations, however, we came to the conclusion that a deliberate attempt at bacteriological warfare was improbable, and our work in consequence has been largely concerned less with bacteriological warfare in the limited sense, than with the wider problem of wound infections and of epidemic diseases resulting from air attacks on the civil population.[23]

And with each rendition of this perspective on the 'true danger' from bacteriological warfare there were implicit and explicit calls for a concrete, public health oriented response.

Emergency response becomes the Public Health Laboratory Service

Topley's advocacy of a bacteriological service during the January 1937 meeting brought rapid action. A few months later, in April, the subcommittee issued a report entitled 'A Possible Scheme for Civilian Bacteriological Service to Operate in Time of War'.[24] The main concern of this document was with public health during conventional bombing. The report maintained that damage to water mains would result in the water supply being cut off and also contamination from the soil through minor fractures in the water mains. When migrating populations were suddenly evacuated from cities to new sites, or in damaged or overcrowded housing when hospitals were full, there would be additional strain placed on sanitary arrangements. Once again the upshot was spelt out in familiar terms:

> As Captain Douglas, Prof. Ledingham and one of us indicated in our earlier memoranda, it is such conditions as these that seems to us to provide one the very few situations in which bacteriological warfare in the restricted sense of the purposeful introduction of bacterial cultures offers some hope of success.... It should however be emphasized that no enemy action of this kind would be required to initiate serious epidemics of typhoid, paratyphoid, or Flexner or Sonne dysentery. These would arise, to a greater or less extent, as the direct result of sanitary disorga-nisation, without any introduction of the causative bacteria. They are always with us....[25]

The long and detailed document also called for laboratory facilities in hospitals and noted the concentration of public health laboratories in London, deemed the most vulnerable area of the country. A 'bacteriological service' was envisaged as a co-ordinated network of laboratories undertaking micro-bial diagnosis and treatment. No further mention was made in the outline scheme of bacteriological warfare in the narrow sense. Instead, a thorough discussion followed about issues such as how the service would deal with wound infections, intestinal infections and respiratory infections; the state of existing bacteriological facilities; the mobilization of the service on the outbreak of war; together with transport, administration and staffing needs.

At a subcommittee meeting in January of the following year, Mellanby put across his opinion that the service 'might, however, be regarded as only a part of a bigger scheme, namely, the institution of a pathological service as a branch of the public health service of this country'.[26] Although Mellanby suggested that the service be made a permanent, peacetime extension of the public health service, this position was not universally supported. Dr Carnworth, the Deputy Chief Medical Officer of the Ministry of Health, while in sympathy with Mellanby, encouraged him to consider the problem from 'a more practical angle'.

Carnworth also noted that Topley's proposal for the Emergency Service was 'inclined to take too pessimistic a view of what might happen'. In his opinion, experience from the First World War and from the Spanish Civil War went to show that 'astonishing as it was, the danger from epidemics was not as great as might be supposed'. From this finding, Carnworth argued that war conditions that encouraged epidemics might be countered by an efficient sanitary, rather than laboratory, service. For example, he proposed that water would just as well be chlorinated as dealt with by bacteriological methods. Finally, he noted that although any war effort may depend on good peacetime services, the Ministry of Health was faced with a range of problems of which Mellanby's current suggestion was not a priority. At this point the chairman stopped the discussion on the grounds that provisions during peacetime were outside the subcommittee's terms of reference, although they all agreed that a subcommittee of the MRC would be asked to discuss the practical implications of the plan for an emergency service.

A version of the outline of the scheme for a bacteriological service was passed on to the MRC and they duly established an Emergency Bacteriological Services Subcommittee, chaired by Topley.[27] This committee's deliberations resulted, not surprisingly, in detailed recommendations for a network of emergency bacteriological laboratories. The Bacteriological Warfare Subcommittee, who now went beyond their remit in their proposals for the Emergency Bacteriological Service, backed these plans: 'Although the organisation of the public health laboratory services in peacetime does not fall within our terms of reference, we would wish to express our opinion that the existing position is extremely unsatisfactory.'[28] This was followed by a plea for an adequate and integrated public health laboratory service.

Within a month the proposals were being considered by the Committee of Imperial Defence who took note of the, by now customary, argument that the present public health arrangements would be inadequate to deal with disease 'produced not necessarily by deliberate attempt at bacteriological warfare – though this might come later – but by the dislocation of sanitary services resulting, not only from air attacks, but also from the strain imposed on them by a large-scale migration of the civil population'.[29] They approved the proposals in July 1938 with only one main proviso. One member of the committee, Sir Samuel Hoare, while agreeing with the idea of a service, complained that 'he would, however, prefer some more colourless title than "Emergency Bacteriological Service" which in his opinion would tend to create an alarming impression in the mind of the general public'.[30]

In a similar vein, because the term 'bacteriological warfare' could 'convey something sinister and alarming to the mind of the layman', the Subcommittee on Bacteriological Warfare had already changed its name in May to the Subcommittee on Emergency Bacteriological Services.[31] Sir Edward Mellanby was approached about the matter and suggested that the title of the nascent bacteriological service should be the Emergency Public Health Laboratory Service. By August the subcommittee had once again renamed itself to keep in line and was now the Subcommittee on Emergency Public Health Laboratory Services.

Intelligence and bacteriological possibilities

While the Subcommittee on Bacteriological Warfare maintained the improbability of a deliberate germ weapon attack, their position was not taken solely with reference to the original memorandum by Topley and his colleagues. During its lifetime, the subcommittee dealt with a small but increasing number of intelligence reports purporting to give covert information on foreign biological weapons programmes. Many of these reports pertained to German activities although the subcommittee cautioned that

> we do not wish to imply that Germany may be the only country in which such activities are being pursued, and appreciating as we do the difficulty of obtaining authentic information on these matters, we would nevertheless emphasise the importance which we attach to a close watch being maintained on similar activities in other countries.[32]

When the Government received notice of Wickham Steed's allegations, very little intelligence information had been gained on bacteriological warfare.[33] Just one month before Steed's story was made public, however, a source 'who has proved reliable in the past' reported that a gas course for advanced gas specialists had opened at Berlin-Charlottenberg in May 1934. Participants were 'surprised' to be told that the course had, in fact, been divided into parts dealing with bacteriological and gas warfare.[34] A further memo recorded a secret report from February 1935 where

> a source was recently told by two persons in touch with chemical research circles in Germany that responsible people had no intention of pursuing experiments in the effect of spraying substances impregnated with bacteria from the air, because of the practically unanimous opinion amongst bacteriologists in Germany that it is extremely doubtful if spraying bacteria in this manner could ever lead to successful results.[35]

By December 1935 it had been reported to British intelligence sources that the German bacteriological course was being run on a 'practically continuous' basis.[36] Although 'no opportunity was lost in reminding pupils that Germany would never start bacteriological warfare ... Germany was preparing to use bacteria in war – but only after the enemy had started such devilish tactics'.

These reports were eventually compiled into a single memorandum for the Subcommittee on Bacteriological Warfare. Its anonymous author added a caveat for the advisors that 'until further evidence is obtained ... it is not conclusive from these reports that Germany is training for offensive bacterial warfare'. Elsewhere, Hankey concurred, describing this sort of information on German activities as 'probably scrappy'.[37]

Sporadic reports of Germany's bacteriological warfare operations continued to reach the subcommittee. A report dismissed as 'doubtful' and issued under 'strong reserve' claimed that anthrax was being investigated at the Military Bacteriological Institute in Berlin, under the direction of the chemical warfare specialist Dr Hugo Stolzenberg.[38] The informant claimed that the 'spore bacilli are liquefied and filled into glass capsules...these glass capsules are dropped from aircraft at any altitude...the glass capsules are intended to be dropped only when the objective is a large or medium large town'.[39] In addition, bacteria were allegedly being sprayed from aircraft or disseminated by a 'detonation-less bomb', which consisted of a parachuted container opening at about 25 metres above the ground to spread the liquid-combined spores.[40] The response of the advisors to this information had been to recommend that Intelligence branches of all Government departments should be asked to maintain vigilance.[41] The particular threat from anthrax against humans and livestock was treated seriously and the subcommittee reported that gas masks would provide some protection, but that the MRC should further investigate the possibility of stockpiling anti-anthrax serum. Both the Air Raids Precautions Department and the Ministry of Agriculture and Fisheries were urged to prepare likewise for a possible anthrax attack.

Only a few other intelligence reports appear to have come before the subcommittee. A series of articles published in French in the Romanian newspaper *Le Moment* in February 1938 expressed the opinion that if war broke out nothing would prevent the use of 'the most effective weapon known at the time', bacterial warfare, which was 'inevitable' and 'a most effective auxiliary weapon'.[42] At the end of 1938, the Director of Naval Intelligence conveyed information that Germany was well aware that Russia would use bacteria in war to poison supplies, and that according to Germany, Spanish 'reds' had already used such methods.[43] The Director added that the Germans had made full plans to retaliate if it became necessary. A month later a paper translated from German reported that, although studies went back as far as using contaminated bullets in the 1890s, military and bacteriological experts varied in their opinion on the feasibility of bacteriological warfare.[44] Most experts, it was claimed, had rejected the possibility and such warfare was denounced as impracticable from 'the purely bacteriological point of view'.

Information about activities abroad was therefore available but provided only a small amount of contradictory evidence, which was treated with suspicion by the British authorities. Although the subcommittee took some action on these reports, the insubstantial nature of the intelligence appears to have permitted Topley and his colleagues to persist with their conception of bacteriological warfare as an indirect threat from more conventional wartime activities. Working within this definition of bacteriological warfare as a public health threat, the main activities of the subcommittee continued to focus on efforts to mobilize support for an emergency public health laboratory service and to stockpile antitoxins as precautionary measures. By 1938 the subcommittee had facilitated the acquisition of some 400 000 doses of tetanus antitoxin ready for the outbreak of war, and made arrangements to accumulate supplies of gas gangrene antitoxin, anti-anthrax serum, insecticides, fungicides and chlorine for water purification.[45] As I have already described, the Emergency Public Health Laboratory Service was to become the foundation of the post-war Public Health Laboratory Service for England and Wales.

Secrecy

The discussions surrounding bacteriological warfare took place in utmost secrecy and the sole attempt by the subcommittee to make its affairs public was quashed. At its opening meeting, Hankey had suggested that questions on bacteriological warfare might arise in Parliament and that the subcommittee should be prepared to 'reassure public opinion'.[46] He even proposed that Topley and Ledingham sign a document based on their original position statement about the topic. This could then be passed on to the Air Raids Precautions Department 'who would thus have the facts and opinions of scientific experts to allay the fears of the general public'.[47] The Committee of Imperial Defence, who did not see matters in such open terms, refused to approve the recommendation and suggested that it was 'inadvisable that any statements should be made in Parliament until the matter was pressed'.[48]

When, in December 1937, a question was eventually raised in Parliament as to what preparations had been made regarding germ warfare, the curt response was that: 'This matter had received consideration in all its bearings in consultation with distinguished scientists and appropriate measures have been decided on. It would not be in the public interest to state the nature of these precautions.'[49] The subcommittee seized this as an opportunity to make their activities more widely known to those outside the Government whom they thought needed to know about their plans for a bacteriological service. The advisors justified this move in terms of a change in their activities. By now, they argued, their original title was a 'misnomer, since, as we have pointed out we are concerned less with the possibility of deliberate introduction of bacteria by the enemy than with steps to safeguard the public health under war conditions'.[50]

In May 1938 the Committee of Imperial Defence took note of this argument and, as already mentioned, allowed the subcommittee to adopt a more innocuous title.[51] In addition, they permitted enough publicity as would allow the subcommittee to continue their work, in particular where agencies outside of Government needed to know about the provisions of antitoxins and sera.

Responding to different bacteriological warfares

The rather modest amount of publicity bestowed upon the Bacteriological Warfare Subcommittee only serves to highlight the extreme secrecy surrounding the topic from the outset. As the role of the independent scientists changed over a short period, from sporadically consulted external advisors to members of an institutionalized committee, the need for secrecy and discretion was stressed at several points, particularly by Hankey. Within this closed world, it is interesting to note how the advice issued by, essentially, just three academics came to frame the entire way in which biological weapons were conceptualized and responded to during this period. What I termed the 'public health' definition of bacteriological warfare dominated even in the light of existing, albeit sketchy, intelligence information. By way of response to this dominant notion, bacteriological warfare as the secondary and indirect effects of conventional bombing, the establishment of the Public Health Laboratory Service made perfect sense.

At one level, it is relatively straightforward to argue that the whole response and conceptualization of bacteriological warfare was refracted through the wider professional interests of the advisors. I have presented evidence that strongly suggests the advocates of 'public health' bacteriological warfare were simultaneously defining their problem and building up the status of, and facilities for, microbiology in Britain. At a more conjectural level, this interest-driven explanation might be integrated with a more local explanation of the activities of these advisors. After all, the solution to the problem of bacteriological warfare, the Public Health Laboratory Service, was presented by Topley as a practical opportunity relatively early in the life of the committee. Advice on bacteriological warfare, once institutionalized, would not survive long if all it amounted to was a talking-shop over the intangible and ill-defined threat presented in intelligence reports. From this perspective it is possible to imagine the stockpiling of sera and antitoxins, together with the Emergency Bacteriological Service, the deliberations surrounding it and the very definitions of what constituted the hazard, as a concrete, pragmatic and instrumental response in the face of alternatively having to cope with and advise on a very different, insubstantial and elusive 'enemy'.

3
Hankey's 'Step Further'

When Britain declared war on Germany in 1939, the Subcommittee on Emergency Bacteriological Services had completed most of its secret preparations for defence against a germ warfare attack. Working with the MRC, the members of the subcommittee had helped to establish the Emergency Public Health Laboratory Service and an attendant stockpile of vaccines and sera. At a time of widespread fear of bombing, the threat of bacteriological warfare had been defined by scientific advisors primarily in terms of an epidemic outbreak caused deliberately alongside, or accidentally in the aftermath of, a conventional bomb raid. This 'public health' perspective framed an unequivocally defensive policy that soon crumbled as the War Cabinet sought a means of retaliation in kind and Britain launched a concerted research effort into biological warfare.

Reorganization and policy revision

Just a few days into the war, a letter on bacteriological warfare was passed to Maurice Hankey, now Minister without Portfolio in the War Cabinet, by the Minister for Co-ordination of Defence, Lord Chatfield. The unsolicited letter from a scientist in Newcastle upon Tyne, H.A. Sisson, requested permission and resources to undertake work on dried anthrax spore production for weapons purposes.[1] Hankey showed the request to Edward Mellanby, secretary of the MRC, who discussed the matter further with 'a number of the best known experts in bacteriology'.[2] They concluded that Sisson's proposal was flawed. In their opinion, anyone breathing in anthrax spores might infrequently develop primary infection but this would hardly spread because the disease was not highly contagious. Mellanby added that this advice, like all previous counsel on biological warfare, was offered from a defensive perspective. He felt

> that this attitude in itself rather inhibits investigation and the question now arises as to whether the time has not arrived when we must reconsider

the whole position and at least undertake experimental work to see what are the possibilities of infection being transmitted to man by various forms of microorganisms through the air.[3]

Mellanby had even gone so far as to allow his coterie of advisors to plan this experimental work, which he invited Hankey to approve. Hankey first suggested that Chatfield write back to thank Sisson but point out that his anthrax proposal would be contrary to the 1925 Geneva Protocol. Mellanby's plans, on the other hand, 'would not be inconsistent' with the protocol or 'our general policy of avoiding resort to illegal methods of warfare and frightfulness in all its forms'.[4] Hankey therefore sought, and soon gained, approval from the Prime Minister, Neville Chamberlain, to initiate the research 'so as to give ourselves knowledge as to how to protect ourselves against such methods. The work was to be conducted in this spirit and not with a view to resort to such methods ourselves.'[5]

Seeking knowledge for protection meant taking a proactive stance towards biological warfare. While this was a step away from the purely reactive policy adopted before the war, it was still intended as a defensive course of action. According to Hankey, Chamberlain had stipulated that his prior approval would be needed if this work was ever to progress as far as preparations for the offensive use of bacteria.[6] The details of the preliminary experiments, carried out at the National Institute for Medical Research under direction of Sir Patrick Laidlaw, are not described in any of the available papers from this period. By February 1940, Mellanby summarized their progress, noting that these 'investigations had already brought out points which were of scientific interest quite apart from bacteriological warfare: other points were relevant to the immediate problem'.[7] The relevant points were listed by Mellanby in very general terms. Spread of bacterial infection, he noted, might create a problem if the necessary conditions existed, such as in the French fortifications along the Maginot Line; for this reason the committee flagged the importance of ongoing work on methods of decontaminating infected air.

Shortly after approval for these early bacteriological warfare experiments had been granted, Mellanby issued a report for the War Cabinet summarizing the pre-war advice on bacteriological warfare. The report was intended as an expert response to various speculative suggestions that were circulating on how Germany might employ biological warfare. The cover note of the report aptly summed up the advisors' position:

It will be seen that the memorandum expresses the view that generally this form of warfare is likely to be less effective than normal methods, but that, if used at all, action by enemy agents would be more likely to cause disease than would the spraying or dropping of bacteria from aircraft.[8]

In the opening paragraphs, this memorandum defined germ warfare in its most apocalyptic form, as the outbreak of an uncontrollable epidemic: 'The one outstanding objective of bacteriological warfare, effectively and intelligently applied, would be to start epidemics of infective disease which would then spread far beyond the particular locality attacked.'[9] The definition adopted by the MRC was important and it informed the authors' eventual judgement on the potential of bacteriological warfare. At the outset, the report outlined the folly of an enemy 'displaying an unexpected lack of knowledge and intelligence' if they chose to spread bacteria at random. Epidemiologically, the report pointed out, this activity would be insufficient to initiate an outbreak of disease. Once again the standard argument was made; disease organisms were 'always with us' but required the right conditions, epitomized by those prevailing after an air raid, to create epidemics. At their most dismissive, the authors rejected the 'aeroplane obsession', that aircraft would be used to deliver a biological attack:

> It is perhaps natural that the spreading of bacteria or viruses by aeroplane should have occupied a prominent place in the suggestions that have been made, particularly from unofficial sources; but the aeroplane is, for most purposes, a very clumsy and inefficient bacteriological instrument, because it cannot usually fulfil the essential condition of depositing the selected infected agent in the right place at the right time.[10]

And, turning to specific diseases, the report promptly disposed of the threat from plague, rabies, cholera, typhoid, anthrax, psittacosis, tularemia, typhus and yellow fever. In particular, the authors rejected anthrax, psittacosis and tularemia as viable agents because they fell outside of their own definition of biological warfare. These diseases, while dangerous for those infected, would not readily spread. Without the potential to cause epidemics, their choice by any enemy would, according to the report, entail 'the sacrifice of the main advantage of the bacteriological weapon'.

On a more threatening note, the report warned of two distinct possibilities, foot and mouth disease targeted at livestock and general bacteriological sabotage. Finally, the report contained a supplementary section warning that germ warfare might be employed in a military context. Here, the authors abandoned their original definition of bacteriological warfare. After noting that epidemics could 'boomerang' back on to friendly troops, they suggested that bullets or shells coated with an organism that did not cause epidemics would enhance the deadliness of these orthodox armaments. Any organism chosen for these purposes, they warned, would have to be hardy and therefore in a class of bacteria that formed resistant spores. Tetanus was ruled out on the grounds that treatment was readily available but, opening up the possibility of further investigation, the authors noted 'whether other spore-bearing organisms such as anthrax, would be effective if used this way is impossible to say'.

Although Mellanby's report persisted with a sceptical view of bacteriological warfare, the danger had not been entirely dismissed and still required monitoring. This role could not be fulfilled by the Subcommittee on Emergency Bacteriological Services because it had been passed to the Ministry of Health on the outbreak of war and was promptly suspended. On 27 November 1939, the War Cabinet agreed to reconstitute the subcommittee under their own auspices with Hankey resuming the chair.[11] This Committee on Biological Warfare had a largely defensive remit: 'To consider in the light of war experience the possible use by the enemy of various forms of Bacteriological Warfare, and to make recommendations as to any counter measures which should be taken in addition to those already adopted.'[12]

These defensive terms of reference were soon challenged. At their first meeting in February 1940, the BW Committee was asked to comment on a lone call to initiate offensive research from the prestigious Canadian scientist, Sir Frederick Banting, co-discoverer of insulin. Banting had prepared this paper for the National Research Council of Canada and passed it on to the British authorities while on a fact-finding mission to the UK. A month beforehand, Banting had met with Hankey and shared a draft of this report to which the Minister had responded enthusiastically, describing it as a 'definite proposal'.[13]

Banting's report warned that bacterial warfare was one of the 'gravest dangers' facing England and France and urged for 'preparedness', drawing a close parallel with the rapid incorporation of chlorine and other poison gases as recognized weapons of war.[14] Banting also intimated that the British scientific advisors were dangerously complacent. After mentioning the dismissive conclusions of the MRC secret document, he added:

> In my opinion, a very great responsibility rests upon the scientists who have so advised the British Government concerning bacterial warfare... it seems to me they fail to realise that upon their advice may rest the security and safety, and even the lives, of the civilian population and fighting forces.[15]

Banting identified the source of this poor advice in the British bacteriologists' construal of disease. He argued that the advisors had thought of diseases produced by germ warfare 'only in terms of the naturally occurring methods of spreading disease'. Believing that this idea was too short-sighted, Banting adopted a far less ecological view of infection, stating that 'under the new conditions of bacteriological warfare, the disease producing bacteria may be scattered anywhere – and it must be remembered that as long as the bacteria gain entrance to the body they produce disease'.[16] While Banting admitted that no research programme in Canada would be sanctioned by their Government unless also sanctioned by the British Government, he concluded that 'if the Germans use bacteria, the Allies should be in a position to retaliate one hundred fold without delay'.[17]

Retaliation would entail a complete change of policy, and Topley was quick to point this out in a written response to Banting's report. Unsurprisingly, Topley also defended the views of the British advisors. His defence rested on the need to provide some measure of advice on the basis of little evidence, while not resorting to exaggeration:

> It would not have been helpful, though it would have been easy, to accept the most lurid forecasts of the effects of bacteriological warfare at their face value, and to warn the defence services that they must be prepared for the consequences. The members of the Sub-Committee were fully aware that they were basing their opinion on inadequate data, and that events may prove them wrong; but it did not seem to them that this freed them from their obligation of giving the closest appreciation of the situation warranted by the evidence.[18]

For Topley the main difference between the MRC and Banting was his 'far more alarmist view ... as to the seriousness of the threat of dissemination of bacteria and viruses by aeroplanes'. The pre-war subcommittee, Topley continued, had never suggested that this threat could be ignored. Nevertheless, he trusted the latest intelligence reports which indicated that sabotage was a far greater hazard than any putative resort to aeroplanes.

When Banting's memorandum was finally discussed by the BW Committee, the general consensus was to side with Topley. Hankey confirmed that Banting's recommendations would entail a change of policy because no offensively oriented research had yet been initiated. Topley verbally reinforced the views he had outlined on paper by stating that, apart from sabotage, he 'saw no reason for changing his opinion that bacteriological warfare was unlikely to produce the devastating results suggested by Sir Frederick Banting'.[19] And while other members of the committee added their agreement, Laidlaw, who was conducting the only biological warfare related research so far sanctioned, added that 'further progress could not be made by purely theoretical discussion, but only by experiments'. This note of dissent initiated a discussion of the finer details of the memo. The committee members agreed that fine sprays from aircraft would disperse and evaporate unless sprayed from quite low altitude. They felt that material in containers dropped from aircraft would 'constitute only a localised danger'.[20] Contaminated shells and bullets, they thought, would endanger those handling them and, in any case, would barely add to the infections that would arise normally from these wounds.

Once these points had been raised, the committee returned to Laidlaw's suggestion that further research was needed. The advisors noted that it would be more straightforward to infect a few individuals in order to create panic and destroy morale, than to initiate an epidemic. Hankey rounded off this discussion on a forward-thinking note, suggesting that

> notwithstanding the general opposition to Sir Frederick Banting's opinions, some further experiments seemed to be desirable.... He would not exclude the possibility of field experiments, preferably with the co-operation of Porton, if these were deemed desirable, but he would have to be put in a position to justify them to the War Cabinet.[21]

At Mellanby's suggestion, Hankey invited Sir John Ledingham to draw up a programme of experiments for the consideration of the committee. While Ledingham was to proceed within the constraints of a defensive policy, yet another step towards widening the scope of the research had been taken. According to Hankey, the scientists should not rule out offensive possibilities if there was a sufficient overlap with defensive needs:

> the programme should be drawn up on the assumption that there was no intention of taking the initiative in offensive measures, but should at the same time not exclude any experimental method, just because it might appear offensive in aim, if it seemed likely to [lead to] improvement in defence.[22]

It is not clear to what extent Hankey was already resolved to shift towards this offensively oriented defence prior to encountering Banting's report. Regardless of what actually precipitated the change, it is evident that prior defensive policy was not dictating the course of events. As the directions of research were planned, and the possibilities for the future were articulated, the scope of 'defensive' measures was recrafted simultaneously. Biological warfare policy and research policy were mutually shaping, or accommodating, each other.

Over the next two months, Ledingham and a small subcommittee consulted with various experts.[23] When Ledingham finally reported on the matter in April, he presented three biological methods for inflicting damage or destroying morale: contamination of bullets and shells with bacteria; distribution of bacteria from the air; and sabotage. All three had, at one time or another over the past six years, featured in intelligence reports. While the subcommittee regarded sabotage as 'far the most effective' means of waging bacteriological warfare, this was not the object of their deliberations. As Ledingham pointed out, 'it is in regard to the possible use of projectiles, explosive shells, dissemination from aeroplanes, that further technical information seems to be required', and therefore were the focus of attention.[24]

First, the subcommittee considered the possibilities for contaminated rifle bullets. They mentioned French literature which suggested that vegetative forms of bacteria, such as *Bacillus prodigiosus*, coated on to bullets could survive temperatures developed on firing and even during impact. While they admitted that these observations could form the basis of further empirical investigation, the subcommittee expressed their own doubts. Contaminated bullets would present a danger to factory workers and, should the organisms actually survive over time, to the soldiers handling them. They dismissed contaminated shrapnel shells for the same reasons. High-explosive shells were thought to be equally dubious by the advisors because the high temperatures involved would destroy bacteria. The subcommittee then turned to consider possible means of distributing toxic material from aeroplanes. Research was already under way at Porton on the physics of sprayed liquids and glass containers dropped from aeroplanes and so the subcommittee recommended that no further research in this area was necessary.

Ledingham's group had consulted various researchers on the use of shells fired from aircraft. They were told that certain types of shells, base-ejection shells, might present an opportunity for practical biological warfare. The temperatures reached by these shells were judged to be less of a problem than for high explosives and this feature, the advisors suggested, could be exploited. In this scenario, bacterial suspensions would be sprayed in the same manner as chemicals from the shells, which would explode at fixed heights above the ground. Although Ledingham's group thought that this means of disseminating bacteria would not give rise 'to mists of the type which would be most effective for producing infections in man', it could still produce sufficient infections for creating panic and destroying morale. In addition, a spray of bacterial suspension could potentially contaminate pastures and pass disease on to livestock.

By the end of their report, Ledingham's group had laid out a plan of action for biological warfare research. Contaminated shells and bullets might be used by an enemy and further research, they believed, would elucidate the issue. They thought that some shells, by analogy with chemical weapons, might also be adapted for use as bacterial bombs. These could induce disease but not epidemics among humans. Generally, however, a note of suspicion over the possibilities of bacteriological warfare ran throughout the report. Only sabotage, especially the use of botulinum toxin, was identified by the subcommittee as a danger against which 'constant vigilance' was urged. And in their final conclusion, as the difficulties rather than opportunities were flagged, Ledingham's group sounded as if they were still not entirely convinced by the threat:

> We have commented on the difficulties likely to be encountered in attempting on the large scale to broadcast pathogenic bacteria by any of the methods discussed in this memorandum, and on the extensive bacteriological organisation that would, of necessity, be required for purposes of offense. In so commenting, however, we can never exclude the possibility that the enemy may really attempt small-scale adventures in this

field, if only to impress, create panic, and destroy morale. All the methods we have considered seem, at the moment at least, more appropriate for the distribution of chemical poisons than of bacteria.

Such scepticism was maintained by the BW Committee even after they received the results from a series of experiments with contaminated bullets. Cultures of the non-pathogenic, sporing bacteria, *Bacillus subtilis* and *B. prodigiosus* had been painted on to the noses of bullets and dried, then fired over ranges of 50 and 500 yards at targets made of sterilized cotton wool enclosed in sterile paper. Investigators had taken samples from the cotton wool in 38 of the puncture holes and then attempted to cultivate the bacteria from the cotton wool. Results indicated that the bacteria had survived, with the principal investigator reporting that 'even the more delicate bacillus, *B. prodigiosus*, survived the majority of tests'.[25] Members of the BW Committee did not argue at all with these results but merely raised a different set of objections, that 'the risks involved in the preparation and handling of organisms of this kind would be such as to make it highly improbable that the enemy would use them for the contamination of bullets or other projectiles'.[26]

Porton Down

Hankey still did not share the evident scepticism of his committee on biological warfare and began to initiate further lines of research. He wrote to Group Captain Elliot, secretary of the BW Committee, in July 1940: 'I recently came to the conclusion that we ought to go a step further in the matter of bacteriological warfare so as to put ourselves in a position to retaliate if such abominable methods should be used against us.'[27] Having met privately with Mellanby and two of the 'leading hands' on the committee, Hankey secured their agreement to move ahead with his plans. Mellanby had indicated that the MRC could provide materials for 'irregular distribution' with only 48 hours' notice, but 'regular methods', which included aircraft, called for more research. The work, Mellanby suggested, might be carried out at Porton Down, Wiltshire, the site of the Chemical Defence Experimental Station since 1916.

Hankey was now faced with a dilemma. He was no longer a member of the War Cabinet, having been made Chancellor of the Duchy of Lancaster when Churchill became Prime Minister in May 1940 and, according to his correspondence with Mellanby, the War Cabinet was far too busy to consider germ warfare. Elsewhere, he informed Elliot that secrecy was a fair reason to sidestep Cabinet approval for his own 'step further' with research:

At first I thought that I ought to get a Cabinet decision because we had always said that we would not go ahead in preparing for its offensive use without such a decision. In view, however, of the extreme secrecy of the matter I am rather inclined to go a certain distance without a Cabinet decision...I should feel justified in taking that amount of responsibility on my own shoulders, but before preparing to do anything on a large scale I should have to go to Cabinet.[28]

Hankey justified this course of action to Mellanby on the grounds that he was acting in accordance with existing chemical warfare policy. It was legitimate to proceed without prior approval, he argued, because: 'in the case of chemical warfare we always took the line that we must carry out the fullest experiments as to methods of using it in order to enable us to discover and provide the means of warding off such attacks'.[29] Hankey spelt out his proposal to 'pursue the investigations we now contemplate on exactly the same basis. This would enable us to try this method of warfare out so far as is practicable.' At this point, and by shuffling past the BW Committee and War Cabinet, Hankey had shifted to an offensive stance in all but name.

Over the summer, Hankey and Mellanby approached Herbert Morrison, the Minister of Supply, and began to make practical arrangements for new research at Porton. It was not until early August that Hankey suggested the rest of the BW Committee might be informed in writing of these activities, and even then he cautioned that 'it would be better, I think, not to suggest in the note that we are preparing for the possibility of retaliation'.[30]

By September 1940 arrangements were complete.[31] Dr Paul Fildes, from the MRC Bacterial Chemistry unit at the Middlesex Hospital, was to head the team and bring two of his research fellows Dr Gareth Gladstone and Dr Donald Woods. Fildes was a pioneer in the field of bacterial physiology, focusing on bacterial nutrition.[32] His team had been instrumental in differentiating this biochemistry-dependent field from the broader discipline of bacteriology during the 1930s.[33] In addition, Ledingham had made available the services of Dr David Henderson and two laboratory technicians from the Lister Institute of Preventative Medicine.[34] Hankey explained to the BW Committee that the research at Porton would be a continuation of work along the lines laid down by Ledingham's subcommittee. This work was to be overseen by a small committee, the Porton Experiments Committee which, according to Fildes, was 'to explore experimentally possibilities of offence'.[35] The new Biology Department at Porton Down was set to become the focus of Britain's biological warfare research.

The programme was eventually approved by the Prime Minister, albeit some time after Hankey had set the research in motion. Hankey used a lever in this effort, a proposal from the Ministry of Economic Warfare to initiate crop warfare. The Ministry's agent in Budapest had been approached by an Austrian emigrant with a plan to use barbary leaves, possibly contaminated with fungus, which would be scattered from aeroplanes in order to poison wheatfields.[36] The Ministry of Economic Warfare, with little enthusiasm for the plan, simply required clarification on Government policy and accordingly had written in October to Hankey.[37] In turn, Hankey wrote to the Prime Minister suggesting the course of action which he had already initiated:

> Broadly speaking my own view is against initiating frightfulness of this kind. I think the right course is to investigate the practicability of the proposals, and the antedote [*sic*], in case they are used against us. By adopting this line we put ourselves in a position to protect our own interests, if they are attacked, and to retaliate if the Cabinet should so decide.[38]

A reinterpreted policy and new research institution now marked the start of a concerted effort towards building and testing a biological bomb.[39] At the time, Hankey explained to the BW Committee that these changes had been brought about by the recent commencement of the 'Blitz'. He reported that:

> In the present phase of the war, in which aerial attack is becoming of primary importance and in which conditions may at any time develop which present some threat to public health, I feel that renewed consideration should be given to the possibility that bacterial methods may be employed by the enemy, and to the counter measures which in that event would be needed.[40]

Later in the war, Fildes wrote that the surrender of France in June 1940 had prompted Hankey to pursue this course of action along with its attendant change of policy. Fildes explained that: 'It was finally agreed that we should press out work in all directions to produce a weapon and that the power of retaliation was the best means of defence. We were specifically instructed to produce a weapon which should be available at short notice for retaliation.'[41]

Whatever brought about the change in Hankey's outlook, the machinery was now in place to begin in earnest the quest for a biological weapon. It was assumed that retaliation automatically entailed an 'in kind' reprisal. And besides the retaliatory nature of these measures, it is also clear that the scientists were expected to produce an interim solution. The new Porton Experiments Committee was to 'agree any offensive procedure which they may think reasonably possible' and this suggestion would be tested by the Biology Department. According to Fildes, if the tests proved to be promising, 'it, and only it, should be put forward as the method of retaliation and this should hold the field while other methods are explored'.[42]

Fildes arrived in November 1940 at the Biology Department, where his team was housed in makeshift laboratories and what he described as 'usually a sea of mud and slush'.[43] Within days, the joint secretary of the

BW Committee, D.H. Rickett, wrote to clarify the present state of thinking on biological weapons and map out the future course of the programme. Anthrax was clearly a candidate disease for the putative weapon, although it was not an unproblematic choice of agent:

> I understand the position to be that until your research work has made some progress we cannot be certain that any offensive procedure will be satisfactory, except in the case of spore bearing bacteria i.e. anthrax. On the other hand, you will probably agree with the animal diseases people that anthrax has certain objections. First we understand that its action is mainly confined to producing primary cases.... Secondly the method of distribution to be adopted is by spraying from aircraft and this, so I gather, involves setting up a fairly large apparatus to produce the infective material. As you yourself point out, this may take a considerable time to develop.[44]

Rickett's account was clearly influenced by the BW Committee view that the primary advantage of a biological weapon would be to cause epidemic infection. Fildes was more sceptical of this view of biological warfare and wrote to the secretary suggesting that the reports of the BW Committee should not be passed to the Porton Experiments Committee. He surmised:

> Although there is nothing in them with which I do not agree, I am nevertheless sure that they had the effect of preventing for twelve months the institution of inquiries which are now in train. When I suggested that experimental work might produce methods which would cause the Committee to take a more serious view of the possibilities of BW, the chairman put the point to Topley. After due deliberation he stated that he would not be altered, namely that BW was not likely to be 'decisive'.[45]

Although anthrax did not meet requirements for an epidemic disease, it was generally recognized as a major scourge of cattle and Fildes regarded this feature as exploitable. The retaliatory weapon would, in the first instance, not be targeted against humans but against cattle.[46] It would be a form of economic warfare.

By the following April, Fildes reported to Hankey that it would be 'futile' to simply spray anthrax over German pastures in a random fashion.[47] Fildes' team had devised another method of retaliation, what Rickett termed 'your special diet for cattle', spreading linseed cattle cakes contaminated with anthrax from aeroplanes in order to infect enemy livestock.[48] This was thought to be the most promising line of enquiry and was soon allowed to set the agenda at the fledgling research station. A year into their research, when Fildes was asked by the chairman of the Porton Experiments Committee for a list of possible methods for waging biological warfare, he apologized and replied: 'I am afraid it will consist of only one item. Other methods may, of course emerge from the work we are doing in a number of different directions.'[49]

The work in other directions included a limited amount of research on toxin X, or botulinum toxin, and some preliminary work on breeding flies to spread contamination.[50] But anthrax, soon code-named N, remained the centre of attention at the Biology Department. In September 1941, Hankey wrote to the chair of the BW Committee seeking a rubber stamp for manufacture of the first usable British weapon:

> Up to the present I have only had authority, namely from the late Prime Minister, to permit experiments bearing on the defensive side of the problem, although I have, on the analogy of the early post-war work on gas warfare, interpreted my authority fairly liberally.... I do not think I am entitled to authorise the preparations, as distinct from plans, for retaliation without a further decision by higher authority. If you and your Committee think that that stage has been reached, I think you should advise me accordingly, and I will make the necessary approach to the Prime Minister.[51]

The approach was made in December and Hankey advocated the cattle cake plan to Churchill as the 'only method technically feasible at the moment' for purposes of retaliation.[52] On 2 January 1942, the Cabinet Defence Committee sanctioned these developments but agreed that

> policy remains as heretofore, namely, that the primary object of research and experiment in bacteriological warfare is to provide effective protective measures.... Lord Hankey is authorised to take such measures as he may from time to time deem appropriate to enable us without undue delay to retaliate in the event of resort by the enemy to the offensive use of bacteria.[53]

However, there was to be no operational resort to these weapons without the express approval of War Cabinet or Defence Committee. Hankey was instructed that if this happened, there should be little doubt that the measures would recoil on their users or allies. Secrecy was also to be paramount and the committee warned that 'all possible precautions must be taken to avoid publicity on the subject'. A day later, a further proviso, that the biological warfare effort should not appreciably divert resources from the rest of the war effort, was added to the list of caveats.[54]

Operation Vegetarian, soon renamed Operation Aladdin, involved the manufacture of cattle cakes on a large scale.[55] Production commenced towards the end of 1942 and was completed on 22 April 1943. Five million cattle cakes were manufactured in London and filled with anthrax at Porton, where they were stored.[56] Special hoppers had been designed and these were intended to attach to aircraft, which would carry and discharge the cakes over agricultural land. The whole operation was evidently an interim measure, and recognized as such by Fildes who wrote to Topley that he wanted 'to be in a position to say that we can retaliate at short notice, as required by our terms of reference, even though our retaliation may be feeble'.[57]

Gruinard Island

Soon after the plans for manufacturing cattle cake were approved at the beginning of 1942, Fildes, who by this time 'had no doubt about the applicability of bacteria in certain directions, if properly used and on a proper scale', suggested that 'academic exploration should now give way to the phase of practical exploration'.[58] Using chemical warfare attack as their model, the Porton scientists launched experiments to investigate the possibility of deploying bacteria as a cloud of 'toxic dust' generated from an explosion.[59]

During March, Fildes deemed his experimental work to have progressed to a stage where 'potential users' might become involved.[60] In order to carry out this task, the Porton Experiments Committee had been supplemented by the Porton Executive Committee who would be 'concerned with the application and development for use of procedures which are found biologically to be possible'.[61] In the notes on the agenda for their first meeting, Fildes presented the committee with his promise to create an anthrax bomb. He briefly described some work by biological warfare researchers in France. This research had shown that inhaling anthrax as 'toxic dust' was only effective when it was mixed with the chemical weapon, phosgene. Fildes disagreed, reporting that he had found pigs and rabbits to be killed in all cases where they had artificially been made to inhale anthrax spores. His team was 'hopeful' that the spores could be dispersed in an explosion and still remain dangerous. But, because any such tests would potentially be hazardous, Fildes suggested that they should first be carried out with harmless spores and only later with live spores.

When Fildes made this proposal, he already had a small isolated island in mind as his test site. Over the summer a large team emigrated from Porton to the 'X-base' on Gruinard Island off the west coast of Scotland.[62] In a series of tests from July to September, the scientists and servicemen filled modified high-explosive chemical bombs with a liquid suspension of anthrax spores, hung them from a frame and fired them from a distance. In the first two trials, sheep placed at distances of 100 and 250 yards were infected with anthrax from the aerosol generated by the bursting bombs. A further trial was performed with a bomb dropped from an aircraft but this failed to produce a result that satisfied the scientists, possibly because the bomb had landed in soft peaty ground.[63] The aeroplane trial was repeated in October, at Penclawdd on the Welsh Gower coast, on a beach firing range usually reserved for chemical weapons testing. The experimenters felt that this time they had produced a far more satisfactory result.[64]

Although the work at Gruinard Island was carried out in utmost secrecy, some months after the trials were completed security became threatened by an outbreak of anthrax on the nearby mainland. By April 1943, 7 cattle, 2 horses, 3 cats and 30–50 sheep had died.[65] Fildes had visited the site and admitted to the Chancellor of the Duchy of Lancaster, now the chair of the BW Committee, that

> there can be little doubt that the outbreak of anthrax that has taken place was due to a carcase [*sic*] being washed up from the island. I approved of the method of disposal, but unfortunately the demolition charge was too great and one or perhaps two sheep were blown into the sea and could not be recovered. This was an unfortunate mischance which will not occur again.[66]

As a precautionary measure, the Security Services had spread a rumour that the outbreak had originated from a carcass which had fallen from a Greek ship at the nearby convoy assembly point.[67] One breach of security had been avoided, but there was still the matter of a compensation claim that had been lodged with the Ministry of Agriculture. With one compromise averted, Fildes was reluctant to admit the claim, protesting that it would 'be a complete exposure of the fact that we have been working with anthrax'.[68] The Ministry of Agriculture representative, Mr Nathan, had also proposed to decline the claim 'on the grounds that we are not responsible for animals thrown overboard from Greek ships'.[69] Instead, Nathan proposed to pay the compensation after the war. Duff Cooper, the chair of the BW Committee, disagreed. The claim was small, a little over £300, and he argued that it should be paid immediately: 'it should be stated that our Government have agreed to pay this sum on behalf of the Greek Government, they being a member of the United Nations, and that settlement between the two Governments will doubtless be made after the war. I do not think that this will compromise us in any way.'[70] While Fildes thought that this course of action was a 'brilliant solution', he also voiced his concerns over the safety of further operations at Gruinard, hoping instead that outdoor tests would eventually be carried out in Canada and the USA.[71]

Special Operations

The anthrax bomb being developed by the Biology Department would have been deployed by the RAF, but they were not the only organization to show an interest in biological warfare. One scientist who appeared on a number of the advisory committees and in ad hoc meetings on biological warfare, Professor Dudley Maurice Newitt, represented the interests of Special Operations Executive (SOE), the clandestine agency formed in 1940 and responsible for sabotage operations. Newitt, a chemical engineer, was their director of research and regarded the emerging field of biological weapons as an ideal choice to assist the SOE's activities.

At the end of January 1942, Newitt met with Fildes and Hankey to discuss the 'position of SOE in the event of retaliatory action in respect of bacteriological warfare being authorised'.[72] During the meeting, Fildes outlined the current situation at the Biology Department and Hankey requested that Newitt and Fildes should undertake any 'investigations as were needed to provide material of suitable characteristics' and to arrange for preparation and storage of 'materials to enable BW to be undertaken without delay should the necessary authorisation be given'.[73] Hankey also authorized some international collaboration. The two scientists were permitted to discuss matters with representatives from the US, who had recently joined the war, and Canada. Any mention of biological warfare research at these meetings had to be accompanied with the explicit declaration that British efforts were 'defensive and protective; that we should in no circumstances initiate these forms of frightfulness, although the possibility of retaliation e.g. under pressure of public demand, could not be excluded'.[74]

Even the ongoing research at the Biology Department attracted Newitt's curiosity. As the plan to develop contaminated cattle cake moved towards full production, the professor seized an opportunity to obtain these materials for the SOE. He requested that, in addition to the 5 million cakes planned, an additional million should be produced for his organization.[75] Botulinum toxin also appealed to Newitt, who informed the Porton Executive Committee that he certainly 'could foresee a number of uses for this material'.[76] By July, Newitt was enthusing over biological weapons in more general terms. In a report passed to the BW Committee, he reminded them that:

> The views of the Committee appear at first to have been influenced largely by medical evidence as to the history of epidemic disease. In 1939 it submitted to the War Cabinet a Memorandum by the Medical Research Council in which the opinion was expressed that this method of warfare was likely to be less effective than orthodox methods, but that the dispersal of bacteria by agents in enemy country might certainly lead to disease.[77]

Newitt added that little empirical work had then been carried out, but now Fildes had made enough progress to merit a 'reconsideration' of the MRC position. He also pointed out that the growth of SOE in 1940–41 had opened up the possibility of their own use of biological warfare. Consequently, liaison with the BW Committee had been maintained and Newitt felt that 'Dr Fildes and his colleagues have been most helpful in assisting various SOE activities and in advising upon technical BW matters generally'. According to Newitt, no reliable methods for spreading contagious diseases in civil populations existed although Fildes had 'made considerable progress' in studies of tetanus and glanders and had even devised 'methods applicable to field operations'. Newitt did not enter into any further details about these studies or methods but wrote that these materials were not presently available, neither were they particularly well suited to SOE. Further work was demanded.

Fildes, on the other hand, was not so willing for his department to become a surrogate research branch of the SOE. In direct response to Newitt's report, he commented that the amount of time devoted to SOE requirements at Porton had actually been quite small. In fact, he added, 'most of our activities have been directed towards trying to produce a weapon for field use and the supply of mere samples of material suitable for SOE'.[78] This animosity between Porton and the SOE resurfaced the following February. As Newitt continued to push for increasing attention from Porton, an irritated Fildes wrote to the new chair of the BW Committee complaining that Newitt was guilty of overstating the health of biological warfare research. Fildes appeared to be perturbed even more by the encroachment of SOE into his research programme. Pleading for autonomy, he wrote:

> I have noted for some time that the relationship between ourselves and SOE is altering. Formerly we learned the conditions under which materials must be used and then set ourselves to find out what we could do. Our projects were then passed to SOE. At the present time SOE is telling us what they want without asking our opinion on the possibilities at all.[79]

Contrary to Newitt's claims that anthrax presented few technical or operational obstacles, Fildes pointed out that problems remained, particularly in relation to maintaining the stability of anthrax. Then, marshalling uncertainty about enemy intentions in his favour, he argued: 'if we are going to credit the Germans with the power to wage BW on us in other directions, without any evidence that they have this power, the whole of our resources will be squandered'.[80]

It is not clear that the evidence that Germany might employ biological sabotage was any more or less substantial than the possibility of their utilizing a bomb. However, by the time Fildes wrote his irate letter in early 1943, the Porton team was convinced of the nature of the threat. Within months of the Gruinard Island trials the concerns of the SOE had been pushed to the margins and anthrax dominated the attention of the Porton team and their advisors. Other projects had slipped behind. In October 1942, Fildes reported to the Porton Executive Committee that 'simple instructions' for cultivating flies had been issued to SOE along with information on infecting the flies with 'preparations' supplied by the Biology Department.[81] Any further research on flies as biological warfare agents was now regarded as 'unnecessary' by the department. Despite SOE requesting a kilogram of botulinum toxin, further work on the subject had ceased as a result of the researchers' admitted 'preoccupation' with anthrax. Even Newitt's request for a million extra cattle cakes had not been met. The original target of 5 million cakes had been achieved and SOE were informed that since they were 'likely to be the first user, SOE should have the first call on the first million tablets charged'.[82] Fildes thus summed up the post-Gruinard situation at Porton: 'at the present time the whole resources of the Biological Section are taken up with research, applications and manufacture of anthrax. This has led to the abandonment of all other applications of BW which were under survey.'[83]

All this optimism over the promise of an anthrax weapon was not confined to the laboratory. At the advisory level, a meeting of the BW Committee was called in October 1942 to consider future policy in the wake of the Gruinard trials. According to Davidson Pratt from the Ministry of Supply, the trials had engendered a shift in position for the biological warfare advisors:

> At an earlier date, the knowledge of available methods had encouraged the belief that this form of warfare, if used at all by our enemies, was not likely to prove more than at worst, a serious nuisance. The result of Dr Fildes' work during the last two years showed that this view needed very considerable revision.[84]

This change in the committee's perception of the threat was used to bolster a case for increased resources, especially personnel and space, and closer links with the United States. Now that the means of offence had been clarified in their minds, the committee members flagged work on defence against anthrax as a future priority. A few days earlier the Porton Executive Committee had also provided a similar appraisal of the potential of the new weapon: 'it was generally agreed that anthrax inhalation was of such superiority over recognised Chemical Warfare agents (100 to 1000 times) that it warranted very urgent and intensive work on both the offensive and defensive aspects'[85] Here, the comparisons had shifted. The experts agreed that anthrax, which had been deemed inferior to hypothetical epidemic-causing armaments, was superior when placed next to chemical weapons. The results of the trials did not speak for themselves until positioned in this manner by the advisors. And now, biological weapons were being positioned as a very real and potent threat.

Soon, Britain's biological bomb was being presented as a sign that Germany could have followed a similar path. The following March, a new

Defence Subcommittee of the BW Committee was informed by their chairman, Duff Cooper, that 'it was possible that the German experiments were further advanced than ours'.[86] No intelligence information was added to support his claim. Duff Cooper also warned his committee that: 'Dr Fildes' experiments had shown that the method most likely to be practicable was the dispersal of anthrax spores, and the Chairman thought that we must assume that the Germans, if they resorted to this type of warfare, would be likely to use this form of attack.'[87]

Four months later, Fildes submitted to the same committee a memo which did nothing to alter this evaluation. The German biological warfare threat, Fildes believed, had not diminished in the light of further experimental work and he had become more convinced of its exact nature: 'it would appear certain that the weapon is an air force weapon, the effectiveness of which will depend upon the mass of its use'.[88] Three years of research, one year after the Gruinard trials, and Fildes was able to present the threat in solid terms based on the mirror of his own research.

The American programme

As the expert advisors used the success of the anthrax bomb trials to lever more resources, their attention increasingly turned to the role that the United States would play in biological warfare research. Between February and March 1942 the Chief of the US Army Chemical Warfare Services had dispatched one of his officers to observe work at Porton. A return invitation was made to Fildes, who went along with his deputy, David Henderson, in November only to find that no work had yet commenced.[89] A meeting of biologists had taken place in October directed by Dr Edwin B. Fred from the University of Wisconsin. This group had acknowledged the potential threat from biological warfare and recommended that both defensive and offensive measures should be pursued. The recommendations were duly passed to Henry L. Stimson, the Secretary of War. According to his report, Fildes had attended this earlier meeting and felt that it had simply explored 'in an abstract manner ground which had already been explored'.[90] Fildes conveyed this sentiment to the head of the new War Research Service, George W. Merck, and claimed that this spurred Merck into initiating a research programme dispersed through a number of university departments.

The US programme grew phenomenally over the following year. A major research establishment was built at Camp Detrick, Maryland and field trials were planned at Horn Island, Pascagoula, Mississippi and Dugway in Utah.[91] Although the British researchers had expressed hopes that the US programme would turn its attention to work on viruses, the American researchers followed the same route as the British and concentrated on botulism and anthrax.[92] It was not long before the US was ready to entertain British advances to mass produce the N-bomb.

Ordering anthrax

In November 1943 the oversight of biological warfare in the UK was rearranged. The BW Committee remained intact and three smaller panels were formed: a Policy Panel now considered matters relating to research, development, supply and security; a Defence Panel replaced the Defence Subcommittee; and an Operational Panel considered matters relating to offence. The post of Chancellor of the Duchy of Lancaster had changed and Ernest Brown succeeded Duff Cooper as chairman of the BW Committee. This move caused some consternation for Fildes who wrote:

> I am sorry to hear that Mr Ernest Brown is likely to be given the Chairmanship of the Committee. I have always understood that he is a strict Methodist, and that seems to me to be a strange background for a person who has to support the less orthodox activities of the Committee.[93]

And another member of the BW Committee, Lord Rothschild, was ready to cause Fildes even greater annoyance. Rothschild, an influential member of many committees, represented the interests of the Security Services on the BW Committee and had become worried that Fildes was being allowed an unprecedented degree of freedom in research, security and policy matters. His anxieties culminated after Fildes announced boldly to the BW Committee that plans were well under way to place an order with the US for the manufacture of a consignment of anthrax bombs. An incensed Rothschild wrote to the War Cabinet secretariat demanding that Fildes be made aware of the security and policy implications of the order and protested that: 'Dr Fildes himself makes no effort to hide his own attitude towards bacterial warfare. His attitude is one which might be described as almost ghoulish scientific interest in the offensive potentialities of bacteria.'[94]

Rothschild was especially concerned about the dangers of storing the anthrax bombs and the consequences if the deadly store was hit in an air raid. Later, Rothschild described Fildes as a 'very good professor' but 'irresponsible to an alarming degree'.[95] With reciprocal animosity, Fildes remarked that Rothschild was uninformed and 'a bit of a nuisance'.[96] Indeed, Rothschild was concerned enough to make a real nuisance of himself and seek further clarification on what he regarded as a significant shift in policy. At the inaugural meeting of the Operational Panel in January 1944, Fildes announced that the Americans had approached Porton for an estimate of the probable requirements for the bombs. The panel members, including Rothschild, queried whether this move from experiment to production was covered by existing authority. Fildes responded bluntly that the development 'was a necessary feature of the instructions given to him'.[97]

The reply failed to placate Rothschild and after the meeting he wrote to Philip Allen of the War Cabinet secretariat, requesting that Allen look back at the War Cabinet minutes to see whether Fildes or the BW Committee had actually been instructed to retaliate at short notice. Even this confirmation, he added, would not end the matter as

> it is easy to make remarks of that type, particularly when the subject was in its early stages, without realising the full implications. . . . Retaliation at short notice in fact involves going into production with all the concomitant storage problems. . . . As soon as serious production starts as opposed to laboratory experimental production, and no amount of verbal quibbling can conceal the fact that Fildes asks that authority should be given for serious production to start in the USA, security problems are immeasurably increased.[98]

Allen encountered some difficulty in reconstructing the prior passage of biological warfare policy. Much had been done in secret and by word of mouth. After examining the written records and consulting with Air Marshal Sir Richard Peck, who had chaired the Porton Experiments Committee and been a member of the BW Committee, Allen was able to piece together some details. In short, biological warfare policy had not been discussed by the War Cabinet or Defence Committee since January 1942 when Hankey was authorized 'in fairly general terms' to proceed with Operation Vegetarian within a defensive yet retaliatory policy regime.[99]

Peck had also echoed Rothschild's concerns that Fildes was pushing matters beyond his remit. In a confidential memo, which he showed to the biological warfare secretariat, he wrote frankly about his disquiet:

> I cannot resist the feeling that the enthusiasm of the scientists, in particular, of course, but not solely, Dr Fildes, has tended to break loose from policy control and that decisions have been obtained and acted upon beyond the knowledge of the matter possessed by the War Cabinet as a whole. I am not sure that their scientific enthusiasm as inventors is not prejudicing their sense of responsibility; and I fear that there is a tendency not to weigh carefully enough the consequences of loosing these inventions upon mankind.[100]

There was obvious pressure on Philip Allen to push matters further. Eventually, the secretary gathered enough material to write a briefing which Ernest Brown could, in turn, condense into a memo for Churchill. Allen's report gave a short history of events and mentioned that the order of biological bombs would put the whole production machinery in motion. Whether or not this amounted to a shift in policy, Allen argued, depended on some keen hermeneutics. After the January 1942 Defence Committee meeting, Allen gleaned, Hankey had issued verbal instructions to Fildes to produce a retaliatory weapon 'without undue delay'.[101] Yet, with no trace of any written instructions to be found, Allen remarked that:

> It is not altogether clear what the words 'without undue delay' mean in this context. Dr Fildes has interpreted it to mean 'at short notice'. The point is of some importance, since, if the bombs were manufactured and stored in the United States, they could not be brought over here and dropped in Germany, if the need should arise, within less than a month. If on the other hand the bombs were brought over to this country for storage, the practical problems involved would be considerable.[102]

While Allen used this confusion to argue that the whole affair was a matter for the Prime Minister, Fildes prepared more of his own ammunition. Research at Porton had largely shifted to defence against anthrax, so there was little chance of Fildes being able to mobilize any new results to aid his bid to proceed with the American order. Instead he took advantage of disturbing intelligence reports arriving from Washington and Berne. Germany, according to this information, had developed the capability of using botulinum toxin in rockets, possibly the pilotless V-1 rockets, and Fildes felt that this was sufficient justification for preparedness.[103] Writing to the chairman of the BW Committee, he acknowledged that there was no way to establish the truth or falsity of the reports, but

> pointed out that specific defence against unknown possibilities was impracticable and that the only defence was the power of retaliation. At present we had no power of retaliation and should have none for a long time unless our opposite numbers in the USA could be stimulated to do their part in production.[104]

By the time this disheartening forecast reached Ernest Brown, he had already put the case to proceed with an order of half a million bombs to Churchill. In a very brief memo, Brown pointed out that the number was 'comparatively small' but marked a transition from experiment to 'serious' production. In policy terms this

> would not be inconsistent with the earlier authority which was given for measures to enable us without undue delay to retaliate in the event of this form of warfare being used by the enemy. It is still true, as it was when that decision was taken, that it would be difficult to take adequate defensive measures against a really large scale attack by the enemy; but, at the present phase of the war, it may well be that you will wish to reexamine the policy which has hitherto been accepted before we enter into a commitment of the kind now suggested.[105]

Following this submission, Fildes was asked by the Cabinet Office to provide further information to convince the Paymaster-General and Churchill's scientific advisor, Lord Cherwell, of the need for the order. Cherwell was concerned with how the bomb compared with other weapons.[106] In response, Fildes noted that the bomb was still experimental but comparable to a chemical phosgene bomb between a hundred and a thousand times heavier. But, he stressed, this was besides the point as the 'only reason for requiring production on minor operational scale is that this weapon is only means of retaliation against a BW attack'.[107]

Cherwell was convinced. In a note to the Prime Minister, he pointed out that properties of anthrax made it a weapon of 'appalling potentiality' and easier to make than 'tube alloys' (atomic weapons).[108] For these reasons, he advised: 'It seems most urgent to explore and even prepare the counter-measures, if any there be, but in the meantime it seems to me we cannot afford not to have N bombs in our armoury.'[109] The case persuaded Churchill, who did not raise the matter with the Defence Committee but instead entered 'most secret consultations' with his military advisors.[110] The Prime Minister wrote shortly afterwards to the chairman of the BW Committee:

> They consider, and I entirely agree, that if our enemies should indulge in this form of warfare, the only deterrent would be our power to retaliate. I therefore approve the proposal of your Committee that an order should be placed in the United States for the manufacturing and filling of the bombs in question. . . . We should regard it as a first installment.[111]

The order had been placed but did not proceed smoothly. During the following months Fildes repeatedly expressed his frustration that everything was slowing down, decisions were being postponed and, more concretely, there was talk of reorganizing the BW Committee. Although a plant for manufacturing the bombs was soon erected at Vigo near Terre Haute, Indiana, it still remained to be tested and made operational. In June 1944, Fildes wrote a short report, entitled the 'Failure of BW Policy in the European Theatre', which gave vent to his anger. Fildes reminded his readers that, as a deterrent, the cattle cake project 'was not considered of much value'; the N-bomb 'was considered to be highly deterrent'.[112] Although Fildes claimed that the United States had agreed to undertake weapon production in July 1943, the aims of their respective programmes had diverged. He believed that the United States were covering a very broad spectrum of research, 'treating it as a subject to be explored *de novo* and with special emphasis on the Pacific theatre'.[113] Fildes then claimed that, despite the 'great difficulties' still ahead, production of the N-bomb could be speeded up if the United States would collaborate in a more co-ordinated fashion and if they would assign production a higher priority over other longer-term projects. Finishing on an ominous note, Fildes warned that without the N-bomb 'it must be recognised that, so far as retaliation by BW methods is concerned, we shall be defenceless against a BW attack unless this is delayed for 6 months or more'.[114]

It is not surprising that Fildes should have remained such a keen advocate of his creation. Later in the year he wrote at length about the moral value of biological weapons. His comments came in response to a short report by a member of the Canadian General Staff, Colonel Goforth, who had claimed that the military on both sides of the war would be deeply suspicious of both chemical and biological warfare. The colonel claimed that, to a military mind, they were unpredictable, 'unsoldierly' and would 'tend to upset his careful staff tables and logistical calculations'.[115] Widening the debate, Goforth also claimed general 'public revulsion' existed towards biological warfare.

Fildes responded by comparing biological weapons with other forms of killing. Like his predecessors on the pre-war Bacteriological Warfare Subcommittee, he argued that his work had produced an exemplary way to kill humanely. He wrote:

> I do not think it true to say that a 'substantial minority' of the population would object to retaliation by gas, microbes or anything else, if an attack in these forms were made on them.... Actually, any moral objections which may exist to BW are based on insecure grounds. Is it any more moral to kill Service men or civilians with HE [High Explosive] than with BW? It may be agreed that it is not, but that BW is more 'horrific' in the sense of introducing unnecessary mental and physical suffering and so should be excluded if possible. The 'horrific' nature of BW is, however, not admitted by those who are competent to judge, on the evidence available from animals.[116]

Fildes then described how animals subjected to anthrax would inhale the invisible cloud of spores, remain outwardly healthy for a few days and then die of septicaemia (blood poisoning) within a few hours, adding that 'observation of monkeys does not suggest that they undergo any more suffering than most people do when they are ill'. In comparison, Fildes continued, any civilian exposed to bombardment by high explosives would undergo 'considerable mental disturbance long before he is buried under a pile of rubble'. This would continue, along with physical distress, upon removal to hospital where

> the suffering he has undergone is often terminated by bacterial septicemia similar to that which has the same effect as BW without the distressing preliminaries. It seems clear to me that a substantial majority of the population would conclude that, if they had to put up with a war again, they would prefer to face the risks of attack by bacteria rather than bombardments by HE.

Bombs and committees

With the anthrax bomb order in place, the British Government and military began to prepare for the transition to biological weapon production in the US. General Ismay had suggested to the Prime Minister that the biological warfare programme should be passed to a subcommittee with representation from the three Services.[117] Scientific experts would be marginalized in this new body and merely be consulted if the military representatives thought it necessary. Intentionally or otherwise, this arrangement would have allowed Churchill to proceed with the acquisition of the anthrax bombs while answering Rothschild and Peck's concerns by wresting control of the programme from Fildes.

When Fildes heard this news he was unimpressed. Writing to the Cabinet Office, he described the proposed committee as 'admirable' but quite incapable of dealing with technical matters.[118] Above all, Fildes felt that the marginalization of experts was indicative of a project immersed in secrecy and wrote: 'We have been too "Top Secret" for my existence to be admitted. The Minister has now been withdrawn, and I am left as a disembodied spirit without admitted existence or apparent authority at all.'[119]

Even after the replacement of the Bacteriological Warfare Committee with the new Inter-Services Subcommittee on Biological Warfare (ISSBW), Fildes continued to complain that he was being 'sidetracked' by the Chiefs of Staff.[120] Fildes' solution to his problem was to request official and formal membership of the new group. Shortly afterwards, the chairman of the subcommitttee, Air Marshal Norman Bottomley, wrote to Fildes and invited him to become the scientific technical advisor to the subcommittee. He also explained why the responsibility for biological warfare had been transferred from the Cabinet Office to the Services. A bomb existed and its use had to be contemplated: 'if an effective use is ever to be made of the weapons which you have developed and if any counter-measures that are approved are to be put into force, the Services must now accept their share of the responsibility and exercise a more direct control than hitherto'.[121]

In response, Fildes continued to defend his position and commented on how previous verbal arrangements with the appropriate Minister had worked to his satisfaction. Since oversight of biological warfare had been moved to the three panels formed in 1943, Fildes felt that he had suffered. He remonstrated that he was victim of 'a fiction that I do not exist', consequently he had frequently been 'overlooked' and 'charged with improper interference' in military affairs.[122] And, asserting his authority as a scientist, he wrote:

> As an expert on the application of Bacteriology to Warfare I am concerned to find that I am invited to be a member of a sub-committee which is to 'keep under review all research'. When I accepted this job four years ago

it was to direct research, and before agreeing to attend this Committee I should like my new duties to be very clearly defined.[123]

A month later, in August 1944, Fildes agreed to join the new subcommittee which had already begun to consider the future of biological warfare once the war ended. Over the next year, planning became increasingly forward thinking as Fildes admitted that the threat of a biological attack from Germany had receded. The order for the biological bomb was continually stalled until events overtook the plans and the war drew to a close before the order could be delivered. At this time it became apparent that Germany had not indulged in a biological warfare research programme on anything like the scale of the Allied effort.[124] Two reports made to the ISSBW in June 1945 spelt out details of this limited research.[125] Hitler had intervened personally to ensure that German biological warfare research remained defensive, a command that was not universally heeded. What little research was performed, in the areas of human and crop diseases, was poorly co-ordinated and, according to intelligence reports, poorly executed. With access to this information, the German threat that helped animate the British biological warfare programme dissipated.

The legacy of world war

The material achievements of the Biological Department Porton, cattle cake and a prototype bomb, are a poor indicator of the significance of the wartime research effort. Britain had launched an organized and concerted effort to produce biological weapons and had shifted from a defensive to an offensively oriented policy regime. When Fildes wrote in 1944 that it 'was finally agreed' to initiate work at Porton, his *post hoc* gloss masked a far more jagged and uneven process of change. At a practical level, Hankey had sidelined the BW Committee and their contrary advice, then established new committees to deal with new research. He had also acted in advance of seeking Cabinet-level approval.

The opposition of the BW Committee could be construed as a product of their opinions on the complexity of establishing epidemic disease. Certainly, this entrenched epidemiological approach was both Banting and Newitt's explanation of the advisors' complacency in the face of the potential German threat. It could be argued that, in contrast, Fildes' approach was underpinned by a more deterministic 'germ theory' in which the presence of the causative agent in a properly formed aerosol was thought sufficient to inflict a militarily significant outbreak of disease. While there is no direct evidence from Fildes that this reductionism was a component of his philosophy, his previous background in laboratory-based bacterial nutrition and his frustration with the BW Committee both point in this direction.[126]

Regardless, the BW Committee was shunted away from influence and Fildes' mission was facilitated by additional pragmatic factors. First, while changing policy by no means determined the course of events, there was sufficient flexibility in the term 'defensive' to stretch the meaning across to research on offensive measures, which under this authorization could proceed without hindrance from any advisors. A second strand of policy, the Cabinet request for a short-term solution and means of retaliation in kind, meant that Fildes would have been able to dismiss the BW Committee's reservations about biological warfare without having to oppose their views directly. An epidemic may have been difficult, even impossible, to create artificially, but this was not required by the Government or military. So long as *some* means of retaliation in kind existed, the details were less important for the authorities. Anthrax, which had been dismissed as a weapon of war by the BW Committee because it was non-epidemic, could now be regarded as an 'obvious' candidate agent in this new policy context.[127] The tangible results from this line of research proved somewhat ephemeral, the stock of anthrax cakes was destroyed soon after the war and the anti-personnel N-bomb never reached large-scale production. But the idea that the means of offence, and the nature of the threat, resided in a targeted attack using a bomb persisted and underpinned the rationale for a flourishing post-war biological warfare programme.

4
The Growth of Biological Warfare Research

What would happen to the British biological warfare programme after the Second World War? It was by no means obvious that research would continue. The anthrax cattle cakes and the rudimentary bomb were significant for their originality, but were nonetheless relatively modest achievements when compared with other wartime technologies such as atomic bombs, radar or operations research. Germany had neither employed biological warfare nor treated their research programme with any seriousness. Furthermore, as this chapter describes, many staff at the Biology Department Porton returned to civilian employment leaving the new Superintendent, David Henderson, with a struggling and emaciated organization.

This said, the present chapter is not about the decline of the British biological warfare research programme. Within a few years, the enterprise had been rejuvenated on a massive scale. Biological weapons research assumed equal priority to atomic science in official policy. Both would be spoken about, and consequently treated together, by advisors as a new class of weapons of mass destruction. A considerable sum of Government money, along with a tremendous amount of hope, was about to be invested in the research programme at Porton. This transformation will be explored in the present chapter as biological warfare in the UK entered a brief 'golden period' for policy-makers and researchers. During this period the pre-war notion of bacteriological warfare as a public health threat was entirely forgotten. The wartime prospect of a biological bomb and the dreadful reality of the atomic bomb placed a changed threat at the top of the agenda. A biological bomb equivalent to the atomic bomb became the central goal of the Cold War research programme in Britain. The Russian threat, portrayed mainly in the same terms, would serve as a spur.

Handing over

When the Inter-Services Subcommittee on Biological Warfare was established in 1944 their ostensible role was to take responsibility for the never realized order of anthrax bombs from the US. Very soon, as the war continued to turn in favour of the Allies, they began to concern themselves with the future of biological warfare. In his capacities as technical advisor and founder of the British research programme, Paul Fildes submitted a report on this subject to the authorities. It is clear from this document that Fildes was already beginning to think about returning to civil work and had framed his forecasts and proposals accordingly. Although, according to its chairman, Bottomley, the ISSBW had been formed because biological weapons were a reality, Fildes presented a different version of the situation. Porton had produced evidence that 'a weapon can be devised for limited use in warfare, but it is becoming questionable whether we shall have proved the possibility of production before the end of the war. In this case it may reasonably be concluded that the feasibility of BW is not yet established.'[1]

This depiction of biological warfare held scope for continued peacetime research in the area, although not necessarily in the same vein as the work to date. Fildes suggested that, in time and 'in the ordinary course of medical research', a more potent weapon than the N-bomb might be developed.[2] In his opinion, cancelling the existing programme of research would be 'unwise, but on the other hand the danger would be too remote to allow great expenditure of energy and resources on the subject in the immediate future'.[3] Having positioned his case by raising the very distant and uncertain possibility of a future threat, Fildes continued by linking biological warfare research firmly to civil medical research:

It is perhaps not generally understood that the basic problems of BW are basic problems of medicine. The applications only are different. Applied medicine is primarily concerned with defence, but defence cannot be arranged intelligently without study of offence. Similarly BW is concerned with the exploitation of offence. Thus both the BW workers and medical workers must know how the microbe carries out its offensive activities before the former can exploit them and the latter protect against them.[4]

Fildes followed up his train of thinking a few months later in a further outline of proposals for post-war research. His vision for the Biology Department at Porton was a group reformed under the Royal Army Medical Corps with close links to the MRC. Most of the work would be 'pure medical research' and the Services would play no role in initiating lines of enquiry.[5] Instead, they would respond to 'offers' made by the biologists. A month later, Fildes revised this proposal and suggested that the MRC take on the sole responsibility for biological warfare. Even at Porton, he mused, most bacterial physiologists would not be working directly on warfare and: 'Owing to the remoteness of the danger and the possibility that BW may later be found to be impracticable, it would be impossible to maintain a staff on this sort of work *unless* it is linked up with work of certain value.'[6]

Next, pushing his argument to an extreme, Fildes suggested that he could use his influence in the Royal Society to establish a Microbiological Research Council.[7] This body would carry out research and education on 'the physiology of all forms of microorganisms'. Fildes presented a similar version of these proposals the following January, arguing this time that ignorance of fundamental bacteriology was the main hindrance to weapon production and that a biological warfare research station must be linked to 'work of admitted national value', which particularly meant 'work on the general physiology of micro-organisms'.[8]

Fildes' vision for post-war research was distinctly long term and oriented to fundamental problems. This outlook can be contrasted with the ideas put forward by Fildes' deputy, David Henderson, on future research policy for biological warfare. In a report that never progressed beyond the draft stage because Fildes took exception to it, Henderson outlined these ideas.[9] Overall, the report placed a greater emphasis on short-term goals than Fildes would probably have found comfortable. Henderson had spent some time in the US and Canada, where it had already been decided that research would be maintained, and he freely admitted that his experience in these countries had convinced him that Britain should continue with biological warfare research. He agreed with Fildes that work to date had been limited by lack of fundamental knowledge and mentioned that the British team had spent much time simply defining the problems to be studied. But, parting company with Fildes, he added: 'Nevertheless, our short term policy research has been particularly fruitful in exposing these problems and it would seem advisable to continue actively in this work until such time as the broadest possible general picture of the fundamental problems in BW has been obtained.'[10]

Whereas a departing Fildes was quite happy to reconstitute the Biology Department, Henderson argued for constancy and a focus on more short-term goals:

> The problems involved are in many ways unique to bacteriological history and the workers already collected for this research have therefore unique experience. To disband the group at this time or to switch its activity to more abstruse problems, allowing the techniques developed and the material resources acquired during the last four years to fall into abeyance, will mean the loss, permanently, of much valuable experience. As noted above, not until such time as the broadest general picture of the fundamental problems in BW has been obtained should most of the short term policy research be abandoned. This applies whether one considers the research purely from the point of view of BW or whether it is viewed as a post-war problem with emphasis on the more ethical idea of advancing medical knowledge, which such research will undoubtedly do.[11]

Fildes rejected Henderson's more immediate goals for biological warfare and his own vision, of a small applied unit at Porton linked to the medical research community, was probably influenced by his own plans for the future. Fildes had already helped secure the future of biological warfare research through his technical advice. In November 1944 the ISSBW acknowledged that 'although this method of warfare had not been developed to the operational stage during the war, sufficient work had been done to indicate that with further research a very deadly form of warfare might emerge'. The committee had recommended, and the Chiefs of Staff agreed, that post-war biological warfare work should continue. But Fildes did not intend to be a part of this effort. Only days beforehand, he had written to the Cabinet Office pointing out that, two years from retirement, he was anxious to revive his work with the MRC and added:

> I had the intention of asking for the release of myself and my personal staff immediately it could be agreed that the danger of a German attack had passed, even before the 'end' of the European War. I doubt whether anyone could suggest that the danger is very great even now, and I question whether it would be to the national advantage to keep up on this sort of work much longer.[12]

Fildes continued to try and release himself from Porton, enlisting the help of the MRC, and continually pointing out that, unless his deputy David Henderson was offered the leadership of the Biology Department, he would be lost to another job at either University College London or the Lister Institute. He wrote once again, in April 1945, to the Cabinet Office asking at least to be given a decision on his release date and asked 'to be taken into account that further internment of a person of my age on Salisbury Plain is not a good way to preserve whatever mental capacity has been left to him after 5 years'.[13]

The pleas were heeded and Fildes left Porton at the beginning of August for the Lister Institute. One of his final acts as head of the Biology Section was to write to the secretary of the ISSBW and warn of the necessity to protect the post-war research programme from the vagaries of adverse publicity or political change:

> there is no doubt that Henderson and other possible recruits with whom I have spoken are seriously concerned about the risk to their professional career attached to an appointment in this new field. They felt that they may suddenly become deprived of the opportunity for work on their selected subject as the result of a decision that an atomic bomb is all that is necessary to insure against war, or some whim of politics or public opinion may lead to closing of research on BW.[14]

Although there is no record of the committee's response to this warning, Henderson's concerns must have been allayed. As Fildes departed in all but an advisory capacity, Henderson assumed the renamed post of Superintendent at the correspondingly renamed Microbiological Research Department.

Organizing biological warfare policy

During 1945, various spokesmen from the wartime biological weapons project met with members of the Chiefs of Staff's ad hoc Joint Technical Warfare Committee to advance a case for biological warfare. Their consultation was part of a much broader review of possible developments in warfare over the next decade. Biological weapons formed only a minor part of the consultation exercise and the achievements made during the war failed initially to convince this senior military panel that such weapons would play any realistic part in future conflicts.[15] Apart from a possible boomerang effect on the aggressors, an objection that traded heavily on an epidemic concept of biological weapons, they concluded that prophylactic measures could and would be developed which would deter enemy employment of germ warfare.[16] Later, in an annex to a report on the future of biological warfare for the same committee, the chemist and army director of special weapons and vehicles, Brigadier Owen Wansbrough-Jones, argued that scientists working in the area had been apt to describe their results 'conservatively'.[17] A final report in December drew attention to the 'probably tremendous increase in lethality in BW agents which may be produced after further research'.[18] The authors flagged the comparative ease of producing a weapon and the possibility of biological warfare being complementary to atomic bombs. All of which added up to a plea for the 'necessity' of continuing research.[19]

Even before the Joint Technical Warfare Committee made their final report, the Chiefs of Staff were ready to pass on their blessing for germ warfare to the Cabinet. In September, they recommended that the Cabinet Defence Committee permit research in the area to continue, writing:

> The Chiefs of Staff Committee are convinced that, in the interests of National Defence, work on BW research should continue in peace time. As an island we are an ideal target for attack by BW methods as our attacker need have no fear that diseases which may spread would recoil upon himself or upon his allies.[20]

After being informed that the US was continuing its biological warfare research, the Defence Committee issued a directive in October 1945 which 'approved the continuation of BW research in peace-time'.[21] Offensive research, according to a statement of biological warfare policy written five years later, was 'implicit' in this general directive.[22] Indeed, a year after the directive was issued, the ISSBW had decided on a broad programme of research maintaining the same policy as a rationale: 'at the time it was emphasised that for the successful development of defensive measures it was essential to study the offensive field'.[23]

One reason for the adoption of this general policy of 'offence for defence' was likely to have been Britain's adherence to the Geneva Protocol of 1925. As described in Chapter 2, the protocol was essentially 'a no first use' agreement applied to chemical and bacteriological warfare. Under the common interpretation of its terms, gas and germ warfare could be utilized against non-signatory states and in retaliation against any state.[24] The policy adopted by the UK during the Second World War and continued into peacetime would have been in accordance with the provisions of the treaty.

In order to advise on policy and the direction of research in biological warfare various committees were rapidly established (see Appendix 1). At the technical level, the Biological Research Advisory Board (BRAB) of the Ministry of Supply was set up in 1946 to provide independent scientific advice on 'biological problems with special reference to micro-biological research carried out in the Ministry of Supply and extra-murally'.[25] It was accountable primarily to the Advisory Council on Scientific Research and Technical Development of the Ministry of Supply but provided technical advice to the ISSBW.[26] The Ministry of Supply, in turn, was responsible for carrying out biological warfare research and development at the Microbiological Research Department (MRD) at Porton.[27] This charge was but a tiny fraction of the vast amount of work carried out by the Ministry, both in research and development (R&D) as well as civil industrial supply.[28]

Located within the Ministry of Defence, the ISSBW, reconstituted as the Chiefs of Staff BW Subcommittee in 1947, consisted of independent scientists, Ministry of Supply, Home Office and Ministry of Health representatives, together with Admiralty, War Office, Air Ministry Staff and medical representation.[29] Its terms of reference stated that it was to be

> the focus for the discussion and formulation of all aspects of BW policy, both offensive and defensive, and [it] reports to the Chiefs of Staff. On technical matters it is advised by the Biological Research Advisory Board and for foreign intelligence it relies on the Joint Scientific Intelligence Committee.[30]

In addition, the BW Subcommittee supplied 'advice on policy and technical matters relating to civil defence against BW' to the Home Defence Committee. It received general guidance on research policy from, and provided advice on 'the policy and technical aspects of Biological Warfare' to, the Defence Research Policy Committee (DRPC). The subcommittee was thus the highest-level committee solely devoted to biological warfare. The DRPC, in turn, was 'responsible for advising the Minister of Defence and the Chiefs of Staff on matters connected with the formulation of scientific policy in the defence field'.[31] The first chairman of the DRPC was Sir Henry Tizard, the civil servant and military scientist who had also chaired the 1945 ad hoc committee which had dismissed the potential of biological warfare in future wars.[32]

A range of committees thus formed a chain of advice and guidance from the laboratory through to the Government, in principle with a division of labour between policy and science. However, the boundary between science and policy is never quite so fixed as such divisions would imply, and various interests can be served by defining any issue in either political or technical terms.[33] As will become apparent, this leakage was certainly used to advantage by the various committees responsible for biological warfare.

Biological warfare takes top priority

Within the new network of committees responsible for biological warfare the post-war programme began to take shape. An early report on the future development of biological warfare research written by the new Superintendent of the MRD, David Henderson, summarized the wartime effort in positive terms, noting that:

> the overall achievement in five years of experimental study has been to raise biological warfare from the status of the improbable, where the difficulties involved were believed by many (without experimental evidence) to be insurmountable, to the level of a subject demanding close and continuous study.[34]

However, later in the report, Henderson qualified this earlier statement further, arguing that 'the imponderables in attempts to set up epidemic disease are so great that such a form of attack by an enemy is probably not a reasonable future possibility'.[35] This reservation eventually justified a research programme that continued to focus on non-epidemic diseases. Henderson also noted that the 'principles which have governed this work have been no more than working hypotheses arrived at by the use of judgement without much experimental backing. In the future more background must be obtained by fundamental and long-term research.'[36] Having outlined this case for further research, the report next discussed possible weapon development and the development and use of simulants and pathogens. It would be the job of biologists to design field trials with pathogens, which could be carried out 'with a sufficient margin of safety to satisfy requirements' or, if the risk was deemed too great, to design special explosion chambers. From the outset, Henderson acknowledged the overall limitations of all trials and reminded his readers that 'the biologist will never be in a position to offer positive proof concerning the effect of any BW weapon against man. He is

---

Box 4.1   Future directions for biological warfare research in the UK (1946)

Offence: more efficient methods of dissemination of agents, knowledge concerning the probable effectiveness of new agents, large-scale production methods, preparation and storage of agents, information of sabotage methods to initiate animal disease epidemics, 'methods to increase the efficiency of the agents already known and tested in the field'.

Defence: immunization, introduction of new antibiotics, large-scale preparation of antibiotics, physical means of protection, information on methods for control of epidemic diseases.

Source: PRO, WO188/667. BW(46)17. Inter-Services Sub-Committee on Biological Warfare. Future development of biological warfare research (memo by Dr Henderson) (30 April 1946).

---

committed to indirect assessment by the use of experimental animals.'[37] In summary, the report functioned as a 'shopping list' of research directions (see Box 4.1). This included offensive and defensive investigations which, according to Henderson, would be best undertaken with the stability afforded by long-term planning and attention to fundamental research.

While the Defence Committee had simply approved the continuation of research on biological warfare during peacetime, a number of factors appear to have contributed to the subsequent high priority and increased scale of research effort in the area. To begin with, policy towards biological weapons was soon couched within a more general defence policy. In July 1947, the Chiefs of Staff agreed on 'a cardinal principle of policy to be prepared to use weapons of mass destruction. The knowledge of this preparedness is the best deterrent to war in peace-time.'[38] Weapons of mass destruction were taken to be atomic, biological and chemical weapons. It is likely that the DRPC were equally content to abide by this taxonomy. The committee had been excluded from almost all decision-making on atomic matters and both chemical and biological warfare held the potential to be the DRPC's 'own weapons of mass destruction'.[39]

Mass destruction

Once biological weapons had been labelled as weapons of mass destruction their fate was firmly tied to that of nuclear and chemical weapons. Yet, there is evidence that this classification was not quite so inevitable as it appears in later policy discussions.

The planning staff for the Chiefs of Staff had stated in 1946 that: 'it may be argued that almost any form of weapon, if employed in sufficient quantity and against suitable targets, is capable of mass destruction'.[40] This remark was made in the context of protracted discussions over what stance to take if the Russians made any mention of biological warfare in disarmament talks at the United Nations Atomic Energy Commission.[41] Although these talks were intended to focus on atomic weapons, the negotiators involved had become alarmed over what would happen if the scope of the discussion spread to other weapons of mass destruction. The Joint Planning Staff soon qualified their wide definition of mass destruction, pointing out that 'to include weapons in normal use in modern warfare would raise issues tantamount to general disarmament which is outside the scope of the Commission'. They restricted mass destruction to atomic and biological weapons on the grounds that 'by their nature' they were 'primarily used for this purpose'. Finally, the staff added the warning that in any disarmament negotiation, every effort had to be made to restrict discussion to atomic warfare.

This position did not hold. By 1948 the situation with the UN Atomic Energy Commission had not been resolved and the matter was referred to the BW Subcommittee, who reported to the Chiefs of Staff that: 'we do not suggest that Biological Warfare should be rated now or in the near future as a means for mass destruction of life'.[42] In their report the BW Sub-Committee justified this position by expressing doubts that bulk production of biological weapons would be possible in the UK within a decade. American weapons, they argued, might be produced within a couple of years but their effectiveness would be 'relatively primitive in comparison with the ultimate potentialities of this form of warfare'.[43] And on Soviet capabilities, 'we have no knowledge of Russia's present ability to initiate Biological Warfare but must assume that she possesses the necessary basic knowledge'.[44]

The BW Subcommittee's conclusion did not temper their more general assessment of the potential of biological weapons. Drawing on the tension between what was feared possible and what was unknown, they warned that:

> Believing in the ultimate potentialities of Biological Warfare and in the impracticability of its international control, in the interests of national security we must be free to devote a great effort to defensive measures in order to reduce the gap between the offence and the defence.... Concurrently, we must also be free to conduct research in the offence in order to possess the power of launching reprisals in kind.[45]

Prevarication over the status of biological weapons was undoubtedly linked to the disarmament context. Whether or not germ warfare was classed as a weapon of mass destruction hinged on whether or not British representatives should be lured into mentioning them in an international arena. The previous year, 1947, the Chiefs of Staff had declared their intentions over preparations to use weapons of mass destruction, a definition which explicitly included biological weapons, and the DRPC had shifted the priority of biological warfare research accordingly. But doubts over the status of biological weapons were not entirely restricted to the exigency of disarmament talks. A similar view was emerging from across the Atlantic. Within a month of receiving the BW Subcommittee advice on arms negotiation, the Chiefs of Staff had also been sent the policy recommendations of the US Committee on Biological Warfare:

> Until adequate measures to preserve the international peace are assured, it shall be the policy of the United States (a) to maintain a research and development program in the field of biological warfare consistent with the necessity of safeguarding the United States against attack with this weapon, (b) to take all possible steps to prepare defences against biological attack, and (c) to be prepared to make effective use of such means of warfare should it become necessary.[46]

Although this statement placed great emphasis on building up a biological weapons capability, the same committee had concluded that it would be incorrect to classify biological warfare under the heading of weapons of mass destruction.[47] Their rationale was based on the complexity that surrounded the initiation of epidemic diseases and the inability of humans to produce and control such epidemics. Although no particular factors were mentioned as contributing to this complexity, the report admitted frankly that any factors affecting the spread of disease were 'poorly understood or perhaps even unknown'.

Non-epidemic disease defied the mass destruction label for different reasons:

> As far as nonepidemic producing agents are concerned, the Committee feels that use of these as weapons would cause no more indiscriminate destruction of life than would, for example, use of incendiary munitions. Also, destruction of property would be practically nil with biological agents.[48]

This comparison with conventional weapons, in terms of loss of life, and the lack of damage to property enabled the committee to extend their discussion into ethical territory. In the light of these comparisons, their argument ran, biological weapons ultimately might be 'more humane and less objectionable than the use of conventional weapons'.[49] This, they thought, would be even more defensible if incapacitating rather than lethal agents were employed.

The British Air Ministry continued to suggest that biological bombs would not be weapons of mass destruction. A cover letter for the Air Ministry's contribution to the 1949 Biological Warfare report stated that: 'It is not suggested that Biological Warfare can be rated now or in the near future as a weapon of mass destruction but undoubtedly progress is likely to increase rather than reduce this fear.'[50] This assessment of the potential of germ warfare acknowledged that the status of biological weapons was open to revision. Nonetheless, two years earlier in 1947, the definition held as a central component of the Chiefs of Staff policy of preparedness.

Promises

As assessments of biological warfare began to trade on the destructive potential of biological weapons, equally and somewhat in contradiction, they also flagged uncertainties that any weapon could ever fulfil that dreadful potential. This tension generated a rationale that helped place biological weapons research at the top of the agenda. Remaining uncertainties would yield to further scientific investigation. The DRPC argued this point to the Chiefs of Staff, noting that:

> Biological weapons are potentially of greater value than chemical weapons and possibly of equal value to atomic weapons for breaking the will of any enemy to fight. But plans should not yet be influenced by the prospect of the availability of such weapons within ten years. There is far too little knowledge available yet to justify this. The whole subject needs the most intensive study, on a far larger scale than is being attempted at present. [51]

This tension between what was still unknown and what was feared possible was not confined to the DRPC and pervades much of the deliberation surrounding these important recommendations. The conclusion of the 1947 report to the Chiefs of Staff on biological warfare echoes the same uncertainties through a contrast with atomic warfare and is worth quoting at length:

> BW is a method of warfare arising out of the normal development of science and is in this respect equivalent to the atomic bomb. It differs from the atomic bomb in one major respect. It is untried. Given that the atomic bomb will function, it follows inevitably without experiment that a blast will be produced destructive to life and property. A BW weapon may demonstrably function, but it is impossible to estimate what effect it will have on life (man) because experiments cannot be carried out on man. Thus, all anticipations and deductions made in the present report are to be accepted only as sound conclusions based on experiments with

animals, it being recognised that results on animals cannot with certainty be applied to man because the necessary quantitative data are lacking and cannot be gathered. Nevertheless it would be hazardous to assume that the estimated danger to man is less than has been concluded in this report. Expert opinion would certainly not support the assumption.[52]

Here, within a single paragraph, was a 'scientific' statement of the magnitude of the threat – equivalent to the atomic bomb – set alongside a commentary on the uncertainty of the threat. The juxtaposition strongly implied that more research was imperative if the two positions were ever to be reconciled. Significantly, this justification of research in terms of the 'fear of the possible' was set to become an influential motif throughout the history of biological warfare research.

Having already drawn on this 'fear of possible' line of argument, the DRPC immediately recommended that 'research on chemical and biological weapons should be given priority effectively equal to that given to the study of atomic energy'.[53] In a later policy statement they added that biological warfare 'may eventually prove comparable with the atomic bomb'.[54] Elsewhere, the BW Subcommittee, in a document primarily expressing concern over the shortage of researchers in biological warfare, had already reported that: 'We have been advised by the Deputy Chiefs of Staff Committee that research on BW is of the highest priority and in the same category of research as atomic energy and research.'[55] During these discussions, Dr Henry Hulme, the Scientific Advisor to the Air Ministry, had acted as an advocate for biological weapons. His advocacy was based on a different facet of biological weapons, their comparatively low cost. When he addressed the DRPC on the priority of biological warfare research, Hulme argued 'that by subtracting one percent from Atomic Warfare costs we could increase Biological Warfare by one hundred percent'.[56]

Another significant factor contributed to the high priority accorded to biological weapons research. Soon after the end of the war, the Air Staff placed a request with the Ministry of Supply for an anti-personnel biological bomb. This was intended for strategic use and, initially, to be in production within five years from November 1946. Commenting on this requirement, BRAB advisors noted that agents and weapons accepted as 'war-time expedients' would certainly not meet the Air Staff requirement without much additional R&D.[57] Members of the BW Subcommittee developed this point and argued that research was not sufficiently advanced to meet the Air Staff requirements in the timescale they had envisaged. Nevertheless, a target-specific bomb, rather than the capability to cover large areas, remained the ultimate aim of UK research policy. Within a year, the DRPC briefly outlined the philosophy behind this stance, arguing that 'in a major war against a highly industrialized country, mass attacks, as opposed to precision bombing, against centres of population and industry will be ineffective and wasteful in manpower'.[58]

Offence or defence?

So, relatively soon after the end of the Second World War, biological warfare research enjoyed the top priority in defence research policy alongside atomic weapons. Within this regime some debate at first ensued over the relative priorities of offensive and defensive research, and particularly over the merit of making any distinction between them. At the first meeting of the BW Subcommittee it was remarked that: 'it was generally regarded as impracticable to dissociate research on the offensive aspect from defensive, and to do so would retard progress in vital research on the latter aspect'.[59] Yet at the same meeting, and in the context of a discussion of poor staff recruitment, committee members drew on the distinction to suggest that biologists might be more likely to work at Porton if 'wholly offensive' research, such as weapon development, took place in Canada.

By March 1947 the policy of 'offence for defence' had prevailed. In pursuing this retaliatory policy, the Chiefs of Staff did not simply elevate the role of offensive above that of defensive investigations. Neither did they draw on previous rhetoric that argued over the impossibility of distinguishing offensive from defensive work. Instead, a third line of argument was employed, as they suggested that adequate defence was *inconceivable* without *first* pursuing research on offensive aspects of biological warfare. At their 45th meeting in 1947, the Chiefs of Staff discussed a report on current staff shortages in biological warfare research and in this context decided: 'that it was essential to proceed with research into the offensive aspect of Biological Warfare, as until sufficient research in this sphere had been carried out, the true problems of defensive measures could not wholly be assessed'.[60]

The priority of biological warfare had peaked. A line of argument based on the 'fear of the possible' had circulated between the BRAB, DRPC and Chiefs of Staff. Expert scientific and military opinion painted biological warfare as possibly destructive yet at the same time had pointed out the need to resolve remaining uncertainties through further research. The Chiefs of Staff had been satisfied that biological weapons rated as weapons of mass destruction and included them in its more general policy stance of 'preparedness'. Finally, the Air Ministry had provided a firm goal for the programme by making a specific request for an anti-personnel bomb. Support for continuing and expanding research at Porton had thus been engineered, the doubts expressed at the end of the war had melted.

The practical outcome from all of these discussions, promises and portrayals of biological weapons, which had ranged across several committees, was a DRPC recommendation that the level of research on biological warfare should be increased. Until then, an estimated 0.25 per cent of the defence

R&D effort had been devoted to this field. Although the extent of the proposed increase was not specified by the DRPC, they indicated that it would need to be sufficient to 'make it possible to bring into service by 1957 biological weapons comparable in strategic effect with the atomic bomb, and defensive measures against them'.[61] Shortly afterwards, the DRPC stated that its objectives for R&D in the biological warfare programme were to be:

(i) A biological weapon for strategic use
(ii) A means of storage of selected agents coupled with a small quality plant, or, alternatively, the means of large scale production
(iii) Defensive measures, including detection, mass immunization, personnel protection and medical treatment.[62]

Imagining the threat

Impetus for continued research on offensive aspects of biological warfare was intimately bound up with expert assessments of the threat. A 1947 Chiefs of Staff report to the Home Defence Committee assessing the future scale of an air attack on the UK considered that no European power was likely to have atomic bombs ready for use by 1951, but would by 1956.[63] However, the report suggested that a potential enemy would be in a position to use a biological weapon by 1951 and would do so more effectively by 1956.

The threat assessments even went as far as to define the nature of the biological weapon. In a statement of information for service personnel on biological warfare, the BW Subcommittee provided an estimate derived from wartime research that one bomber load of cluster munitions would affect one square mile in the open or a quarter of a square mile in a city with a 50 per cent risk of death.[64] This estimate is repeated in several other documents issued by the committee at this time. The information for Service personnel noted that the method of dispersion would be 'invisible airborne clouds from bombs, rockets or other devices' or saboteur weapons such as infected reservoirs or foodstuffs. However, in terms of the most immediate threat, the warning was: 'the most likely form of generation would seem to be from aircraft clusters containing small bombs, thus getting as wide an area of scatter as possible.[65]

A year later, in 1948, a similar assessment of the nature of the threat was proposed by an ad hoc panel of the BW Subcommittee:

It is not possible at present to forecast the form which a biological weapon might take. The present indications are that spraying the agent in a particular form or in a liquid medium from the air is not practical. As far as we can see, the form of weapon most likely to be used would be some form of container, equipped with an ejection device, which would be dropped to earth or conveyed to the target in a vehicle or rocket or shell type.[66]

Spraying was dismissed further in the detailed annex to the 1948 annual report on biological warfare prepared, in consultation with military and scientific advisors, for the Chiefs of Staff Committee:

It might appear at first sight that aircraft spray tanks as used for smoke and CW chargings might be an effective means of dispersing BW agents. This weapon might conceivably prove of value for massive contamination if such were ever required, or for the destruction of crops on a limited scale.... Mainly for the reason that it cannot be aimed, aircraft spray is not therefore being considered at present as a possible weapon for airborne clouds of BW agent.[67]

The report explained that sprayed charging might not reach the ground in any predictable fashion, unless it was released at 'zero feet'. In addition, fitting spray tanks on to jet aircraft and the fear that the safety of aircrews and aircraft could not be guaranteed provided more barriers to exploring spraying any further. Apparently, other methods of dissemination, shell, mine fragments or bullets had not been 'seriously considered'. One further line of development had been explored by Canadian scientists who experimented with contaminated darts and found the weapon to be 'technically feasible'. On the other hand, the authors of the report pointed out that the difficulty of finding suitable targets, 'men in the open', meant that dart guns presented a poor comparison with other methods of dissemination.

These various assessments appear to have been based heavily on the results of UK research; the 50 per cent casualty figure had been 'made in the light of experiments carried out under the stress of war'.[68] By 1948, the United States' Committee on Biological Warfare, while recognizing the contingencies surrounding the estimates, had also adopted them as a basis for their future plans.[69] The US committee noted a revised UK estimate that, taking into account improvements, 100 square miles of city would require 2000 tons of agent to bring about 50 per cent casualties. This, and a forecast tenfold improvement in bomb efficiency and agency potency, was judged by the Americans to be 'the best estimate that can be furnished at this time'.[70]

The US committee's views on how biological agents would be spread also echoed British assessments: 'by military attack BW agents could be carried to the enemy in bombs or other missiles'.[71] Sabotage, enhanced by the tiny quantities of agent needed to effect an attack, was mentioned as a potential threat in another assessment.[72] The report also recognized that contamination of surfaces and water supplies, and the use of insect vectors, were possible means to employ biological warfare but the authors dismissed them as either easily countered or poorly researched.

Sabotage was not ignored in the British context, but was generally mentioned only in passing. In one letter from Wing Commander George Lamb, Henderson had to be reminded not to discount entirely this means of waging germ warfare: 'I have been talking to our "cloak and dagger" boys, who suggest that the use of BW as a sabotage weapon should not be lost sight of, although it is not regarded as a very suitable weapon for general employment.'[73] Despite this reminder, sabotage remained in the background of the threat assessments and in the shadow of the potential effects of a biological bomb. In a meeting with one visiting US scientist, Dr Caryl Haskins, the BW Subcommittee informed him that 'in view of the different circumstances in this country, we do not attribute such importance to its use by saboteurs as is the case in the United States'.[74]

Wider input from foreign intelligence into these assessments was rather slight. In 1949, Dr D.K. Blount of the Joint Intelligence Bureau reported to the DRPC that, regarding biological warfare:

> many of the appreciations of Russian development were founded on presumption and not on real facts. Fairly sound information was available as to what equipment the Russians had at the present moment, but there was little reliable intelligence about the position in the scientific and technical fields.[75]

A Joint Intelligence Committee (JIC) report summarizing what was known of the Russian situation provides some indication of the types of presumption that had been made. One key inference was based on 'reliable information' that penicillin was in short supply in Russia. This was, in part, thought to be because of a lack of scientific and technical personnel and equally the 'backward nature of the Russian fermentation industry'.[76] On the basis of this information, the JIC conjectured that: 'it would be reasonable to assume that if Soviet industry could have manufactured large-scale production of BW agents it could also have manufactured the plant necessary for large-scale penicillin production by the most modern methods'. Other evidence of the status of germ warfare in Russia proved elusive. The report admitted that

> we have no firm evidence concerning any BW organisation in Russia. There are, however, indications suggesting that a small group of scientists and technicians is carrying out BW research under the control of the Soviet Army, that their work is only on a small scale, and that the scientific and technical abilities of the group are not of a high order.[77]

According to the JIC, no information existed of any biological weapons R&D or trials. The committee had also undertaken a survey of the scientific literature which they believed revealed widespread Russian interest in microbiology and related subjects, 'but the scale and scope of their work are such as might be fully justified by the legitimate requirements of public health and agriculture'. The report also acknowledged that there was some Russian interest in sabotage, a conclusion supported by a report from a few months earlier which stated: 'There is no firm indication of the use by saboteurs of BW agents by the Russians. There are numerous reports from German and Russian sources attributing outbreaks of disease to Russian saboteur action, but in no case can these charges be regarded as having been substantiated.'[78]

Scraps of evidence pointing towards a Russian interest in sabotage were then assembled in this report. F.G. Krotov of the Soviet Army Medical Service had published 28 literature reviews bearing on biological warfare. Major-General Schreiber of the German Army Medical Corps had been captured by the Russians in May 1945 and interrogated in Moscow about contamination of pastures with anthrax sprayed from aircraft and the treatment of surfaces of objects with plague bacilli in order to infect those handling the objects. During the 1937–38 purges against Soviet microbiologists, many were charged with and convicted of sabotage against farm animals by spreading infectious disease, 'and the intention to cause infectious disease of selected human subjects. . . . The Soviet authorities evidently believed in the efficacy of saboteur BW methods.'[79]

The broader JIC summary of possible Russian activity concluded that 'the Soviet Union is probably capable of waging BW by sabotage methods, but up to 1948 had not advanced very far with any project for large-scale BW as envisaged in the West'.[80] This was followed by a crude attempt to predict future Russian capabilities based on knowledge of the timescales involved in the US project. After openly acknowledging the difficulty of applying these estimates to Russia, the committee proclaimed that

> there can be little doubt that the USSR could, if such were its policy, achieve the United States level of production of 1945 by about 1952. Any threat which may develop subsequently will depend, *inter alia*, on policy decisions on which at present we have no evidence, and we are unable to assess its probability, magnitude or details.

The BW Subcommittee, with a possible hint at the recent Soviet atomic bomb trial, regarded this report as sufficient evidence of a security threat to demand some response. After some discussion, they concluded:

> While it was fully realised that the Joint Intelligence Committee could not be more specific in their appreciation of the threat . . . the general feeling was that the USSR had considerable leeway to make good before that country would be in a position to employ this weapon offensively; nevertheless in the light of recent events; the Joint Intelligence Committee's broad conclusion could not be lightly disregarded, namely that the

USSR could achieve the United States level of production of 1945 by about 1952.[81]

In the vacuum left by such reports, assessments were frequently based on the assumption that UK and US possibilities reflected Russian capabilities. The risk was used by the BW Subcommittee to hammer out further proposals by way of a policy response. They recommended a 'firm and consistent policy for research', as they argued that constant changes in policy were disruptive.[82] Subcommittee members also felt that there was no need to change priorities from those adopted by the DRPC in 1947. Rapid detection and 'development of, and production research on, selected agents and weapons for strategic use' were to remain of 'supreme' importance for completion by 1955.[83] Moreover they were both classed among 'projects which are so important as to call for continuous effort regardless of date of completion'. Any vestiges of the pre-war, 'public health' terms through which these possibilities were defined had by now disappeared. Pragmatic definitions and targets based on a biological bomb now dominated the UK programme and the assessment of the foreign threat.

The place of civil defence

Defensive measures for protecting the civilian population were not entirely neglected by advisors in the deliberations about biological warfare research. In 1947, the Home Defence Committee approached the ISSBW and BRAB to solicit their opinions about a possible germ warfare attack on the UK. They wanted some indication of what agents might be used, what vaccines existed, and whether it was feasible to mass-produce any vaccines for stockpiling.[84] BRAB replied that it was impossible to list the likely agents, but that research into the problems of large-scale production, processing and storage of one unnamed antibody should begin, and that 'probably four different types of production plant would be required for the various types of vaccines etc'.[85] BRAB subsequently asked the Ministry to commence 'high priority' research on the production, processing and storage of the antibody and also sought the co-operation of the MRC.

A year later, in 1948, the BW Subcommittee passed the matter of mass immunization over to an ad hoc advisory committee in the Ministry of Health, chaired by the Chief Medical Officer. Their discussions produced little practical advice. The Chief Medical Officer's pessimistic report read: 'the committee is driven to the conclusions that these difficulties would, indeed, be so immense that to inoculate the population against a number of diseases, and before the event of hostilities, would not be within the bounds of practicability'.[86] Even assuming that immunization against any agent might in principle be found, the logistics of mass immunization were daunting. Many months' training of a large number of people would be required.

Centres to carry out inoculation would have to be established. More than one injection might frequently be needed, and with time taken for immunity to develop, 'mass immunisation would have to be started sooner than it might be judged politic to signify governmental expectation of war or to create public alarm about conjectured assault with biological weapons'.[87] Even persuading people to volunteer for injection without any imminent danger of war could prove difficult for the authorities. Having outlined such a depressing menu, the committee could only recommend that the Government rely on therapeutic measures and on provision of gas masks.

In the light of the Ministry of Health comments on mass immunization, the BW Subcommittee was left to suggest that measures which were impracticable during peacetime 'might not be so under the stress of an emergency or in time of war'.[88] In such an event, they contended, any effective defence would most likely be a combination of mass immunization, detection of agents, physical protection such as gas masks and protective clothing, together with therapeutic treatment after infection. During 1949 the Civil Defence Committee of the Cabinet proceeded to ask the Ministry of Health to undertake research on 'measures necessary to immunise the population in the more vulnerable areas, and of the facilities which would be required for the therapeutic treatment of BW casualties'.[89] The MRD, 'owing to lack of staff and facilities and to its numerous other commitments' was unable to assist the Ministry of Health except to provide results of research that had already been carried out. The BW Subcommittee therefore sought help from the MRC through its secretary, Sir Edward Mellanby.

Mellanby's response was swift and unenthusiastic. The MRC was devoted to both fundamental research and to the broad aim of curing disease. Mellanby regarded the BW Subcommittee's request as a diversion and wrote of the council's reluctance to return to biological warfare research. Their input would have to be 'really necessary', over and above that provided by existing expert advisors.[90] The BW Subcommittee responded courteously to Mellanby, informing him that BRAB had discussed the matter and would be quite capable of providing advice. Actual research on immunization and therapy, however, was 'beyond the capabilities of the Microbiological Research Department' and the BW Subcommittee would continue to seek the MRC's assistance on these issues.

The BW Subcommittee adopted a more personal approach and Hankey eventually met with Mellanby. They decided to appoint a small panel to 'advise on research in immunisation and the therapeutic treatment of casualties'.[91] This was to become the MRC BW Defence Committee with a remit to advise the Ministry of Health on measures for civilian defence against biological warfare, such as mass immunization. It was also to initiate research for solving such defence problems. This defence remit was quite circumscribed and members of BRAB did not feel that it overlapped with their own work.[92]

The pre-war Subcommittee on Bacteriological Warfare had been pre-occupied with stockpiling and provision of prophylactic and therapeutic measures against biological warfare. These activities, I have argued, were directly influenced by their predominant definition of bacteriological warfare in terms of the threat to public health in the aftermath of conventional bombing. While the BW Subcommittee and BRAB did not ignore civil defence entirely, it is evident that the issue was not their primary focus and was readily farmed out to the Ministry of Health and MRC. What remained was a remit that revolved around the high priority accorded to offensive research, within the framework of the race to develop a biological bomb for retaliatory use.

Recruitment

While research planning made rapid progress, the advisors were faced with poor staff recruitment as a major practical obstacle to implementing these plans. At the end of the war many of the staff at the Biology Department, including the project leader Paul Fildes, had returned to civilian research although some maintained contact through membership of BRAB. Until the end of the war, staff had remained attached to the MRC although work was reported only through the Ministry of Supply. Once the ISSBW was established towards the end of the war, the biological warfare research programme became more formally linked to the activities of the Services. After 1945 the MRC no longer wished to be the main agency associated with biological warfare research and responsibility for the staff had moved to the Ministry of Supply. According to Fildes, the shift was contrary to advice from the ISSBW and was perceived as a threat to the freedom of the biological warfare scientists.[93]

With the staff numbers depleted, it became essential to recruit new staff during peacetime. By the end of 1947 there were 42 scientific staff employed at the MRD, only a few people short of the wartime maximum of 45 workers. The BRAB still felt that this would not be enough to sustain the expanded post-war programme and complained that 'Porton would continue to suffer from the national shortage of trained biochemists, biophysicists and micro-biologists'.[94] BRAB members took an active interest in rectifying this short-age and rallied to promote efforts for building up microbiology departments in universities through postgraduate training and extramural contracts. The DRPC lent their support by suggesting that non-military applications of biological warfare research might appeal to biomedical researchers. In their view, 'so far as we are competent to judge, research in the defence field may result in important contributions to the broader field of medical science'.[95]

Fildes, in a separate note to BRAB, also drew attention to what he saw as a neglect of research on the physiology of pathogenic bacteria and viruses.[96] Arguing that this focus was narrower than that of general microbiology, he declared that 'practically all advances in the direction we require have come, in this country...from schools of "bacterial chemistry"'.[97] The two 'most hopeful' schools he identified were at Oxford ('two small rooms and a passage') and Cambridge ('a small hut').[98] Birmingham was added to this list by the vice-chairman of the University Grants Committee as it had a Department of Industrial Fermentation.[99] All of which implied that more resources should be devoted to the specific field of bacterial chemistry.

All such efforts to rejuvenate the field, in any event, would take time to show results. And in the mean time, the new Chief Superindent at the MRD, Henderson, complained to the BW Subcommittee via BRAB that, whereas a 'serious research programme had been outlined', there were few indications that it could be executed.[100] It was important for BRAB to address whether Porton research could continue along the same unrealistic lines, or in the Superintendent's words whether they wanted to 'stagnate for six years as a result of a lack of proper facilities'. Plans had been made to build extensive new facilities at Porton and building was to commence later in 1948. Henderson noted that construction of new facilities was planned to take three to four years with additional time to get them up and running. Howard Florey, a senior BRAB member, added that the pilot experimental fermenter was experiencing setbacks and the new laboratories should not suffer similar delays otherwise staff would be lost:[101] 'Scientific staff could not be expected to keep their enthusiasm indefinitely....Whilst a bacteriological department at Oxford might well be housed in huts as a temporary measure, the work at Porton could not be done in huts.'[102] Other members of BRAB echoed these concerns, particularly that staff could not be expected to 'mark time' for four or five years. They would instead return to working for universities. The board decided that a direct approach would need to be made to the Minister of Defence in order to convey their anxieties.

The discussion of staff morale and delays in obtaining facilities afforded ample opportunity for Fildes to emphasize the unique nature of the research being undertaken at Porton. He explained that:

> Outside Porton, the medical approach was largely directed towards cure of or protection against disease. In contrast, an essential Porton approach was to enhance the action of the microbe. This different approach was necessary not only to produce weapons but to design rationally a defence against BW in the worst form that could be achieved by research.[103]

As the anxieties about staff recruitment and retention became entangled with the slow progress on the new facilities, the DRPC responded with a report to the Minister of Defence, Viscount Alexander of Hillsborough, which attached the highest importance to the construction of new laboratories. The Minister, in turn, forwarded it to the Production Committee of the Cabinet with an endorsement that high priority should be accorded to 'certain defence projects' in order to protect the national interest.[104] He also recommended that the Cabinet committee should take steps to inform civil departments of the weight now attached to building up the MRD.

With direct support from the Minister of Defence it became possible for Henderson and his advisors to set new targets for staff recruitment with some degree of confidence. By April 1948, the MRD stated that it was now aiming for a total staff of 24 scientific and 30 experimental officers. Already, 20 scientific and 25 experimental officers had been recruited and a proportion of these were undertaking a training course in bacteriology at the Postgraduate Medical School, London University.[105] Nevertheless, the lack of highly qualified specialists remained a general concern.

Two years later, a report on biological warfare policy maintained that adequate salaries, levels of personnel and overall research expenditure were all necessary to the success of the research programme.[106] The topic occupied the advisors' focus of attention at the next two BRAB meetings. A general 'wage freeze' policy had been adopted by the Treasury and attempts by BRAB to recruit and upgrade staff at the MRD were not proceeding well. Board members regarded this situation, and especially a lower than requested salary granted to the Chief Superintendent at MRD, as a comment on the status of biological warfare research in general.[107] This opinion was voiced by several board members despite a letter in their possession from Sir Kenneth Crawford, Controller of Supplies at the Ministry of Supply, which affirmed that the area remained of high priority.

Recruitment problems continued and Fildes wrote a memorandum on the subject in May 1951.[108] The memo contains a rare reflection on the ethical status of peacetime research into germ warfare. Fildes mentioned how it originally had been thought that recruitment through the personal contacts of the board would be sufficient to attract good scientists and 'cause it to be known that first class work could be done at Porton, that professional careers would not be jeopardised and even that there was no moral obliquity involved in preparing to defend one's country'.[109] Rather than pursuing this moral line, Fildes blamed the present failure of personal approaches on the fact that medical salaries had recently been raised above those for the scientific Civil Service, making it difficult to recruit medically trained staff. Fildes' radical solution to this problem was to propose, yet again, a new research council specifically to deal with problems of biological defence. The memo was discussed at the 20th meeting of the board a month later and it was decided that setting up a new council would be impractical and expensive.[110] The board acknowledged, however, that whereas the MRC was a 'prestigious employer', the Civil Service had a reputation for impinging upon the autonomy of its employees. Here, prestige was equivalent to allowing researchers the freedom to pursue their own lines of investigation.

Apart from morality and pay conditions, there had been one other suggestion to explain the lack of enthusiasm among the scientific community for careers in biological warfare research. Occasional reports about biological warfare research had appeared in the press and had begun to irk those connected with the work. One condemnatory article, singled out by the BW Subcommittee, appeared in the *Lancet* on 5 March 1949.[111] Owen Wansbrough-Jones, the Scientific Advisor to the Army Council, spelt out his disdain for the article, and its possible long-term consequences:

> this article typified the need to educate scientific opinion regarding the humanitarian aspects of BW research and the all-important need to provide adequate defences against this form of warfare . . . the article also ignored the possible development of a highly civilized technique using non-lethal BW agents. . . . If such articles were permitted to pass unanswered they would result in the building up of a mass of opinion in scientific and medical circles hostile to BW which would in due course affect public opinion and be in turn reflected in government policy.[112]

Later, the BW Subcommittee expressed its regret that the *Lancet* article had been 'discourteous to those, who through a sense of duty, were engaged in BW research'.[113] Their condemnation was accompanied by a more practical suggestion to host an informal meeting to 'educate' journal editors, a proposal taken seriously by Sir Henry Tizard, chairman of the DRPC. Tizard also considered whether the media might be directly responsible for staff shortages, but concluded otherwise:

> Since at the present time there is little or no evidence to suggest that the recruitment of staff is being adversely affected by unfriendly criticism in the press, it would be unwise to launch what would be an obvious and perhaps provocative propaganda campaign to convert the heretics of the medical world and the scientific press.[114]

For Tizard, maintaining secrecy was more important than any publicity exercise thought necessary to recruit new staff. Against such evangelistic zeal, Tizard recommended instead that personal contacts should 'sow the seed quietly', that a public pronouncement on biological warfare should be in preparation for release if necessary and that monitoring of press activity on the topic should be maintained.

Biological weapons ascend

Whatever the causes and effects of disappointing recruitment, more money and a great deal of political and military support had been injected into the post-war biological warfare research programme. Although it is not clear quite how much extra money was eventually awarded, there are several signs of the impetus that had been given. Around £2.25m. was spent on a huge new building, which opened in 1951, for the MRD.[115] Sufficient staff were recruited, in spite of difficulties, to carry out an ambitious programme of research at Porton. Beyond the laboratory, Operation Harness, a large-scale field trial at sea using pathogenic organisms, was approved and carried out in 1948 off Antigua. A series of further 'hot' trials followed. In addition, plans were soon in place to build an expensive new experimental plant to study the bulk production of pathogenic organisms. The cost of this Experimental Plant No. 2 was estimated to be between £1m. and £1.3m., and its contested fate was to become a key indicator of the general status of biological warfare as an element of Britain's defence.[116]

5
Project Red Admiral

The rapid expansion of the British biological warfare research programme was, in part, a response to the perceived threat of a similar attack against the nation coupled with the broader position of the Chiefs of Staff on their preparedness to use weapons of mass destruction. Growth was also driven by a more proximate Air Staff requirement, dating from immediately after the Second World War, for an anti-personnel biological bomb to be in operation by 1955. This programme of research, code-named 'Project Red Admiral', was carried out mainly at the renamed Chemical Defence Experimental Establishment (CDEE) at Porton.[1] Much of the work at MRD was intended to underpin the quest for a biological weapon. In this respect, sea trials and the mass production of agents were most directly related to this task, but not the only pertinent activities. Nonetheless, under the 'offence for defence' regime which had emerged in the late 1940s, these three components of the UK programme, namely Red Admiral, the experimental fermentation plants and outdoor pathogen trials commanded a prominent role in plans for the future of British biological warfare.

Yet, despite the favourable policy environment and general momentum with which the post-war biological warfare research programme was launched, it was not long before the first signs appeared that biological warfare would not always remain a high priority. By the mid-1950s all three elements of the most directly offensive part of the germ warfare programme had been abandoned or, at the very least, modified beyond recognition. This chapter and the next chart the decline of Project Red Admiral and the biological work most directly related to the development of a bomb. At every stage, these changes were symptomatic of a steadily fading regard for biological warfare in the UK policy arena.

Negotiating Red Admiral

The reasons behind top secret Air Staff Requirement OR/1006, the request for an anti-personnel biological bomb, do not appear in the public record.

What is evident is that it was planned to be 'comparable in strategic effect with the atomic bomb' and that even the more fundamental aspects of work at the MRD would be oriented towards achieving this end.[2] Henderson pointed this out in an early report on the future of biological warfare research, as he reported to the Chiefs of Staff that no satisfactory weapon existed for distributing dry powders of biological agents and 'an early decision on the possibilities of solution of this problem will materially influence the course of the more purely biological aspects of this work'.[3]

By November 1946 the Air Force had formulated a clear request outlining the characteristics it wanted from the biological weapon. This initial request was treated with no small amount of scepticism from scientific quarters and was promptly sent back to the Air Staff by the advisors on the newly formed Biological Research Advisory Board (BRAB). The original requirement had stipulated, in fairly broad terms, the significance of the weapon and its probable means of employment. With an early target date for 1951, the weapon was envisaged for strategic use against civilian targets (see Box 5.1).[4]

The military thinking behind this specification was elaborated in an Air Staff assessment of biological warfare drafted a few months after the weapon requirement had been issued.[5] Its authors suggested four possible roles for a biological bomb: besieging strongly held positions; industrial attacks; waging economic warfare; and use in tactical situations. Not all were reckoned to be equally feasible.

Rendering isolated strongholds uninhabitable and the siege of cities and ports were judged by the authors to be the most suitable roles for a biological bomb, although they added a reservation that friendly forces would be unable to enter the contaminated areas immediately. At a later stage, however, specially immunized personnel might be employed to launch an offensive using conventional arms. Next, the disorganization of industrial areas was considered in the report. The authors envisaged this disruption taking place far behind enemy lines and it was therefore thought to be particularly suited to the Air Force:

> Botulism toxin dropped into reservoirs and the infection of natural fauna of such areas e.g. rats, mice, dogs and cats with Bubonic Plague, rabies etc, are all suitable methods of attack. Airborne types of agents may also be employed in this role, owing to the fact that the majority of people will be concentrated indoors.[6]

Thirdly, a scorched earth policy involving destruction of animals and crops was mentioned as a less attractive option for the Air Staff, on the grounds that it would require large amounts of agent and numbers of aircraft to put into action. Finally, tactical applications of biological weapons were considered most unlikely by the authors, although the report suggested a possible situation where an immunized force could 'take by storm, a position which

---

Box 5.1   Top Secret Air Staff requirement for a biological bomb (1946)

1. The Air Staff require the development on HIGH priority of an anti-personnel bomb containing a biological agent.

2. The bomb is intended for strategic use against industrial targets and should contain the most effective biological agent for the incapacitation of workers.

3. The bomb should be designed to achieve the most economical distribution of the biological material on the assumption that the aircraft will be able to make only a single run over the target.

4. The bomb should be capable of being aimed from heights of up to 50 000 feet and at speeds of up to 500 knots. The contents should not be adversely affected by atmospheric conditions at these altitudes nor by temperature or humidity conditions in any part of the world.

5. If possible the outer container of the bomb should permit its stowage in the space required by one of the series of ballistically stable bombs now under design. The bomb should not need special precautions in handling and loading.

6. In selecting the biological technique, the necessity should be borne in mind of later occupying the contaminated area with our own forces.

7. The bomb should be available for carriage in the B3/45 and the long-range and medium bombers now being schemed. To this end, development should be completed in 5 years' time.

PRO, AIR 20/8727. OR/1006. Air Staff Requirement
for a Biological Bomb (November 1946).

---

would normally require a full scale air and ground attack, involving vast numbers of men and material and incurring many casualties'.[7]

The Air Staff report, unsurprisingly, stayed clear from suggesting particular biological agents except in the most tentative terms. It did, however, mention the differences between persistent, non-persistent and highly infectious non-persistent organisms. It was also sensitive to the problems of delayed effects when bacteria incubated after initial infection. Moreover, the report drew attention to limitations that would be placed on any choice of agent by the supposed susceptibilities of an enemy and by possibilities for counter-immunization:

For example, it is assumed the Russians are more lice and parasite ridden, than we are, therefore it would be to our advantage to attack Russia with bacteria from the parasite borne groups i.e. bubonic plague, typhus etc. Russia would perhaps, appreciate this, and therefore should in theory immunise against this possibility.[8]

An outline of possibilities for attack was also provided in the report. Low-level bombing was accurate but susceptible to anti-aircraft fire. High-level bombing would engender problems of accuracy, compounded by the effects of cold on the living agents in the bomb. In contrast to most other contemporary UK assessments available in the open literature, the authors accepted the possibility of deploying germ warfare by spraying the agent. In order to succeed, researchers would need to obtain a number of things, including accurate meteorological reports, suitable temperature conditions and agents. They would also have to find the means to surmount the 'great inaccuracy' of sprays. That all this could be achieved was supported, apparently, by the 'theoretical fact' that within ten years only a small amount of agent, 800 lb per 3 square miles, would be needed to cover large areas of open country.

Although these different modes for disseminating biological agents were discussed in the report, the primary focus remained on a germ warfare bomb. This weapon would take the form of a 1000 lb cluster bomb, a parent bomb which contained smaller 'child' bombs each housing a live and deadly load. The parent bomb would break up at a predetermined height and the cluster of child bombs would be pushed out so as to cover as wide an area as possible. Readers were provided with a familiar estimate of the damage that could be wrought by this type of bomb:

> It has been estimated that approximately 200 tons of this type of bomb would be required to cover an industrial city of 100 square miles in order to produce a 50 per cent risk of death. This figure is based on the assumption that each individual weapon produces a 50 per cent risk of death over a square mile of city.[9]

In their conclusion, the authors of the report claimed that initiating a biological warfare attack would run 'against the teachings of the civilized world'.[10] Yet, they insisted, it remained 'essential however that the study and preparations mentioned in this paper should go on, in order that we in this country will be fully prepared for any emergency'. From the Air Force perspective, a biological weapon of the type envisaged in the report would be 'by far the most economical method of waging war'. But it was to be a last resort. The final point made in the report was a plea that 'moral, physical and political factors' should ensure a general prohibition of the use of germ warfare altogether.

Scientists from BRAB responded within months to the Air Force request with a detailed and carefully worded condemnation. Their initial rejection of OR/1006 hinged on the feasibility of using any agents, lethal or non-lethal, within the time frame that the military had requested.[11] Of the agents then under investigation, the advisors argued that anthrax was too persistent and would contaminate the ground; the non-lethal fever, brucellosis, was regarded as unsuitable because there was insufficient information on its storage and because no effective immunization existed. Finally, BRAB declared that botulism was also not suitable. Insufficient research had been carried out to put the agent into large-scale production in a form suitable for storage and distribution. The choice of agents was not the only aspect of the Air Staff requirement to receive criticism. The board also pointed out that technical difficulties and the danger to operatives associated with pathogen production had never been fully overcome. Additionally, they mentioned the need to develop better methods of dispersion and distribution than the emergency 'retaliatory weapon', which had been accepted in the war despite 'its known very low efficiency'.[12]

As to the future, the advisors noted that although their scientists were pursuing research into improved methods of agent dispersion, they had yet to produce anything practical. According to Henderson, the scientists were aiming principally for a method to distribute airborne clouds of organisms.[13] In the interim, field trials and explosion chamber tests would be necessary as would research on the properties of biological warfare agents. BRAB members in particular advocated more research on these properties because they regarded the available agents as far too fragile for deployment. If they were to be used, they argued, it would have to be under intolerably stringent transport and storage conditions. Overall, BRAB concluded that research on biological warfare agents and their distribution had not reached the stage where the Air Staff requirement could be satisfied by the stated time limit. Using this judgement as a call for stepping up the pace of the nascent biological weapons programme, they noted how: 'researches since the end of the war have made it clear that while certain agents and weapons were accepted as war-time expedients they would not meet Staff requirements without considerable further research and development'.[14]

BRAB's call to heighten the research effort was timely given the struggles of the early post-war programme in terms of personnel and resources, which were discussed in Chapter 4. In the face of these challenges, the mere promise of a biological bomb could serve a useful purpose for the beleaguered MRD. The role of the Air Staff requirement in promoting research at the MRD was referred to directly by the Air Staff representative on the Chiefs of Staff BW Subcommittee, Air Vice-Marshal Gerard Combe, in a note written in May 1947 and presumably intended for Henderson. In the letter, Combe defined his main role as being to 'try and jerk the MOS into attending the wants of the Microbiological Research Department'.[15] Combe wrote that the 'short-term' Air Staff requirement for a bomb seemed to have achieved 'a lot of good' in this respect since it 'focused attention on the plight of the MRD'. This does not appear to have been mere flattery on behalf of the Service which had requested the bomb. Combe admitted realistically in this memo that he was 'certain that there is very little chance of meeting this short-term requirement – the best that we could hope for would be the present 4 lb BW bomb with, possibly, a more powerful agent'. Despite these private doubts, the promise remained as crucial justificatory rhetoric that helped mobilize support for the biological warfare research programme.

By October the Air Ministry had reconsidered their demands. A detailed draft Air Staff requirement was circulated which cancelled both the requirement for a biological bomb together with a parallel request (OR/1002) for a strategic gas bomb.[16] The replacement requirement, OR 1065, was passed on 17 November 1947 and referred to the need for a strategic toxic weapon.[17] There was no particular designation whether or not this was to be a chemical or biological weapon but elsewhere the change was justified in terms of the emergence of intermediary agents not readily classifiable as either potential gas or germ weapons.[18] Although not mentioned by name, these agents were in all likelihood inert, yet highly potent, chemical toxins derived from living organisms.[19]

According to the final version of the new requirement, the strategic toxic weapon would cause 'widespread incapacitation of the workers' and produce 'maximum adverse effects on morale'.[20] The Air Staff wished to see a weapon developed with alternative fillings, which could either induce temporary incapacitation or produce a high percentage of deaths or permanent disability. The target was specifically intended to be personnel in industrial areas but would also include pockets of resistance and lines of communication.[21] Alternatively, two different weapons could be produced with priority going to an incapacitating weapon. A lower priority, lethal weapon would target places such as atomic plants, armament centres and research establishments: 'The purpose of the lethal filling would be for attacks on organisations vital to the enemy's war effort, with the aim of eliminating personnel such as highly skilled scientists and technicians, upon whose ability the efficiency of the organisation is largely dependent.'[22]

The Air Staff requirement asked in somewhat general terms that the fillings for the toxic weapon or weapons should be difficult to detect; be only so persistent as necessary to affect the enemy; should possess a maximum of a few weeks' incubation time; and, in the case of the incapacitant, have a 6–12 month effect. Finally – and again in fairly broad terms of safety and efficacy – the conditions of storage, transport and delivery were to be taken into account during the design of the weapon. With some indication that the Air Staff had been stung by BRAB's rebuttal of their initial request, the draft permitted some degree of flexibility over the precise characteristics of the weapon. Rather than making every point of the requirement mandatory, the weapon would now merely be one that could 'most completely fulfil the aim'.[23]

Priorities and target dates for completion were officially the province of the DRPC who set these after consulting the Air and Supply ministries.

Within a year, the DRPC had issued a set of detailed forecasts for toxico-logical research. With a sense of urgency, the committee pointed out that 'the requirements will be met by 1957 with no margin of time and only if development meets with no serious difficulties'.[24] The biological weapon development programme was laid out in detail and included production by January 1955 of 100 000 child bombs per week (for a war reserve of 7 million bombs), together with 200 biological cluster bombs per week (for a war reserve of 10 000 parent bombs). Britain was preparing itself for a serious stake in what it considered to be a most deadly new mode of waging war.

Biological and atomic bombs

Even as the biological bomb project was taking shape, comparisons were being drawn with atomic weapons. An Air Ministry paper from 1948 attempted to make some theoretical headway on this question, although it acknowledged from the outset that a direct comparison between atomic and biological weapons was not practicable. There was, it conceded, 'no defin-able measure whereby strategic effects may be gauged or compared'.[25] The primary effects of the two weapons differed radically. Moreover, biological weapons were still in the research stage and untried in operational condi-tions with great uncertainties surrounding the spread of disease initiated by such weapons. As such, 'estimates of their potential effectiveness in war are therefore reasoned guesses based largely on theory supported by experiments of limited scope'.[26]

Scientists working on biological warfare defined the potential effectiveness of future germ weapons 'in terms of the weight of weapons likely to be required to cause a certain chance of death or incapacitation over a unit area'.[27] The report drew on the most recent estimate in circulation: a 1000 lb cluster bomb dropped in 'favourable conditions' would cause an even chance of death or incapacitation over 1 square mile of open country. These figures had been extrapolated, without any clear justification, to a further estimate of the effectiveness of germ weapons against personnel in indus-trial cities by applying a factor of four to the calculation. This suggested that 4000 lb of biological bombs would be required to cause a 50 per cent casualty risk to exposed persons for every square mile in the built-up area of a city. The author admitted that this estimate was 'arbitrary and likely to undergo considerable revision', but nevertheless would be used in comparison with the atomic bomb.

In making the comparison, the report noted that the main advantage of the biological weapon over an atomic bomb was its ability to leave buildings intact. An attempt was made to compare the number of 'ideal sorties' required to inflict damage over 27 key Russian cities, each with population over 100 000 people. The damage required was different for the two types of weapon. For atomic weapons, the calculation attempted to predict destruction or serious damage to 80 per cent of the main built-up area of each city. With biological weapons, the figures were based on the weight needed to cause an even chance of casualties over both the main built-up areas and then both the main and outlying built-up areas. The answers were 59 ideal sorties of atomic weapons, 203 ideal sorties of biological weapons (just against the main built-up areas) and 296 sorties of biological weapons to take in main and outlying areas.

As mentioned, this report did not place a great deal of faith in its own calculations, noting that: 'the application of the arbitrary factor of four to any calculation may be completely wrong, and is only based on present theoretical knowledge of the effectiveness of the various agents, and on the assumption that they can be effectively dispersed by air weapons'.[28] Such caution notwithstanding, 59 atomic bombs were evidently more expensive than 296 biological bombs. Each aircraft would carry ten biological bombs, so the report concluded that: 'when operational factors of loss rates, abortive sorties, and aiming errors have been applied to either the atomic attacks or B/W attacks, there will be no significant differences in the effort required to deliver either one or the other'.

Huge assumptions were involved in drawing this conclusion and parallel arguments about costs and relative effectiveness resurface in other contemporary documents.[29] It remains impossible to trace whether or not these estimates had any significant role in justifying the nascent biological weapons programme. Generally, the date by which a biological weapon was predicted to become comparable to, or even surpass, the effectiveness of atomic bombs remained as 1957 in most documents which made reference to the matter. There is also evidence, from a draft contribution to the Chiefs of Staff 1949 Report on Biological Warfare, that a year after these comparisons were made the Air Ministry had settled on the idea of biowarfare as a retaliatory complement to atomic weapons:

We assume that, as a party to the Geneva Protocol of 1925, this country will not initiate biological warfare but will resort to its use only as a retaliatory measure. However, lest over-optimistic results should be expected from retaliation on a massive scale, it should be borne in mind that the large-scale use of biological warfare from the air as a weapon of war has not been tried nor will it have been possible to test experimentally its effect on men. In these circumstances it would be unwise to expect decisive results from an all-out offensive with such a totally untried weapon. It should therefore be regarded, not as a competitor with the other types of weapon in our armoury, but as a complementary weapon to be used when its peculiar characteristics can be fully exploited.[30]

Perhaps of greater significance is that biological weapons were even contemplated alongside atomic weapons. Clearly, as the author of the Air Ministry report commented, they were very different modes of warfare. In the last chapter, I pointed out that parallel discussions were taking place in the Chiefs of Staff BW Subcommittee about whether biological weapons could be classified as weapons of mass destruction. Now the parallel was being drawn merely by an attempt to make *some* comparison, albeit based explicitly on a wide range of assumptions. Furthermore, this was not the last time within the policy arena that the military would solicit expert opinion on the similarities and differences between biological and atomic weapons. The fates of these two types of killing were not automatically coincident but instead were being knitted together through these various discussions, calculations and investigations.

Tripartite collaboration and the biological bomb

Work related directly to the bomb took place at the CDEE, and by 1950 research had been classified into three areas: fundamental research on the disruption of droplets by supersonic air blasts; studies of the explosive dispersion of liquids from experimental bombs; and the design and development of experimental munitions.[31] These projects were all aimed at understanding the behaviour of liquids during a blast and of controlling the agent survival and size distribution of the resulting particles.[32] In March, the Air Staff requirement for a strategic toxic weapon was amended to specify that the weapon was once again to be specifically for biological warfare.[33]

The progress of the bomb project was linked with ongoing tripartite research collaboration. At their fourth meeting during 1949 the BW Subcommittee had discussed the whole matter with US and Canadian delegates in attendance.[34] The US in particular showed the most hawkish attitude; Major-General Waitt of the US Chemical Corps mentioned that

> from the American point of view, the time factor was becoming increasingly important; he was under pressure to produce munitions for operational use, although these might fall short of the staff requirement and of potential achievement. The E48 bomb, which was not entirely satisfactory, was now ready for testing, and he was anxious to carry out toxic trials with it this year; using certain agents he was advised that it would be practicable to carry out these trials on land.[35]

While Henderson agreed with the need for open-air trials of bombs under operational conditions, he also added that in the UK lack of resources and a suitable test site meant that his staff were 'best employed on laboratory research for the next year or two'.[36] On the other hand, in the course of the same debate, the Director-General of Armament for the Air Ministry, Air Vice-Marshal Geoffrey Pidcock, reminded Henderson that there was also a requirement in the UK for a toxic weapon to be in service by 1957, and if laboratory-bound work resulted in no biological weapon being available then he dissented from Henderson's proposal. Wansbrough-Jones responded that 'if a worthwhile weapon was to be produced in time', then the UK should concentrate on basic research as a complement to US and Canadian fieldwork.

Henderson remained anxious to keep his staff occupied in the laboratory rather than the field and had to be reassured in a telling letter from Wansbrough-Jones in 1952. The correspondence referred specifically to an ongoing DRPC appraisal of biological warfare, which will be described fully in Chapter 7. Wansbrough-Jones, in his capacity as Principal Director of Scientific Research for the Ministry of Supply, felt it necessary to allay the Superintendent's fears, informing him that research at Porton would continue to focus on basic issues. He wrote:

> The examination of the present position of BW must be undertaken. I should think that the people who have been nominated to do it will certainly keep clear of immediate Service and [Civil Defence] needs, and do it calmly. I agree that we do not want short-term Service requirements to play a part in it at all.... I do not think you need to worry at the moment anyway, at the thought that you may get pressed too much to produce a weapon when other things may be important.[37]

Indeed, the tripartite division of labour established during the Second World War had held, with the UK concentrating on fundamental research while bomb trials continued in both the US and Canada. During 1950 and 1951, these were undertaken using non-pathogenic simulants to discover why discrepancies of up to 100-fold less efficiency had been revealed between laboratory results and the field with a so-called 'baby 4 lb bomb'.[38] The experimenters concluded that the particles in the 4lb bomb were too large to be effective. Other trials, using *Brucella suis* against animals, reinforced findings regarding the inefficiency of the bomb despite experimenters successfully generating an infective cloud.[39] Trials also took place with tularemia bacteria which had been subjected to only one previous 'cursory field test' on Operation Harness in 1949 yet had been judged to offer 'considerable possibilities'.[40] The experimental British bomb received a bout of preliminary testing during this spell of trials at the Suffield testing range in Alberta, Canada. It was reported to have given 'equivocal results, but seems likely to give a better dispersal efficiency than the 4 lb bomb and a remarkably high infection rate'.[41] Besides the bombs, a spraying device for agent dispersal that had been designed at Camp Detrick was tested in the field during 1951 but 'showed little promise'.[42]

Other trials, at Dugway in Utah, aimed to perfect an American biological bomb.[43] The problem of distributing the units from cluster bombs over an optimum area had led to American field studies using rotating clusters, including ones for the E48R2 (4 lb) bomb that was soon standardized by the

United States as the M114.[44] With regard to production, it was reported to the British BW Subcommittee that a plant capable of manufacturing 1 million bombs a month was being built in the US and it was expected that the plant would be ready by spring 1952.[45] By 1953 the US charging plant had been completed and tested with simulants, and an associated weapon-filling plant had been tested with water.[46] Plans were under way to set up two further plants of the same size and possibly a third for virus production. The US were also devoting considerable effort to the production and dissemination of dried rather than liquid agents and the US Air Force had put in an operational requirement for a biological bomb containing a lethal agent by 1 July 1954. Correspondingly, attention shifted from the incapacitating brucellosis, briefly to plague, which was soon judged 'insufficiently stable', and it was decided at the eighth Tripartite Conference that a 'combination of *B. anthracis* and the $\frac{1}{2}$ lb bomb should be the objective'.[47] More generally, the BW Subcommittee reported that 'promising results' had been obtained, for distributing unit bombs, with discus-shaped bombs ejected from a rotating cluster. These were supposed to distribute agents over an 'appreciably greater' area than had been achieved before.[48]

Killing the bomb

While scientists embarked eagerly on the initial stages of the tripartite weapons programme, by 1953 the situation in the UK had altered dramatically as the Air Ministry signalled an increasing scepticism about the biological bomb. In response to a request for contributions for an update on the 1950–51 Biological Warfare report, the Air Ministry noted that the estimate for the effectiveness of the 1000 lb biological bomb had been amended to 1 square mile. The memo added further qualifications, based on a 500 lb bomb, which reduced this figure to one-ninth of a square mile:

> However, whilst this estimate may be theoretically sound, weapon development has advanced sufficiently to show that the practical problem of dispersion is such that it is very unlikely that this theoretical limit can be reached in the foreseeable future. In fact, to date the best scatter to be achieved by a British 500 lb. cluster has been of the order of one-ninth of a square mile (i.e. at least nine bombs will be required per square mile). Recent American operational suitability tests have led to the conclusion that 14×500 lb. BW bombs will be required per square mile.[49]

This appraisal of the effectiveness of the bomb provided a first hint that the Air Ministry was disappointed with the progress of the biological weapons programme. A top secret Air Ministry document was issued the following year in July 1954 which altered the terms of the standing requirement for a bomb. This paper opened on a reassuring note for the research programme, stating that 'to implement the national policy of retaliation in the event of biological warfare being initiated by an enemy the Air Staff will ultimately require toxic biological weapons'.[50] The document then changed tone, noting that the initial target from 1947's OR/1065 would not be met:

> It is now apparent that because of the magnitude of the problem a great deal of research still remains to be done in both the agent and weapon fields before a satisfactory weapon can be recommended to the Service. Moreover, it appears that the storage, transportation, testing and preparation for use of the weapon and its agent will present new problems to the Service and may necessitate the provision of special skills and equipment. The Air Staff considers that until problems associated with the toxic biological weapons are better appreciated it would be unwise to state definite requirements for weapons and other equipment. This A.S.T. [Air Staff Target] is therefore issued to replace ASR [Air Staff Requirement] No. OR/1065 which is hereby cancelled.[51]

The new aims of the Air Force were then spelt out in broad and general terms:

> The Air Staff requires research to determine effective agents and suitable weapons for waging biological warfare. They also require investigation of the associated problems connected with the storage, handling, transportation, testing and preparation for use of such agents and weapons with a view to determining what is required in the way of skills, equipment and procedures in the Service.[52]

Yet, in principle, the Air Staff were still 'interested primarily in the strategic use of an anti-personnel toxic biological weapon and it is upon this aspect that they wish to be informed first'. Such weapons would be carried in medium bombers, in the normal stowages and with no special equipment needed; the weapons and agent would need to withstand atmospheric conditions from ground level to 60 000 ft; and specialist skills for storage, handling and transportation were to be kept to a minimum. Any bomb was ultimately for 'use in any part of the world' and if it could not be stored in any region, 'the Air Staff wish proposals to be made on means of enabling the weapons to be prepared for use anywhere with the shortest possible delay'. Finally, the Air Staff requested that 'this AST be given high priority so that there may be no undue delay in determining a solution to this problem'.[53]

But the requirement for a biological bomb for use in the foreseeable future had been unceremoniously cancelled. Project Red Admiral was effectively terminated. The revision of the operational requirement into a more nebulous request may have been welcomed by Henderson, judged by his earlier reluctance to concentrate on short-term Service requirements. The cancellation of the bomb, however, indicated that biological weapons no longer occupied the same position of priority they had enjoyed straight after the war. Before exploring in Chapter 7 how the policy context was beginning to alter during the early 1950s, it is necessary to outline the parallel fate of the other central aspects of the post-war vision for biological weapons research, the means for large-scale agent production and trials. Scientists and advisors regarded an effective biological warfare research programme in the UK as thoroughly dependent on a supply of pathogenic bacteria. In order to achieve this end, plans had been rapidly tabled for a fermentation plant which could cope with the production of disease-causing organisms. As plans to build this plant faltered, recovered and faltered yet again, 'Experimental Plant No. 2', like the bomb, became a crucial indicator of the wavering fortunes of the British biological warfare programme.

Experimental Plant No. 2

An experimental fermentation plant for the production of large quantities of non-pathogenic micro-organisms was discussed at the inaugural meeting of BRAB in 1946.[54] Even at this early stage, it was apparent that researchers regarded this pilot plant as an interim measure. Between 1947 and 1955 additional recommendations were made by BRAB to construct a second large-scale fermenter that could cope safely with the manufacture of quantities of pathogenic organisms. This so-called Experimental Plant No. 2 was intended to make a major contribution in research on methods of production. In its turn, the plant was to act as a step on the route to the bulk production of agents for waging biological warfare.

Immediately before the initial discussions on this matter by BRAB members, the ISSBW had affirmed the necessity of the experimental plants, noting that

> offence development will require intensive study and methods in large scale production of disease producing organisms.... The solution of these problems is as important in the general development of microbiological research and therefore, defence development, as it is in the field of offence.[55]

Henderson's written case for the first large-scale plant at Porton rested on fairly general grounds. Initially, he argued that the non-pathogenic plant would be an ideal response to an MRC request to the Ministry of Supply for help in developing production plants for antibiotics. In connection with this request, Henderson thought that Porton would be the perfect location, there existed a 'dearth of qualified personnel' so the establishment of more than a single centre for the work would be 'impossible at this time'.[56] Additionally, he appealed to the progress of academic research in microbiology as a whole, writing of the past barriers created through a 'lack of sufficient quantities of biological material for the chemical and immune-chemical study'. Henderson was unable to give a firm indication of costs, but concluded his memo by stating that, spread over five years, the cost may be £1m. or more, 'the price of a few aircraft or the quarter deck of one battleship'.[57]

By the end of 1947 the DRPC had incorporated these proposals into their stated objectives for biological warfare research, which included, as alternatives, either a small plant coupled with agents which could be readily stored, or a large-scale production plant.[58] Yet the effects of this endorsement remained confined to defence-related quarters. The chairman of BRAB complained that in obtaining facilities, such as the planned non-pathogenic experimental plant:

> the Board was informed that the Chiefs of Staff and the Defence Research Policy Committee accorded to it [BW] the highest priority. It appeared, however, that this priority was binding in the Defence, Service and Supply Ministries only. Other Ministries, such as the Ministry of Works and Industry were concerned with the provision of research facilities and with these there appears to be no priority for any kind of project.[59]

The board had, at that time, been informed only that the Ministry of Defence would be looking into the matter.

Even in the face of such delays, Experimental Plant No. 1 was placed among the official aims of the MRD research programme for the following year, along with bacteriology and experimental pathology; biophysics; chemistry; field trials; joint work with the Chemical Defence Establishment; and extramural projects.[60] Early in 1948, the new plant was still making slow progress and Henderson was growing impatient. In expressing this frustration to BRAB, he complained that while a 'serious research programme had been outlined', there were few indications that it could be executed.[61] It was important for BRAB to address whether Porton research could continue along the same unrealistic lines, or in the Chief Superintendent's words whether they wanted to 'stagnate for six years as a result of a lack of proper facilities'.[62] Henderson was not alone in raising these concerns. Howard Florey, supported by other BRAB members, insisted that staff would soon lose patience with the situation and would drift back to academia. The chairman of BRAB tried to appease Henderson by reminding him that biological warfare research occupied the highest priorities of the Chiefs of Staff, and DRPC. On the other hand, the supply of materials and labour by industry was 'governed by the Prime Minister's priority list in which biological warfare had no place'.[63] The solution agreed by the board was to approach the Minister of Defence directly.

Whatever the outcome of this resolution, Experimental Plant No. 1 was completed in May 1949 and was in partial operation by November.[64] A year later, the plant had been used to study simulant agent growth and the maintenance of purity in continuous flow production.[65] By the close of 1951 it was reported that Pilot Plant No. 1 was now ready for production and plans had been made to produce the antibiotic streptomycin in collaboration with the Distillers Company.[66]

Even before Experimental Plant No. 1 was fully operational, its successor was facing opposition. Discussions focused, in part, on costs. The estimated £1m. budget for Experimental Plant No. 2. was a cause of concern for several BRAB members and deemed by Florey 'a sum as great as, or greater than, the whole annual expenditure by the Medical Research Council'.[67] Nevertheless, as a backdrop to the financial considerations, the board also saw the decision as contingent on two broader questions of policy.

The first question concerned the status of the UK programme relative to the US research effort. To what extent should the UK rely on the US for their supply of pathogens? Experimental Plant No. 2 would certainly grant the British scientists and military a degree of independence from the US in this area. Another related consideration was the extent to which the plant was to be judged a crucial adjunct to Project Red Admiral. The proposed plant was described by the board as offering 'the only possibility' for obtaining full-scale production of biological warfare agents in time to meet the Air Ministry's target date of 1957 for an operational bomb. Without the target date, the board members suggested that the new plant could be delayed until experience was gained from Experimental Plant No. 1.[68] The latter option was endorsed strongly by Trevor Lord Stamp, a senior bacteriologist who had worked at Porton between 1943 and 1945, who argued that policy should revert to that of the Second World War when all mass production of pathogens was to be undertaken by the US.

Throughout this entire debate the BRAB members readily acknowledged that these options were regarded as policy decisions and beyond the scope of their responsibilities. The BW Subcommittee equally made a clear and overt distinction between what they considered as technical matters and the 'policy aspect' of the proposal to proceed with the plant.[69] This subcommittee had discussed the plant at several junctures. They had then passed their positive consideration of the matter on to the DRPC, noting that

> even if the target to date of 1957 for the completion of the development of a BW weapon and its production were open to doubt or amendment, this would in no way invalidate the conclusion that the construction of a pilot plant for the experimental production of toxic organisms was a matter of urgency.[70]

The DRPC, who had a wider portfolio of research priorities to juggle with than just biological warfare, were a little more circumspect about Plant No. 2. The committee was asked to 'consider very seriously' whether the plant was worth the estimated cost, which by this point had risen to £1 300 000. Its chairman, Tizard, noted that 'while in the long run much information for

civilian purposes might well be obtained from a plant of this kind, its potentialities for war purposes were still very speculative'.[71] At this juncture, one
member took the opportunity to remind his colleagues where the sense of
urgency arose from, noting that 'the necessity for proceeding with the construction of this plant at the present time arose entirely from the 1957 planning date' for the bomb. In the light of these concerns, the DRPC suggested
somewhat ominously that work continue on design of the plant but that
a further decision would need to be made regarding the erection of the plant.

The suggestion was passed back to the BW Subcommittee who stoutly
responded that research was concentrated on 'fundamental problems' which
made it impossible to forecast whether a weapon would be in production by
1957. Nonetheless, the subcommittee still continued to view Plant No. 2 as
a high priority.[72] Undaunted, they continued to propose reasons to the
DRPC as to why the plant should proceed. To begin with, the members
lamented how 'in several past field trials, either the quality of the agents
provided from American sources was found to be inferior, or else we were
compelled to use agents of our own manufacture because those having the
required properties were not available in the United States'.[73] They compounded the complaint further, calling the Americans superior in the 'exe-
cution of large-scale industrial products', but 'pedestrian' in their biological
warfare research.[74] Moreover, they argued, the prospects of the Americans
solving the difficult problems involved in production plant design were
'remote'. Even as part of a reciprocal exchange, the loan of technicians and
designers to the US would not 'serve any useful purpose' as they did not
have sufficient 'status to influence' American views.[75]

The BW Subcommittee also drew a firm distinction between research on
techniques and equipment for bulk production and the production itself.
The implication appears to have been that Britain would engage in the former
using Experimental Plant No. 2 and obtain results that could then be
applied either in Britain or the US. This conceptual distinction equally
implied a firm geographical division of labour between research and design
(stage II) and bulk production (stage III):

> the object of stage II is to acquire 'know-how' and to develop techniques
> and equipment which will be applied in the construction of stage III
> plants. The location of the latter is an entirely different problem in which
> industrial potential and strategic security are among the primary factors
> to be considered.[76]

What appeared to be at stake was not simply the plant itself, but the freedom
of the researchers at the MRD to carry out research but stop short of what
they evidently regarded as the more pedestrian aspects of applied work.

Although the subcommittee acknowledged that collaboration with the US
had been very close in the past there had 'been some signs of coolness'

recently.[77] For example, the US had been planning to carry out trials of biological weapons without consulting the UK. The committee ended their plea to the DRPC with an open admission of the strategic value of a British plant for restoring Anglo-American relationships:

> there is no doubt that the greater our contribution at the present time, the more likely are we to secure their collaboration and their assistance at a later stage in the bulk production of agents. In this connection we are of the opinion that the existence in this country of a plant for the experimental production of agents would represent a valuable bargaining counter.[78]

All of these arguments had been informed by reports from across the Atlantic. Early in 1950, Sir Henry Tizard passed a note on the American situation along to the BW Subcommittee. The note, from sources in Washington, confirmed the poor progress made in the United States' research on production, most notably that they had failed to prevent leakage from valves in the production machinery.[79] The note also reported that, while the Americans would be likely to welcome offers of technical assistance from the UK, any written agreement to allow British access to the products of US research would be less forthcoming, then added portentously:

> if we drop our building programme, this may have repercussions on our general Biological Warfare collaboration, which as you rightly say is happier than is the case in most other fields. Part of this is undoubtedly due to the feeling Americans have that we are making a major independent contribution to the common cause; and if we reduce our direct experimental effort we may lower our bargaining status.[80]

The BW Subcommittee finally put forward a bargaining counter of their own to the DRPC. A reduced-scale experimental plant should be built. Whereas the original plant was to have comprised four different production units, this was now reduced to two units (one for experimental production of spores and one for the production of vegetative organisms). A further reduction to one unit was possible but, according to the subcommittee, would not be 'sound policy', although it was still deemed to 'be better than none at all'.[81]

BRAB, likewise, continued to advocate the centrality of the plant and protested that delay would engender major alterations to the entire MRD programme.[82] With respect to the relationship between the US and the UK, the distinction between research and bulk production previously drawn by the BW Subcommittee was now adopted by BRAB to place new and expensive equipment at the heart of British biological warfare policy. Apart from storage and transport of pathogens which, anyway, might not be of the 'required quality' or 'sufficient quantity', the board was keen to stress that

Experimental Plant No. 2 was necessary for fundamental research under the current policy directive which had been in place since 1946.[83] They added that Experimental Plant No. 2 was necessary in order to maintain a retaliatory capability and that offensive research would have to cease without the plant.

By May, the DRPC appeared to have completely abdicated their enthusiasm not merely for the new fermentation plant but for the entire direction of the research programme. At a BW Subcommittee meeting the dismissive views of the DRPC concerning the 1949 Report on Biological Warfare were reported: 'doubts had been expressed whether there was sufficiently convincing evidence on which to base a decision to make a special effort to continue research and development in the offensive sphere, or that Biological Warfare would be used against us'.[84]

In the light of this alarming pronouncement, the DRPC had asked the new chairman of the BW Subcommittee, Lieutenant-General Sir Kenneth Crawford, for an update on the advantages and disadvantages of offensive biological warfare research. The reasons behind this enquiry were not concerned solely with the level of financial commitment involved. Crawford, in turn, consulted BRAB 'as a body with full scientific background and as men of common sense' and asked them to justify biological warfare, not so much in terms of economics, but against the likely use of atomic bombs as the major strategic weapons of the future.[85] The explosion of the first Soviet atomic bomb in August 1949 had severely shaken Western assumptions about the state of Russian defence research and this unease probably lay behind the changing attitudes of the DRPC.[86] The board was also asked about the division of labour between America and the UK with respect to pathogen production and fundamental research. In association with this division of labour, the BW Subcommittee also wished to know BRAB's views on the necessity of Experimental Plant No. 2, 'even for defensive purposes alone, quite apart from any question of pilot production'.[87]

The discussion and answers to these questions demonstrate how uncertainties could be drawn on as strategic resources by the expert advisors. Fildes, in this manner, asserted that 'years of fundamental research were still required to prove the possibilities of BW' and that it was necessary to be prepared for offence in order to deter an enemy.[88] Likewise, Henderson argued that although untried, the potential of biological warfare as a strategic weapon was great and that the UK was particularly vulnerable to a putative attack. Several other board members added their view that germ warfare should be seen as both cheaper than and complementary to atomic warfare. So, although the uncertain potential of biological warfare was openly acknowledged by the board, this was used as an argument in favour of continuing research.[89] While many analyses of scientific expertise emphasize how advisors advance their interests by appealing to scientific certainty and authority, in this instance the scientists were quite capable of using uncertainty openly to defend the status of their research. In a report which followed from this discussion the board declared in a somewhat bewildered tone that

> in their view there was at present no justification for looking at BW as other than a form of warfare which might, by further research, be shown to be either practicable or, on the other hand, impracticable... on the balance of evidence, the development of a dangerous weapon was not improbable and certainly not impossible, but only if active research, including field trials, was continued along the lines which had already been approved.[90]

BRAB's views were duly passed on to the BW Subcommittee in writing and verbally by Henderson. The Superintendent reported that for initial field trials the small quantities of agents required meant the plant was not essential. But, for final trials of full-scale weapons the plant would be needed, initially to produce simulant chargings. Apart from the role of the plant in devising new weapons, other members of the Subcommittee felt that they would be able to 'demonstrate whether or not an agent could be produced in bulk, a fact which could not be determined in the laboratory where conditions differed'.[91] Such knowledge would be invaluable, they believed, in assessing the accuracy of intelligence reports. The members also repeated the suggestion that the plant could also be used for defensive research to test characteristics such as storage and viability of organisms. The chairman, Crawford, summed up the discussion by appealing to the comprehensive utility of the plant. He concluded that 'it was evident that the offensive aspect must be studied if defensive research was to proceed on a sound basis. The meeting endorsed the view of BRAB that Plant No. 2 was a necessary tool in fundamental research.'

Crawford's eventual submission to the DRPC in May 1950 followed an equally commendatory route, openly in favour of maintaining the existing programme. Nevertheless, as chairman of the BW Subcommittee, he was keen to outline arguments both for and against continuing offensive biological warfare research. He flagged the failure of the DRPC to endorse the proposal for Experimental Plant No. 2 as a fundamental challenge to the prevailing regime. This failure, he wrote, raised 'far wider issues and the whole BW research policy is now in question especially the offensive part of the programme'.[92] In his memo, Crawford stated that although 'scientific opinion cannot guarantee that the development of a BW weapon is practicable', the available evidence certainly pointed towards success. Moreover, on the basis of best estimates biological warfare was 'of the same order of magnitude as the atomic bomb' and could be used to complement atomic weapons.

In favour of changing the existing policy and terminating offensive research, Crawford's memo listed six points.[93] Present 'financial straits' necessitating a concentration of resources into projects 'essential to a hot war';

difficulty of recruiting good staff; uncertainty surrounding biological warfare; difficulty of assessing the results of a biological attack in a war situation; the theoretical possibility of antidotes being developed for all agents; and the Geneva Protocol prohibiting the initiation of biological warfare. It is worth noting, in the light of BRAB's prior discussion of this matter, that uncertainty could be used in different contexts as justification for the continuation or the termination of offensive research.[94]

Nine points were put forward in favour of maintaining the status quo.[95] Although knowledge of biological warfare developments in Russia was 'extremely meagre', it was believed by intelligence sources that a small research effort existed which might result in a Russian capability by 1952. This was thought possible even though Crawford reported that: 'the general standard of open bacteriological research in Russia is not rated highly'. Moreover, Crawford added that 'the Russians will not hesitate to take risks in the production of agents which would be unacceptable to Western Powers, nor is it likely that they will hesitate to carry out BW trials on human beings'. He drew this point to a close by confessing that accurate intelligence of the threat was probably unobtainable. In the absence of this knowledge, a 'mirror' was instead proffered to the DRPC: 'we are on the firmest ground if we base our appreciation on deductions from our own work'. Not only would this approach have offered a means to overcome uncertainty and construct an assessment of the threat, it also created a self-perpetuating rationale to continue offensive research. Put bluntly, if we could potentially do something then so too might the enemy; so, the only way to be sure would be through research that attempted to actualize that potential.

Crawford's memo to the DRPC also maintained that, in view of the threat, defensive research should also proceed. Experimental Plant No. 2 would be invaluable for this work and could even 'be justified on defensive grounds alone' as it was 'probable that the extra cost of making limited preparations for the development of BW weapons is relatively small and will pay good dividends'.[96] Plant No. 2 was judged 'not essential to fundamental research in microbiology, [but] is essential to fundamental work in BW'. In particular, the plant would be useful to determine if agents could be bulk produced. This said, considering defensive measures in isolation would be inadequate and even dangerous, given the 'general experience with chemical warfare'. Experimental Plant No. 2 would indicate which agents were likely to be used in war together with some clues to their strategic and tactical potential.

Offensive biological warfare preparation was also advocated as a deterrent by Crawford. Defence, while possible, could be overcome by the development of strains of micro-organisms resistant to countermeasures and 'the practical difficulties of producing a defence may prove almost insuperable, and more probably to Russia than to Western Powers'.[97] Offensive research, the chairman argued, could also lead to the development of an incapacitant, 'a powerful weapon which is far more humane than existing weapons'. Furthermore, offensive biological weapons using highly persistent agents would be useful for putting atomic plants, experimental establishments and underground installations out of action. The final reason that Crawford provided against a change in policy was that the UK was 'committed fully though informally to close collaboration with the United States and Canada in this subject'. The memo closed by emphasizing that the work must not be 'skimped' and a long-term policy would be important for recruiting and maintaining staff.[98] In terms of timescale, the chairman urged, 'if there is to be any chance at all of producing BW weapons by 1957, there is no time to lose'.[99]

Crawford went to the DRPC personally on 16 May 1950 to advocate offensive biological warfare research in general, and the proposed new plant in particular. He was minuted as having sold biological warfare to the committee in the following terms:

> after consulting a number of impartial individuals with great knowledge of bacteriology, he had been convinced that the case for going ahead with our existing policy of research and development on biological warfare was made out. Admittedly there was no guarantee that a weapon would be successfully developed but the possibility of success was greater now than it had been in 1945 and could be said to be greater than that of failure. In view of the new importance attaching to land operations, moreover, it would be well to bear in mind the tactical possibilities of BW which might turn out to be a big casualty producer in an opposing army. Its potentialities in sabotage might also be very great. He had been convinced that the construction of Plant No. 2 at Porton was fundamental to the continuation of BW research.[100]

Tizard, the DRPC chairman, put it to Crawford that sufficient justification of the committee's support for long-term policy was already evident from the effort and expenditure invested in building the new laboratories at Porton. Crawford remained resolute, Plant No. 2 was essential and staff 'would not be convinced that our policy was firm until that project was approved'.[101] But, retorted the chairman, 'in view of the financial stringency to which we were at present subject, the timing of such a project was of great importance'. So, what was the point of producing organisms in bulk when 'fundamentally there was nothing new about the process'? Crawford fell back on the strength of his tripartite allies and replied that 'he had been assured that the proposed scale was the minimum which would give us the information we needed and that the Americans were of the same opinion'.[102] Further discussion by the committee connected with the more general DRPC remit of balancing defence R&D priorities. How did Experimental Plant No. 2 compare with other defence R&D expenditure priorities? And, having previously invoked the Americans, whether 'this was not a field of research and development which we ought to leave entirely to them'.[103]

Whether as a delaying tactic, or in deference to the gravity of these decisions, the DRPC did not resolve the matter in the course of the May meeting.
Instead, they instigated efforts to collect evidence from further afield. The
committee recommended that a delegation be sent to the US to discuss the
operational value of biological warfare and the division of labour between
the two nations, including the possibility of passing the whole programme
over to the Americans. Although the US were eventually consulted on these
matters, there is no record in the open British archives pertaining to the
advice obtained.[104] On the other hand, an external report was both sought
and gained by the Ministry of Supply from the Technical Director of Glaxo,
Dr F.J. Wilkins. He concluded that the proposed size of the plant could be
maintained but at the expense of other aspects such as stores, a workshop,
laboratories, changing rooms and offices. As a consequence the estimated cost
was reduced from £1.3m. to £0.95m.[105] At this point, Crawford told the BW
Subcommittee that he now 'felt confident' of DRPC approval, and they in turn
were likely to recommend to the Chiefs of Staff that the project go ahead.[106]

And indeed, the Chiefs of Staff had already, in June, agreed in principle to
construction of Experimental Plant No. 2 pending advice from the DRPC on
their priorities.[107] Their rationale apparently rested on the undesirability of
leaving production research entirely to the United States. By the end of
1950 the decision to defer had been reversed by the DRPC, although with
the former proviso that other aspects besides the plant itself were limited in
order to make significant savings.[108] The new plant would be built at a cost
not exceeding £950 000.[109] Such encouraging news for the biological warfare
programme was, however, to be but a temporary reprieve.

Two years later and the plant had still not been constructed, although the
US were reported to be proceeding rapidly with their own plant. A further
reversal of fortunes looked imminent for the British biological warfare
research programme as a few of the scientific advisors attempted to stall
events and cancel the plant. In its defence, Florey was keen to remind his
fellow BRAB members that they had hardly been decisive when they recommended the plant and therefore another reversal of policy should not be
taken lightly. Fildes repeated the argument that the new plant would help
determine whether countries other than the US could produce operational
quantities of pathogens. In this respect, he argued, the success or failure of
the UK would be taken to mirror Russian abilities. In the end, Fildes and
Florey prevailed, the board did not capitulate and continued to affirm the
necessity of the plant for germ warfare research.

Their recommendation sank. In May 1952, it was announced to the board
that building work on Experimental Plant No. 2 would definitely not be
started that year.[110] The position was to be reconsidered in the 1953 spending
estimates but would, in any case, have to fit in with other Ministry of Supply
defence commitments.[111] The possible repercussions from the latest delay
were spelt out by the scientific advisors. Although the Air Staff requirement

for a biological bomb still existed in July 1952, according to indignant BRAB members postponement of Experimental Plant No. 2 also entailed a post-ponement on meeting the Air Staff request.[112] The BW Subcommittee had already acknowledged BRAB's complaint and soberly noted the implications for Project Red Admiral, that 'in view of the Chiefs of Staff's decisions, OR 1065 would have to be reviewed'.[113] And at that time, the Ministry of Supply were even negotiating with the Air Ministry for an alternative interim weapon to be delivered in stages.

The decision over the future of the plant was taken in the light of the developing capabilities in the United States. When the Chiefs of Staff made the decision to postpone the plant in April 1952, Crawford had

> informed the Committee of the progress being made in the United States in the development of the means of production of toxic agents and in the development of Biological Warfare weapons. He suggested that, in view of this fact and of the present vital necessity for economy, the erection at Porton of Experimental Plant No. 2 – for the experimental production of toxic Biological Warfare agents – should be postponed.[114]

As I will discuss in Chapter 7, these developments in the US were also linked to a broader shift in the thinking of the UK Chiefs of Staff. In June 1952, they had announced that future work was to be restricted to 'long range offensive possibilities about which the United States had less information'.[115] The fate of the experimental plant and the fate of Project Red Admiral were now tied together. 'Long range' implied fundamental research and was 'purposely worded to give latitude in formulating future Operational Requirements'.[116] As we saw earlier in the chapter, this latitude meant that the specific require-ment for a biological bomb could eventually be dropped by the Air Ministry and replaced with a far more diffuse request to continue research.

A delegation from the BRAB visited the US in October 1952.[117] They noted in their report back to the board that the staff at Dugway had 'not really got into their stride', despite their 'elaborate facilities'; also that they were disap-pointed with the work at the Naval Research Laboratory, San Francisco.[118] The large-scale production plant which the Americans had constructed at Pine Bluff was enough to convince the delegation that they would not be disadvantaged through their own lack of a pilot plant.[119] This was admittedly a good reason for abandoning Experimental Plant No. 2, although the board continued to recommend that research on continuous flow should continue albeit with lowered expectations. They suggested that a smaller plant could be built when it was financially practicable, although as one BRAB member, Davidson Pratt, observed, this change would force the UK to rely on the US for their pathogen production.

BRAB continued to recommend the plant over the next two years. In 1954 Fildes was still arguing that field trials, Experimental Plant No. 2 and a workable bomb filling were 'essential to determine whether BW was a real risk or not'.[120] At this time, the plant had not been cancelled but was still a deferred item. Henderson's own view was that the collapse of Project Red Admiral had removed an encumbrance and created an impetus for going ahead with the plant. He noted how 'in previous years he had been pressed because of an operational requirement' but, presumably without now being pushed towards this concrete goal, the knowledge was now available to specify requirements for bacterial continuous culture 'without taking chances'.[121]

Contrary to the reasoning from other committees elsewhere in the British biological warfare hierarchy, the fact that the US had achieved bulk production was not regarded by BRAB as counting against Experimental Plant No. 2. Fildes, drawing on an older distinction, pointed out that the UK was not contemplating production but nevertheless required the 'know-how' as a 'purely research measure'.[122] Hankey added that that was a matter for the BW Subcommittee and that 'if attacked, we must be in a position to retaliate. We must have the knowledge and the apparatus for acquiring it.' The debate concluded with the board recommending the plant as 'a necessary instrument of research'.

By November 1954 a new specification of the buildings and services needed had been drawn up.[123] But, a year later, the plant was coming under the pressure of the reduced status of biological weapons research. At its 33rd and 34th meetings, held in 1955, BRAB discussed the Experimental Plant No. 2 in the light of a policy directive by the Minister of Defence that had lowered the general position of biological warfare in the overall military research and development programme. Nuclear weapons had been elevated to take pole position, thus relegating all other means of waging war. In the face of these developments, the scientific advisors from BRAB remained adamant 'that it would be entirely wrong to stop production research on disease-producing organisms, that the plant would have wider use than the culture of pathogens, and that the plant was an essential piece of apparatus for pursuing microbiological studies'.[124]

Even though BRAB retained its support for the plant, the justification behind the plant had been transformed. As Henderson put it: 'he had always maintained that the Plant would have uses outside that of the culture of pathogenic micro-organisms'.[125] This comment was intended to raise the possibility of obtaining additional civil support for the plant. However, although funding from the Defence Vote had been unforthcoming, Wansbrough-Jones noted that the alternative of seeking funding from bodies such as the Ministry of Health, MRC or Department of Scientific and Industrial Research would 'entail a loss of direct control'. The board continued to claim the centrality of the plant for the biological warfare programme, concluding 'that they considered the provision of Experimental Plant No. 2 to be an essential part of the apparatus of MRD. It would prove a necessary and most valuable complementary facility for the furtherance of basic research.'[126] Yet by now, Experimental Plant No. 2 had been repositioned, in line with the shifting status of offensive biological warfare, as a tool for fundamental work.

These attempts to align ongoing plans with changing policies failed to secure the plant. By the end of the year, the DRPC had 'recommended that BW research should be restricted to that required for defensive measures'.[127] As a consequence, Experimental Plant No. 2 had been deferred yet again. Within a year, BRAB were informed bluntly that this deferral was to be construed as indefinite.[128]

Other events overtook the decision about whether to proceed with the plant. Work on continuous fermentation processes had continued at Porton Down despite the shifting fortunes of the proposed bulk plant.[129] The Annual Report of the MRE for 1956–58 noted that an 'entirely new' apparatus had been developed for producing quantities of around 100 litres or a kilogram of dry weight cells per day.[130] The fermenter had a volume of 20 litres and held 10 litres of culture. Its output was 'normally' 5–10 litres/hour (100–250 litres/day) depending on the growth rate of the organisms used. The new plant had a key advantage over its unrealized predecessor. Components for this new plant were available entirely from commercial sources, thus reducing the need for specialist engineering.

By the end of the decade, a laboratory-scale continuous flow pathogen plant had been used to produce quantities of virulent plague.[131] An estimate of the cost of the 100 litre plant for pathogen production was provided at the 43rd meeting of BRAB and the minimum would be £28 000. At this juncture, the board formally recommended that this new plant should be constructed and a proposal was submitted to the Ministry.[132] At last approval was granted and building finished in August 1962.[133] But this was not Experimental Plant No. 2 as originally envisaged, neither was it used for the same aims or in the same policy context as had been planned in the 1940s. Somewhere between 1949 and the mid-1950s biological warfare policy had shifted from an offensive to a wholly defensive regime. The bomb had been cancelled and the experimental plant 'reinvented'. A similar fate would befall the ambitious series of sea trials that were launched as a crucial component of the post-war research programme.

6
Trials for Biological Warfare

The tests on Gruinard Island carried out during the Second World War were but the first open-air trials to be conducted under the auspices of the British biological warfare project. Towards the end of the war, Paul Fildes had made approaches to his advisors and to the Navy to carry out weapon trials at sea as an extension of the land trials.[1] Early strategic plans for the post-war biological warfare research programme included discussion of further trials and as to their status, the Superintendent of the MRD, Henderson, even entertained the notion that 'no clear division' could be drawn between offensive and defensive research, with the 'possible exception of field trials'.[2] I will argue in this chapter that the trials were significant, not simply for the time and resources devoted to them, but equally because they generated as many, if not more, problems than they solved for fundamental research. And, in the broader context, like the aspects of the programme described in the previous chapter, the series of trials held between 1949 and 1955 were a pivotal indicator of thinking not only about the nature of biological warfare but also its relative positions in Government, scientific and military policies.

Operation Harness

By the end of 1947 the Chiefs of Staff had approved and obtained Treasury consent for a large-scale operation at sea involving tests of pathogenic agents. It was not long before the advisors on the BRAB declared their approval to proceed with Harness as 'a valuable and bold step forward'.[3] They code-named the trial 'Operation Harness' and the naval officer's report on the mission later noted how 'high priority having been accorded to the project, the magic word "Harness" unlocked departmental store cupboards without questions being asked'.[4] While all of this enthusiasm indicates that Harness was a central component of the post-war research programme, this was not a view that was shared by Henderson. He was quick to complain to the BW Subcommittee that the trial would be disruptive and was likely to curtail work back at the establishment. In a separate report, he called on BRAB to ensure that staff who undertook to spend time away from the laboratory bench on the 'unsatisfying routines' of trials should be given 'exceptional privileges'.[5] Moreover, he regarded the trial as potential threat to the prestige of his researchers and wrote:

> there is no group of workers whose whole time of duty it will be to conduct trials. In fact, it is difficult to foresee the development of such a group because I can think of no scientist of the right calibre who in peacetime would be willing to sacrifice his career on such unproductive work.[6]

Henderson's protests notwithstanding, planning for the trial proceeded throughout 1948. Security for Harness was divided into three parts: the fact that trials were being carried out at all, the nature of the biological agents used, and the association of the US and Canada with the trials. All were classified 'top secret'. There was to be no official press release made in connection with the operation, but an emergency press release alluding to chemical weapons had been prepared by the BW Subcommittee as a contingency plan:

> The Admiralty and Ministry of Supply are taking the opportunity of concluding some uncompleted work in connection with the latest poisonous gases which were known at the end of the last war, principally with a view to perfecting modern designs of gas masks to counter the use of these gases. For obvious reasons, these experiments will take place well out at sea.[7]

This disingenuous statement was only to be released from Whitehall if absolutely necessary. Chemical weapons trials were felt by the BW Subcommittee to be more palatable than biological weapons because 'the public is somewhat bored with the well known aspects of gas masks and chemical warfare, and such trials have little scare news value'.[8] Although, as the Ministry of Supply soon pointed out, this cover would be rendered far less credible by the presence of well-known bacteriologists at the test site, the BW Subcommittee decided that the remote nature of the trials provided sufficient anonymity for those entering and leaving the site.[9] The chemical weapon story was adopted but, in the event, never needed.

In fact, several remote sites were surveyed for their potential suitability for trials. Antigua, one of the Leeward Islands off the Bahamas, St Thomas in the Virgin Islands, Roosevelt Roads and Vieques Island in Puerto Rico and Goat Island in Jamaica were all targets of reconnaissance missions.[10] One site on Antigua, Parnham Sound, was eventually chosen by the BW Subcommittee as a suitable headquarters for the trials, especially as it was the site of a disused American military base. The acting governor of the Leeward Islands agreed to the use of Parnham Sound 'provided this would incur no danger to the local population and that their interests were safeguarded'.[11]

Although the conduct of the trials remained entirely in the hands of the British scientists and military, the United States agreed to provide additional supplies and personnel, and the Canadians were to supply additional scientific officers.[12] Operation Harness was thus to be a genuinely tripartite collaborative experiment.

The request that the scientists at Porton Down had originally put to the Admiralty provides a succinct overview of the methods employed in Operation Harness:

> We wish to operate on the open sea, where our biological warfare agents cannot infect land, and use a 'layout' similar to the type we have used on land. We wish to release biological warfare agents in suspension or cloud form upwind of the layout. The layout must be loaded with animals, and must also contain apparatus which can be controlled remotely so as to suck air through sampling bottles (impingers), which will be fixed to each animal point on the layout. After a trial we must recover the contaminated layout with immunity, remove and hold the infected animals and the impingers, subsequently carrying out analyses in laboratories which must be provided. We must be able to sterilise all equipment after a trial. We must have quite stable weather conditions over a period of three months.[13]

All of these requirements added up to an elaborate, albeit makeshift, experimental system. Up to 35 inflatable rubber dinghies, each mounted with an aluminium animal crate and glass sampler, would be floated out to sea. Each crate could house one sheep in the main body and a monkey in a separate box on top. In addition, side arms could be slid on to the main body, each containing three guinea pigs. The entire apparatus, dubbed the 'trot', was towed into position by two motor boats. A bomb for each test was mounted on a float and fired by remote control, thus releasing an infectious cloud over the trot. Two parent ships were responsible for entry and exit into the test. HMS *Narvik* acted as the 'clean ship' from which animals and equipment were floated out to sea, and the 'dirty' ship, HMS *Ben Lomond*, was where infected animals and contaminated equipment were taken after exposure to agents. The dirty ship also contained accommodation for the scientific staff, an enlarged sick bay and laboratory space. Finally, a further ship was also needed to operate downwind of the trot and warn off any shipping which strayed within range of the trials.

During the planning for the operation, secrecy and safety played a combined role. Any serious ordinary casualties were to be admitted to hospital in St John, the main town 7 miles from Parnham Sound. Cases resulting from the biological warfare trials were to be treated in the hospital accommodation at the base or flown out to Camp Detrick in Maryland, which was the US's main biological warfare research facility.[14] Anthrax would be treated in around 10–14 days at the shore base, but anyone with more protracted illnesses would have to be evacuated. The longer-term illnesses were identified as brucellosis and tularemia, both incapacitating diseases. As a precautionary measure, Porton scientists and their advisors made provision for isolation facilities that could cope with around ten cases of infection. Henderson made an additional suggestion that the Admiralty might consider inoculation of naval personnel with Porton's still unproven anthrax vaccine. In reviewing these preparations, Henderson endorsed them and reported 'that in the light of past experience, the safety precautions planned for the trials were adequate'.[15]

The cover story and safety aspects of the trials had been dealt with early in 1948, and trials were set to begin on 26 October. The two ships involved in the trial, HMS *Ben Lomond* and HMS *Narvik*, were specially fitted out at Portsmouth Dockyard, a substantial task demanding a considerable amount of overtime from the dock workers. Two weeks of preliminary trials also took place at Portland on the south coast of England from 18 September, using resistant spores of the non-pathogenic *Bacillus subtilis* to contaminate equipment.[16]

By October the final preparations for the operation were still not complete, and several problems had arisen for the scientists and their advisors. The strain of anthrax developed for the trials, for example, had caused test animals to react in an 'unexpected and perplexing' way.[17] Other organisms which had been suggested for the trials, *B. pestis*, *B. mallei* and *Psittacosis* virus [sic], had been refused on safety grounds by the Inter-Service Medical Panel on Safety Precautions for Operation Harness.[18] To compound these problems, security had been breached on several occasions. Various press reports had appeared concerning the unusual fitting out of the ships at Portsmouth, although none made any explicit link with biological warfare. And, as if the various incidents with the bacteria, other committees and the press were not enough, several of the 250 monkeys specially flown into Britain from India managed to escape. 'Most' were recaptured, the press reported on the incident and this coverage resulted in questions in the Commons together with some sorely unwanted attention from anti-vivisectionists.[19] The BW Subcommittee decided, in spite of these setbacks, that the trial should proceed as planned.

On 5 November a small flotilla, with 454 personnel on board, set sail from Portsmouth for Antigua, stopping off in Gibraltar for repairs. The transit to Antigua is recorded in the operation's naval report as having being notable only for 'the exceedingly foul weather' and 'the good behaviour and well-being of the monkeys'.[20] Crew had initially been informed that the trials would incur some danger but had been led to believe that the tests were for chemical warfare purposes. Officers only revealed the biological nature of the trials to the rest of the crew once the ships had set sail. The news did not disrupt the trials, only one crew member was reported to have taken exception to the change of circumstance and refused to work in the most dangerous part of the ship.[21] By the end of the month, the party had arrived at Parnham Sound to ready themselves for the large-scale and largely untried logistic operation.

After a nine-day series of tests using non-pathogenic organisms as simulant agents, the experimenters proceeded to 'toxic' trials with pathogens. The first agent tested was *Brucella*.[22] Four days before Christmas, the trot was laden with guinea pigs and monkeys and positioned ready for the trial. As the trial was being prepared, two adjacent dinghies suddenly capsized, apparently taken by sharks. By way of a solution, the experimenters ordered special shark-repellent bags from the US Navy and on arrival these were duly attached to the trots. Although this prevented the problem from recurring, the naval officer's report wryly observed that 'sharks were plentiful, and provided plenty of fun'.[23]

Seventeen further trials were carried out by the scientists and their naval assistants between 7 January and 17 February using *Brucella*, tularemia and anthrax. The full apparatus, involving all 35 dinghies stocked with sheep and guinea pigs, was used in just two anthrax trials. Throughout, the labour was arduous as the tropical temperatures, protective gear and elaborate manoeuvring of animals, people and equipment all conspired to make life difficult. It was, as one naval officer recorded, 'hard work, sweating in balloon fabric suits and gas masks for periods of up to three hours, with the outside temperature at 80 deg. F'.[24]

The scientific report of the trial concluded that the logistics of the operation were too complex, at times exposing 'an excessively large number of men to "risk"'.[25] Although the report favoured future sea trials, it emphasized the difficulties of using a mobile layout in open sea, particularly because the wind speeds in the Caribbean had turned out to be higher than expected. A particular problem during the operation had been ground swell which made setting up and recovering the experimental equipment hazardous. As a consequence, the safety of the open sea was quickly abandoned for 'an area just off the lee shore of an island with many small fishing craft in the vicinity'.

In the mean time, another sort of germ warfare was being fought ashore. The medical report of the operation records the degree of concern that officers had over the behaviour of their crew:

> It was known before arrival that the Leeward Islands were noted for the prevalence of venereal diseases of all types.... It was expected that this menace, hand in hand with cheap rum and a comparatively young and inexperienced ship's company, might entail at least an appreciable loss of manpower. Little could be done to influence this apart from instruction which, including precautionary measures, rather emphasised control by abstinence; and provision of alternative sources of entertainment to avoid idle minds.[26]

Eight cases of venereal disease were reported to the medical officer. The figure compares with a single infection of a laboratory technician with brucellosis, a case dismissed in the final medical report as an inevitable part of routine contact: 'where cultures of this organism are being handled in the laboratory, infection can be taken almost as a matter of time'.[27] The relatives of this unfortunate technician were informed only of the 'common name' of his disease and that it was frequently contracted in tropical climates.[28] Illness even delayed Henderson from visiting the site of the operation due to his having 'picked up a bug' at Camp Detrick in Maryland.[29] The illness was not named, except as a laboratory infection, and was said to have responded to treatment.

The main findings in the technical report of the trial remain closed. The report was keen to stress 'that the operation was not primarily designed to test weapons or weapon design'.[30] Instead, the trial had aimed to locate a suitable base and refine research techniques for future tests. Of the 22 toxic trials attempted, 15 were judged by the experimenters to be completely successful, 3 partially successful and 4 were a 'complete failure'.[31] Success here meant a trial being carried to completion without being interrupted by events such as poor weather conditions, the bacterial cloud missing the trot or equipment failure. From the successful trials, the report noted, the higher toxicity of biological over chemical warfare agents could be cautiously accepted. Additionally, the 'blunderbuss method' of field trials was judged inappropriate for improving on the inefficient distribution of the biological agents.

Two short reports to the BW Subcommittee reveal the optimism with which the operation was viewed. The general tenor was that the lessons learned from the implementation of the trials were more important than the experimental data obtained. This, in itself, would be sufficient evidence of success for those involved to warrant further trials in future. BRAB were of the opinion that:

> The operation has confirmed the value of BW. The laboratory work since the previous field trials has been confirmed. It has provided information regarding the behaviour of new types of bacterial suspensions with certain experimental animals, and brought out the value of monkeys in this type of research. It will be unnecessary, in future, to rely on such clumsy animals as sheep in trials with bacterial clouds. The trials have brought out many administrative and scientific problems.[32]

In a similar vein, the tripartite assessment of the trials concluded that

> the sea trials were necessary and fully justified. Owing to the novelty of the techniques adopted and the limited time available to perfect scientific co-ordination for sea requirements, the quantitative data obtained was

limited. On the other hand the qualitative data of the operation confirmed and extended the results of previous trials. The conference considered that the operation substantiated and to some extent augmented previous estimates of the potentialities of Biological Warfare...there was unanimous agreement that the ultimate objective should be full scale field trials of toxic weapons and agents.[33]

The trials were unique and there was little stock of experience on which the participants could draw. Such ignorance applied as much to the experiments themselves as to the logistics that made any experiments possible. While this was no Manhattan Project for biological warfare, the operation had taken up a great deal of effort in terms of personnel, resources and time. At a logistical level, there were many constraints upon the conduct of the field-work. In particular, the continuing importance of elaborate secrecy, implemented to shield Harness from unwanted domestic and foreign attention. Although the scientists, technicians and crew may well have taken the Gruinard Island trials, and possibly chemical weapons trials, as a starting point for their experiments, setting up a floating trial was not a straightforward task. The personal tone of the naval and medical officers' reports may have suggested a farcical element in the conduct of the operation, but this should not mask the amount of work needed to keep everything on track despite sharks, escaping monkeys and itinerant crew. Furthermore, this was not simply an attempt to recreate the conditions of the laboratory in the field. Work back at Porton Down was at a rudimentary stage and Henderson had complained of the diversion that the operation would create. The trials were not therefore simply tagged on to the end of a laboratory research process, instead they were intended to provide some guidance for the basic research back at the MRD.

Operation Cauldron

Operation Harness in the Bahamas was judged a success by the scientists involved and by their advisors. Then, only days after the final tests had been carried out, the Chiefs of Staff approved the continuation of sea trials for the following year.[34] Once the scientists had returned to their laboratories, however, they reported to the BW Subcommittee that more time would be needed to assess the results from Harness and to design new equipment for future trials.[35] In addition, Henderson was keen that the British contribution to the tripartite research collaboration should remain fundamental and laboratory based. No sea trials were carried out in 1950 but pressure was mounting from another direction for a renewed effort in this area.

Within a year of completing Operation Harness, upheavals in the US and Canada began to make an impact on the British programme. The impetus came from Caryl Haskins, who had visited Britain in April 1948. He issued an influential report during 1950 in his capacity as the chair of an ad hoc investigation into biological warfare for the US Secretary of Defence.[36] Biological, chemical and radiological weapons were grouped under the acronym CEBAR and portrayed as a significant threat should the Russian effort overtake that of the United States. While the general tenor of the report provided impetus for an expanded US biological warfare research programme, one practical upshot, according to British advisors, was that a decision was made to concentrate American field testing at Dugway in Utah.[37] Consequently, no new areas were to be considered for future field trials and only *Brucella* would be used at Dugway. The Canadian programme was being similarly curtailed as workers at their Suffield trials site had not yet managed to justify the sums invested by their Government. At Suffield, trials were undertaken during the summer of 1950 to discover why discrepancies of up to 100-fold less efficiency had been revealed between laboratory results and the field with the 4 lb bomb.[38] Beyond this, very little progress appears to have been made. Although Canada and the US had struggled successfully to pursue their outdoor trials, according to the BW Subcommittee, neither 'was prepared to accept the responsibility for the conduct of trials of a full range of BW agents'.[39]

These limitations on the field programmes of Britain's two tripartite allies also coincided with local problems. Although Porton scientists proposed to set up an enclosed steel 'bursting chamber' for testing potential biological agents at Porton, it had transpired that in practice this could only be considered as a long-term project.[40] The US and Canadian scientists had already constructed bursting chambers but these were incapable of dealing with toxic agents. An alternative was for BRAB to once again consider the possibility of trials in British waters. No site was named, although Gruinard Island was mentioned as a possible site for a few months of the year. The matter was referred to BRAB's Scientific Committee, which endorsed the views of the board adding that the proposed trials must take place at sea.[41]

The endorsement from BRAB, in the context of the serious limitations that had been imposed on the Canadian and US field test programmes, meant that Henderson had a case to submit to the DRPC requesting that trials be resumed.[42] Initially these British trials were intended simply to develop equipment for use on a smaller scale than during Harness. Success in these preparatory exercises would lead the Porton team into Operation Cauldron, a series of 'toxic trials' with pathogens 'in Scottish waters with relatively simple equipment, with few men and few ships' during the following year.[43] Besides being considered by the DRPC, the BW Subcommittee also approved preliminary trials in UK waters for 1951 but passed the matter of toxic trials on to the higher authority of the Chiefs of Staff. This initial display of reluctance by the BW Subcommittee was attributed by its members to the 'the strong competing claims on Admiralty manpower and resources'.[44] By February, this hurdle had been overcome as the Chiefs of

Staff approved trials for the following year and provisionally approved the trials for 1952.[45]

In the interim, experimenters at Porton had carried out large-scale tests over the city of Salisbury.[46] The experiments were designed to investigate travel of clouds through built-up areas. No further details are provided in the open literature about the logistics of these field trials, or the nature of the clouds generated for the tests. It is likely that they used inert particles or possibly non-pathogenic organisms intended to simulate a biological weapon attack. The main conclusion drawn from the test was that the probable dosage inside buildings would be similar to that in the open, as victims would be exposed to agents for long periods albeit at lower concentrations. Also, the experiments indicated that a bomb bursting at rooftop level would have comparable effects to those of a ground-burst bomb. These conclusions, highlighting the vulnerability of cities to a biological bombing raid, could only encourage the planned water-borne trials with living agents.

Preliminary trials for Operation Cauldron took place between 20 and 24 August 1951 in Shanklin Bay on the Isle of Wight. Cauldron, while on a smaller scale than its predecessor, still involved the use of a 200 by 60 foot artificial floating island on which the test animals were placed, rather than the 'trot' of dinghies deployed in Harness.[47] Although the majority of this work was concerned with the behaviour of this pontoon at sea, a 'small trial' was carried out on 23 August which probably employed an inert simulant. The trials were encouraging and deemed by the BW Subcommittee to have been 'very satisfactory'.[48]

It was now the BRAB's responsibility to advise on whether the case for field trials was stronger than relying on alternative tests in bursting chambers. The argument in favour had been advanced in a memorandum from Henderson, the Chief Superintendent of the MRD, before the board met in August shortly after the pontoon testing.[49] The case rested on the difficulties of extrapolation of data from the laboratory and cited the example of *Brucella suis*. Aerosols of this organism had been found to be only one-quarter as effective in the field as in the laboratory.[50] Extrapolation across species from simulants to pathogens was also reported as an unreliable source of data. Nevertheless, according to the Chief Superintendent, data from the field would provide a firm basis for future laboratory work. In addition, three changes were mentioned which were deemed to have made field trials necessary: recent weapon developments; improved survival of vegetative organisms; and progress with novel agents.

Henderson, who had previously called field trials 'unjustifiable and in many ways needless', was now converted.[51] More generally, the field trials proposal marked a shift in biological warfare research policy. As the board noted:

> In the 1949 Report the opinion was stated that field trials should come at the end of a development programme; other authorities have maintained

that an earlier appeal to the field test is essential to guide fundamental research and development, and further experience has convinced us that this is so.[52]

The preceding details of the discussions and debates over the availability of field sites in Canada and the US provide a note of caution in taking this statement at face value. It is evident that the shift in research policy was precipitated as much by such contingencies as site availability as by its necessity for fundamental research and development.

In the hastily arranged meeting after the trials at Shanklin Bay, BRAB members rested their arguments in favour of proceeding with trials at sea on the successful development of the relatively cheap and simple trial technique using the pontoon. Another argument in favour of field trials was made by one BRAB scientist who pointed out that field trials would give an 'absolute assessment of a weapon', whereas bursting chambers provided only comparative data.[53] Furthermore, the minutes of the meeting somewhat cryptically record that there was 'also now an added sense of urgency, and the situation could be said to have been altered by new factors, and the time was ripe for the acquisition of new knowledge'.[54] Whether this statement referred tangentially to the Korean War, atomic weaponry or other more proximate developments remains a matter of conjecture. The outcome of the board's discussion was that it concurred with the Ministry of Supply's Principal Director of Scientific Research, Wansbrough-Jones:

> certainly for the present and probably also for the foreseeable future, properly conducted field trials with weapons and with hot agents will be necessary for the interim and final assessments, and that they are an essential complement to small scale trials in laboratory conditions in bursting chambers, coupled with large scale trials with simulants.[55]

Field trials had originally been regarded by scientists and advisors as the end point of the research process. So, during the Second World War, the Gruinard trials were depicted by Paul Fildes in particular as the culmination of research, at which point production should follow ineluctably. The new research policy still saw the trials as integral to the invention of a bomb, but also as feeding back into the basic research taking place in the laboratory.

A potential site for the trials had been found in a bay around 20 miles north of Stornaway on the Isle of Lewis in Scotland. Towards the end of the year this location had been confirmed and a request from the Ministry of Supply was put to the Air Ministry for an aircraft to transport stores, personnel, experimental animals (including 1000 guinea pigs) and visitors to Stornaway.[56] In the words of the BW Subcommittee, Cauldron was 'to be regarded as an extension of the MRD laboratories for exploratory testing of new agents and weapons'.[57] The scientists involved echoed this rationale through BRAB, stating that 'for the first time agents that cannot be handled at land bases' would be used, in particular *Pasteurella pestis* the bearer of plague.[58]

This was to prove a controversial choice. The following April, there was a fierce debate among BRAB members over the use of *P. pestis* in Operation Cauldron.[59] The fact that in combat *P. pestis* might give rise to an epidemic and 'boomerang' back on friendly troops was seen as highly disadvantageous. In the light of these factors, Lord Stamp proposed that more readily controlled agents, such as those causing brucellosis and tularaemia, should become the focus of attention. Moreover, Wansbrough-Jones pointed out to the board that the Service requirement was for a non-lethal agent. Keen advocates of *P. pestis*, Fildes and Hankey acknowledged that its use was contrary to established policy, which focused attention on non-epidemic diseases, but argued that for 'political and defensive purposes' it was important to ascertain its effects in case an enemy employed the pathogen. The final decision of the board was to recommend the use of *P. pestis* in the trials for these very reasons.[60] The negotiation surrounding the choice of *P. pestis* underlines an important point about the role and functioning of this expert board. Work at Porton was officially harnessed to Service requirements, especially through the Air Staff requirement for a bomb, and in turn was linked to broader biological warfare policy. Contrary to this, however, BRAB, or at least senior members of BRAB, were quite capable here of 'subverting' research in a direction that ran contrary to policy.

With the trials approved and preparation under way, it remained for the Chiefs of Staff to decide on the degree of secrecy that would surround Cauldron. At their meeting in January 1951, the BW Subcommittee had already acknowledged that 'there might be some small risk to fishermen, and it would be necessary to keep the area clear'.[61] Wider publicity, such as a press release, was eschewed unless considered absolutely necessary:

neither they [the trials] nor the draft press announcement would involve a security risk since there was no likelihood of an enemy being able to glean information. A cover plan was not therefore required nor worthwhile. If an advance statement were made, there was the possibility of opposition from bodies such as anti-vivisectionists; but, more important, there was the general effect upon the nation. Any misrepresentation of the trials might be a serious embarrassment to the Government. It was pointed out, however, that with the attention of the Press focused on the Royal Funeral and the Accession, it was unlikely, in the next few weeks, that publicity would be switched to BW.[62]

Although there was some disapproval from the BW Subcommittee over this stance, the policy held. Fishermen would be officially warned and no public announcement would be made about Cauldron unless the trials received unwelcome publicity, and even then any release would require direct approval from the Minister of Defence.[63] Certainly, from the Chiefs of Staff perspective, this does not appear to have been a matter of national security. Animal rights protesters and embarrassed politicians seemed to pose more of a threat than Soviet intelligence agents.

As with Harness, a short press release was prepared to be held in reserve. The statement placed a great emphasis on defence. It opened with a very brief and general paragraph noting that biological warfare research had taken place during and after the Second World War that established its potential, that reports in the public were frequently exaggerated and that it was, nonetheless, necessary to keep a watch on the topic. The release continued with an apologia that

> in order that effective means of defence may be developed, every possibility must be studied, not only in the laboratory but in the field. To this end, for example, highly specialised laboratory apparatus has been developed for the study of the mode of infection of many forms of respiratory disease. Furthermore, the results so obtained are to be tested this year by experiments in the open; for safety these experiments will be carried out at sea. Only by such means can the risk from biological warfare attack be adequately assessed and specific defence measures perfected.[64]

Behind the press release, policy was still aimed at defence through retaliation and Operation Cauldron was a crucial embodiment of this policy. The operation was due to be carried out at the end of April 1952 although the detailed reports of the trials still remain secret. Although the operation was hampered by poor weather conditions, the scientists were able to 'carry out short range trials with dangerous agents and to investigate the long range travel of clouds downwind'.[65] *Brucella* and plague were the only organisms involved in these tests.

In August, Sir Paul Fildes and Lord Stamp issued two joint memos on the preliminary results of Operation Cauldron.[66] Although they praised the efficiency and simplicity of the new pontoon techniques, the two board advisors flagged several drawbacks and discussed one particular limitation, the range of wind directions that could safely be used for toxic trials in home waters. By way of an alternative, Fildes and Stamp then drew attention to recent, unspecified, developments in long-range trials using simulants.[67] They argued that such trials, testing the properties of agents over extended distances, would provide information regarding 'weathering of organisms' and safety distances. Toxic long-range trials, they hoped, might eventually be carried out to 'provide a more dramatic demonstration of the potentialities of BW' and, at a more concrete level, add to knowledge from current short-range trials investigating the infective power of brucellosis.

In reply, Henderson argued that a wholesale shift to long-range trials would be undesirable; his conclusion was drawn primarily on the grounds that Cauldron was not designed for such tests.[68] Despite Henderson's protest, some preliminary long-range trials had already taken place during Cauldron and were mentioned explicitly in the second memo from Fildes and Stamp, where they made further proposals for conducting long-range trials.[69] They suggested using a 'so-called' avirulent strain of *Brucella abortus*, an organism which had been used both as a living vaccine in North America and as a simulant in field trials at Suffield.[70] Stamp and Fildes were aware that this was not an entirely safe proposal. The authors noted how others had considered it possible that the bacteria 'might regain virulence in the animal body', but added that protective clothing, a 2 mile range and an onshore breeze should reduce the risk of contamination. If, in spite of these protective measures, the organism was still considered too much of a risk, they conceded that other non-pathogens could be substituted for the *Brucella* strain. This debate over the role and place of long-range trials would return later in the year and occupy more of BRAB's energies.

Operation Hesperus

Even before the results of Cauldron had been fully assessed, plans for a further series of trials, now dubbed Operation Hesperus, were tabled to take place at Stornaway. In addition, Kenneth Crawford of the BW Subcommittee reported that the Prime Minister had approved a reconnaissance mission to find a different site for future trials beyond Hesperus.[71] The scientists needed better weather conditions and wanted to undertake experiments on a larger scale than Cauldron or Hesperus. Yet further doubts about the direction of these trials were raised at the December 1952 meeting of BRAB. Stamp continued to suggest an investigation of simulant survival in the field. He envisaged that this might entail cancelling the Hesperus trials which, he added, were to be curtailed anyway. On the other hand, Henderson pointed out that the Americans had not had any success with their long-range pathogen field trials and therefore the UK should continue work on pathogens the following summer. The final decision of the board was to follow Henderson and recommend continuing with the 1953 trials.

Possibly because of his vociferous opposition to the directions in which Hesperus appeared to point, Stamp was invited to produce a paper on the future of field trials which was received by BRAB at the end of December.[72] The paper, described by John Morton of the MRD as 'written in genuine if slightly boisterous enthusiasm', set out alternative possibilities for the field trials programme. It argued for long-distance trials over a quarter of a mile as the best route forward with fieldwork. Morton's comments on this work are attached to this document and the 'dialogue' between the two scientists provides further useful insight into some of the uncertainties that surrounded this phase of biological warfare research.

Stamp's paper opened by pointing out that relatively little attention had been paid to long-distance trials. He attributed this neglect to the evolution of biological warfare research from chemical warfare, where local effects were the focus and therefore the cloud was 'bracketed' by placing sampling apparatus and animals close to the bomb. Even, he continued, in early tests using anthrax and botulinum toxin, the stability of agents over long distances was of little importance for the experimenters. Stamp argued that this neglect did not extend to work with vegetative organisms, where scientists had taken seriously the possibility that much of the cloud might be lost soon after the samples were taken. As Morton recognized, the significance of this consideration depended on the purposes behind the weapon. It was only of importance if the users were actually concerned about what happened outside the immediate area of effect.

Stamp's argument continued by maintaining that long-distance simulant trials were needed for scientists to fully assess the potential of germ warfare. Morton added drily that this was in fact what Hesperus intended to achieve. He also added that there were drawbacks to using simulants, believing that none existed for *Brucella*, then adding that avirulent *Pasteurella pestis* might not be the same as the pathogenic strain, 'and anyway we aren't terribly interested in that organism at the moment'.

Stamp also suggested that trials at sea might differ in kind from trials over land. Because of this complication he continued to advocate land-based simulant trials at Porton. Although Morton agreed with the utility of such research, he pointed out that such trials would be more difficult to carry out and would further load already heavy commitments at MRD. With a keen eye on priorities, Morton noted that sea trials with simulants would compete directly with the time for toxic trials, both requiring comparable meteorological conditions. Stamp finished his argument by mentioning that short-range trials on dispersal efficiency would continue to be necessary as an integral part of the development of an operational weapon.[73] He also pointed out that fusing was one of the greatest obstacles to be overcome in obtaining a practical and economic bomb. Morton dissented. Apart from fusing, he added, 'we cannot produce charging; and manufacture, filling and sealing of bombs present problems equal at least to fusing'. Stamp had, he finished, overestimated the weapon testing aspect of the UK trials. In the light of this involved debate it seems obvious but necessary to point out that the 'trajectory' of the research programme was not mapped out in advance by previous scientific advances. The comments by Morton and Stamp serve to emphasize how alternative courses were open to the developing programme.

Eventually, over a year after completion, BRAB judged Cauldron as having been 'extremely successful' in establishing the new pontoon technique, despite adverse weather conditions during the trial.[74] Nevertheless, other results were less promising. The trial data appeared to demonstrate the ineffectiveness of the agents tested.[75] Fildes declared plague to be a 'failure' and *Brucella* 'had not increased its reputation as a dangerous agent'.[76] He also felt that vegetative organisms were not stable enough to be used as biological warfare agents and that Cauldron had not advanced the assessment of the 'true risk' of biological warfare, merely shown that the risk was lower than originally thought. In spite of such doubts, Hankey argued shortly afterwards in the same meeting that Cauldron had justified the expense and contributed to 'consolidation of thought'. This point was unanimously agreed on by the BRAB. Further work, they agreed optimistically, 'would almost certainly result in an ultimate evaluation of the risk'.

A draft programme for Hesperus was issued in January 1953 which proposed a mixture of short- and long-range trials with the bacteria responsible for brucellosis, tularemia and also Venezuelan equine encephalitis (VEE) virus.[77] Stamp also appeared to have won a degree of success – an additional series of long-distance tests on downwind travel of clouds of simulants was planned. The draft emphasized, however, that the proposals were tentative and would need to be modified depending on local contingencies. On these grounds, the plan provides little guidance as to what actually occurred in the Hesperus trials. It does, nonetheless, give some indication of priorities. The plan specified that *Bacterium tularense* and downwind travel of pathogens and simulants would be accorded highest priority.[78] This was repeated at the 28th meeting of BRAB, where Henderson reported that cloud decay would be the main focus of the operation.[79]

One unresolved aspect of the programme for Hesperus was revisited during the February 1953 meeting of BRAB, the question of whether or not to proceed with land as well as sea trials.[80] Wansbrough-Jones argued that it was first necessary to understand the variables affecting organism survival under relatively controlled circumstances before attempting land trials. Alternatively, he felt that extrapolation of results from sea to land would not be possible. Later in the same meeting, it was announced that land trials had been planned at Porton that year. Porton scientists intended to employ two simulant agents, *Bacillus prodigiosus* and avirulent *Pasteurella pestis*, in tests to measure the effects of light on the organisms.

An incidental point, made by Henderson during this general discussion, indicated the role of the bombs used in these trials. The Chief Superintendent pointed out that development of a British weapon was still 'some considerable time' away. Therefore, he argued, Hesperus would concentrate on the US weapon, although it appears that eventually both a British and an American bomb were tested. Hesperus, like Cauldron, was therefore a continuation of existing policy and practice, heavily oriented to producing a bomb.

The proposed use of VEE virus in Hesperus marked an interesting development away from bacteria in the trials series. This highly infectious, debilitating but rarely lethal disease had been mentioned briefly in connection with Cauldron but only received serious consideration by BRAB during their planning for Hesperus. After the disappointing results with vegetative bacteria in Cauldron, Fildes had raised with BRAB the issue of using viruses in the outdoor trials.[81] He believed that these were not so susceptible to weathering, although one board member Edward Spooner, Professor of Bacteriology at the London School of Hygiene and Tropical Medicine, pointed out that there was enormous variation in the ability of viruses to remain active in the open. Survival of micro-organisms had also been postulated to be dependent on light and Hankey raised the issue as to whether travel of bacterial clouds in darkness had been investigated; by way of response he was referred to the proposed land tests at Porton. In spite of these discussions, VEE was never employed in Operation Hesperus.[82] The only organisms employed at sea in 1953 were those responsible for brucellosis and tularemia. BRAB decided that VEE might pose risks to livestock via infection of birds, even though the risk was thought to be very small. Certainly, this risk posed no obstacle to the board in recommending that VEE should instead be used in forthcoming trials in the Bahamas.

Virology

VEE was one of several viral pathogens which were candidates for biological warfare agents. The focus of the MRD research programme had begun to shift towards the possibility of using viruses in the early 1950s. At this time, virologists were beginning to establish their work as separate from cognate fields such as bacteriology and pathology. Viruses were increasingly being characterized as distinct from other micro-organisms and a range of improved techniques, such as cell and tissue culture and advances in electron microscopy, aided the study of viruses.[83]

An intelligence report from 1951 drew attention to the problems that might be involved in virus production for biological warfare: 'it is probable that if the Soviets include viruses in their BW programme, they could produce them with no greater difficulty than the Western powers. Virus production is, however, a laborious and expensive process which would not be productive of large quantities.'[84] It is not clear how influential or widely read this secret report would have been. Regardless of the intelligence position, a year later the MRD was pursuing its own plans to investigate viruses as potential agents of war. At the 26th meeting of BRAB a working party headed by Fildes was established to 'consider the form of a virology unit and how best to implement it'.[85] They were asked not to discuss financial matters relating to the unit.[86] The working party met at the end of October 1952 and had recommended that a virology unit be formed at MRD.[87] Despite chairing the working party, Fildes had openly opposed this recommendation on the explicit grounds that the work was especially dangerous. Fildes seems to have had several objections to the virology unit apart from the danger. He stated at the next BRAB meeting that the risks were likely to deter an enemy from virus research and that field trials with these pathogens would be impossible. Later in the debate he added that starting a new department would divert resources and personnel from the already understaffed parts of the MRD. It appears that Fildes was as concerned with safety as to maintain existing strength in his own field of bacteriology and not to weaken the MRD position through diversification. His position was not accepted by the board, which recommended the establishment of the unit. One reason for this support was voiced by Wansbrough-Jones who saw it as a solution to the staff freeze imposed by the Treasury. A new virology unit meant that four scientific officers and seven experimental officers could be hired.

In the light of the decision to establish a virology unit, Wilson Smith of BRAB and Professor of Bacteriology at University College Hospital, was asked to write a report expressing his personal opinions on viruses as warfare agents.[88] He took the opportunity to complain from the outset that there had already been problems recruiting any personnel in advance to the unit. Afterwards, Smith outlined the key qualities that would required of a virus weapon: high virulence, high infectivity, ready transmissibility, infectivity by the respiratory route, lack of effective means of prophylaxis, ease of production and stability. Smallpox, psittacosis, influenza, typhus, Q fever and encephalitis viruses were all listed by the professor as potential human agents and he mentioned ongoing US investigations into Q fever and typhus.[89] Animal viruses were also named in the litany of agents and included foot-and-mouth, rinderpest, Newcastle disease and hog cholera.

Constraints on the proposed project were also suggested by Smith who envisaged a unit with capacity to research four viruses. He recommended field tests as a first step in order to avoid commencing work on viruses that would later prove to be unworkable in the field. The report also considered the problems of choosing suitable non-pathogenic simulants. The problems were those of how close, and in what respects, any simulant would have to resemble its pathogenic substitute. This paper on the potential of viruses was accepted by BRAB as a statement of research policy at their meeting in November 1953.[90] The virology unit formed on 1 January 1954 with the expectation of employing three researchers by the end of the year.[91]

Return to the Bahamas: Operation Ozone

By June 1953, about a month after commencing, progress in Hesperus was quite poor owing once again to bad weather. Two days of trials out of a possible 22 had been made.[92] In the mean time, reconnaissance for the 1954 trials near Nassau in the Bahamas had taken place during March.[93] A site had been selected and Henderson proposed that Hesperus might be abandoned by the end of August because of the poor conditions, with the new trials starting in

January or February 1954.[94] During Hesperus, the scientists, assisted by 195 naval crew, did manage some innovation with routine long-range toxic trials extending to ranges of up to 1200 yards.[95]

The preliminary results from Hesperus were made available to BRAB in October 1953.[96] Besides studies of travel and survival of vegetative pathogens, two other objectives of the operation were specified in the field report. Firstly, the experimenters had gained more outdoor experience with *Bacterium tularense* and secondly, they had been able to compare the British B/E1 experimental bomb and American E61 bomb designed to spread anthrax spores. Many of the trials had involved animals at short ranges because the sources were too small to establish infections at longer ranges. The shorter of the long-range survival trials, at distances around 450 metres, were judged successful by the experimenters, although beyond this distance they were deemed 'far less good than expected' with aerosols of organisms surviving only for very short periods.[97] In particular, the long-distance trials were not a success with *B. tularense*. This organism proved to be 'very disappointing' as very few organisms survived dispersal. Bombs provided poor results but alternative spray-generated data provided some positive results. Spray tests indicated that the tularemia bacteria could survive two minutes after being sprayed over 1100 metres – although even this feat entailed some loss of live organisms. The experimental spray technique was concluded to be 'fundamentally sound' if used in an undisturbed topographical environment with a controllable spray generator. Despite some disappointing results, it was concluded that *Brucella suis* was not affected adversely by prevailing meteorological conditions. *Bacterium tularense* was 'probably more affected' but not to the extent that it could be dismissed as a potential agent. There was no discussion of how badly an organism would have had to perform to be discarded as an agent.

In general, the advisors dubbed Hesperus as 'productive of experiments and less productive of positive conclusions', with a 'fair number' of negative results among the 72 toxic runs. Nevertheless, BRAB members did not take this as a setback but skated over it as 'an inevitable concomitant of most researches', especially when viewed as a component of a longer-term project. In the BRAB annual report for 1953 an additional but brief assessment attributed the poor success of the long-range trials to the poor weather and nearby cliffs. It remarked, however, that there was evidence to 'suggest that organisms are less damaged by half a mile travel than by explosive dispersal'.[98] This passing remark appears to be an early endorsement, albeit tentative and conceptually embryonic, of the idea that a spray of organisms allowed to drift towards a target might show more promise than a bomb.

Henderson reported elsewhere that the forthcoming research in the Bahamas, Operation Ozone, would be likely to focus on spray sources.[99] This would involve long-distance trials of up to 2 miles for *Brucella suis* and *Bacterium tularense*. Henderson proposed that a shorter amount of time would be spent studying how clouds of these two organisms decayed following dispersal from the British experimental bomb. A third strand of Operation Ozone was planned with field trials of VEE and *Psittacosis*, both at that time believed to be viral in origin.[100]

These two viruses were chosen for Ozone largely on the grounds that the Americans were able to produce them in a stable form. As with other aspects of the trials, the choice of viruses did not pass unchallenged. Wilson Smith expressed concern at the December 1953 meeting of BRAB that the tests with viruses were being performed before a virology unit at Porton had been established. Both Smith and Spooner made the further objection that *Psittacosis* was an especially dangerous agent to be using in the first field trials and in follow-up laboratory tests. Henderson, nevertheless, was satisfied with the safety precautions developed during Cauldron and Hesperus but welcomed further suggestions by the two professors on the matter. They recommended that training in virus techniques should be provided for the MRD technicians.

One BRAB member also pointed out during the discussion on viruses that, although it might have been better to work with a simulant first, financial restrictions threatened to render Operation Ozone the last field test for the foreseeable future. Even at the reconnaissance stage of Ozone this possibility had arisen. The minutes of the BW Subcommittee meeting in June 1953 recorded that:

> It was impossible, at this stage, to say whether there would be an annual or future requirement for field trials. Much would depend on the information forthcoming from trials in the Bahamas if agreed. It might be possible as a result of the Bahamas trials to reassess the risks from BW.[101]

On a more positive note for the research programme, the subcommittee believed that security would be no more or less of an issue in the Bahamas than at Stornaway. They added enthusiastically that 'it was felt that there would be no adverse effect on the tourist trade' from testing and dispersing pathogenic organisms in the area. Finance again appeared to be the key restriction as the Admiralty and Air Ministry had indicated that, unlike the Scottish trials where no charges had been made, these Services were now more reluctant to bear any costs of the operation.[102]

Senior figures in the Admiralty had distanced themselves from the trials quite considerably, arguing several times that while the Navy had no wish to obstruct the trials, they had little or no direct interest in their outcome. The most strident argument to this effect came in an unsigned memorandum from August 1953:

> Admiralty participation in BW trials is in a certain sense accidental, consequent upon the fact, first demonstrated by Operation 'Harness' in

1948, that trials of this nature can be more conveniently carried out at sea. The Ministry of Supply, of course, is the Department responsible for BW research and they must therefore be the protagonist in arguing the case for the importance of the successful operation of trials.... However, with this proviso it is suggested that it is the duty of the Admiralty, as of all the Service Departments, to speak strongly in favour of measures which will enable BW experiments to be fruitful; although the War Office and the Air Ministry are much more likely to be involved in the actual use of BW weapons than the Admiralty, if that unhappy event should occur.... Our support, however, should not be so unqualified as to implicate the Admiralty in any way in sharing the costs of these trials.[103]

This is perhaps the clearest statement in the open literature of the attitude held by any of the Services towards biological warfare at this time. It is quite clear that, finances aside, the support of the Navy was lukewarm, and it saw itself as largely unaffected by any future developments in biological warfare research.

Even the Cabinet Defence Committee wavered in its approval of the trials, although their objections were less concerned with financial matters. In urging for a more suitable location to be found, 'they recognised that the results of the trials were essential for defence against biological warfare, but that the security and other objections to holding these trials at the Bahamas were considerable'.[104] Yet shortly afterwards, in August, they did agree that Operation Ozone would be held between February and May the following year.

Once again, the perennial questions of publicity and security had arisen in connection with the trials. Press statements were intended to be released by the Government before the trials in the Bahamas but this course of action was rapidly curtailed. In January 1954 the new Governor of the Bahamas and his Executive Council agreed unanimously that no announcement should be made until absolutely necessary. The demand was conveyed to the British authorities although it did not prevent a short article from appearing in *The Times* on 12 March 1954, at the outset of the operation, which provided a positive coverage of the trials. This piece drew heavily on a Ministry of Supply press release, quoting defensively: 'Her Majesty's Government cannot neglect consideration of the precautions which would need to be taken should this form of warfare be applied to us.'[105] With a nod in the direction of safety, the article stated that 'the area chosen is out to sea, at least 20 miles away from any inhabited island and is widely removed from any normal shipping channel'. While the article was short on detail and strong on official rhetoric, it marked an unprecedented lowering of the obsessive secrecy that had surrounded all previous trials of biological warfare agents.

Following a three-week delay, due to damage to the pontoon, Operation Ozone commenced early in 1954 some 60 miles south of Nassau. Trials proceeded according to the plans, except that *Psittacosis*, which was declared unstable following explosion chamber tests in the US, had been abandoned as a test organism. Instead brucellosis and tularemia bacteria were used, with an additional debut from VEE. Initial and tentative results were revealed to BRAB at their June meeting. All but 6 of the 80 trials had been carried out by spraying organisms. *Brucella suis*, *Bacterium tularense* and VEE had all been tested as aerosols in bright sunlight and had half-lives ranging from a few seconds to two minutes. Overall, Fildes in particular, was positive about the progress of the trials and gave his opinion that 'if trials were to be carried out for three or four years, it might be possible to assess the BW risk'.[106] This opinion became the official position of BRAB and was passed along the advisory hierarchy to the BW Subcommittee.[107]

A later report on the trials also noted that the susceptibility of pathogens to daylight demonstrated in Ozone was 'of great importance in relation to the possible use of seaborne attack employing onshore winds. Other attack is likely to be by night.'[108] This idea, of an attack without a bomb but with a cloud sprayed and left to drift across a target, is possibly the first solid hint of the new conception of the threat that would become dominant in British research and policy in a few years' time.

The last trial: Negation

Fildes' optimism over the future of trials was to be short-lived. Approval for the next series of trials, Operation Negation, to be carried out in the Bahamas between October 1954 and March 1955, came from the Chiefs of Staff in August. This approval was issued with an ominous proviso; the Chiefs of Staff had 'stipulated, however, that the continuance of trials beyond 1955 must be subject to further consideration at the appropriate time'.[109] Although not linked in any direct way to this warning, the previous month had seen the Air Ministry issue their revised target cancelling the immediate request for a biological bomb.

During Negation, Henderson intended to use the same organisms and possibly also eastern equine encephalitis 'as it was more lethal'.[110] He proposed to supplement the virus work by using *vaccinia* virus, responsible for cowpox and proposed as a simulant of smallpox, in order 'to break new ground'. Wilson Smith noted that the virus programme was new and that in the absence of laboratory work 'the best guess of a suitable agent had to be made'.[111] Vaccinia, in particular, required further laboratory investigation. The possibility of using variola virus, the smallpox virus, offensively was also raised by the board but doubts were expressed as to its potential danger.

Further Operation Ozone results became available to BRAB early in 1955.[112] Despite poor weather conditions, 70 separate trials had been carried out with *Brucella suis*, *Bacterium tularense* and *vaccinia* virus. This included observations under varying conditions of daylight, temperature and humidity.[113] Low solar radiation improved the half-life of *Brucella suis* and *vaccinia* but *Bacterium tularense* remained susceptible to radiation and humidity and BRAB members concluded reluctantly that: 'it might well be that *Bact. tularense* is of no value as a BW agent'.[114] By June, BRAB members could summarize the key conclusions they had drawn from Negation. Scientists were now sensitive to the 'extreme dependence of survival of airborne micro-organisms on external conditions: the life in unfavourable circumstances was very short, in favourable circumstances very long'.[115] BRAB's discussion of the early results from Negation was rounded off with a telling statement from Fildes who, on considering the results of the operation, noted pessimistically that 'it was becoming clear that the hazards of biological warfare, as distinct from sabotage, were not as great as has been thought. A statement should be made to this effect.'[116] Although minuted, any official statement of this opinion was not made by the board in their recommendations from the meeting.

On land, during 1955, a further series of trials took place away from the MRD to ascertain the vulnerability of Whitehall to a germ warfare attack. There is very little detail about these Special Operations trials in the public domain. Assistance from the Post Office and MI5 was obtained and at least two trials took place. The first trials simply investigated the air currents in the building and had found leaks throughout the system. The following trial was 'more ambitious' and MRD staff had distributed spores of the simulant *Bacillus globigii*.[117] Two weeks after releasing the bacteria, experimenters took samples at various points and concluded that the Air Ministry Citadel and the Whitehall telephone exchange had been contaminated. BRAB were also informed that a later test had succeeded in contaminating the Cabinet Office.[118] After this initial investigation which seemed to have confirmed any fears that existed about sabotage, no immediate follow-up trials were planned. These do not appear to have been the only trials connected with a potential sabotage attack. Henderson elsewhere referred in passing to 'contamination work' which had been carried out on the London Underground, suggesting that this form of attack could be 'applied to the whole country'.[119]

Sea trials sink

The series of sea trials was voluntarily interrupted as the researchers at Porton paused to consider their results. Dr Walter Cawood, from the Ministry of Aviation, reported to the Ministry of Supply's Scientific Advisory Council in June 1955 that trials in the Bahamas would not be carried out at the end of the year.[120] He had a reassuring excuse for this decision, 'the mass of data accumulated needed to be correlated with laboratory results and there was much stocktaking to be done before arrangements could usefully be made for further trials'.[121] An expedition for the end of 1956 might be required. As Henderson explained matters, 'he had come to the conclusion that it would be better to concentrate during the coming year on laboratory studies aided by the new bursting chambers...no new agents had materialised which called for trials in the field at present'.[122] Henderson's decision was by no means unreserved, he was concerned that if trials were suspended then the Admiralty might take away HMS *Ben Lomond* and the pontoon, making them unavailable for future trials. Cawood assured Henderson that it was the availability of sailors rather than the particular naval facilities which would present problems. He pointed out that it had even been suggested that the Ministry of Supply should investigate the possibility of assembling a civilian crew: 'had the trials been continuous and of a more permanent nature this might have been possible; but in the circumstances it did not seem practicable'.[123]

By October 1956, Henderson's concerns had been realized. Further sea trials for 1957–58 had been agreed in principle by the Scientific Advisory Council, but the committee noted that they might need to be deferred because of difficulties in providing a crew for HMS *Ben Lomond*.[124] Indeed, within the Ministry of Defence, Admiralty representatives had stated categorically that HMS *Ben Lomond* would not be made available for future biological warfare field trials.[125] The chairman of the Defence Research Policy Staff (DRPS), who serviced the DRPC, still wished to know, despite the Admiralty position, whether there was any technical need for the trials. Several members of the DRPS 'doubted whether research had progressed far enough and that sufficient technical data had been obtained to enable anyone to make a decision to stop'.[126] They also thought that several more trials were necessary. During the debate on the trials, one member of the DRPS, Air Commodore Lance Jarman, noted that 'the Air Ministry considered BW purely as a global war weapon and, even in that sense, its value was doubtful because of the effect of nuclear weapons'. He recommended that trials should be stopped and effort devoted solely to defensive research.

The Air Commodore's remarks capture the overall change in the position of biological warfare from its previously exalted status. The plans for a biological bomb had been all but abandoned by the Air Ministry as attention turned towards nuclear weapons. By this stage, Experimental Plant No. 2 had been postponed indefinitely and during the past decade, according to Henderson, the work at the MRD

> could point to little concrete information on biological warfare but a considerable volume of knowledge on techniques and field methods...the information which they now had clearly indicated that the covert use of biological warfare would be the simplest and most serious form of attack and the most difficult to combat.[127]

The threat itself now appeared to be confined to sabotage and the series of trials at sea was finished. There would eventually be future trials at sea and future trials with simulant agents. But, whether or not as a direct result of the DRPS deliberations, Operation Negation was the final large-scale, outdoor trial with pathogens to take place under the auspices of the British biological warfare research programme.

7
The Drift of Biological Weapons Policy

The previous chapters described the fate of the key elements of post-war biological warfare research. An initial burst of enthusiasm by the military and their advisors had provided the momentum for an expanding post-war research programme, yet the biological bomb and Experimental Plant No. 2 never materialized and the ambitious series of seaborne trials was terminated. While these were not the only research activities in biological warfare at Porton, they had occupied the attention of various advisory committees where it was frequently argued that they underpinned the existing retaliatory policy. Yet broader changes appeared to be shunting biological warfare to the bottom of the military agenda and the major components of the research programme suffered as a result. In this chapter I will chart in some detail these changes in the policy regime during the early 1950s. The detail is necessary since there are few unequivocal statements of policy during this period to act as beacons in the narrative. Instead, during the early 1950s open statements regarding policy tend to drift in an ambiguous and ambivalent manner. The drift, nonetheless, was in the direction of defensive in preference to offensive priorities.

Some doubts

The initial signs that faith in the powers of biological weapons might be faltering appeared in discussions about a 1949 report by BRAB to the Chiefs of Staff. This had suggested that:

> An accurate assessment of the potentialities of Biological Warfare cannot, of course, be made until this weapon has been used on a large scale in warfare, and it may well be that when the actual trial is made against man – if ever it should be – it may prove relatively ineffective if not completely so. Nevertheless, a study of the potentialities of BW agents by the only available means (i.e. by trials on experimental animals) has shown that agents can be dispersed from aircraft bombs, and that the toxicity of

three agents at least is many times greater than that of any known chemical agent.[1]

Any suggestion that biological warfare might prove ineffective was potentially damaging. The following year, the new chairman of the BW Subcommittee, Kenneth Crawford, tried to rescue this report from any such negative interpretations. He pointed out that estimates about the practicability of a biological weapon were 'the honest opinions of our technical advisers. Scientists by nature tend to be conservative, and the Report may give a misleading impression that there are very long odds against BW ever being a practical proposition.'[2] Yet, Crawford was still willing to consider a shift in policy for quite different reasons and admitted to the subcommittee that continued delays in building Experimental Plant No. 2, coupled with staff shortages, had raised problems:

> As I see it the main issue is whether in view of the present state of national finances, we can justify the continuation of research and development in the offensive sphere. There are may factors to be considered, amongst these being the extent to which the Americans are relying upon us and the repercussions for collaboration with that country if we discontinued offensive research; the deterrent factor and so forth.[3]

In view of these doubts, the DRPC and Chiefs of Staff quickly instigated a review of the advantages and disadvantages of offensive biological warfare research. As I described in Chapter 5, Crawford, in turn, consulted BRAB in April 1950 and asked them to justify biological warfare against the likely use of atomic bombs as the major strategic weapons of the future.[4] Since the two weapons were now regarded as weapons of mass destruction, the need for a comparison was unsurprising. Although the first Soviet atomic bomb explosion in August 1949 was never mentioned explicitly in any of the debates on biological warfare at this time, it is no great conjecture to suggest that this event affected the status accorded by the Chiefs of Staff to the other weapons of mass destruction. In addition, the DRPC who had originally been excluded from decision-making over atomic warfare had started to be given some influence in that domain.[5] After the end of 1949 the DRPC were given authority to formulate policy on atomic matters as they related to non-atomic R&D projects.[6] This new and promising responsibility may further explain the turn from their initial championing of chemical and biological warfare.

The BRAB advisors responded to Crawford's request in positive but not wholly supportive terms. They argued that biological weapons could be regarded as cheaper than and complementary to atomic bombs. On the matter of whether a biological weapon was feasible, however, they had been unable to offer unequivocal assurances yet had, at the same time, called for more research. Crawford, reporting back to the BW Subcommittee, added his own gloss to BRAB's flourish of ambivalence. In the first instance, he drew attention to how the 1946 estimate (that a 1000 lb cluster bomb would cause 50 per cent chance of death to unprotected personnel over $\frac{1}{4}$ square mile in a built-up area) had been revised to cause an equivalent risk over a square mile. And, added tantalizingly, that there were 'reasons to believe that this latter estimate may be conservative'.[7] He concluded that while there was no guarantee, there was every reason to suggest that a biological bomb equivalent to the atomic bomb could be constructed.

On finance, Crawford noted that the DRPC were reluctant to spend money on germ warfare research because there were shortages for the defence research programme as a whole. Any additional expenditure would now be at the expense of other projects. Brushing this matter to one side, he added: 'I do not consider that the problem of how to find the money should be allowed to obscure the main point of consideration, which is, whether or not our future defence may be jeopardised if we do not pursue the full BW research project wholeheartedly.'[8] Crawford finished by providing the Chiefs of Staff with a stark choice, inviting them to decide in principle between two options. Either the existing policy for offensive and defensive R&D should be endorsed, or offensive research should be postponed 'and the risks involved accepted'.[9]

Throughout all of these discussions held by BRAB, the BW Subcommittee, the DRPC and the Chiefs of Staff there was remarkably little input by way of intelligence information. The JIC had admitted to 'extremely scanty' knowledge of Russian activity in biological warfare. The only information that they were prepared to endorse was that a small group of scientists and technicians appeared to be carrying out research on biological warfare problems under the control of the Russian army.[10]

In June 1950, the Chiefs of Staff met to consider Crawford's two options. They affirmed the existing retaliatory policy, at the same time agreeing in principle to the construction of the new fermenter, Experimental Plant No. 2.[11] Nonetheless, this decision was not quite a straightforward continuation of 'business as usual'. At this meeting, the Chiefs of Staff discussed the developments and recommendations that had arisen since the 1949 Report on Biological Warfare was issued, specifically in the context of the division of labour with the UK's tripartite allies. A research policy dealing with this matter had already been settled between the countries during the previous year such that:

> The United Kingdom for the next few years should devote its main effort to fundamental research on the development of agents. The United States would press on with field trials of interim weapons, and at the same time would continue with fundamental research and investigations in the explosion chamber with simulants and chargings. Canada would

endeavour to assist by the provision of facilities for the testing and development of weapons. These three programmes were complementary to one another, and formed the basis for a fully integrated and economic research policy, having regard to the individual resources of each country.[12]

In their June 1950 meeting, the Chiefs of Staff, at the same time as sanctioning existing national policy on biological warfare research, simultaneously endorsed a separate policy for the UK to concentrate on fundamental research.[13] The British share of investigations had 'been interpreted as laboratory work up to and including work on the experimental production of small quantities of pathogens'.[14] Tizard, the chair of the DRPC, also pointed out to the Chiefs of Staff that the magnitude and potential of biological warfare could not be ascertained without the construction of Experimental Plant No. 2. The plant would demonstrate whether the agents could be produced safely, readily handled and still remain viable. All of which fell within this definition of fundamental investigation.

Although, as we have seen in Chapter 5, much of this discussion about the second experimental plant revolved around the proposed cost and the desirable degree of independence from the US, straightforward military matters were not absent from consideration. As the debate of the Chiefs of Staff ranged over the matters which had already been raised by their subordinate committees, Lieutenant-General Brownjohn contributed by saying 'that it would be unwise, particularly as we had so few weapons with which to strike at our potential enemy, and were in this particular field ahead of the United States, not to press on with research into offensive possibilities'.[15] Admiral of the Fleet, Lord Fraser, summed up by echoing this opinion and 'said that it seemed wrong either to ignore the threat or to avoid the conclusion that we could not assess the defences we required without investigating the offensive potentialities of BW. The Chiefs of Staff therefore should endorse the policy outlined in the 1949 Report.'[16] For the time being the 'offence for defence' policy had won out, while at the same time subsuming a commitment to one particular version of fundamental research.

These decisions were soon conveyed directly and personally to the Americans. The BW Subcommittee were informed that 'when the Chiefs of Staff considered Biological Warfare Policy they had, *inter alia*, instructed the VCAS (Vice-Chief of the Air Staff) to acquaint the US Chiefs of Staff of the importance which they attached to BW and in particular to the offensive as well as the defensive aspect of research'.[17] At their meeting, the US Chiefs of Staff hinted to the VCAS that they were experiencing the same uncertainties that had occupied the British. The Americans had 'intimated that they found it impossible as yet to assess the operational value of BW or state with certainty whether it was a practical and worthwhile weapon'. The US Chiefs of Staff were uncomfortable with this situation and remained keen to have their judgement on the potential of biological warfare clarified. Crawford, at least, did not regard this development as a worry. He pointed out to his subcommittee that they could not assume the US were sceptical about biological warfare and associated research, otherwise why would they have recommended further expenditure on the area?

Further information on US attitudes towards biological warfare was gleaned from Major-General A.C. McAuliffe, Chief of the US Chemical Corps, at an informal meeting with members of the BW Subcommittee in July 1950. McAuliffe pointed out that the US had reaffirmed its policy of remaining 'purely retaliatory' despite objection from the ad hoc Stevenson Committee which had reported recently to the Secretary of Defence.[18] As a result, both biological and chemical warfare had received a low priority for funds. Additionally, the visitor reported that the US military and scientists now regarded nerve gas as a more promising weapon than germ warfare and this was receiving the greater share of funding as a consequence. All of this news pointed to a negative conclusion. McAuliffe summarized his own position, saying that 'he wanted to see weapons in being, but development in weapons had been disappointing, time and funds having been expended with little result to show'.[19] Later in the meeting, he added to this pessimism when he informed his audience that

> much concern was felt in the United States at the sabotage threat inherent in BW. This was being explored actively and was considered to be a very real danger. The potentialities of BW agents in a strategic role, disseminated from aircraft, remained however still to be demonstrated. Until this could be done he saw little hope of the low priority enjoyed by BW in the US being raised.[20]

By way of reply, Crawford and his compatriots eagerly tried to convince McAuliffe of the potential of biological warfare. Crawford reassured the Major-General that, despite the uncertainties surrounding biological weapons, that the subject still held a 'fairly high priority' in Britain. Then, blurring the boundaries between offensive and defensive research, he added 'that it was most dangerous to ignore the defensive aspect of BW and that for this reason alone it was essential to go a fairly long way into a study of offensive possibilities'.[21] The chairman reiterated several times that a high status had been accorded to biological warfare policy in the UK, with top priority awarded to a means of defence against a biological attack and a lower priority assigned to purely defensive measures. His case was bolstered with what could only be described as 'conversion' testimonies. Crawford

> assured Major-General McAuliffe that he had shared his scepticism of the value of BW when he had first come into contact with it, but he was now convinced that it was so potentially a powerful weapon that it could not

be neglected. A similar change of opinion had occurred to many eminent scientists after a brief contact with BW research.

This confession elicited similar testimonies from around the table. Wansbrough-Jones, now the Scientific Advisor to the Army Council, added

> that it was found that new bacteriologists who were brought into BW research from time to time, became converted to its very great potential importance as they gained knowledge of what had been done, and to the fact that it might prove practicable. This experience, of the unanimity of all scientists who came into contact with BW, was one of the factors which had influenced British judgement of its potentialities.

Henderson also contributed by remarking how

> a group of bacteriologists assembled under the auspices of the Medical Research Council, and none of them with any previous experience of BW, had been asked one by one whether they thought that BW was likely, or whether there was nothing in it. They had all replied that they thought that BW might well justify itself.

This evangelistic barrage did not appear to have had any immediate effect on McAuliffe, who continued to make sceptical remarks throughout the rest of the meeting. Henderson, for instance, reported that although there had been no great improvement in an actual weapon since the war, their research had produced substantial gains in the potency of the available biological agents. McAuliffe merely noted that 'though this might be so he had not himself witnessed convincing field trials to substantiate it. Considerable sums had been spent on BW in the United States and as yet no weapon had been produced other than the 4 lb bomb which was not thought very effective.'

Crawford also mentioned the assessment of biological against atomic weapons. The original calculations had indicated that biological weapons would be considerably less effective than the atomic bomb. Air Commodore Heard, the Director of Weapons for the Air Ministry, then repeated figures from a more recent assessment which gave an encouraging fourfold increase in its estimate of the lethality of biological agents. Additionally, an aircraft carrying just a single atom bomb could carry ten 1000 lb biological bombs, although he soberly reminded his audience that no such weapon as yet existed. Nevertheless, he continued, the latest theoretical calculations indicated that a germ weapon distributed across a single square mile would be four times as effective as one atomic bomb. Theory, Heard confessed, rested on 'a great many imponderables'. Particle size and degree of protection in particular needed to be taken into account but the calculations still, he believed, provided some indication of the potential of this inexpensive weapon.

Moving on, Crawford raised the possibility of a tactical use for biological weapons, possibly with rapidly acting botulinum toxin in mind.[22] McAuliffe replied dismissively that: 'the United States had not considered this aspect of BW since they were preoccupied with the question of whether it was possible to make BW into a worthwhile weapon at all. When they solved this problem they would turn their thoughts to its other possible uses.'

The chairman summed up this meeting by stating that 'it was clear that no final answer could be given on the potentiality of BW until more research had been carried out'. What is evident is that, in the face of McAuliffe's doubts about biological weapons, the members of the BW Subcommittee did not surrender their enthusiasm. At this point, biological warfare was still sufficiently important for this committee to mount a fairly strong defence of its potential. This positive view was not confined to the BW Subcommittee. Within a few months of the meeting with McAuliffe, Brigadier H.T. Findlay, the Director of Pathology at the War Office and a member of the BW Subcommittee, visited the Suffield Experimental Station in Canada and reported his 'opinion that the present grading of BW in the USA was temporary and that undue attention should not be paid to it as it may be changed at any time to a higher one'.[23] The priority was based on its status as a retaliatory measure 'and had little to do with its potentialities as a weapon'. This assessment of the situation may have had some foundation; within two years biological warfare had shuttled up the priorities of the US military but in a manner which was equally unpalatable to the British advisors.

Divergence and change

In March 1952 a Chiefs of Staff appraisal of biological warfare was issued. It noted that British research had primarily attempted to gauge the danger of biological warfare. The report drew attention to alarming changes taking place in the United States that appeared to be moving their collaborators in a completely different direction. Information exchange remained 'nearly perfect' but changes in management combined with financial pressures meant that research establishments had now to provide 'concrete evidence of their value'.[24] As a consequence, the push to concentrate on offensive aspects of biological warfare, and weapons development in particular, had become 'intense'. The prognosis was equally gloomy:

> Military management has largely superseded scientific control. . . . BW is in danger of becoming a prize for which all three Services now compete, and from now on any appreciation of its value made by the Services received from the USA must be suspect. There is a real danger of the basic scientific aspects of BW receiving scant attention.[25]

On the more practical side, the report predicted that a strategic germ weapon with 'uncertain capabilities' would be available to the US Air Force within a year. In addition, the technical barriers to mounting an attack against the Soviet Union with anti-crop agents, particularly wheat rust, were being rapidly overcome. The report added portentously, 'this country might indeed prove to be more vulnerable than the USSR if, of which there is no important evidence, Soviet interest had been directed towards crop destruction'.[26]

As any attempt to influence US policy in this area would be improper, 'dangerous and probably futile', the report's author recommended that Britain look towards modifying its own policies on biological warfare. A number of suggestions were made which would reappear in various guises over the coming months. Firstly, resources should be devoted to the 'immediate defensive problems' facing civil defence and the Services in the UK. Next, some appreciation should be made of the 'military and strategic consequences of the probable United States weapons'. An important third proposition was to 'diminish our effort on short term offensive problems but we should strengthen them on research aimed at very long range offensive possibilities'. Finally, research should be directed at 'learning all we can of the ultimate dangers of BW, and dealing with short and long term defensive measures'.[27]

Within a month the Chiefs of Staff were suggesting that with the recent change to a new Conservative Government, a 'reaffirmation' of biological and chemical warfare policy would be timely.[28] In the same context, the United States plans for a biological weapon were discussed and Sir Kenneth Crawford informed the Chiefs of Staff that 'expert opinion in this country was that such precipitate practical action was akin to running before one was able to walk'. He also added that the plans had come about, in part, so that the Chemical Corps could 'justify their existence'. Crawford felt that there was still plenty of work to be done on more fundamental aspects of biological warfare and put before the Chiefs of Staff a set of recommendations not dissimilar to those from the March appraisal.[29] These recommendations, Crawford suggested, should be considered in the upcoming review of global strategy.

This review was issued in June 1952 and placed a strong emphasis on Britain being prepared to use atomic weapons should war occur. War would most likely be a short and intense affair and all preparations outlined in the document were geared towards this possibility.[30] In this context, a strong line was also taken by the Chiefs of Staff over biological and chemical warfare: 'The Allies should not take up a position which would deprive them of the ability to use Bacteriological Warfare or Chemical Warfare in retaliation, if such were to their advantage.'[31] In the wake of the Global Strategy paper, the Chiefs of Staff drafted a more detailed report for the Cabinet Defence Committee on 'Biological and Chemical Warfare Research and Development Policy'. Although the final version is not in the public domain, a top secret draft provides some insight into the stance adopted by the Chiefs of Staff in the Global Strategy paper. In particular, the authors recognized the need for continued research effort on both defensive and offensive features of both biological and chemical warfare.[32] After suggesting that there was no reason why the Soviet Union would honour its pledges under the Geneva Protocol, the report also pointed out that it was believed the Soviet Union had 'devoted considerable effort to furthering her knowledge of these forms of warfare'.[33] The report admitted that biological weapons were untried but asserted that research to date clearly pointed to the dangerous nature and efficacy of germ warfare.

Whereas appraisals from the end of the 1940s had downplayed bacteriological sabotage, this report dubbed it 'already a menacing weapon' to be used against targets such as headquarters or livestock. The potential power of a biological bomb was also flagged. Unlike the previous ambivalent attitudes towards germ weapons as 'weapons of mass destruction', this report placed a biological bomb clearly within such an ambit:

> At present, no weapon which could be relied on in war has been developed but we are advised that it is not beyond the bounds of possibility that weapons can be produced which would place BW as a casualty producing weapon against an unprotected population in the same class as the Atomic Bomb.[34]

The report continued by describing the unrestricted tripartite exchange of information on the topic, the considerable sums spent by the United States in the field, and the fact that the UK remained 'superior' on certain aspects of fundamental research. In conclusion, the Defence Committee was asked to agree on the threefold biological warfare policy which was, by now, thoroughly discussed: 'Research and trials to determine the true risk of biological warfare should be continued; Research to establish the best defensive measures should be continued; offensive research should be concentrated mainly on the study of long range possibilities.'[35]

Yet this recommendation appeared to place far greater emphasis on defensive biological warfare, a position which did not immediately mesh with the more offensive stance outlined in the Global Strategy paper. Difficulties over the interpretation of British policy had already emerged after Henderson visited the US and, on his return, expressed concern to BRAB in March 1952 that 'American colleagues of long standing had become offensively minded', wishing to end the Korean War as soon as possible.[36] Similarly, Henderson felt that the US Services had developed a 'most aggressive outlook' with the consequence that their focus had shifted to short-term projects on anti-personnel and anti-crop weapons. BRAB members regarded the divergence in the two countries' attitudes as problematic and expressed concern at the May meeting of the board that the US might use biological weapons in Korea. UK policy, it was stated, was not to initiate biological warfare and this might leave the country in an awkward situation vis-à-vis the Americans. Not to concur with the US might entail scientific ostracism, whereas concurrence would signal both a change in UK policy and would raise moral dilemmas for the staff at Porton. The board concluded this discussion by requesting an assurance on British Government policy 'that BW would in no circumstances be used except in retaliation'.[37]

The Minister of Supply, Duncan Sandys, requested the authority to provide this reassurance directly from the Cabinet. However, concern was expressed at this level that the request could turn out to be 'somewhat embarrassing'.[38] It was noted that the recent report by the Chiefs of Staff on Global Strategy had recommended that the Allies should be prepared to use bacteriological and chemical warfare in war when it was deemed 'advantageous'. Moreover, this was to be reflected in the Government's public attitude to the employment of these forms of warfare. The problem arose because it was

> not clear what the last part of this recommendation implies. Any sudden announcement of a modification of our previous policy of adherence to the Geneva Protocol would, of course, be a very severe shock to public opinion and would raise political storms domestically and internationally. No doubt, therefore, it was intended that any change in our *public* attitude should be made only gradually and should be related to what could be discovered of the activities or intentions of the Russians. Even so, if that is to be Government policy, it seems out of the question to give a responsible and eminent body of scientists and others a private assurance in a contrary sense.[39]

BRAB was considered to be free from 'well-known communists or fellow travellers' but this was insufficient to justify additional reassurances. The Prime Minister and the Foreign Secretary had

> thought it important to maintain our freedom to use weapons of biological warfare in *retaliation* if they were used against us. This does not go nearly so far as the recommendation by the Chiefs of Staff and would not appear to be contrary to our existing obligations under the Geneva Protocol.[40]

The issue was clearly one of the mismatch between the sought assurance of one policy, use only in retaliation, and the more general endorsement by Ministers of the Chiefs of Staff Global Strategy which apparently pushed biological warfare policy in a more offensive direction. It may well be that this was a misunderstanding, as the final version of the Global Strategy paper explicitly mentioned retaliation. Certainly, the matter was eventually resolved in favour of the Minister of Supply who provided assurance of the no first use policy to BRAB in a letter which was read out at the board's following meeting.[41]

The move away from an offensive biological warfare policy was therefore apparent but still in its early stages at this time. On balance, the Government still maintained the need for an offensive retaliatory capability. Nonetheless, in the course of BRAB's discussion of the worrying American situation, a change in direction for the British research programme was proposed by Wansbrough-Jones, now the Ministry of Supply's Principal Director of Scientific Research.[42] He announced that building work on Experimental Plant No. 2 would not commence that year and future research should concentrate on the general rather than the particular. For example, 'work should be directed, not to manufacture any particular size of bomb but rather to discover whether any bomb was of value'.[43] Although this statement suggests a move away from a programme broadly applied to and guided by Service needs, Experimental Plant No. 2 was still linked by BRAB with an offensive capability. The Air Staff still had a requirement for a complete biological bomb and the target date had apparently moved from 1957 to 1955.[44] While BRAB argued that the postponement of Experimental Plant No. 2 entailed postponement of this Air Staff requirement, the Ministry of Supply were negotiating instead with the Air Ministry for an alternative interim weapon.[45]

Carter and Pearson provide further evidence of a drift towards a more defensive outlook over biological warfare. They mention that, at the 1952 tripartite meeting, the general research policy of Britain on chemical and biological weapons was said to stem 'from the military thesis that the employment of toxicological weapons would be justified only if they showed marked advantages over conventional weapons'.[46] The report of the following year's conference also mentioned that lack of funds for chemical and biological weapons research hampered the more general policy of building a retaliatory capability.

Yet momentum for some offensively oriented research was maintained at this time by a DRPC working party on biological warfare led by Sir John Cockcroft, Scientific Advisor to the Ministry of Defence.[47] This small group contained a number of supporters of biological warfare research, including Henderson, and was established because Sir Henry Tizard, the DRPC chairman, had expressed doubts over the value of germ warfare research in Britain.[48] Their investigation ran independently and in parallel with the Chiefs of Staff review of biological warfare. One member of the party, Robert Cockburn, Scientific Advisor to the Air Ministry, had already expressed Tizard's doubts about the value of biological weaponry, arguing to the DRPC that 'there were no grounds for making a comparison between biological and atomic weapons and...the most that could be said was that biological weapons might have a useful strategic application'.[49] The investigation thus appears to have reflected a degree of impatience from the, previously supportive, DRPC over the progress of the research programme at Porton. The working party concluded that biological warfare research was justified, recommended that the research required by the Chiefs of Staff 'should continue along the lines originally indicated' and were 'convinced on the facts presented to them that a potential danger existed'.[50] Possibly reflecting Henderson's disdain for being pushed into applied work, the group recommended against mounting operational biological weapon production in the UK as there were still 'far too many unknowns'.[51] Although the working party had met to investigate whether or not biological warfare research was a 'waste of money', this remit was not regarded by all advisors as a great threat.[52] In Hankey's opinion, the working party had performed a useful public relations function as a wide range of authorities had been made aware of the dangers of biological warfare, a fact he thought likely to protect research status and funding in the area.[53]

Directives

Despite, or possibly because of, these developments during 1952, the details of policy remained far from clear at all levels of discussion. The scientific advisors, in particular, felt ostracized by secrecy as ambiguity over policy emerged once again, this time during a BRAB debate at their December meeting.[54] Discussion at the meeting soon strayed from the supposed topic of field trials into more general issues.[55] Fildes reported that he had been involved in disagreements with Ministry of Supply officials which he attributed to his 'lack of knowledge of changing policies'. He expressed his dissatisfaction with a 'rather nebulous directive of the Chiefs of Staff' and called upon Wansbrough-Jones to make matters clear.[56] Wansbrough-Jones pointed out by way of reply that the Chiefs of Staff, who were not scientists, 'could give broad direction only and had agreed on a policy that research and trials to determine the true risk of BW should be continued, the best defensive measures should be established, and that we should concentrate mainly on the study of long range offensive possibilities'.[57] He added that because there had been a change of Government, the Chiefs of Staff and the Ministry of Supply were currently seeking clarification on their biological warfare policy.

The clarification demanded by Fildes finally arrived for BRAB early in 1953 in the form of a Chiefs of Staff directive.[58] It stated that Experimental Plant No. 2 should be postponed for a year and that close collaboration should continue with the USA. A threefold UK policy, concentrating on defensive aspects of biological warfare, was specified in almost the same terms as Wansbrough-Jones had put to the board the previous December.

A second, more detailed, section of the directive had been drawn up by a working party chaired by Wansbrough-Jones.[59] This was done in response to the earlier requests by BRAB – Fildes in particular – for greater clarification of policy. The directive stated that 'so far as the true risk of a lethal agent can be determined experimentally', research should aim to investigate three features. First, bulk production of stable agents for Service purposes. Experimental Plant No. 2 was deemed to be necessary for this aim, although its postponement was acknowledged. The second research question was 'whether agents can be distributed and reach the target in an effective form'. The importance of improving weapon performance was flagged as a key part of this objective. The final area of research would be 'whether the results on the target are likely to warrant the effort'.

Defensive measures were also mentioned. In this respect immunization, physical protection, decontamination, early detection, rapid identification and secondary infection were all regarded as important research topics. It is notable, however, that although a proportion of the work at MRD was to be channelled in a defensive direction, Wansbrough-Jones pointed out that the Chief Superintendent 'must have discretion according to the availability of staff'.[60] Besides this mention of discretion, an even broader plea for research autonomy was made in the directive. The difficulty in distinguishing biological warfare from other research was taken as grounds for including work with no immediate biowarfare application in the MRD programme. Moreover, in direct connection with this statement, 'purely ad hoc work' was mentioned in the directive as a disincentive to recruitment of scientific staff.

The directive concluded with a paragraph dealing with risk assessment. While it was acknowledged that 'wide assumptions which cannot be scientifically established must be made to present a reasonable picture of probabilities', it was proposed nevertheless that a summary of the risk from biological warfare should be included by the Chief Superintendent in each MRD annual report. The data would be available to the Services but without the Chief Superintendent incurring responsibility. Henderson was not entirely satisfied with this proposal and at the 28th meeting of BRAB voiced this opinion. The only reason recorded for Henderson's objection was that it would not be wise to supply an estimate of risk 'in the light of recent research'. This objection was not accepted by BRAB on the grounds that no other authority could make the assessment, a view which was most certainly in line with the members' opinion of themselves as an extremely specialist unit consisting of 'eminent members in a circumscribed field'.[61]

The Board approved of the Chiefs of Staff directive at its 28th meeting when it was still to be commented on by the Minister of Supply. Matters were complicated because the Minister was also preparing his own general directive on biological warfare policy.[62] By June, however, the Chiefs of Staff directive, which had not been altered further, reached a stage where no major modification by any of the advisory committees was expected before it was approved at Ministerial level.

The Minister of Supply issued his separate directive on biological warfare research in November 1953 and although much of its content appeared to consolidate the various deliberations from the previous year, there were some significant changes of emphasis.[63] Certainly, the directive had not gained a particularly easy passage past the Chiefs of Staff. In July, a draft version suffered delays as doubts were expressed in various departments about its 'timing and suitability'.[64] A further draft was issued in August and a few months later was submitted to the Cabinet Defence Committee for approval. From the Admiralty perspective, the new draft had successfully shifted emphasis towards a defensive policy. Moreover, because the Navy was the Service 'least concerned with the offensive and defensive aspects of this form of warfare', the new draft had advantageously reigned in the scope and economic scale of activities about which it had only marginal concern:[65]

> A change of wording...and a rearrangement of the order in which the objects of research are set out...both combine to put the emphasis on the defensive aspects of this work rather than on offense and retaliation. Further a paragraph in the earlier directive which might have been taken as authority for scientists engaged in biological warfare research to range rather widely over their subject, has disappeared entirely. As the draft now stands, it does not appear to be much more than an orderly statement of what is in fact going on, and it does not contain instructions which could be held to cover the Minister of Supply in demanding an unreasonable share of resources for this purpose.[66]

The same alterations were duly noted by BRAB members. They were keen to point out that the order of tasks had changed from the original draft and 'priority appeared to be given to the defensive and research aspects rather than to the building up of BW offensive potential by weapon development and production investigations'.[67] The revised version of the directive nonetheless echoed the Global Strategy paper by announcing that, in the event of war, Britain should be able 'to protect her civil population and Service personnel, as well as crops and livestock, against attack by biological methods, and to retaliate by those methods against the enemy should the Government of the day decide to adopt this course'.[68]

Research was to concentrate on six areas. Protection and treatment were the first two items on the list followed by: 'practical potentialities of biological methods of warfare' relative to the cost and effectiveness of other means of warfare, obtaining suitable agents, bulk production techniques and the determination of appropriate weapons. Close collaboration with the US was encouraged for the purposes of 'economy and efficiency'. Complementarity was also mentioned at this point, specifically with respect to weapon R&D: 'since the Americans are concentrating mainly on the development of weapons capable of early introduction into the service, our programme of weapon development should put somewhat greater emphasis on the study of long term projects'.[69]

Further divergence from the United States

While the directives allowed a number of strands of thinking from the DRPC, Chiefs of Staff and BRAB to coalesce and provide a very brief period of stability, the situation across the Atlantic appeared worse. By February 1954 the situation in the US was described at a BRAB meeting as 'chaotic' and Henderson was shortly due to visit and seek clarification on the state of affairs.[70] Plans had been laid to transfer the American biological warfare research effort to industry but had failed. As a result, Camp Detrick was still 'nominally' in the control of the Chemical Corps although staff had resigned in large numbers. Service requirements had also altered and production of incapacitating *Brucella suis* at Pine Bluff was once again favoured after the possibility of superseding it with anthrax had receded. According to Henderson this situation was the result of disagreements between the Air Force, who favoured anthrax, and the army who wanted *B. suis*. He believed that the final decision would depend on the strength of influence of the respective Services.

In the light of all this confusion, BRAB discussed whether or not the US situation would have repercussions for the UK research programme. Henderson had already informed the American Assistant Secretary for Defence, Dr Quarles, that the UK were not relying on the US for biological weapons, which Henderson considered to be 'not yet perfected'. Wansbrough-Jones argued that the UK Chiefs of Staff should be advised that as a result of the US confusion 'there was progressively less probability that a weapon capable of early introduction would be produced in the USA'.[71] In addition, Fildes, presumably pitching for Experimental Plant No. 2, voiced the opinion that the UK should not rely on American pathogen production.

The situation became so troubling that Fildes requested an ad hoc gathering of the BW Subcommittee soon afterwards. The chaos in the US was likely to have repercussions for British policy, in particular the division of labour that had been agreed four years earlier. Both Fildes and Henderson were concerned especially about the 'serious confusion' in US thinking and the loss of autonomy that might result if the military adopted responsibility for scientific research.[72] It looked as if this was to occur through a transfer of accountability from Edgewood Arsenal to Camp Detrick with a colonel as director of the programme. Wansbrough-Jones observed that if present policy was to change, some consideration would have to be given to the consequences if the UK no longer relied on the US for operational research. In reply, Fildes added that a reappraisal would entail revisiting the desirability or otherwise of Experimental Plant No. 2. It was agreed that Dr Walter Cawood and Henderson should appraise the situation, since they were due to visit the US, and other members of BRAB should visit the US in October or November. The subcommittee also pointed out that UK policy on biological warfare would need to be reconsidered later in the year and that the

Ministry of Supply should formulate the problems that would arise if a break from the US took place.

In June 1954, Henderson reported back on his trip to the States where the situation at Detrick 'had never been worse'.[73] Staff were continuing to leave at a disturbing rate. Fortunately, he thought that there was a greater degree of stability in Washington where the Defence Department had revised their policy. This would cease to emphasize weapon development and take the form of a broader assessment of biological warfare. Cawood added that the assessment exercise, code-named 'Exercise St Joe', was due to report in mid-1955 and was being treated seriously by the group undertaking the work.[74]

More atomic weapons

As offensive biological warfare research moved down the ranking of research priorities, the degree to which atomic weapons were now overshadowing other weapons of mass destruction came to the fore. In 1952, the Chiefs of Staff Global Strategy paper had marked a shift in defence policy towards reliance on a nuclear deterrent. Echoes of this change appeared in a DRPC review of defence R&D in March 1954. Developments in weapons of mass destruction were reported only to have had fundamental effects on the defence programme with regard to atomic weapons.[75] The review continued:

> It is still too soon in so new a field as biological warfare to forecast with any certainty what developments may yet arise....Development of offensive biological weapons has been largely disappointing. We still know too little of the behaviour of agents under operational conditions to make the detailed quantitative assessments which could allow a strategic offensive based on biological techniques to be developed. Apart altogether from the political issues which must be faced before biological warfare could be initiated, the use of such weapons must be limited even in the strategic role to attritional forms of warfare.[76]

Although this was a negative statement about the achievements of the biological weapons research programme, the report went on to maintain that the UK could still be subject to a biological weapon attack. It would be essential therefore to keep up to date with developments in the field in order to make countermeasures available.[77]

So, suggested policy for R&D, while not abandoning offensive research altogether, called on various uncertainties to recommend assigning it an unequivocally low priority. The defence review concluded that biological warfare research should concentrate on: methods of protection against contamination or infection; methods for the treatment of human or animal casualties and for decontamination; 'the practical potentialities of biological methods of warfare and, in particular, their relative effectiveness and cost as compared with other methods of attack'; determination of suitable biological agents for use in different roles; research on processes and techniques for the bulk production and storage of agents and for the filling of weapons; and finally investigation of suitable forms of weapons for the delivery and distribution of agents upon various kinds of targets.[78] In short, a primarily, though not exclusively, defensive agenda.

Although the Air Staff requirement for a biological bomb was not effectively abandoned until July 1954, the review judged the situation with a degree of prescience. With regard to the future, the prediction for the state of development by 1957 pointed out that

> sufficient knowledge of the behaviour of organisms may have been acquired for the potentialities of biological warfare to be assessed but this is by no means certain. No attempt will have been made to develop offensive weapons in the UK but the research will have continued to find suitable agents for different roles and suitable forms of weapons for their delivery and distribution.[79]

Yet several extant versions of a further DRPC 'Review of Defence R&D' by its programmes subcommittee reveal that the position of biological warfare in defence policy had still not been entirely resolved. The draft report states that although the Chiefs of Staff had asked the subcommittee to pay particular attention to chemical and biological warfare, 'only a small part of this problem is a scientific matter but, in the hope that we can help the Chiefs of Staff reach a decision, we have reviewed the problem in rather wider terms than those that are strictly our business'.[80] Government policy, in this draft version, was that:

> we must be ready to defend ourselves against chemical and biological attack and that we must be prepared to retaliate with *chemical* weapons if they are used against us; with regard to biological warfare, basic research is to be carried out primarily to identify and estimate the threat against us and only secondarily and then in the long term with a view to offensive use of biological agents.[81]

The Ministry of Supply pushed for a more general offensive interpretation of policy, suggesting that retaliation should be with 'similar', rather than just chemical weapons.[82] They also added that 'at present we are relying on the United States for the short term development of biological weapons'.[83] Only the latter amendment survived to the final version of the review.

The statement of Government policy, which survived alteration by the Ministry of Supply, implied that no retaliatory capability was required for biological warfare. The argument for this position was made by drawing a rhetorical and conceptual separation between offensive and defensive research, albeit underpinned by the same fundamental studies:

> with regard to biological warfare, we believe that for some time the same basic research is essential for a proper assessment of the problem of defence as for offence, except perhaps in a limited field of development of actual weapons to distribute biological agents. We believe however that against this background of the legal, moral and political factors involved and taking into account our financial situation it is unlikely to be decided that any activity in this field is justifiable in this country which is not directed primarily to the solution of the fundamental problems of defence against biological attack.[84]

This line of argument developed into a damning recommendation for both the chemical and biological weapons research programmes. Once the further possibility was taken into account that, in the nuclear age, retaliation in kind might be an inadequate response to chemical and biological warfare, 'it might be held that no work whatever in the field of biological warfare whether offensive or defensive could be justified' and that little more than a 'watching brief' could be devoted to chemical warfare.[85] Chemical and biological warfare were then left off a list of ten fields and techniques where basic research effort was deemed to be 'vital'.[86]

By October, the Ministry of Supply had submitted its proposed substitute version of this report to the DRPC.[87] As already mentioned, this advocated a more offensive stance in biological weapons policy. In contrast to the DRPC version, the Ministry of Supply conflated offensive and defensive research in order to ground the justification of continued biological warfare research in scientific authority:[88]

> Research on both offensive and defensive aspects of chemical and biological warfare must continue if we are to be able to protect ourselves against methods of attack which may be used against us and further to deter an enemy from launching such attacks because of the knowledge that we would be able to retaliate. In any event, no rational division can be made between that part of the research and development which is directed towards offensive ends and that part which is required for defensive purposes.[89]

In the Ministry of Supply redraft, an ensuing list of various areas of defence research meriting priority was extended to include chemical and biological warfare, 'dependent on policy to be stated by higher authority'. The implication of this qualification was only partially clarified. A paragraph following the list stated that all of the fields deserved 'very high priority', but due to selectivity pressures, 'we have indicated some directions in which we think further research is not required'. These changes survived to the final version submitted to the Chiefs of Staff.[90]

The Ministry of Supply redraft was discussed by the DRPC shortly afterwards.[91] Air Marshal Thomas Pike the Deputy Chief of Air Staff, who had recently taken over the chair of the BW Subcommittee, voiced his preference of the Ministry of Supply redraft. He also wanted the concluding paragraph, which the Controller of Munitions at the Ministry later wanted to drop, included.[92] This conclusion had pointed out the shift in outlook needed before abandoning offensive research. It also questioned the assumption that had held since the beginning of the Second World War that retaliatory measures would entail retaliation in kind:

> any change in the present research and development programmes in chemical and biological warfare must be dependent on fundamental changes in Government policy, on the possibility of the use of these forms of warfare and the necessity or otherwise in a nuclear age of preparing retaliatory and defensive measures against them.[93]

The Controller felt that the statement added nothing to the report. Pike, on the other hand, doubted whether the DRPC 'was in a position to state whether BW and CW should be considered as major weapons or whether they should or should not be developed as an insurance'.[94] Nonetheless, the chairman pointed out, the committee had been asked specifically by the Chiefs of Staff to cover this subject in the report. It was agreed that biological and chemical warfare would be dealt with as separate issues and that both would remain as priority areas of basic research, with the continuing proviso that 'this was dependent on a ruling from higher authority'.[95]

The final version of the research review was submitted to the Chiefs of Staff in November 1954. It opened with a statement of 'new' defence policy which was 'interpreted' as meaning that: 'to prevent global war we need a deterrent that includes nuclear weapons and their means of delivery; we must be prepared for warm wars, which we define as peripheral wars of the Korean or Indo-China type'.[96] The report dealt mainly with chemical warfare – apart from a statement highlighting the overlap between defensive and offensive research, and a conclusion that

> in present circumstances we would be justified in limiting our activities in this field to the solution of problems of defence against biological attack. In doing so we accept the position that on the outbreak of a future war it would be unlikely that we would be able to develop any offensive BW in time for it to be of any use.[97]

By June 1955 a directive from the Minister of Defence was discussed by the BRAB. During this meeting, the Ministry of Supply's Principal Director of

Scientific Research, Cawood, pointed out that strategic nuclear weapons were now 'the only items in the first level of importance'.[98] He added that 'the general position of biological warfare was now considered to be fairly low in the list of potential weapons'. This demotion had been foreshadowed on 14 October 1954 when the Cabinet Defence Committee endorsed the annex to a paper on biological warfare research and development policy which 'put defensive preparations first but also included a retaliatory capability'.[99] It encouraged collaboration with the US and 'directed British attention to long-term projects'.[100] With the Air Staff requirement for a bomb completely revised the previous July, any mention of retaliatory capability was bound to be a mere token.

Defending biological warfare

There had been a major, but by no means direct, transition to a defensively oriented policy regime in the early 1950s. What remained constant was the widespread secrecy surrounding UK biological warfare policy. This deliberate policy of concealment did not go unchallenged, particularly among scientists. Some expert advisors even thought that a foray into the open would be a vital way of promoting and controlling a positive public image of germ warfare.

Early in 1950, the BW Subcommittee undertook a small study of the articles that had been published in the press on biological warfare.[101] They concluded that there had been an increased interest in the subject since 1946, as indicated by both the dailies and the scientific and medical journals, such as the *Lancet*.[102] The interest, however, was not deemed to be particularly healthy and the authors of the study complained:

> These articles make it necessary to keep in mind the need to condition public opinion, for articles especially such as that in the *Lancet* may result in the growth of opinion hostile to Biological Warfare, with a consequent adverse effect on the recruitment of staff and perhaps on the collaboration of the public in defensive measures at a later stage.[103]

In order to counteract this possible threat to the research programme, the report suggested that informal contacts should be utilized to the full in order to give influential scientists the 'true facts'. It recommended that suitable information should be passed on to individuals through the instruction of Civil Defence personnel; also that some public announcement should be made to 'correct misapprehensions and to put the subject in its proper perspective'. Although the authors did not believe that it was timely to issue this public announcement, they did express the need to have a statement ready in reserve.

A draft public announcement designed to allay any anxieties was prepared accordingly for the BW Subcommittee. It defined biological warfare as 'the use of germs to cause sickness or death to human beings and livestock and to destroy food crops' and then provided a compact historical summary, noting that early in the Second World War

> it was learnt that investigations were being carried out in other countries to explore the value of Biological Warfare. After the fall of France it was decided that experiments should be carried out to assess with greater accuracy the possible effects of secret weapons of this nature and to design defences.[104]

Presently, it noted, research was carried out in the UK 'by a team of highly qualified scientists'. Germany, Japan and Italy were named as countries which had been conducting biological warfare research: Japan on a 'considerable scale', Germany had 'very large establishments' engaged in the work but it was 'treated as less important than the development and production of the well known "V" weapons.' Next the draft announcement stated that the public had been furnished with 'an exaggerated impression of the potency and general state of development of Biological Warfare'. It then dismissed an example of claims that a small biological bomb could wipe out an entire city and an ounce would kill 200 million people and added that there were 'no facts to support these grossly exaggerated and misleading claims, though it would be unwise to underestimate the potentialities of this form of warfare'. This disparaging comment set the scene for the main message in the announcement. Because this form of warfare could not be underestimated, 'it has, therefore, been necessary to continue research to explore all aspects of Biological Warfare, and so to develop measures for the protection of the Services, the civil population, and the livestock of the country'. The announcement ended by claiming that the research might not only eliminate biological warfare but also have a 'direct bearing on the prevention of disease'.

Even the modest degree of candour in this draft unsettled the Chiefs of Staff who 'considered that it tended to give an unduly alarmist impression, and that it was too long'.[105] A revised version was soon put together by the secretary of the Chiefs of Staff Committee in consultation with Tizard of the DRPC and the official committee of Civil Defence. This was a far shorter announcement, again to be held in reserve and released if necessary. The definitions remained the same, as did the declaration of the medical benefits that could arise from the research, but all references to the history of biological warfare and activities of other countries had been omitted. Also, the specific examples of exaggeration over biological warfare were deleted and instead the paragraph read:

> It is the view of His Majesty's Government that the aggressive nature of this form of warfare has been exaggerated; nevertheless it is their duty to

do all in their power to safeguard this country against possible attack of this nature. It has therefore been necessary to develop measures for the protection of the Services, the civil population and the livestock of this country.

The announcement went through a further redraft and by November 1950 the specific example of hysterical exaggeration had returned, while research was now promised to 'minimise the significance of BW' rather than eliminate it. The key paragraph dealing with the need to continue research now read:

It is the view of His Majesty's Government that there is no clear evidence that any form of Biological Warfare hitherto suggested would be of major military significance in a country provided with efficient Health Service. However, with the advance of knowledge this may not always be true and it is, therefore, the duty of the Government to do all in their power to safeguard the country against any possible future attack.

Eventually the BW Subcommittee decided that both of these two latest versions should be held in reserve by the Minister of Defence, should their release become necessary 'to correct authoritatively any spate of criticism about BW'.[106]

Less formal attempts by members of the public to glean information about germ warfare activities were met with unqualified rejection. Henderson had been approached for information by the editor of the popular science journal, *Penguin Science News*, and also the Secretary of the Association of Scientific Workers. Kenneth Crawford warned him sharply against risking a security breach. In a letter to the Superintendent, Crawford described the Association of Scientific Workers as 'a highly dangerous organisation'. He also berated the editor of the *Penguin Science News* for wanting to keep his circulation figures high and being 'more concerned with that than with the education of the public'.[107]

Not surprisingly, if information was to be released at all by the Government then it would be done so in a controlled manner. The following year, plans were under way to invite a 100 scientists to inspect the new laboratories at Porton on 14 December 1951. The invited visitors would be free to inspect the whole establishment. There had been a suggestion that the press might also be asked to be present, but the advisory bodies rejected this idea, even though there was nothing, in principle, to prevent the press from covering the event. This novel excursion into the previously hidden world of the MRD, coupled with the imminence of a further open-air trial, Operation Cauldron, meant that it might be necessary for the Government to issue some sort of explanatory press release. Any such release was likely to entail a change of policy on public mention of biological warfare. The JIC, in particular, had been 'disturbed by the difficulty of reconciling the policy of not mentioning BW with the fact that Cauldron in particular could not possibly be kept secret'.[108]

The DRPC considered this debate and concluded that it would be 'most unwise' to invite journalists to Porton or even issue a public announcement on biological warfare.[109] They agreed however that the present policy on publicity about biological warfare ought to be reviewed, particularly in connection with Operation Cauldron. The JIC had commented that 'if journalists were in the privileged position of being invited to visit MRD they could be told *not* to publish anything'.[110] Returning to the theme of 'educating' the public, Wansbrough-Jones commented that this stance 'appeared to ignore the object of the Press statement. It was not, as appeared to be thought, to focus attention on the MRD but to enlist the aid of the Press in educating the public about BW.' Wansbrough-Jones pressed his case further, arguing that

> the moment seemed ripe for being more liberal towards publicity on BW. In the past, information had been withheld because we were not certain what to publish rather than on grounds of security. But we now knew what ought to be taught and the teaching of measures of defence against bacteriological warfare was more likely to allay alarm than to cause it.[111]

He continued, arguing that any press release was to 'guide' the journalists and would not be used verbatim. And in case his previous comments on the purpose of the exercise had been ignored, he repeated that 'neither should the object of the visit of the scientists be confused with that of the press. The purpose of the former was to assist recruiting; the latter was to enlighten the public about BW.'[112] Henderson added that the press statement was sufficiently anodyne and unlikely to provide Russia with any new information.

Members of the Services were less sanguine. Air Commodore Sydney Bufton objected that 'although the Public had been given very little official information on BW they appeared quite content'. While Lieutenant-Colonel Pritchard who was representing the Director of Weapons and Development at the War Office described the draft press release as 'dull and feared that it might, through not giving enough information, leave the imagination to run riot'.[113] Only the Admiralty were in favour of a more liberal policy on release of information about germ warfare, largely because this would be likely to stifle any speculation when Operation Cauldron was carried out at sea the following year.

At the close of this discussion, the subcommittee agreed to put a case to the Chiefs of Staff for relaxing the current policy of not mentioning biological warfare to the public and a report summarizing the need for 'education of the public' was hastily drafted and then redrafted.[114] The final version argued for a reversal of policy on the grounds that the press would be 'easier to control' if information were freely provided rather than leaked.[115] No vital information would be released in any event. The press were also seen as a key means to evangelize the public and so the report recommended 'that the method of indoctrinating the public should be, in the first place, by inviting the Press to Porton'. In the interim, the visit of the scientists to Porton took place and five days afterwards the press had made no mention of the event.[116]

All these moves towards a more open environment were to be short-lived as the proposed policy changes were quashed at the highest level. In a letter from the secretary of the Cabinet, Sir Norman Brook, to the Prime Minister, Sir Winston Churchill, a firm recommendation was made not to allow a press release of any kind. Brook wrote frankly:

> The scientists engaged in this work suffer from a sense of sin which makes them itch to justify what they are doing. Some months ago they sought authority to release a statement claiming that it is more merciful to kill a man by inducing mortal disease than by blowing him to bits with an explosive. I see no reason to suppose that we will have to justify our 'biological warfare' research. And, if we have to do so, I hope we shall not squirm and cringe in the pretence that it is all 'defensive'.... I suggest that these people might get on with their work and stop bothering about publicity for it.[117]

Hand-scribbled at the bottom of this letter is the dry response 'please let them itch a little longer'. And indeed, a few days later formal notice was provided for the waiting advisors that no draft press statement would be approved.[118]

These moves towards openness on the part of the scientific advisors reveal much about their attitude towards the public.[119] The scientists were aware that their message would only succeed if their depiction of the scientific work was presented hand in hand with a particular depiction of the political context. The draft press release portrayed the British research as benign, not because it was biological warfare research, but in virtue of being part of the defensive activities of a caring nation state with the best interests of all the population at heart.

Sabotage

Although the concerns of the various committees responsible for biological warfare remained focused on offence with, and defence against, biological bombs, the possibilities of sabotage were not entirely ignored during this period. Most debate on this matter among the advisors focused on reservoir safety, following an approach to the BW Subcommittee early in 1950 by the Director-General of the Security Service. His request for an expert assessment is not in the public domain, although it appears that the Director's concern was over sabotage for assassination purposes rather than to target large numbers of people.

This matter was referred to BRAB and then the MRC BW Defence Committee, whose members concluded that large reservoirs could not be considered immune from attack simply on account of their size. With smaller reservoirs the threat was described in more concrete terms, the BW Subcommittee had envisaged a scenario in which a 'crash' dose by one person might be used to overcome chlorination.[120] A short report by the subcommittee also provided two arguments against the possibility of such an attack. First, the safeguards provided through the variation of human reactions to disease and second the indiscriminate effects on an entire community in 'hope of liquidating the significant few'. The BW Subcommittee report on these issues added 'that these considerations are unlikely to weigh heavily with the Soviet Union'. On the basis of these threatening conclusions, the BW Subcommittee was expected next to consider the repercussions and provide some policy guidance for the Security Service.

With no sense of urgency, the matter was passed over to Porton. A year later, Brigadier H.T. Findlay from the MRD met with the BW Subcommittee to outline their risk assessment of reservoirs. Porton's main concerns were focused less on the properties of reservoirs or biological agents and more on the intentions of any saboteur. Would a putative saboteur choose to deliver biological agents using water sources and, if so, would those sources be reservoirs? Findlay regarded these as key uncertainties. A further contribution to the debriefing was made by Fildes who, unable to attend through illness, had submitted a letter to the subcommittee. He argued that there were few grounds for regarding this form of sabotage as a danger; any risk was minimal and ought to be acceptable. His letter concluded that 'it was imperative not to allow administrative action to get ahead of proved facts'. Once the letter had been read out, Crawford poured further doubt on to the suggested threat with comments about the difficulty in performing this act of sabotage and whether

> it would really vitally affect our war effort if a saboteur succeeded in killing a few selected persons. Of course it would be a great coup if the saboteur were able, in one blow, to poison for example the Prime Minister and the Chiefs of Staff. But it was possible that merely to cause sickness or death to a small number of unessential persons would not be worth the effort.[121]

The subcommittee also considered whether chlorination would provide sufficient protection against sabotage. The Director of Water Examination at the Metropolitan Water Board was attending the meeting purely for this discussion and noted that it would not be feasible to keep a large reservoir sufficiently chlorinated to ensure protection. He also pointed out that a saboteur would probably introduce any agent along with chemicals to neutralize the effects of chlorine. In response to these pessimistic conclusions, Lord Stamp raised the possibility of setting aside a reservoir and using it to undertake trials to resolve any uncertainties. Henderson, however, was not in favour of the idea due to the imposition on staff time at the MRD.

In summing up, Crawford 'said that no method was known at present of preventing a saboteur introducing BW agents into a water main'. He thought that the subcommittee had given the Security Service some indication of the vulnerability of water supplies but admitted that further experimental work was needed. By way of action, the subcommittee invited the War Office to prepare a report for the Ministry of Supply on methods of ensuring water purity and for the Ministry to then report on which methods would be likely to succeed in defence against biological weapons. At this point, whatever scepticism had been expressed by the advisors, the BW Subcommittee looked ready to give reservoir sabotage further serious consideration.

But for some, all this emphasis on sabotage was misplaced. Fildes had already expressed his disdain and within days of the meeting was supported by Dr J.F.S. Stone, one of the joint secretaries of BRAB, who wrote to the Ministry of Defence that 'the subject is getting out of hand . . . the important point . . . is whether this method of attack is a worthwhile one and this will have to be settled before all sorts of administrative actions and committees are called in'.[122] Such dissent notwithstanding, the War Office soon supplied their report detailing available methods of water purification. Quite independently, the MRC BW Defence Committee had been asked to investigate the same problem by the Ministry of Health. Their letter to the Ministry admitted that there had been differences of opinion among committee members, but that 'the majority view' was that public water supplies could be a viable target for a bacteriological warfare attack.[123]

After this short flurry of activity, the administrative circus resented by Fildes and his allies was eventually forestalled. Certainly, at the time of these debates, there were few arrangements in place to deal with sabotage, but the BW Subcommittee barely discussed the matter again except to revive one safeguard from the war. No successor had been appointed for Bruce White, a chemist and bacteriologist at the National Institute of Medical Research. During the Second World War, the late White had been responsible for dealing with any items suspected of being contaminated with biological agents. The BW Subcommittee requested that their joint secretaries seek authority for a replacement and recalled how White's 'wide knowledge and fertile imagination . . . was able to deal with the numerous objects that were sent to him'.[124] Eventually, after further discussion, the subcommittee decided that any suspicious articles could first be inspected by bacteriologists attached to the Regional Scientific Advisor's staff, part of the Civil Defence network. Only objects still under suspicion after this test would be sent on to the MRD for further investigation.[125]

Concerns over sabotage were echoed in a lone intelligence report from 1951, which reminded readers that sabotage attacks would not require any mass production capability. The authors stated baldly that 'we have no firm evidence of the existence in the USSR of any BW project, whether concerned with research, the mass production of BW agents, or the development of the special weapons and equipment required'.[126] Their warning on sabotage was far more strident: 'the Soviets are fully capable of producing a variety of BW agents for such purposes: the only difficulty would be that of delivery'.[127] According to the report, epidemic disease remained 'beyond the power of man' and sabotage activity could only occur on a limited scale. The report did, however, warn that epizootics, diseases capable of infecting livestock, such as foot-and-mouth and rinderpest, could still present a threat.

Although water-borne sabotage remained the focus of much discussion of sabotage during this period, there is some evidence that more far-reaching trials had been carried out by scientists into the threat. The 1951–53 Chiefs of Staff report on biological warfare briefly mentioned that certain experiments had been carried out in the US and UK that had established the vulnerability of air conditioning systems in large governmental office buildings, such as the Pentagon, to a biological sabotage attack.[128] As efforts to produce a bomb were curtailed and policy faltered towards a defensive regime, Henderson published a revised evaluation of the threat. In August 1956, he argued that 'the covert use of biological warfare would be the simplest and most serious form of attack and the most difficult to combat'.[129] In this statement, for a fleeting moment, Henderson argued for the primacy of sabotage as the main biological warfare hazard.

Losing the BW Subcommittee

Debates over biological warfare policy during the early 1950s had included economics as a significant factor. The outbreak of the Korean War in 1950, together with a range of other overseas commitments, had undoubtedly stretched the overall defence budget to its limits.[130] Nonetheless, economics was not the only consideration. The role of chemical and biological weapons in the light of nuclear weapons and, to a lesser extent, the legal position of the UK with respect to the Geneva Protocol featured in many discussions of biological warfare. After 1955 economic matters, while still not the sole consideration, became predominant in deliberations over biological warfare policy.[131]

In November 1955, the chairman of DRPC considered instructions from the Minister of Defence to discuss a reduction of the Ministry of Supply defence R&D budget from £204m. to £170m. in 1958–59.[132] Part of this 'exceedingly difficult' task involved biological warfare research, for which the chairman had a severe proposition:

> I understand the minimum cost of maintaining the MRD as an establishment is of the order of £300 000 p.a., but that if it is kept going, it would be necessary to incur considerable additional expenditure at intervals

of 2 or 3 years for trials etc. I therefore reluctantly propose to stop all expenditure in this field.[133]

The proposal was not adopted but remains significant simply because such a move could now be contemplated. A later Defence Research Policy Staff (DRPS) paper notes some reasons why the suggestion was not implemented:[134]

> the Committee [DRPC] came to no conclusion on the development of offensive weapons but noted that the abandonment of MRD was not involved in the MoS suggested savings. The money involved was small, there was no competition for the effort or facilities and the team was earning prestige and co-operation in its exchanges with the US.[135]

It is also worth noting that, despite previous directives indicating a general attenuation of the offensive research programme, weapon development was still a topic of debate with the DRPC.

MRD had survived and offensive capabilities were not entirely excluded from discussion but policy had drifted further. A significant event was the dissolution of the BW Subcommittee in 1955. The official reason given by Pike, the chairman, was that the committee had regressed to a rubber-stamping operation. Certainly, the amount of information in the open files of the BW Subcommittee supports this position with much of the papers from the previous year being taken up with extended discussions of attempts to harmonize US and UK security classifications. Pike, not feeling it was worthwhile calling a final meeting, wrote to subcommittee members in July:

> For some months I have felt that the work of the Biological and Chemical Warfare subcommittees has, in the main, amounted to little more than the settling of rather mundane points of administration and that this does not really justify calling together so many eminent members. I therefore thought it right to bring the matter before the Chiefs of Staff, suggesting perhaps the work of the Subcommittees could be undertaken effectively by other existing Committees or bodies and with less inconvenience to so many busy people.... I only regret that I am unable to convey my thanks to you personally at a last gathering around a table.[136]

Operational questions were now to be referred to the Chiefs of Staff, security matters to the JIC, R&D was to be the ambit of the DRPC and matters of production would be discussed by the Joint War Production Committee. At an organizational level, a key link between the policy-makers and their technical advisors was thus severed. At a symbolic level, removal of the committee can be construed as an indicator of the waning regard for biological weapons in the minds of defence policy-makers.

In the same year, the 1955 DRPC review of defence research reported that biological research was now 'mainly defensively aimed'.[137] This was a reinvention of the scope of defence. Officially, by subsuming retaliation under defensive measures, British policy had always been 'defensive'. What was emerging was a policy under which no measures for retaliation were actively being sought as biological warfare assumed a minor role in military thinking. Henderson had announced that sabotage was still a major threat, thus providing some rationale to continue research on biological warfare. But a shift to a defensive programme was, in effect, a shift to a delimited programme. A delimited programme, in turn, implied decreased resources, status and autonomy for researchers at the MRD, not to mention its elite scientific advisors. There could be no doubt that the biological warfare research programme was under threat.

8
A New Threat

No Cabinet-level decision to abandon an offensive biological warfare programme appears to have ever been taken. Nonetheless, in the previous chapter a close reading of the open statements on policy among various advisory and policy-making committees revealed an uneven gravitation towards a defensive posture. The 1955 DRPC review of defence research reported that biological research was now 'mainly defensively aimed'.[1] In the same year BRAB, the MRD's advisory board, discussed the establishment's future research plans 'in the light of a policy directive by the Minister of Defence, which lowered the general position of Biological Warfare in the research and development programme'.[2] By December, the DRPC had 'recommended that BW research should be restricted to that required for defensive measures. The work of the MRD would be substantially unchanged.'[3] This declaration of autonomy referred mainly to the basic research being conducted in MRD laboratories; one area that advisors acknowledged would be affected by the new policy was the pursuit of field trials.

Practical demonstrations of the growing power of atomic weapons, the explosion of the first Soviet atomic bomb in 1949 and the British equivalent in 1952, had marked a gradual overshadowing of Porton's tentative and patchy progress towards a biological bomb. The Chiefs of Staff BW Subcommittee was dissolved in 1955, dismantling the arena exclusively devoted to discussion of biological warfare policy. Gradually, after 1955, economic considerations came to the fore and even the survival of a chemical and biological warfare research programme was, for a time, in doubt. By this time the plans for Experimental Plant No. 2 had been 'deferred indefinitely'.[4] Sea trials planned for the end of 1955 had already been postponed. By the end of the following year the Admiralty had stated that the ship used in the trials, HMS *Ben Lomond*, would not be made available for future biological warfare field trials.[5] Postponement had become indefinite deferral and the same judgement seemed to symbolize the general attitude of the Government and the military towards the entire field of biological warfare.

Abandoning offensive chemical warfare

In July 1956, the Cabinet took a highly secretive decision to abandon an offensive chemical weapons capability.[6] This radical shift in policy had originated in a report from the DRPC issued on 9 November 1955 which had recommended 'that the means of large-scale production of nerve gas and the development of weapons and ammunition to use it should be discontinued'.[7] As Carter and Pearson note, no parallel Cabinet decision was made concerning biological weapons.[8] Instead, during 1956, the status of germ warfare became a matter for inference. A brief on the matter to the First Lord of the Admiralty immediately prior to the Cabinet discussion on chemical warfare had ended by assuring him that: 'There is no naval requirement for nerve gas. It would not be effective in war at sea....He may also like to assure himself that the decision on chemical warfare would apply in principle to biological warfare agents.'[9] The DRPC staff, in particular, interpreted the Cabinet decision over chemical warfare in broader terms, contending:

> The arguments which led to the cancellation of weapons for the offensive use of chemical warfare agents largely apply to BW weapons. The Ministry of Supply paper to be tabled at the next DRPC meeting stresses the covert use of BW agents but the Staff may feel that the time lag between dispersal and effect rules them out in any war concept which involves atomic weapons. However, until the directive mentioned in para.1 above is altered, it will not be possible for the Service Departments – in particular the War Office and the Air Ministry – to delete BW offensive weapon requirements and targets from their lists.[10]

The directive the DRPC referred to was the 1954 Defence Committee decision to place defensive biological warfare research at the top of the agenda but not to abandon a retaliatory capability. No mention at all of biological weapons had been recorded in the minutes of the Cabinet decision on offensive chemical warfare. The diminished role of biological weapons was only implicated when it was noted that general policy was to rely on a nuclear deterrent.[11] The DRPC, nonetheless, communicated their 'recommendation... that BW research should be restricted to that required for defensive measures' down the advisory chain to BRAB.[12]

At the same time the US were revising their biological warfare policy in the opposite direction.[13] In 1956, their long-standing though frequently contested policy of refraining from first use was secretly abandoned in favour of a more offensive policy. The President could now take the decision to use biological weapons and therefore a policy of preparedness for such an eventuality was substituted. The shift marked an expansion in the US biological warfare research programme, a change which threatened to leave the British partners in the tripartite alliance looking impoverished.

New trials, new danger

Within the newly emerging, defensive policy environment the threat to the biological warfare research programme at Porton was considerable. The 1955 DRPC proposals to close the entire programme had been unsuccessful, and may possibly have been made only part seriously, as a lever during the annual financial haggling for the Defence Research Vote. Nonetheless, a defensive programme would have implied a downward path for the future of research at the now renamed Microbiological Research Establishment (MRE). Whether as a deliberate strategy, or through more indirect means, it was imperative for those involved in the area that the status of biological warfare should be revived within the ambit of a defensively oriented policy regime.

As biological bombs became of less interest to both scientists and policy-makers, Henderson, the Director of the MRE, attempted initially to refocus attention on sabotage. Early in 1957, he reported to BRAB how he had attended the 11th tripartite conference and argued 'that the manufacture and dropping of bombs was not the best way to employ BW, and that sabotage in its various forms was probably the most effective method'.[14] Henderson, however, remained sceptical about whether this opinion would even be minuted in the conference proceedings.

A few months later, in the June meeting of BRAB, mention was made of new possibilities for waging biological warfare. During the meeting, Henderson reported to the board that collaboration with the US was being threatened by shifting policy in the UK, noting that 'the Americans had begun to regard us as poor allies owing to their belief that we were retrenching in BW policy'.[15] The US were continuing work in an offensive direction and according to the Ministry of Supply's Chief Scientist, Owen Wansbrough-Jones, US 'production was keyed to policy and was directed at the manu-facture of bomb fillings'.[16] In response, the chairman, Sir Charles Dodds, reiterated the view that these cluster bombs were unlikely to be effective and Wansbrough-Jones continued to elaborate this theme, at the same time making an oblique reference to a change of outlook at Porton.[17] He proposed that 'the new concept having arisen, should the air-weapon project be abandoned?'[18] This novel concept was discussed briefly and in veiled terms by the advisors, but it is clear that it involved a 'long distance travel method' in preference to dropping bombs.[19]

Following the Chief Scientist's lead, the board proceeded to 'recommend that work on the development of bomb clusters should cease'.[20] Although there is no open record of whether this recommendation was endorsed at higher levels, BRAB did not discuss bombs again. It is not even clear how much work was being performed on bombs at this time, since the Air Staff target had been watered down in July 1954 from a specific requirement for a bomb to a general request for long-term research on the topic.

The 'new concept' noted by the Chief Scientist soon received serious attention from scientists and advisors on other committees. In June 1957 a new Offensive Evaluation Committee, previously the Offensive Equipment Committee, held its first meeting within the Ministry of Supply. Although the primary concern and lines of responsibility of this advisory committee were in the field of chemical warfare, the members of the committee were also concerned with the potential of biological warfare. At the inaugural meeting:

> Consideration was given to proposals that direct attack by conventional weapons limits the effectiveness of BW and that clandestine, off-target methods fully utilizing the insidious nature of biological agents would possibly enable a single aircraft to attack effectively tens of thousands of square miles.[21]

This new threat, dubbed the Large Area Concept (LAC) by scientists, envisaged an aircraft or ship spreading a line of pathogenic biological agent some miles away from an area (off-target) and thus spreading a deadly cloud across an entire region. Large area coverage had been discussed as a general possibility at recent tripartite conferences. Delegates had recommended that Canada carry out field trials with live avirulent strains of agents over 10 000 square miles; and theoretical calculations had indicated that even greater distances, up to 40 000 square miles, could be achieved, albeit under 'undesirably restricted' conditions.[22]

In a later report, John Morton of the MRE claimed that interest in the LAC had originated in the US some ten years previously but 'did not catch on' in spite of trials with a ship which spread a cloud over tens of thousands of square miles.[23] It is most probable that this trial referred to tests in San Francisco Bay which had taken place in 1950.[24] Morton suggested that the possibility of a large attack was still not taken seriously because it was linked to quite particular meteorological conditions which would require a 'lid' of air to prevent upward diffusion of a large cloud; also because 'contemporary opinion underestimated potential survival of BW agents'. According to Morton, interest had been 're-awakened' during 1955 because of three developments. Firstly, calculations at the Chemical Defence Experimental Establishment (CDEE) 'suggested that the meteorological requirements need not be so stringent'. Work in the laboratory had demonstrated that some agents could survive for long periods whilst airborne. Finally, Morton pointed out that there had been 'growing dissatisfaction with the inefficiency of on-target attack by cluster bombs, which gave an extremely low ratio of effective cloud to total weight and also sacrificed one of the outstanding characteristics of BW – the difficulty of rapid detection'.[25]

Researchers from both the chemical and biological sections at Porton put forward the case that the UK was especially vulnerable to the new threat in a detailed report to the Offensive Evaluation Committee.[26] The report discussed possibilities and problems concerned with maintaining an aerosol cloud of organisms over a long distance, keeping the organisms alive and also their means of dissemination. It concluded that: 'In general, the feasibility of effective attack of very large areas with BW agents is far from proven, but evidence is available which would make it dangerous to assume that it is not possible.'[27] This recommendation carried with it an implicit call for further research. The threat was likely but still needed to be proven. Whether or not this was deliberately implied in order to rejuvenate the trials programme, a proposal to investigate and evaluate the large area threat would have aligned with the new defensively oriented regime in biological warfare policy. Within a short period of time, scientists at Porton had embarked on a renewed series of open-air trials underpinned by the rationale of the LAC as a defence threat.

Zinc cadmium sulphide

The first series of trials that related to the LAC involved the use of fluorescent tracer particles to simulate a biological agent cloud.[28] Two aircraft field trials using zinc cadmium sulphide particles as simulants took place in the UK in 1957.[29] Zinc cadmium sulphide was also being used in parallel tests in the US, Operation Large Area Concept, where it had been selected and used for various tests since 1950.[30]

The first tests in the UK involved the release of 300 lb of the particles along a 300 mile line over the North Sea with samples taken at meteorological stations in England and Wales.[31] In the trial, the fluorescent powder

> was laid from an aircraft whose track ran from a point west of Newcastle out into the northern part of the Irish Sea, thence southwesterly to a point a few miles off Wexford. The dispersion height was 1000ft above sea level when flying over the sea, the offshore distance varying considerably in consequence of the irregular western coastline.[32]

Further details of what appear to be the same trials were reported to the Offensive Evaluation Committee.[33] The investigators deemed the results of the second study better than the first, being more in accord with what had been predicted: 'the northern edge of the cloud was shown to be sharply marked; no particles had been collected at a station estimated to be 30 miles outside that edge'.[34] Samples were taken at 56 locations by the experimenters and also by three sampling aircraft. Their conclusion, 'if the samplers gave a true picture', was that 28 million people would have received a dose of 100 particles.[35] Volunteer trials in the US had indicated that such a dose would have been effective for tularemia and Q fever.

The trials progressed but not without difficulties. Commenting on the MRE Annual Report for 1956–58, Henderson informed BRAB that: 'work in the field was very slow because of the unfavourable weather. Results in the open compared well with the laboratory but were far too few.'[36] Additional problems existed. Biologists, the board members noted, had 'not run parallel' with meteorologists. Despite Henderson's report, other BRAB members expressed their view that correlation between work at Porton (using a rotating drum and a test sphere) and field results were equally problematic. The effects of light on the survival of micro-organisms also presented problems for demonstrating the threat from large area coverage.

While these obstacles were being discussed, the impossibility of undertaking large-scale toxic trials was also acknowledged. One member of BRAB, Dr R.W. Pittman, noted that: 'it was not possible to carry out large scale trials in this country with pathogens, and probably not with simulants either'.[37] However, it was mentioned that potential trials could be discussed with the US and Canada at the forthcoming tripartite conference in Canada. At the close of the discussion the Chief Scientist identified large area coverage as the 'essence of the BW programme'.[38]

Strategic insignificance

The 'essence' of the biological warfare programme, however, was not universally acknowledged and germ warfare remained a low priority in defence policy. As a result of Defence Research Policy Staff (DRPS) deliberations about general chemical and biological warfare policy, an ad hoc working party was established in 1957 to consider 'a closer examination of both CW and BW against the background of use of the megaton bomb and the possible limitation of nuclear tests'.[39]

Shortly afterwards, a draft review of the overall defence R&D programme highlighted the precarious position of chemical and biological warfare.[40] The review considered military needs in relation to the restriction of the Ministry of Supply R&D expenditure to £190m. for that financial year. Under the heading of chemical and biological warfare were listed: studies of virulence; causation of respiratory infections; viruses; the sampling, detection and identification of biological warfare agents; the therapy of nerve gases; the exploitation and discovery of the V-gases; detection of nerve and V-gases.[41] Finally, in a section on what might happen if the budget were further reduced to £150m. in 1959–60, abandonment of R&D on biological and chemical warfare was listed as the first item in a list of seven measures. This was still likely to constitute a drastic measure as indicated in a brief for the Chief of the Air Staff which portrayed chemical and biological warfare research as 'relatively cheap insurance', therefore not worth terminating.[42]

Again, while the overall programme of research survived, the status of biological weapons continued to decline. The DRPS ad hoc working party established in 1957 issued a report which was circulated among its members the following February.[43] The section on biological warfare opened by stating: 'we accept that direct attack of population centres is inefficient'.[44] Despite such a dismissal, the working group's enthusiasm for biological weapons soon picked up. With a nod towards the LAC, the report noted that an alternative use of pathogens, long-distance travel in air of sprayed organisms, might work, although it added that there 'is no proof that such a method is effective (and there probably never can be complete proof in real circumstances)'.[45] The statement was qualified by pointing out that existing scientific data suggested 'no reason to doubt that, given the right circumstances and weather conditions, large areas could, with economy, be covered with infective doses of pathogenic organisms, e.g. a single aircraft might cover an area of the order of 100 to 200 miles square'.[46] The report warned that the effects would be delayed; that while respirators might afford protection, mass immunization would be impractical; that a biological weapon attack caused no material damage; a large-scale attack would be highly dependent on the weather; and that effects could range from death to incapacitation in humans, animals or crops.

The working group summed up its scientific material by affirming the reality of a potent threat and alluding once again to the LAC:

> Our judgement therefore is that it would be scientifically possible on selected occasions to deliver a devastating attack with biological agents. If the disseminating vehicles were unobserved and unrecognised, it is improbable that it would be realised that attack would be made until disease symptoms started. If the attack were recognised precautions could be taken but in practice are unlikely . . . to prevent large-scale infection.[47]

Scientific possibility, however, did not equate with practical possibility. The report went on to relate the technical judgement to the 'military and political practicalities in the light of the existence of nuclear weapons'.[48] Retaliation by nuclear means against a biological weapon attack was thought ethically justifiable, while the UK 'could not openly use the threat of biological warfare as a deterrent' in the light of the Geneva Protocol. The working party acknowledged that the undoubted Russian knowledge of UK, US and Canadian work on germ warfare probably did act as a deterrent, but they also suggested 'that biological warfare cannot make a significant addition to the present deterrent capability of the Western powers'.

In warfare, delayed effects and lack of precise control were reasons given by the DRPS why no tactical application for biological weapons could be envisaged.[49] Likewise, in a global war, delayed effects which were susceptible to the weather would discount a biological counter-attack against the USSR. Although biological warfare was potentially useful in this scenario as a follow-up weapon, 'the remaining delivery effort would be better employed in carrying nuclear weapons'. Russian use of germ warfare was also discounted because 'it would be unlikely that the Russians would be so confident that their delivery would remain undetected until disease had taken a firm hold'.[50] Only the lack of a nuclear deterrent, the DRPS thought, would prompt the Russians to initiate biological warfare. So, they concluded: 'on balance, therefore, we think that so long as nuclear retaliation is poised on both sides, use of BW either by the West or against the West, is unlikely in view of the delays and uncertainties and risk of premature discovery inevitably associated with this form of warfare'.[51]

With this general dismissal of biological warfare, only a limited defensive effort remained as an option. The report finally recommended that 'it would be unwise for the West as a whole to renounce all Defence interest in bio-logical warfare. But we doubt whether the sum of the effort in the US, in Canada and in the United Kingdom is justified by the importance of the subject in the present circumstances.'[52]

The working party report quickly became an official DRPC report which was later quoted by the Chiefs of Staff.[53] This was in the context of a paper with three aims: to comment directly on the DRPC report; to respond to a Home Office request for an assessment of the same topic; and as a response to a letter from the Admiralty suggesting the abandonment of any chemical and biological weapons reserves.[54]

The DRPC report reiterated the working party consideration 'that it would be scientifically possible on selected occasions to deliver with economy a devastating attack on large areas with biological agents'.[55] The report also evaluated biological warfare, stating that it possessed a 'negligible additional deterrent effect' next to the megaton bomb, and had the disadvantages of delayed effects, susceptibility to the weather conditions, lack of precise control and carried the risk of premature discovery.[56] Again, echoing the report from which it was derived, the DRPC concluded: 'because of these disadvantages, BW is unsuitable for the initiation of war, counter attack or tactical use, although it could be very useful to increase dislocation in the follow-up stages if effort were available'. Finally, the committee felt that some military interest in defensive research was still justified in order to keep abreast of new technical developments.[57]

The Chiefs of Staff Planning Committee next considered the DRPC paper on chemical and biological warfare together with a report on the intelligence situation.[58] Their conclusion was quite dismissive of both the threat and potential of biological warfare: 'we believe that the insignificance of BW as a deterrent to global war is due not only to the existence of nuclear weapons, but in particular to the practical difficulties of delivery and the uncertainty and delay in its effects as well as to the legal aspects of its use'.[59]

Given these considerations the deterrent effect of biological weapons could 'not be regarded as credible'.[60] Even a future partial or complete ban of nuclear weapons was deemed to offer no significant change in the cred-ibility of a biological weapon deterrent. Additionally, it was pointed out that there existed 'the political difficulty of posing a threat based on a weapon whose initial use is contrary to the Geneva Convention'.

Strategic uses of chemical and biological warfare against the UK were likewise dismissed. Soviet chemical and biological offensives against nuclear retaliatory bases would serve 'no strategic advantage'. Against civilian targets, it would depend on the 'conditions of post-nuclear devastation'; the high concentration of UK targets in a relatively small area meant that it was 'not likely that BW and CW follow-up to nuclear attack would be considered profitable'. The report recommended that this factor should also be taken into account in any future consideration of 'the scope of defensive measures'.[61]

On the tactical side of matters, the Chiefs of Staff were unequivocal: 'we agree with the Working Party Report that biological agents show little tactical promise'.[62] Likewise, on offensive policy:

> We agree with existing policies that the United Kingdom needs no offensive or retaliatory capability in either BW or CW, provided that capability is retained by the West as a whole. There seems little doubt that in the near future the United States will continue to have such an offensive capability.[63]

The 1954 Chiefs of Staff directive had included a retaliatory capability as part of biological warfare policy and 'existing policies' appears in this context to have conflated biological and chemical warfare together under the 1956 decision to abandon offensive chemical warfare.

With respect to defensive measures for the Armed Forces, the Chiefs of Staff judged the risk 'so slight as not to justify special personal defensive measures'.[64] Western research on chemical and biological warfare, as an international task, was felt to be important for defence and possible offence:

> research into their offensive possibilities will be needed primarily to point to the best measures for detection and protection, and also to provide adequate background for intelligence assessments and to facilitate production of stockpiles without delay if future assessments show the need.[65]

It was also noted that future changes, such as nuclear disarmament, might affect the relative importance of chemical and biological warfare. Periodic reviews of the area were recommended therefore to keep abreast with such developments.

In summary, the report concluded with several points, the key items being:

> The strategic value of BW in present known forms is insignificant.

There is negligible risk of BW or CW being used against the United Kingdom which ought to be accepted when deciding upon the scope of
defensive measures.
The West must continue to possess an offensive capability in BW and
CW, but this does not require the United Kingdom itself to possess such a
capability.
The degree of risk does not justify defensive measures against BW or CW
being taken by units of armed services, based in the United Kingdom, or
by ships at sea.
The West as a whole must continue some co-ordinated research and
development effort into the offensive and defensive aspects of both BW
and CW.[66]

Once the Chiefs of Staff had all but dismissed biological weapons from the
defence agenda, the possibility of abandoning all UK research in the area
was again raised. A full report by DRPS on this matter was issued early in
1959.[67] This split the enquiry into the financial saving (no more than £1.6m.
per annum) and the 'political and scientific consequences' of terminating
the UK research effort in the field.

The discussion of the political and scientific consequences of giving up
the UK research programme focused on the degree of co-operation that had
resulted from the tripartite conferences. These were described as 'a model'
where 'information flows more freely between the three countries in these
subjects than in almost any other'.[68] Based on contacts at technical and
military level, the report added that should the UK cease its research on
chemical and biological warfare then the US would soon stop supplying
information. The final part of the discussion raised an unresolved issue
which had left the status of the UK programme less than clear:

When our Services decided three years ago that they could no longer
support UK manufacturing capacity for BW or CW agents, nor work on
the detailed design of weapons to deliver them, the then Prime Minister
took the view that it would be necessary for him to consult the US President
personally before the UK work stopped; but the Suez crisis intervened
before he did so and it was subsequently decided not to pursue the matter.
Officially, therefore, the US authorities have not been told that the UK is
planning to rely on them to provide agents and munitions if it is decided
to mount offensive BW or CW.[69]

Some US scientists had been informed of these changes and 'expressed
considerable apprehension'.[70] In response, three courses of action were outlined in the DRPS report: to continue the research programme without alteration; to delay a decision and ask the Ministry of Supply to provide a more
accurate figure on the savings that could be made by stopping chemical and

biological warfare research; to ask the US directly what their reaction to the UK withdrawal from chemical and biological warfare research would be. Simply making the latter enquiry was potentially harmful and the Ministry of Supply investigation was judged likely to entail considerable time and effort. This left only the first option of maintaining the status quo.

The DRPS finally recommended that the DRPC inform the Chiefs of Staff Committee that a saving 'of not more than £1.6m p.a. – possibly much less – could be achieved by ceasing research on BW and CW. The political and scientific advantages that would flow from this course are such however that the DRPC cannot recommend its adoption.'[71]

The DRPC discussion of this document is minuted briefly. Much of the discussion focused on the Ministerial action delayed by the Suez crisis. Wansbrough-Jones, hinting that the Chiefs of Staff had not entirely abandoned the possibility of offensive biological warfare, pointed out that 'a question still unsettled was whether we intended to rely on the USA for production and weapons. If so they ought to be told.'[72] The document and its recommendations were approved by the DRPC 'subject to greater emphasis on the fact that the saving to be obtained by closing down this work would be very much less than £1.6m'.[73] These arguments appear to have been cogent enough to rescue both the chemical and biological warfare research programmes although there could be no doubt that they had fallen to an extremely low priority.

The insignificance of biological warfare was soon flagged down the advisory hierarchy to members of BRAB. On the occasion of Wansbrough-Jones' retirement from the post of Chief Scientist in 1959, he noted optimistically that 'the present situation of toxicological warfare seemed to him rather healthy' and read out a personal letter from the Chief of Air Staff to BRAB. The Chief of Air Staff enthused over the work at Porton, having visited in July, and commented that: 'there was no cause for any criticism that it is an extravagant dissipation of our limited scientific resources. As regards the wartime application, it is clearly wise that we should continue to participate in research in this field however remote the possibility of bacteriological and chemical warfare.'[74] These somewhat backhanded compliments could only indicate to BRAB that the perceived threat of biological warfare, and consequently their own importance, had diminished drastically since the early 1950s.

Change and anxiety

More general defence cuts were also beginning to have an effect of the emphasis of work at the MRE. An extensive discussion in late 1957 of the role of civil work at MRE highlighted these changes to the BRAB. One member, the chemist Sir Eric Rideal, pointed out that 'military projects might be more limited in the future' and consequently civil work should be undertaken such as producing biological materials or carrying out animal-based drug tests.[75] Dodds suggested that the colonial office might make a suitable 'customer' for any civil work undertaken at MRE. During the discussion, the annual report from the civil equivalent of the DRPC, the Advisory Council on Scientific Policy, was quoted to support the latest moves. The council was 'ready to accept the general principle of the use, where appropriate, of defence research establishments for civil work...where, as a result of defence cuts, it would otherwise be impossible for full use to be made of equipment and facilities or of research teams'.[76] Wansbrough-Jones felt that a compromise policy should entail 'best national use of MRE, while retaining its BW commitments'. Later in the debate, he reiterated bluntly that 'it was a question of economics: defence funds were being reduced, and civil projects must be entertained'.

Fildes pointed out the possible implications of such a policy. If it were implemented, he argued, the MRE should shift from the Ministry of Supply to the civil-oriented Department of Scientific and Industrial Research. Civil work could then be carried out in an institution parallel to, but separate from, the MRE proper. Another advisor, Wilson Smith, objected, pointing out two barriers to a full-blooded adoption of civil work: the reliance of MRE on the defence budget and secrecy. This objection was linked to research strategy, as he argued that 'a great part of microbiological work could be said to bear a BW complexion, but...most of the work at MRE was not *ad hoc* BW'. This, in turn, was linked to the type of work the board envisaged taking place under civil contracts. The work should not simply involve research where products were 'churned out'. In short, this shift towards civil research was linked here with concern over academic freedom, suggesting not so much that military research was regarded as essentially any more or less autonomous than civil work; but that disturbing the status quo might have presented a threat to the MRE's control over its working environment. Regardless of these fears and objections, the MRE was to become increasingly involved with civil projects from the 1960s onwards.[77]

Further changes were on the horizon. The Ministry of Supply was dissolved in 1959 and the MRE was transferred to the War Office on 23 November, having had a very brief spell under the Ministry of Aviation.[78] This change was perceived by BRAB as more than a simple administrative shuffle. Within the shifting context, the 'gravity' of staffing problems at the MRE was debated at length by BRAB, with much of the discussion relating to the future character of the MRE.[79] Wansbrough-Jones, supported by a number of other board members, felt that the nature of the War Office, as a Service department, would not fit well in the long term with taking charge of 'a scientific research institute of national status'.[80] In particular that 'the real objection was not to association with the War Office, but to being directly under a Service Ministry with its label attached'.[81] A recurrent theme in this and other similar debates was the need to maintain the scientific standing, not to mention the autonomy, of MRE by recruiting good staff who might not wish to work for Government, particularly the Services.[82] And, although Wansbrough-Jones insisted that the War Office would continue to require BRAB's advice, there remained a problem. The Scientific Advisory Council (SAC) was now split between the Ministry of Aviation and the War Office, with the latter amenable to the notion of a hybrid body reporting to both, but the former being hostile to the idea. Moreover, the chairman continued to voice his opinion that under the reorganization BRAB might be seen as 'superfluous', especially if, as proposed, one possibility materialized, that the MRE was taken over by the MRC. BRAB agreed that ceding MRE to the research council was not a good solution as there might then be too many experts involved. A 'less technically informed body' of scientists could, they felt, do more damage if BRAB reported to them than if they reported to an administrative body which would execute their recommendations without further discussion.

The board passed on their warning of the possible effects of a 'Service' label on staff and the 'threat of instability to a research programme with wide Service and civil commitments' to the Permanent Under-Secretary of the War Office.[83] But BRAB continued to be disgruntled by the changes that were occurring. Professor Wilson Smith declared to the board that he could no longer recommend MRE in terms of 'quality of research, freedom of research and security of tenure' as he had previously.[84] Fildes also voiced his concern that long-term research needed to be free from 'political upheaval', with another member, Professor Arnold Ashley Miles, Director of the Lister Institute, drawing attention to a tension between the job security of staff and the 'dependence of BW on defence policy'. A letter from BRAB was now drafted for the Permanent Under-Secretary of State for War, to be consulted by other colleagues in the Ministry of Defence. It pleaded for an assurance of some long-term stability in order to maintain the reputation of the establishment and asked to be immunized from 'fluctuations of defence policy and spending'.[85] The board then asked for present arrangements to be given urgent consideration. They recommended BRAB be placed under entirely civilian control with Service liaison carried out through a body akin to the dissolved Chiefs of Staff BW Subcommittee.[86]

After the reorganization of the ministries, the SAC was left with three boards (BRAB, Chemical Defence Advisory Board and the Weapons and Explosives Board).[87] In the 1960 annual review of the BRAB before the council, all the concerns over the changes were repeated and members added that the shift would 'be likely to lead to difficulties as the work of the Establishment moved away from its purely military potentiality'.[88] By April 1961, however, BRAB were informed that the prospects of shifting the MRE to civil control had 'if anything, become more remote'.[89] At the same meeting, Fildes' anger was now directed at the overall status of biological warfare and the general impotence of the scientific advisors. He expressed his dissatisfaction with the 'efficacy of the Board's resolutions'.[90] Because they no longer had direct contact with the 'users', he felt that their advice was now ignored. Florey also joined in and 'criticised the remoteness of the final advisors from the source of first hand information, and felt strongly that the Board might expect to be told what decisions had been reached and on what grounds'. BRAB may well have assumed an extremely close relationship with their 'constituency' at MRE, the Chief Scientist even commented on how board members had 'virtually assumed the role of supervisors of each section', but the advisors continued to suffer from the more general neglect of biological warfare.[91]

More trials

In spite of the disregard for germ warfare among military planners, a further five long-distance trials of fluorescent particles were carried out between October 1958 and August 1959.[92] Yet towards the end of this series, BRAB were informed that resources for future trials should be obtained on an informal basis, the DRPC 'would not allot a high priority to the work, and the official priority might in fact be less effective than the present loosely defined arrangements'.[93]

BRAB continued to remonstrate to higher authorities and in its 1959 annual report noted the slow progress of aircraft trials in the UK.[94] The board also 'reaffirmed its belief that large area attack with BW agents constituted a major threat to the country's defences, and its profound dissatisfaction with the low priority accorded to this threat'.[95] It is notable that this degree of certainty was not universally expressed by the committee members. In amending the minutes of their 44th meeting held in October 1959, Fildes argued that the draft minutes implied that the threat from a large area attack had been proven. The words 'what he believed might prove to be a massive threat' were altered to 'reaffirmed its belief that large area attack with BW agents might prove to be a massive threat'. This in turn meant that a line in the paper on BW Potential 1959, and presumably the annual report too, needed changing from 'constituted a major threat' to 'might prove to be a massive threat'.[96] These alterations served to indicate both the likelihood of a threat, but equally one requiring further research to substantiate. It further underlines the 'negotiated' character of BRAB's scientific recommendations and judgements about the threat.

Henderson expressed his own frustration over research on the LAC at a meeting of the SAC, reporting that progress on aircraft trials of long-distance cloud travel had been hampered

> by the low priority of the project and the fact that other demands for aeroplanes had the prior call. As far as he could gather, the failure to obtain the needed high priority stemmed from the decision of the

Defence Research Policy Committee that biological warfare had no direct strategic importance and that it therefore carried a relatively low priority.[97]

At the same meeting Sir Charles Dodds added that the DRPC decision was difficult to understand given the high priority of biological warfare in the US. Sir John Carroll, a member of the DRPC and Deputy Controller of Research and Development for the Admiralty, replied that although the DRPC were aware of this, they wished to rely on American work in order to conserve limited resources.

Henderson would not allow the matter to drop and raised it again in a separate report to the SAC. He complained that evaluation of the threat from a large area attack was impeded and added that Porton could only obtain an aircraft for trials from the Ministry of Aviation at full cost.[98] The effect was to produce a supportive statement in the SAC annual report:

> We referred last year to experiments which had been carried out both in this country and the USA in the dispersion of toxic agents released from aircraft. Results in both countries had shown that particles so dispersed were deposited over very large areas. It is the view of our Biological Research Advisory Board, with which we concur, that these results indicate that that method of attack could constitute a major threat to the defences of this country. Further work to evaluate the magnitude of the threat has been seriously delayed by the low priority which has been given to it.[99]

A report on the matter had also been forwarded to Sir Owen Wansbrough-Jones, 'who had expressed sympathy with MRE's view but reiterated his doubt that seeking higher priority would give better results than the present reliance on goodwill'.[100] While Henderson admitted in response that the air force had their own priority programme, 'the time had come for the DRPC to face squarely this issue of what he believed to be a massive threat'.[101]

Despite these setbacks the tests continued. Trials with tracer particles from aircraft eventually succeeded in covering 'areas of the UK with not less than 1 million and up to 38 million inhabitants'.[102] Major problems had been encountered in forecasting the travel of the cloud and in the loss of particles from the cloud, which suggested a lower agent dosage than the experimenters would have predicted.[103] Yet, by July 1960 a total of 12 such trials had taken place; the last two had been from on board ships.[104] In these cases, releases of fluorescent particles were made 'simulating a breathable BW cloud as regards particle size' – one in the English Channel (8 November 1959) and the second in the Irish Sea (10 November 1959).[105] The clouds were sampled at permanent sampling stations across England and Wales operated by Meteorological Office, Ministry of Supply and USAF staff. No great loss of particles into the sea was observed, and this was taken to demonstrate that an attack from off the coast was a potential threat:

> It may therefore be concluded, that subject to the availability of BW agents which could not suffer a substantial loss of infectivity during dispersion and night travel for some 10 hours, a biological attack, mounted from a ship at sea, against the UK would have been feasible, and is likely to have been effective on this occasion over a very substantial area of sea and land.[106]

Once the likelihood of a threat under these conditions had been demonstrated to the satisfaction of the experimenters, the Offensive Evaluation Committee decided that a 'sufficient' number of long-range trials had now taken place and resources should be diverted to smaller-scale studies of particle loss from clouds.[107] One notable trial of this type did not attempt to spray a very large area as before but to target a city. This trial, using a spray of powdered zinc cadmium sulphide fluorescent pigment, took place over Norwich on 28 March 1963.[108] The aim was to test whether the heat emitted from industrial and domestic services in the city would disrupt the flow of a large cloud and whether the aerosol material would be deposited on the ground locally in larger concentrations than in the open countryside. Norwich was thought large enough to generate sufficient heat and had the advantage of being located in a flat area. The line source released was 62 miles in length with the centre of the line 24 miles upwind of Norwich. Sampling took place at 30 locations in the city 'mostly in the yards of adjoining police buildings and in the gardens of private houses' and at ten locations in the surrounding countryside.[109] The results of the trial were inconclusive although further trials were planned.

From inert to living simulants

It was mentioned earlier that BRAB had explicitly dismissed the possibility of large-scale trials using live pathogens or simulants in the UK. This view did not persist and a year after this comment had been made, BRAB members discussed UK trials in the context of the slow progress that was being made in US and Canadian field trials. These tests had aimed to monitor the airborne survival of micro-organisms in relation to the LAC.[110] During this debate, the joint secretary of the board, Morton, suggested that a paper requested by BRAB at the previous meeting might, on delivery, constitute a preliminary estimate of the scope and type of trials that MRE could undertake in a similar vein. Members noted that any such future trials would have to be performed at night to enable maximum survival of the simulants and further debate ensued about the difficulties of extrapolation and generalization. One advisor, Professor Miles, raised these points in terms of whether a simulant might not differ less from a pathogen than pathogens from each other. Henderson responded that 'close simulation of any particular pathogen was of no importance provided the general behaviour was of the same kind'.[111]

As this debate moved away from the purely hypothetical, Henderson raised the distinct possibility of conducting trials of non-pathogenic organisms over populated areas, 'on a much larger scale than ever before in the UK'.[112] The Chief Scientist was less sanguine and responded that 'in view of possible objections' the Ministry's desert ranges, such as Maralinga in Australia, should instead be proposed as possible sites for trials. The debate closed with Henderson remaining enthusiastic and saying that 'successful simulant trials were an essential prelude to pathogen trials'. BRAB then firmly recommended that priority should be accorded to simulant studies in both the laboratory and in large-scale field trials. They also proposed that a costing of simulant and pathogen trials should be prepared for the board by MRE.

Meanwhile, Morton's report provided detailed plans for outdoor pathogen and live simulant tests. Laboratory tests with pathogens were thought to be 'unreliable' because it was difficult to extrapolate results from the laboratory to the field. Equally, it was difficult for scientists to recreate the field in the laboratory. Morton made these points frankly, arguing:

> Which, then, is the laboratory test most closely representing the field, and have we any assurance that the field will not also show some idiosyncrasy? Clearly tests with simulants alone will not give us full confidence in answering these questions. Secondly, we are not at present able to define 'field conditions' sufficiently closely to simulate them in the laboratory.[113]

Consequently, laboratory tests could only play a 'supporting role'. Morton's plans for pathogenic tests involving the LAC envisaged night-time sampling of a toxic cloud over 20 miles within a safety range of some 200 miles. These requirements, scale and safety, suggested that any such trials would take place at sea.

The idea for pathogen trials returned in 1960 during a discussion of a paper entitled 'BW Potential' by the Offensive Evaluation Committee, whose members noted that 'it was hoped, eventually, to carry out large scale trials with pathogens'.[114] The committee had flagged the contradictory positions of BRAB, who held that 'large area attack might constitute a major threat', and the Chiefs of Staff policy that 'there was a negligible risk of BW attack against the UK'.[115] 'BW Potential' had also listed areas where scientists required more information to assess the magnitude of the large area threat. These topics included the effects of anti-personnel biological warfare agents on domestic and wild animals, field aspects of the stability of clouds of agent, and agent detection. The chairman, Professor Reginald Fisher, a biochemist from the University of Edinburgh, pointed out that as 'most was known about agents which were merely incapacitating, he considered that more lethal agents should be looked for'.[116] However, Morton pointed out that not only did MRE wish to avoid duplicating searches for agents taking place in America, but also the establishment 'had no directive for development of agents or weapons'.[117]

In the interim another advisor, Pittman, proposed that a single large-scale trial with non-pathogenic bacteria could tie together the biological and physical/meteorological aspects of the problem of cloud dissemination. The committee raised a number of problems with extrapolation. There was insufficient information to correlate the number of fluorescent particles collected during trials with the number of live organisms that would be inhaled during an attack. Nor could correlations between trials in bursting chambers and the field necessarily be extrapolated from simulants to other organisms.

Linked to problems with extrapolation, the choice of a suitable simulant for the proposed tests was also open to negotiation by scientists. Field trials using aerosols at Porton had been 'steadily reduced in magnitude' as testing of pathogens, testing over large areas and steady meteorological conditions were not available at the site.[118] A previous trial at Porton 'with the simulant *Serratia marcescens* has not been satisfactory chiefly because of poor stability of laboratory prepared suspensions...a more stable source of simulant would overcome this problem but would not erase doubt as to the applicability to pathogens of the information obtained'.[119]

There was no discussion of safety per se but the Offensive Evaluation Committee noted that: 'it would be difficult to get political agreement to releasing a cloud of simulant bacteria over populated areas. Fairly large scale trials had already been carried out with non-pathogens.'[120] Safety was also a flexible consideration for the scientists as they decided on what constituted a suitable simulant for trials. Morton had already reported that

> when we come to consider 'simulant' trials...the only big difference from pathogen tests is the freedom from need for stringent safety restrictions. The question then is, how far can one go in relaxing precautions?...A decision is therefore required as to what organisms we could use over populated areas and whether further detailed investigation of their harmlessness is needed.[121]

Even a suitable test site seemed elusive, with the Australian range at Marlinga proving 'unpromising' and Christmas Island being 'likeliest but would be very expensive because of logistic difficulties'.[122] However, despite the BRAB's previous recommendations, the search remained a preliminary investigation 'as there was no present intention to conduct trials'.[123]

The LAC had also generated a search for suitable methods to disseminate agents and simulants. Preliminary testing of spray devices had been initiated in 1957 and carried out jointly by CDEE and the National Gas Turbine Establishment.[124] A number of trials with different designs of sprays using killed bacteria took place at Cardington and, when this site was found to be polluted and unsuitable, at a non-operational RAF station at Odiham, some 50 miles from Porton. By 1960, various trials had also taken place back at Porton with live spores of the non-pathogenic *Bacillus globigii* in the cloud.[125] In terms of safety procedures, Henderson had informed BRAB that: 'the material had been tested for non-virulence and in view of the ample precedent for such releases within the range he had not thought it necessary to seek permission'.[126] Here, the previous use of *B. globigii* at Porton appeared to have played a key role in its definition as 'harmless'.

Large Area Concept, early warning, defence and renewed interest

At about the same time as live simulant trials were being proposed in scientific and advisory arenas, the LAC became characterized quite specifically as a problem related to defence. A 1961 report discussing prospects for an early warning of a biological warfare attack warned that:

> It can now be accepted that the principle of 'large area coverage', by the dispersal of bacteria from aircraft, guided missiles or sea-borne craft, is satisfactorily established. A BW attack by this means may or may not commend itself as a strategic weapon; as a threat from a potential enemy it must certainly be taken seriously.[127]

The report added that pursuit of detection devices to warn of a biological weapon attack had been largely the province of the US rather the UK researchers, as 'the result of a policy deliberately adopted about 10 years ago, when the principle of large area coverage was unknown'.[128] The US had been assigned the task of developing the sophisticated technology for detection, while the UK were assigned to investigating identification rather than detection methods. The report continued by outlining recent changes: 'But when the possibilities of the newer offensive principle were recognized, it became clear that the UK would have to take a less detached interest in the question of rapid detection.'[129] Henderson had already flagged to the SAC the shift in research direction that the threat of large area attack, as distinct from a biological bomb, implied for the MRE:

> Until relatively recently the Establishment had thought the only type of detection needed would be rapid identification of material dropped by bombing but the long range dispersion possibilities had made clear the need for some form of continuous early warning system capable of indicating the presence of a dangerous biological agent in the air.[130]

Later, BRAB members stressed that early warning was essential if those attacked by large area coverage were to gain protection from gas masks. In an emergency, the 10 million civilian respirators in store would be rationed to those 'whose duties made it essential for them to be in the open'.[131] Early warning experiments aimed to provide at least a two-hour respite in order get 85 per cent of the population under protection. Whereas BRAB had previously flagged the LAC as the 'essence' of the biological warfare research programme, the same committee now dubbed the problem of early warning as 'the outstanding BW defence problem'.[132] The rationale for trials thus became one of assessing the threat through an evaluation of the dissemination *and* detection of agents.

So, the scientists' sense of urgency to provide an early warning of attack and their perceived threat of a large area attack merged under the defensively oriented research programme to create a degree of impetus for further trials. At the same time, the increasing prominence of the LAC in quarters beyond BRAB provided additional rationale and direction for the defensive programme. In 1960, the DRPC had become a little more convinced about the notion of a large-scale attack and reported that

> it was now clear that potent bacteriological agents existed which could be produced cheaply and might be disseminated over a wide area from a small number of delivery points by night. There were however still gaps in our knowledge; in particular about what happened to the organisms after release – and to find out, field trials would be needed. For the moment research and development should continue at the same level with the proviso that if a breakthrough should occur the matter would be raised again.[133]

This renewed perception of the threat, combined with what the chair of the DRPC, Sir Solly Zuckerman, saw as the slight possibility of the abolition of nuclear weapons, promised some reprieve and resulted in another review of biological (and chemical) weapons policy in 1961.[134] The Chiefs of Staff had already asked for an operational assessment of chemical and biological warfare and had not entirely dismissed the possibility of manufacturing chemical and biological weapons at some point.[135] This move had already been interpreted positively by one BRAB member as an 'awakening of interest' in the area.[136] Dr William Littler of the BRAB had ventured this opinion after Professor Wilson Smith had detected similar changes across the Atlantic. Reporting to the board on his recent visit to the US, Wilson Smith said that he 'had been impressed by the increased interest in bacteriological warfare that had resulted from the nuclear stalemate'.[137] Once again, the fate of biological warfare research and policy could not be entirely divorced from that of other weapons of mass destruction.

In parallel to the Chiefs of Staff assessment, Sir Solly Zuckerman established a panel chaired by Sir Alexander Todd 'to consider the potentialities in warfare of biological and chemical agents, and to make recommendations about the scope of the programme devoted to their study in the UK'.[138] The papers for these assessments were completed by the end of the year but were deemed 'too complex' for the Chiefs of Staff.[139] In order to remedy the situation, the Chief Scientist, now Dr Walter Cawood, established a subcommittee of the DRPC to prepare a 'single, simplified short paper'.[140]

The operational assessment of biological warfare had concluded that 'while we cannot foresee the need for this country in isolation to acquire an offensive strategic potential, BW if further developed might be used . . . ' as an incapacitating weapon in limited war, a clandestine weapon or 'a weapon in the exploitation phase in Global war, and on rear target areas in all phases of global war'.[141] The Todd Panel had concluded that Russia was not a suitable target for biological attack and had ruled out the potential of germ warfare in tactical situations. Cawood's ad hoc group, drawing on these conclusions, agreed that 'an expansion of effort on investigations of the offensive aspects of CW and BW is warranted', although added that no strategic offensive *capability* in either chemical or biological warfare was required. They also added that the statement that Russia was not a suitable target for a germ warfare attack was too categorical and might change given future technical advances.[142]

The Todd Panel had also made an organizational recommendation with respect to 'the lack of continuous service guidance, together with the defensive basis of current policy, [which] has led to uncertainty and diffusion of the BW and CW programme of R&D'.[143] As a solution the panel called for the establishment of a standing policy-making body in this area. This recommendation was not endorsed by the DRPC subcommittee, who insisted that 'the existing machinery operates efficiently and that there is nothing to be gained by the setting up of another advisory body'. Any attempt here to reconstitute a body similar to the Chiefs of Staff BW Subcommittee had been rapidly quashed.

The result of these deliberations over the various reports on chemical and biological warfare was for the Chiefs of Staff to suggest to the Minister of Defence that there should be renewed efforts which would 'increase somewhat the level of our activity in this area' if it was politically and financially acceptable.[144] This was to amount to about £1.294m. additional expenditure over five years. In addition a political decision was called for on the proposal to conduct large-scale dissemination trials using microbes.[145]

These recommendations met with some initial degree of resistance. A brief for the Vice Chief of the Air Staff notes that he had intended to 'urge that no additional funds should be devoted to BW and CW, and that we should continue to rely very largely on the Americans'.[146] In the event, all that survived of this opposition was a clause that the commitment to increase funds would be limited by the priority of chemical and biological warfare relative to other items in the defence programme. This had no effect and the proposals were approved at Cabinet level.[147] Policy from 1963 was later summarized in a three-point plan:

> a. 'The UK should develop a limited chemical retaliatory capability ... '
> b. 'Research should be carried out on biological agents with an author-ised expenditure of £0.47 million over 5 years'
> c. 'The production of equipment for defence against chemical and biolo-gical agents at a rate of £17.5 million for the three services over the next 5 years'.[148]

The amount allocated to biological warfare research was split between £0.37m. over five years for research on biological agents and £0.3m. over three years for trials.[149] Possible opposition in Cabinet to large-scale bio-logical warfare trials had been outlined and promptly rejected in a brief to the Minister of Defence:

> Experience in the past has shown that such trials cannot be kept entirely secret. The fitting in dockyards of naval vessels with hutches for guinea pigs etc. invariably attracts excited notices in the press. The consequent Parliamentary questions are bothersome but need not be more since the purpose of the trials is basically defence.[150]

The purpose of all of these trials would be to continue to gauge the feasibil-ity and nature of a large-scale biological weapons attack on the UK. Despite the firmly defensive justification for these tests, it is worth pointing out that in the mind of the Prime Minister at the time, Harold Macmillan, the new chemical and biological warfare priorities 'were firstly research in order to keep up to date with techniques and American information, secondly the development of offensive capability as a deterrent against such agents being used against us and thirdly, defensive measures'.[151]

The increased allocations to chemical and biological warfare were justified to Cabinet as a response to a NATO Supreme Headquarters Allied Powers in Europe (SHAPE) recommendation that all nations should possess a retali-atory defensive capability in chemical and biological warfare.[152] The Cabinet Defence Committee noted that this did not imply a readiness to use such weapons, any agents produced as a result of the renewal of effort 'should not be deployed at present'.[153] Overall, the UK plan was to 'be reasonably well prepared defensively to meet any known Chemical and to a lesser extent Biological Warfare threat by 1967, if we continue our current re-equipment and training programme'.[154]

Sea trials with simulants

The proposed single large-scale trial with non-pathogenic organisms mentioned earlier had now become a series of trials for which preliminary work
was already under way. A year before obtaining Cabinet approval for trials,
BRAB had sanctioned the use of live non-pathogens in trials which might
involve exposure of members of the public 'subject to vigorous testing of
every batch of material in animals'.[155] During the year 1962–63 the aerobiology and early warning groups at Porton were integrated, by which time
Porton was using live organisms 'wherever possible' in cloud tracking and
sampling fieldwork.[156] Local trials, presumably at Porton, took place to
assess the viability of airborne organisms and test detection methods, while
plans were made to conduct full-scale trials using ships and aircraft.[157] These
included a CDEE trial at Portsmouth to study the penetration of biological
agent simulant into a ship.

Then, in May 1963, the Chief Scientist, Cawood, reported that, following
the local trials at Porton on early detection of biological warfare agents, it
was now 'necessary' to extend the range of the trials so that the decay of the
cloud and its microbial contents could be tracked.[158] In addition, investigators wanted to check if the dead or dying organisms could be detected using
techniques that worked in the laboratory. Consequently, trials had 'been
planned to simulate more realistic BW attack from the sea and air at distances of up to 50 miles from the south coast'.[159] Further approval for use of
living organisms in trials by the Secretary of State for War was not required,
although he was to be kept informed of events by the Chief Scientist.[160]
Cawood justified the trials on the grounds that the release of 'harmless
micro-organisms presents no special hazards' and that routine release of
organisms from brewing, sewage disposal and agricultural operations happen 'on a vast and frequently uncontrolled scale, without public comment'
and involved 'organisms which have, potentially a greater health hazard
than the strictly controlled trials referred to in this note'.[161] His note also
mentioned that harmless micro-organisms had been used on Porton ranges
for years to 'simulate BW agents in field trials. They are no more harmful
than the normal background material of the air and are at a very low
concentration by the time they have cleared the range area.'[162]

A progress report on field trials undertaken in 1963 and 1964 noted that
'it can fairly be said that it is now usually possible to conduct an early
warning or viability trial with a close approach to technical perfection;
imperfect knowledge of the structure of the atmosphere is the cause of most
failures'.[163] By this time, ten trials had been carried out, mainly at night,
using a ship as a source vehicle along the south coast of England. Initially
these trials had used dead, stained organisms.[164] Most of the other trials
used a mixture of live *E. coli* (162) and *B. globigii* spores, the latter being used
as a tracer.[165]

More details of experimental procedures are available for the later trials and provide some indication of the extent to which simulants were used. Between October 1964 and May 1965 13 trials took place at night in Lyme Bay and Weymouth Bay on the south coast.[166] The bacterial suspensions of *E. coli* (162) and *B. globigii* were released along a line between 5 and 20 nautical miles long and were released between 5 and 20 nautical miles from the shore. A cloud was generated by four spray heads spraying bacterial suspension at about 4 litres per minute for between 55 and 113 minutes; the cloud was tracked by simultaneously releasing balloons carrying radar reflectors. Sampling of the cloud was performed on land at distances of up to 37 nautical miles downwind as the cloud spread across the southern coast.[167]

Scientists drew several conclusions from this series of trials.[168] Primarily, that *E. coli* survived better when airborne in large particles than in small ones. The later trials had also used a novel technique that involved using 'microthreads' of spiders' webs to hold the micro-organisms and study their viability in a simulated airborne state.[169] At the same time as the trials with sprays, sets of *E. coli* held on microthreads were exposed to the atmosphere in both exposed and sheltered sites. The experimenters concluded that survival of *E. coli* on microthreads was better than for airborne *E. coli*, but was still in better agreement with field results than any other method which would be used back in the laboratory. Finally the experiments confirmed 'that the viability of *E. coli* is influenced by the previous history of the air mass'.[170]

Test tube

Despite the dominance of the LAC in the thinking of BRAB and the work of the MRE, not all of the tests performed outside Porton were concentrated on large-scale outdoor attack. Covert attack by biological weapons had been declared a major threat at the 12th tripartite conference in 1957 and all three participant nations had agreed to heed this warning in their defensive research.[171] Possibly as a direct result, 'continuance' of so-called 'ventilation trials' was recommended in mid-1958 by the BRAB.[172] Such tests were intended 'to determine the risk of covert BW contamination' after a sabotage attack. Tests had previously been carried out in places such as GPO tunnels and admitted difficulties with extrapolation were used by the BRAB to justify further tests: 'it was now desired to investigate the London Underground, which was a more realistic environment for assessing the threat. Conditions were different from those in the laboratory and the risk might be very serious or negligible.'[173]

These early plans for ventilation trials in the London Underground were suspended until 1961 for unspecified 'political reasons'.[174] Even then, when BRAB attempted to reopen the topic, Cawood voiced his opposition on the grounds that there was a lack of need and probable political opposition to their conduct. He also mentioned that, in terms of priorities, there were far more pressing threats, especially 'in relation to large area attack, local sabotage was a trivial hazard and adequately predictable from existing knowledge'.[175] This view was objected to on several grounds. The chairman, Dodds, and another board member, Professor Miles, argued that the two types of attack might be used in conjunction. Henderson reminded the board that trials in the US had shown very effective spread of a vegetative simulant through the Pentagon and similar results had been obtained in the 'underground citadel' of UK Government buildings. Because these previous tests could not be taken as 'completely representative of the London Underground' further trials would be needed.[176] The proposed trials were deemed to be small-scale, cheap and 'could be done unobtrusively and without public disturbance'.[177] Also, professors Wilson Smith and Spooner argued that the board could not properly advise on the threat and countermeasures without the trials. It was agreed by the board to seek permission to conduct trials 'on the travel and survival of simulants in the London Underground'.[178]

Henderson intimated that the trials were inevitable, arguing that ventilation trials and early warning trials 'must eventually involve the use of living non-pathogens and the exposure of the public to them'.[179] In seeking the board's approval to proceed with such tests, especially for early warning trials, another advisor, the microbiologist and biochemist Professor Donald Woods, stated that 'no doubt full checks would be made of the harmlessness of the simulants'. Henderson responded that there had been no adverse indications in animal tests using far higher doses of bacteria than would be employed in the field. The board concluded by approving 'the use of living non-pathogens in trials which might involve exposure of members of the public, subject to rigorous testing of every batch of materials in animals'.[180]

Eventually, as further approval was sought for the ventilation trials, the possibility of sabotage became subsumed as a component of a large-scale attack. A 1962 SAC warning, that a large area biological warfare attack might be 'supplemented by an intense local attack...which might dislocate metropolitan life', led to renewed proposals to carry out trials on the London Underground.[181] The trial would be designed to 'predict the risk to the travelling public of the release of a BW agent in the London Underground Railway System'.[182] The medical advisor to the London Transport Executive was approached by the Ministry of Supply, followed by the vice-chairman who eventually gave his permission to proceed.[183] London Transport's main concern seems to have been whether a suitable cover story could be provided to allay public suspicion. There was also some concern expressed by the Secretary of State for War, Peter Thorneycroft, that living organisms were being used, although Cawood explained to BRAB that these concerns were less to do with safety as the 'Minister was concerned solely about public reaction to tests'.[184] However, these concerns do not appear to have swayed him from allowing the tests to proceed.

At lunchtime on 26 July 1963 the trial supervisor dropped a small face powder tin, containing 30 g of *Bacillus globigii*, from the window of a train travelling between Colliers Wood and Tooting Broadway in south London. The report of the trial stated that this bacteria was 'not pathogenic and does not cause food spoilage or have other undesirable properties'.[185] The test itself was so straightforward that no scientists were actually involved in carrying it out. Only London Transport personnel were needed. Their job was to collect samples over a period of 12 days from the air and from dust throughout the Underground. These samples were then examined back at Porton Down in order to determine the spread of the bacteria. The report concluded that 'bacterial spores can be carried for several miles in the tube system', having been found ten miles north at Camden Town, and that 'trains travelling through an aerosol became heavily contaminated internally'.

By October 1963, scientists were planning for further tests on the Underground system.[186] They envisaged using less hardy organisms which more closely resembled pathogens. Yet in their discussions they could provide no suggestions for ways to counteract a sabotage attack. Only one member of the BRAB was able to make a suggestion, the closure of floodgates in the Underground system.[187] Even this measure would work only if the gates were made airtight. No further trials were carried out before the following March and some setbacks had appeared.[188] The Assistant Chief Engineer of the London Transport Executive had retired and the replacement needed to obtain security clearance. Also, the trainee engineers who undertook the sampling in the 1963 trial were no longer available. It was proposed that a coliphage would be used in the next test which was planned for April 1964. Previously, sabotage had been taken with various degrees of seriousness by the scientific advisors on biological warfare. Under the new regime which focused on defence and the LAC, sabotage retained a strong presence as a potential hazard but primarily as an adjunct to the off-target, wide-area threat.

Surviving and redefining policy

As the defensive regime stabilized in the mid-1950s and the threat of biological warfare was dubbed 'insignificant' by the Chiefs of Staff, the biological warfare research programme appeared to be heading for equal insignificance. While the LAC was neither invented *ex nihilo* nor completely fabricated just to maintain interest in biological warfare, it was certainly seized on by the scientists at Porton and their advisors. The threat provided rationale and a direction which meshed with the aim of defence against a similar attack. Moreover, the same tension that had sustained the quest for a biological bomb, between what was feared possible and what was unknown, also sustained the research into large area coverage. The advisors, particularly Fildes, were careful to present the LAC as unproven but potentially devastating.

The LAC and early warning against a threat were woven in as defining strands of the new regime, while the ubiquitous threat of sabotage became linked to the aftermath of a large-scale biological attack. By the mid-1960s more funds had been injected into the biological warfare programme as the sea trials continued. Rather than succumbing to an imposed defensive biological warfare policy, the MRE scientists and their advisors had succeeded in making sufficient contribution to the scope and content of that policy to ensure their continued survival. The threat had been perpetuated and so had the research programme.

9
Making Threats

The possibilities for biological warfare are chilling. But these possibilities should not lure us into the oversimplified notion that the threat from biowarfare grew linearly with the growth of scientific research. I have argued throughout this book that the role of experts and the construction of threat was not such a straightforward matter. Once advice was formalized, the imperative grew for experts to feed their knowledge about germ warfare into the flow of decision-making. But this knowledge was always fragile and constantly slipping from the grasp of the advisors, researchers and their patrons. As circumstances changed over time, the nature of the threat altered as a complex mixture of technical, economic, political and legal considerations combined to provide for successive changes in outlook. And even at any one time, the palpability of the threat often varied between the different groups in the policy arena.

To recap briefly, by the mid-1960s with a programme of large-scale trials in place, biological warfare research in the UK was justified in terms of defence.[1] During the previous 30 years advisors and policy-makers had construed the primary source of threat in changing ways and set research and policies to respond accordingly to that shifting threat. The inter-war period witnessed the formalization of advice on biological warfare, with experts positing threat in terms of disease resulting from a disrupted public health system. Such disruption, they argued, would not require any special means of attack beyond a conventional bombing raid. In order to defend against this breakdown in public health, the advisors were well placed to argue for improvements which materialized in the Emergency Public Health Laboratory Service.

During the war this view of the dangers prevailed for a short time among some experts. They were sidestepped by Maurice Hankey who was instrumental in setting the biological warfare research programme in motion independently of these advisors. Alongside this more proactive approach, a retaliatory policy emerged from deliberations between Hankey and Chamberlain. Both policy and research were fuelled by suspicions about German activities. Scientists at Porton responded to the Prime Ministerial request for a retaliatory weapon at short notice and soon settled on anthrax cakes and the biological bomb as their research targets. After the war, a bomb remained as the goal around which offensive and defensive policies were formulated as the British research programme expanded. During the late 1940s, policy became increasing tied to the fate of atomic weapons as biological warfare was defined as a weapon of mass destruction. Then, as policy shifted slowly to defence in the 1950s, the expert advisors became acutely aware of the implied loss of resources, autonomy and status that would accompany change. Seizing on the notion of the LAC, they repositioned the threat within the new defensive regime. Large-scale trials to explore the new hazard were organized by scientists and the results were eventually presented for policy-makers in a successful attempt to spur them into restoring some of the lost status to biological warfare.

This periodization needs qualification. I have not suggested that at any time other types of threat disappeared without a trace, merely that at different times BRAB and the other committees were heavily preoccupied with a particular type of risk. Moreover, biological sabotage remained a ubiquitous threat. At different times sabotage was viewed as more or less pressing, although it never strayed far from the advisory agenda. A second caveat concerns the parochial nature of this study. When a fine-grained history of US biological warfare research and policy becomes available it may be easier to see where the UK programme developed purely in terms of local technical and political considerations, and where it was reacting to changes in the American programme. My suspicion is that this US history will enrich, but not substantially alter, my interpretation of events. Even in my geographically limited account, the state of US biological warfare research and policy was never entirely absent from ongoing discussions among British advisors and policy-makers about the future of germ warfare. So, for instance, the LAC in the late 1950s certainly had experimental roots in the US biological warfare programme. Whether or not the US were as equally enamoured as the UK scientists with the concept remains a moot point, but this does not alter the way in which the concept was deployed opportunistically by the British advisors to rescue the UK programme.[2] Thirdly, it is important to remember that scientific advice was not exclusively about threat definition and assessment. Experts were called on to advise on a range of issues at Porton Down from staffing through to the agents to be used in outdoor trials. However, the principal advice that they passed in the direction from Porton to Whitehall concerned the nature of biological warfare.

Advice on biological warfare was marked at all times by uncertainty and secrecy. Germ warfare research was such a clandestine activity and policy was so guarded that the different committees involved were not always fully cognizant of the activities and decisions of their counterparts. Moreover, these counterparts formed a very restricted network within which flows of information were tightly controlled. This secrecy threatened the coherence of any policies concerning biological warfare. Fildes, for example, was able to take his Second World War bomb project so far as placing an order with the US despite the late objections that this was tantamount to a change in policy. Fildes' success can largely be attributed to secret dealings with his superiors by word of mouth and the resultant difficulties of his objectors in piecing together an alternative history with which to challenge his authority. Likewise, the indecisive drift of biological weapons policy throughout the 1950s was certainly exacerbated by the restrictions on communication within the advisory and policy-making web.

The prevalence of uncertainties in science policy is not unusual, although with biological warfare the advisors would freely admit their ignorance when it suited them. This situation contrasts with the depiction of scientific expertise in both popular and academic literature, where certainty is generally taken to be the source of authority and power for science.[3] In many accounts of expertise in political settings, uncertainty exists but is glossed over by advisors or only revealed by opponents intent on weakening particular claims. Lack of knowledge is equated with loss of power. Yet, knowledge and power were not always so closely linked during the formulation of biological warfare policy. To be sure, this separation was sometimes in the hands of those receiving advisement, particularly as expertise could be treated on a 'take it or leave it' basis. At the outset of the Second World War, Maurice Hankey, for example, was not compelled to follow the advice of the BW Committee when its members remained sceptical about the prospects for bacteriological warfare. Nor did Hankey need to muster contradictory arguments directly against their position. He simply ignored them.

Advisors also willingly separated knowledge from power by employing an alternative resource, namely uncertainty. According to their assessments, the hazard may or may not have been real but the scientists' solution to this uncertainty was always to perform more research. The threat almost always carried a corollary promise from the scientists to help deal with the threat. This rhetoric played on the 'fear of the possible', the tension between what remained unknown and what terrible possibilities might transpire. How often this research produced answers is less interesting in this context, than the underlying plea by the advisors to maintain an active research programme. Here, rather than the scientific advisors' authority being grounded in practical demonstrations of the efficacy of biological warfare, a very general and diffuse appeal to scientific authority formed the epistemological underwriting of their advice. And this 'fear of the possible', alongside scientific reassurances to resolve those fears and uncertainties, acted as a crucial mechanism by which the biological warfare research programme became a self-sustaining institution throughout this entire period.

Henderson retired in 1964; Fildes severed his links with biological warfare after 1968.[4] After 1965 the work at the MRE became increasingly defensive and influenced by civil contracts. The US soon followed suit and in 1969 President Nixon made a historic public announcement: his country would unilaterally abandon biological weapons. Shortly afterwards, in 1972, the international Biological and Toxin Weapons Convention was opened for signature. The convention moved to ban the development, production, stockpiling and acquisition of biological warfare agents.[5] The BRAB was dissolved in 1977 and its functions fell to the Chemical Defence Board. Work at the MRE continued but now under threat of successive reviews of its future and in 1979 the establishment was reconstituted.[6] A small Defence Microbiology Division was created within the Chemical Defence Establishment to focus on defensive research. The majority of staff from the MRE remained within a new Centre for Applied Microbiology and Research (CAMR). In doing so, a historical loop was completed as CAMR came under the responsibility of the Public Health Laboratory Service, itself a product of early concern about the biological warfare threat.[7]

Towards the close of last century, the end of the Cold War and the 1990–91 Gulf War marked a resurgence of political and military interest in biological warfare. Once again, the threat has changed. Various southern countries have replaced the USSR as the source of potential danger and ubiquitous sabotage has been sublimated into a fear of bioterrorism. It would be complacent to deny the reality of this threat. But, looking back over the history of scientific advice on the threat in the UK, it might also make sense to reflect further. While scientists did not conjure their assessments of the threat from thin air, neither did the menace become real all by itself. It is difficult, but not impossible, to begin to ask about the institutional, social and material sources which operate to bestow a sense of reality and urgency on the most recent manifestations of the potential danger. In particular, how scientific advice, uncertainty and authority operate to depict the threat in more or less concrete ways. Again, this reflection should not be for the sake of complacency or empty academic exercise, but hopefully in order to gain a more sober understanding of just where our anxieties originate when, to paraphrase Camus' quote from the opening of this book, we think about just what dreadful and fantastic possibilities science has put into biological warfare.

Appendix 1   Organization of Advice on Biological Warfare (1947)

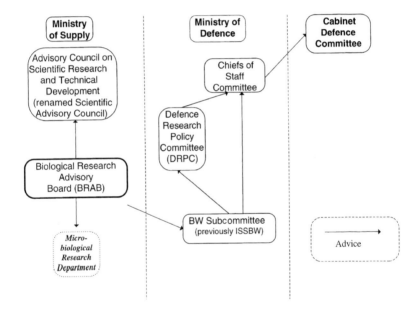

Outline Chronology

1925		Geneva Protocol for the Prohibition of the Use of Gas and of Bacteriological Methods of Warfare
1934	July	Wickham Steed publishes allegations of German biological warfare testing on London Underground and Paris Metro. Ledingham, Douglas and Topley write a secret report on the Wickham Steed allegations for the Committee of Imperial Defence
1936	November	Committee of Imperial Defence Subcommittee on Bacteriological Warfare. First meeting
1937	April	Committee of Imperial Defence Subcommittee on Bacteriological Warfare proposes Emergency Public Health Service. Eventually becomes Public Health Laboratory Service
1938	May	Subcommittee on Bacteriological Warfare renamed Subcommittee on Emergency Bacteriological Services
	August	Subcommittee on Emergency Bacteriological Services becomes Committee on Emergency Public Health Laboratory Services
1939	September	Start of Second World War: Germany invades Poland
	Sept.–Feb. (1940)	Prime Minister Chamberlain approves of defensive research to be undertaken on biological warfare at National Institute of Medical Research
	November	War Cabinet establishes BW Committee
1940	February	War Cabinet BW Committee. First meeting. Considers Banting's memorandum proposing offensive biological warfare research. Hankey invites Ledingham to draw up a research plan with no intention of taking offensive measures but which was not to exclude offensive research which might improve defence
	May	Churchill becomes Prime Minister
	July	Hankey proposes his 'step further' to expand the biological warfare research programme without consulting War Cabinet
	November	Fildes arrives at new Biology Department Porton
1942	January	Cabinet Defence Committee affirms policy to undertake research in order to be able to retaliate without undue delay with biological weapons
	July, Sept.	Tests of anthrax (N) bomb on Gruinard Island
	October	N-bomb test at Penclawdd. Meeting of US biologists under Edwin B. Fred marks the start of the US biological warfare research programme
1943	April	Operation Vegetarian (renamed Operation Aladdin) completed: 5 million anthrax-filled cattle cakes produced
	August	Tests of anthrax (N) bomb on Gruinard Island
	November	BW Committee supplemented by Policy Panel, Defence Panel and Operational Panel
1944	March	Churchill approves order of US anthrax bombs to be placed

	c. June	BW Committee dissolved. Inter-Services Subcommittee on Biological Warfare (ISSBW) established
1945	May	Second World War in Europe ends as Germany surrenders
	July	Atlee elected Prime Minister
	August	Fildes leaves Biology Department Porton. Henderson becomes Superintendent of renamed Microbiology Research Department (MRD)
	October	Cabinet Defence Committee approves continuation of biological warfare research in peacetime
1946	July	Biological Research Advisory Board (BRAB) established
	November	Air Staff issue first requirement for a biological bomb (OR/1006)
1947	January	Defence Research Policy Committee (DRPC) established. ISSBW report that biological warfare had highest priority and research was of equivalent priority to atomic science
	March	Chiefs of Staff label research on offensive aspects of biological warfare as essential
	April	ISSBW reconstituted as Chiefs of Staff BW Subcommittee. BRAB reject feasibility of initial Air Staff requirement for a biological bomb
	July	Chiefs of Staff set policy of preparedness to use weapons of mass destruction
	August	Soviet Union test explode their first atomic bomb
	November	Air Staff Requirement for a strategic toxic weapon (OR/1065) approved. DRPC objectives for biological warfare R&D reported to the Chiefs of Staff: a strategic biological weapon; means of storage or large-scale production of agents; defensive measures
1948	December	Operation Harness trials commence off Antigua
1949	February	Operation Harness ends
	June	BW Sub-Committee informed of Tripartite division of labour in biological warfare research
	November	DPRC report that Experimental Plant No. 1 in partial operation at MRD. DRPC recommend work to continue on design of Experimental Plant No. 2 but defer approval to erect plant
	Year end	Annual Report on Biological Warfare to the Chiefs of Staff flags uncertainties over potential of biological weapons. DRPC request from BW Subcommittee an update on advantages and disadvantages of biological warfare in comparison with atomic warfare
1950	February	BW Subcommittee propose a reduced scale Experimental Plant No. 2
	May	BW Subcommittee respond to DRPC request for update on biological warfare with recommendation to continue offensive research and to build Experimental Plant No. 2
	June	Start of Korean War as North Korea invades South Korea. Chiefs of Staff affirm existing biological warfare retaliatory policy and agree to construction of Experimental Plant No. 2 subject to DRPC approval
	December	DRPC approve building of Experimental Plant No. 2
1951	Summer	New facilities open at the MRD. Churchill re-elected as Prime Minister

1952	April	Operation Harness trials off coast of Scotland
	May	BRAB informed that DRPC had reversed decision to commence building of Experimental Plant No. 2
	June	Chiefs of Staff Global Strategy paper issued recommending increased reliance on nuclear deterrent and that the Allies should be able to retaliate with chemical or biological weapons. Chiefs of Staff restrict offensive biological warfare research to long-term possibilities
	July	BRAB informed that Government policy was to deploy biological warfare only in a retaliatory capacity
	October	British atomic bomb test
1953	February	Chiefs of Staff issue a directive on biological warfare: continue research to determine the risk of biological warfare; defensive measures to be established; offensive research restricted to long-term possibilities
	May	Operation Hesperus trials off coast of Scotland
	July	Korean ceasefire signed
	November	Minister of Supply issues a directive on biological warfare emphasizing defensive research but still affirming that some retaliatory capacity was required
1954	March	DRPC Review of Defence R&D reports that development of biological weapons has been disappointing. Operation Ozone trials off the Bahamas
	July	Air Staff Requirement OR/1065 cancelled by Air Ministry. Replaced by more general Air Staff target to continue research on problems associated with biological weapons with no definite specification for weapons or other equipment
	October	Cabinet Defence Committee agrees to put defensive preparations against biological warfare first but to continue to endorse a retaliatory capability. Programmes Subcommittee of DRPC suggests defensive and offensive biological warfare research unjustifiable. Operation Negation trials commence off the Bahamas
	November	Revised DRPC Review of R&D recommends that UK limits its research to defence against biological attack
1955	March	Operation Negation ends. Eden becomes Prime Minister
	July	BW Subcommittee dissolved
	November	Sir Frederick Brundrett, chair of DRPC, proposes to stop all expenditure on MRD. Proposal not adopted by DRPC.
	December	BRAB informed of DRPC recommendation that biological warfare research be restricted to defence. Experimental Plant No. 2 deferred
1956	January	DRPC Review of R&D for 1955 reports that biological warfare research was mainly defensively aimed
	July	Cabinet agrees to abandon large-scale production of nerve gas, the development of nerve gas weapons and destroy the residue of the Second World War stockpile of other chemical weapons and agents
	October	DRPC interpret the Cabinet decision regarding chemical agents as applying to biological warfare and request that Cabinet alter requirement for a retaliatory capability

	November	Admiralty refuses use of HMS *Ben Lomond* for future biological warfare sea trials
1957		MRD renamed the Microbiology Research Establishment (MRE)
	January	Macmillan becomes Prime Minister
	February	DRPC Staff ad hoc working party to investigate significance of chemical and biological warfare
	May	Britain test explodes hydrogen bomb
	June	Offensive Evaluation Committee first meeting mentions possibilities of Large Area Concept (LAC)
1958	February	DRPC Staff ad hoc working party reports significance of LAC as a potential threat but that the overall research effort of tripartite allies was not justified
	July	Chief Scientist, Wansbrough-Jones, labels LAC research as the essence of the biological warfare programme.
		Chiefs of Staff Planning Staff label the deterrent effect of biological weapons as insignificant and the threat of an attack as negligible.
		Report of first large-scale trials to test LAC using zinc cadmium sulphide during BRAB meeting. Mentions that two trials had taken place in 1957
1959	January	DRPC consider abandonment of biological and chemical warfare research but reject this proposal
	November	MRE transferred to War Office after dissolution of Ministry of Supply
1960	September	DRPC acknowledge their acceptance of the threat from LAC and recommend that research continue at the same level until further progress had been made
1961	April	Chiefs of Staff request an operational assessment of chemical and biological warfare
	September	The Chief Scientific Advisor and Chair of DRPC, Solly Zuckerman, orders a review of biological and chemical weapons policy (the Todd Panel)
	November	BRAB label the need for early warning of a biological warfare attack as the outstanding defence problem
	December	Chief Scientist, Walter Cawood, establishes a subcommittee of DRPC to combine findings of Todd Panel and Chiefs of Staff operational assessment
1962	May	Cawood's ad hoc subcommittee recommends an expansion of research on offensive aspects of biological and chemical weapons but no offensive capability in biological warfare
	August	Hundred litre experimental plant for pathogen production completed at MRE
1963	May	Cabinet Defence Committee approves expansion of biological warfare research programme including outdoor trials
	July	First in a series of outdoor trials along the south coast of England using sprays of living non-pathogenic organisms
1964		Henderson retires from MRE

Notes

1 Biological Warfare and Scientific Expertise

1. PRO, WO 188/705. Biological and Chemical Warfare Research and Development Policy. Report by the Chiefs of Staff. Draft. No date (1952).
2. Weart, S. (1988) *Nuclear Fear: a History of Images* (Harvard: Harvard University Press); Boyer, P. (1985) *By the Bomb's Early Light: American Thought and Culture at the Dawn of the Atomic Age* (New York: Pantheon Books); Haber, L.F. (1986) *The Poisonous Cloud: Chemical Warfare in the First World War* (Oxford: Clarendon Press).
3. For an overview of research prior to the Second World War see Geissler, E. and van Courtland Moon, J.E. (eds) (1999) *Biological and Toxin Weapons: Research Development and Use from the Middle Ages to 1945* (Oxford: Oxford University Press). A recent journalistic account of the US programme is Regis, E. (1999) *The Biology of Doom: the History of America's Secret Germ Warfare Project* (New York: Holt). For the Japanese programme see Harris, S. (1994) *Factories of Death: Japanese Biological Warfare 1932–45 and the American Cover Up* (London: Routledge). On the early Canadian programme see Bryden, J. (1989) *Deadly Allies: Canada's Secret War 1937–1947* (Toronto: McClelland and Stewart).
4. The official histories of Porton Down are Carter, G. (1992) *Porton Down: 75 Years of Chemical and Biological Research* (London: HMSO); Carter, G. (2000) *Chemical and Biological Defence at Porton Down 1916–2000* (London: The Stationery Office). See also Harris, R. and Paxman, J. (1982) *A Higher Form of Killing: the Secret Story of Gas and Germ Warfare* (London: Chatto and Windus) and Carter, G. and Balmer, B. (1999) 'Chemical and Biological Warfare and Defence, 1945–1990' in Bud, R. and Gummett, P. (eds) *Cold War, Hot Science: Applied Research in Britain's Defence Laboratories 1945–1990* (Amsterdam: Harwood Academic Publishers).
5. The accounts of specific diseases have been distilled from Mandell, G., Bennett, J., and Dolin, R. (eds) (1995) *Mandell, Douglas and Bennett's Principles and Practice of Infectious Diseases* (4th edn) (New York: Churchill Livingstone); Franz, D., Jahrling, P., Friedlander, A., McClain, D., Hoover, D., Bryne, R., Pavlin, J., Christopher, G. and Eitzen, E. (1997) 'Clinical Recognition and Management of Patients Exposed to Biological Warfare Agents', *JAMA*, 278 (5), 399–411.
6. Finer divisions of micro-organisms, such as the *rickettsiae*, are recognized but lie beyond the concerns of this book.
7. The division between pathogenic and non-pathogenic is not hard and fast. Few organisms invariably cause disease when they encounter a host, those that do are classed as strict pathogens. Other 'harmless' organisms can become opportunistic pathogens in the right conditions. For example, the bacterium *Bacillus subtilis*, used as a harmless test organism in many biological warfare experiments, has been associated with disease in otherwise sterile conditions e.g. in hospital cases when dialysis machines have become contaminated and affect patients on haemodialysis. See Shanson, D.C. (1999) *Microbiology in Clinical Practice* (Oxford: Butterworth Heinemann).
8. Chemical warfare agents include any substance used with the primary intent to inflict harm by means of the toxicity of the substance (rather than, say, explosion,

etc.). Examples include chlorine, mustard gas and the nerve agents such as sarin.

9. See Dando, M. (1994) *Biological Warfare in the 21st Century* (London: Brasseys); Lederberg, J. (ed.) (1999) *Biological Weapons: Limiting the Threat* (Cambridge, Mass.: MIT Press); Zilinskas, R. (ed.) (2000) *Biological Warfare: Modern Offense and Defense* (Boulder: Lynne Rienner).

10. See Pile, J.C., Malone, J.D., Eitzen, E.M. and Freidlander, A.M. (1998) 'Anthrax as a Potential Biological Warfare Agent', *Arch. Intern. Med.*, 158, 429–34.

11. Not all species of bacteria have the ability to form such spores.

12. For a detailed account of a recent Russian outbreak of anthrax, related to biological weapons research facilities, see Guillemin, J. (1999) *Anthrax: the Investigation of a Deadly Outbreak* (Berkeley: University of California Press).

13. See Sontag, S. (1989) *AIDS and Its Metaphors* (New York: Anchor) for an account of how the strong metaphorical associations that surround plague have been transferred to other diseases such as AIDS.

14. SIPRI (1971) *The Problem of Chemical and Biological Warfare* Vol. II: *CB Weapons Today* (Stockholm: Almqvist & Wiksell). In addition, Geissler lists 32 biological agents that were under consideration in the US research programme in 1956. See Geissler, E. (ed.) (1986) *Biological and Toxin Weapons Today* (Oxford: Oxford University Press).

15. As most people who would have been party to these documents would have been senior in both rank and age, few if any are still alive.

16. As to the value of the account, I would concur with Virginia Berridge in her history of recent AIDS policy when she writes that 'contemporary history . . . has its own implications, both in structuring further interpretations, and in creating and presenting documentation on which future workers will base interpretation'. Berridge, V. (1996) *AIDS in the UK: the Making of Policy, 1981–1994* (Oxford: Oxford University Press); see also Doel, R.E. (1997) 'Scientists as Policymakers, Advisors and Intelligence Agents: Linking Contemporary Diplomatic History with the History of Contemporary Science' in Söderquist, T. (ed.) *The Historiography of Contemporary Science and Technology* (Amsterdam: Harwood).

17. This linguistic device has been exploited to useful effect in a variety of studies of science. See, for example, Latour, B. (1987) *Science in Action* (Harvard: Harvard University Press) and Latour, B. (1988) *The Pasteurization of France* (Harvard: Harvard University Press).

18. See MacKenzie, D. (1993) *Inventing Accuracy: a Historical Sociology of Nuclear Missile Guidance* (London: MIT Press) for a thorough case study of the way in which the meaning of 'accuracy' was decided on in this way. Negotiations over 'what counts' have been subjected to rigorous empirical and theoretical analysis in Clarke, A.E. and Fujimura, J.H. (1992) *The Right Tools for the Job: At Work in Twentieth Century Life Sciences* (Princeton: Princeton University Press).

19. See, for example, Spinardi, G. (1997) 'Aldermaston and British Nuclear Weapons Development: Testing the "Zuckerman Thesis"', *Social Studies of Science*, 27(4), 547–82.

20. MacKenzie, D. (1999) 'Theories of Technology and the Abolition of Nuclear Weapons', in MacKenzie, D. and Wajcman, J. *The Social Shaping of Technology* (2nd edn) (Buckingham: Open University Press).

21. Mukerji, C. (1989) *A Fragile Power: Scientists and the State* (Princeton: Princeton University Press); Gummett, P. (1980) *Scientists in Whitehall* (Manchester: Manchester University Press).

22. Deliberate bias may or may not occur at times, but the phenomenon here is more endemic. See, for example, Nelkin, D. (1992) *Controversy: the Politics of Technical Decisions* (London: Sage); Collingridge, D. and Reeve, C. (1986) *Science Speaks to Power: the Role of Experts in Policymaking* (London: Pinter); Englehardt, T. Jr and Caplan, A. (1987) *Scientific Controversies: Case Studies in the Resolution and Closure of Disputes in Science and Technology* (Cambridge: Cambridge University Press).

23. See, for example, Jasanoff, S. (1990) *The Fifth Branch: Science Advisers as Policy-Makers* (Harvard: Harvard University Press); Irwin, A. (1995) *Citizen Science: a Study of People, Expertise and Sustainable Development* (London: Routledge); Yearley, S. (1992) *The Green Case* (London: Routledge).

24. Gieryn, T. (1983) 'Boundary Work and the Demarcation of Science from Non-Science: Strains and Interests in the Professional Ideologies of Scientists', *American Sociological Review*, 48, 781–95; Gieryn, T. (1999) *Cultural Boundaries of Science: Credibility on the Line* (Chicago: University of Chicago Press); Jasanoff, S. (1987) 'Contested Boundaries in Policy-Relevant Science', *Social Studies of Science*, 17, 195–230.

25. Douglas, M. (1992) *Risk and Blame: Essays in Cultural Theory* (London: Routledge); Douglas, Mary (1986) *Risk Acceptablility according to the Social Sciences* (London: Routledge); Douglas, M. and Wildavsky, M. (1982) *Risk and Culture: an Essay on the Selection of Technical and Environmental Dangers* (Berkeley: University of California Press).

26. Lupton, D. (1999) *Risk* (London: Routledge); Lupton, D. (ed.) (1999) *Risk and Sociocultural Theory: New Directions and Perspectives* (Cambridge: Cambridge University Press); Caplan, P. (ed.) (2000) *Risk Revisited* (London: Pluto Press).

27. This diagnosis paraphrases Jan Golinski who provides a balanced and far more detailed analysis of the arguments surrounding constructivism in the history of science. See Golinski, J. (1998) *Making Natural Knowledge: Constructivism and the History of Science* (Cambridge: Cambridge University Press).

28. This approach has been adopted in the defence field through some sharp analysis of how the US conceived critical moments in the Cold War. See Johnson, R.H. (1994) *Improbable Dangers: US Conceptions of Threat in the Cold War and After* (Basingstoke: Macmillan – now Palgrave). Johnson's study is excellent, although he tends to regard social and psychological processes as leading to threat exaggeration, an approach which assumes that there is a historical 'spectator's gallery' from which to assess the validity of actors' conceptions. It also assumes that the only role of social and psychological processes is negative, which unintentionally implies the odd claim that any 'correct' assessment of the threat would entail *no* social or psychological processes whatsoever.

29. This is typified by the uncertainty expressed in the Chiefs of Staff quote opening this chapter.

30. And this is classic social construction rather than a mythic and stereotypical version which reduces everything relentlessly to a cultural mirage. See Berger, P. and Luckman, T. (1966) *The Social Construction of Reality: a Treatise on the Sociology of Knowledge* (London: Penguin), esp. Chapter 1; Sismondo, S. (1993) 'Some Social Constructions', *Social Studies of Science*, 23, 515–53.

31. Hilgartner, S. (1992) 'The Social Construction of Risk Objects: Or How to Pry Open Networks of Risk', in Short, J.F. Jnr and Clarke, L. (eds) *Organizations, Uncertainties and Risk* (Boulder, Colo.: Westview Press).

32. Derbes, V.J. (1966) 'De Mussis and the Great Plague of 1348: a Forgotten Episode of Bacteriological War', *JAMA*, 169, 59–62.

33. Poupard, J.A., Miller, L.A. and Granshaw, L. (1989) 'The Use of Smallpox as a Weapon in the French and Indian War of 1763', *American Society of Microbiology News* 55(3), 122–4.
34. Tomes, N. (1998) *The Gospel of Germs: Men, Women and the Microbe in American Life* (Harvard: Harvard University Press); Porter, R. (1997) *The Greatest Benefit to Mankind: a Medical History of Humanity from Antiquity to the Present* (London: Harper Collins); Brandt, A.M. and Gardner, M. (2000) 'The Golden Age of Medicine?' in Cooter, R. and Pickstone, J. (eds) *Medicine in the 20th Century* (Amsterdam: Harwood Academic Publishers) pp. 21–37.
35. In the early nineteenth century, predating the emergence of germ theory, rioting occurred in such places as Russia, France and England, spurred by rumours that doctors and other officials were deliberately spreading cholera either to reduce the poor population or to boost the supply of bodies for anatomical dissection. See Porter, D. (1999) *Health, Civilization and the State: a History of Public Health from Ancient to Modern Times* (London: Routledge) p. 88.
36. Mendelsohn, E. (1997) 'Science, Scientists and the Military', in Krige, J. and Pestre, D. (eds) *Science in the Twentieth Century* (Amsterdam: Harwood Academic Publishers) pp. 175–98.
37. See Bud, R. and Gummett, P. (1999) 'Introduction: Don't You Know There's a War On?' in Bud, R. and Gummett, P. (eds) *Cold War, Hot Science: Applied Research in Britain's Defence Laboratories 1945–1990* (Amsterdam: Harwood Academic Publishers).
38. Edgerton, D. (1990) 'Science and War' in Olby, R.C., Cantor, G.N., Christie, J.J.R. and Hodge, M.J.S. (eds) *Companion to the History of Modern Science* (London: Routledge); Whittemore, G.F. Jr (1975) 'World War I, Poison Gas, and the Ideals of American Chemists', *Social Studies of Science*, 5, 133–63; Sturdy also makes the point that scientific and administrative innovation accompanied each other in the case of chemical warfare during the First World War: See Sturdy, S. (1998) 'War as Experiment. Physiology, Innovation and Administration in Britain, 1914–1918: the Case of Chemical Warfare' in Cooter, R., Harrison, M. and Sturdy, S. *War, Medicine and Modernity* (Stroud: Sutton) pp. 65–84.
39. This argument has been succinctly made in a more general form by Bruno Latour who argues: 'The social history of the sciences does not say "look for society hidden in, behind or underneath the sciences". It merely asks some simple questions: "In a given period, how long can you follow policy before having to deal with the detailed content of a science? How long can you examine the detailed reasoning of a scientist before having to get involved with the details of policy?"' Latour, Bruno (1999) *Pandora's Hope: Essays on the Reality of Science Studies* (Harvard: Harvard University Press) p. 87.
40. For a brief overview of the research carried out at Porton Down, see Carter, G. and Balmer, B. (1999), 'Chemical and Biological Warfare and Defence, 1945–1990' in Bud, R. and Gummett, P. (eds) *Cold War, Hot Science: Applied Research in Britain's Defence Laboratories 1945–1990* (Amsterdam: Harwood Academic Publishers).
41. Rogers, P., Whitby, S. and Dando, M. (1999) 'Biological Warfare against Crops', *Scientific American*, 280(6), 61–7.

2   Bacteriological Warfare as a Public Health Threat

1. Hugh-Jones, M. (1992) 'Wickham Steed and German Biological Warfare Research', *Intelligence and National Security*, 7(4), 379–402.

2. Wheelis, M. (1999) 'Biological Sabotage in World War I' in Geissler, E. and van Courtland Moon, J.E. (eds) *Biological and Toxin Weapons: Research Development and Use from the Middle Ages to 1945* (Oxford: Oxford University Press).

3. See Falk, R. (1990) 'Inhibiting Reliance on Biological Weaponry: the Role and Relevance of International Law', in Wright, S. (ed.) *Preventing a Biological Arms Race* (Cambridge, Mass.: MIT Press) pp. 240–66; McElroy, R.J. (1991) 'The Geneva Protocol of 1925', in Krepon, M. and Caldwell, D. (eds) *The Politics of Arms Control Treaty Ratification* (New York: St Martin's Press – now Palgrave) pp. 125–66. The term 'bacteriological' reflected the state of knowledge at the time, rather than any deliberate attempt to exclude other living organisms such as viruses.

4. In addition, Carter and Pearson note that sporadic but poorly supported intelligence reports about bacteriological warfare appeared throughout the 1920s and 1930s. See Carter, G.B. and Pearson, G.S. (1999) in Geissler, E. and van Courtland Moon, J.E. (eds) *Biological and Toxin Weapons: Research Development and Use from the Middle Ages to 1945* (Oxford: Oxford University Press).

5. Hugh-Jones, M. (1992) 'Wickham Steed and German Biological Warfare Research', *Intelligence and National Security* 7(4), 379–402.

6. Hankey, Maurice Pascal Alers (1877–1963). Hankey was a senior civil servant who held posts on many committees including secretary of the Committee of Imperial Defence (1912–39) and secretary of the War Cabinet during the First World War. He was responsible for the formation of the Cabinet Secretariat in 1916 and was secretary to the Cabinet until his retirement in 1938. He was also clerk to the Privy Council from 1923 to 1938. In 1939 he came out of retirement and entered the War Cabinet as Minister without Portfolio. After Churchill was elected Prime Minister in May 1940, Hankey left the Cabinet and was appointed Chancellor of the Duchy of Lancaster and then Paymaster-General from 1941 until March 1942. He continued chairing various committees until 1952. See Roskill, S. (1970, 1972, 1974) *Hankey: Man of Secrets* (3 vols) (London: Collins).

7. The MRC had been responsible for administering the state funding of medical research since 1911.

8. Ledingham, Sir John Charles Grant (1875–1944) was a scientist with wide interests in bacteriology, pathology, haematology, immunology and virology. He was a professor of the University of London from 1920, elected FRS in 1921 and took up directorship of the Lister Institute in 1931. Topley, William Whiteman Carlton (1886–1944). Topley was a bacteriologist who carried out pioneering studies on experimental epidemiology. His co-authored work with Dr Graham Selby Wilson, *The Principles of Bacteriology and Immunity*, became a key reference work, with the ninth edition published as *Topley and Wilson's Microbiology and Microbial Infections* in 1998. Topley was elected FRS in 1930 and became secretary of the Agricultural Research Council in 1941. Douglas, Capt. Stewart Ranken (1871–1936) published in the fields of bacteriology and immunology. He held the post of Deputy Director and Director of the Department of Experimental Pathology at the National Institute for Medical Research from 1921 and was elected FRS in 1922.

9. PRO WO188/648. Appended to CBW2. Committee of Imperial Defence Subcommittee on Bacteriological Warfare. Note by the Joint Secretaries (4 November 1936). Comment on Mr Wickham Steed's Article in the July Number of 'The Nineteenth Century' (27 July 1934).

10. Currently classified as *Serratia marcescens*.

11. PRO WO188/648. Committee of Imperial Defence Subcommittee on Bacteriological Warfare. 1st Meeting (17 November 1936).
12. PRO WO188/648. Appended to CBW2. Committee of Imperial Defence Subcommittee on Bacteriological Warfare. Note by the Joint Secretaries (4 November 1936). Memorandum on bacteriological warfare (13 April 1934).
13. PRO WO188/648. Appended to CBW2. Committee of Imperial Defence Subcommittee on Bacteriological Warfare. Note by the Joint Secretaries (4 November 1936). Memorandum on bacteriological warfare (13 April 1934).
14. These were respectively Professor Pfeiffer of Breslau, Professor J. Bordet of the Pasteur Institute in Brussels, Professor T. Madsen of Copenhagen and Professor W.B. Cannon of the Harvard School of Medicine. The scientists were among several who had replied to an appeal for expert information on the possible effects of bacteriological warfare by a subcommittee of the League of Nations Temporary Mixed Commission. The final report of the Temporary Mixed Commission was dated 30 July 1924. SIPRI (1971) *The Problem of Chemical and Biological Warfare.* Vol. IV: *CB Disarmament Negotiations 1920–1970* (Stockholm: Almqvist & Wiksell).
15. Mendelsohn, J.A. (1998) 'From Eradication to Equilibrium: How Epidemics Became Complex after World War I', in Lawrence, C. and Weisz, G. (eds) *Greater Than the Parts: Holism in Biomedicine, 1920–1950* (Oxford: Oxford University Press) pp. 303–31.
16. PRO WO188/648. Appended to CBW2. Committee of Imperial Defence Subcommittee on Bacteriological Warfare. Note by the Joint Secretaries (4 November 1936). Memorandum on bacteriological warfare (1 April 1935).
17. Members at the first meeting were: Colonel Sir M.P.A. Hankey (Chair), Sir E. Mellanby (MRC), Sir John Ledingham (Lister Institute); Mr G.E.A. Grey (Treasury); Prof. W.W.C. Topley (London School of Hygiene and Tropical Medicine); Major H.M.J. Perry (Royal Army Medical College); Dr F. Griffith (Ministry of Health); Dr P. Hartley (National Institute for Medical Research); Dr A. Landsborough Thomson (MRC); Mr N.K. Johnson (Chemical Defence Research Department).
18. Mellanby, Sir Edward (1884–1955). Mellanby was secretary of the Medical Research Council, the organization responsible for Government funding of medical research in Britain since its establishment as the Medical Research Committee in 1911. He previously held two posts as chair in pharmacology at the University of Sheffield and a honorary physician to the Royal Infirmary since 1920. He was elected FRS in 1925. His research was on biochemistry and physiology, the most significant work being on the cause of rickets. He held the post of Medical Research Council secretary from 1933 to 1949.
19. PRO WO188/648. CBW 1. Committee of Imperial Defence Subcommittee on Bacteriological Warfare. Composition and Terms of Reference. Meeting (2 November 1936).
20. PRO WO188/648. Committee of Imperial Defence Subcommittee on Bacteriological Warfare. 1st Meeting (17 November 1936).
21. PRO WO188/648. Committee of Imperial Defence Subcommittee on Bacteriological Warfare. 3rd Meeting (22 January 1937).
22. PRO WO188/648. CBW12. Note by the Secretary (22 February 1937). Appendix A. Technical Memo by Ledingham, Topley and Griffiths (1 February 1937).
23. PRO WO188/648. CBW29. Committee of Imperial Defence Subcommittee on Bacteriological Warfare. Second Report (29 April 1938).

24. PRO WO188/648. CBW 14. A Possible Scheme for Civilian Bacteriological Service to Operate in Time of War (22 April 1937).
25. Ibid.
26. PRO WO188/648. Committee of Imperial Defence Subcommittee on Bacteriological Warfare. 5th Meeting (31 January 1938).
27. Williams, R.E.O. (1985) *Microbiology for the Public Health: the Evolution of the Public Health Laboratory Service* (London: PHLS) pp. 1–7.
28. PRO WO 188/650. Committee of Imperial Defence Subcommittee on Bacteriological Warfare. Proposals for an Emergency Bacteriological Service (17 May 1938).
29. PRO WO188/648. 1438-B. Committee of Imperial Defence. Proposal for an Emergency Bacteriological Service to Operate in War (June 1938).
30. PRO WO188/648. Committee of Imperial Defence. Extract of Minutes of the 329th Meeting, held on July 19 1938.
31. PRO WO188/648. CBW29. Committee of Imperial Defence Subcommittee on Bacteriological Warfare. Second Report (29 April 1938).
32. Ibid.
33. PRO WO188/648. CBW3. Committee of Imperial Defence Subcommittee on Bacteriological Warfare. Note by the Joint Secretary (4 November 1936).
34. Ibid.
35. Ibid.
36. Ibid.
37. PRO WO188/648. Committee of Imperial Defence Subcommittee on Bacteriological Warfare. 1st Meeting (17 November 1936).
38. PRO WO188/648. CBW20. Committee of Imperial Defence Subcommittee on Bacteriological Warfare. Note by the Joint Secretary (25 October 1937). PRO WO 188/650. 1382-B. Committee of Imperial Defence. Chemical Warfare. December 1937.
39. PRO WO188/648. CBW20. Committee of Imperial Defence Subcommittee on Bacteriological Warfare. Note by the Joint Secretary (25 October 1937).
40. A recent historical account of German biological warfare contradicts these reports. Deichmann argues that there is little evidence of German interest in biological warfare before 1940. See Deichmann, U. (1996) *Biologists under Hitler* (Cambridge, Mass.: Harvard University Press) Chapter 6.
41. WO 188/648. Committee of Imperial Defence Subcommittee on Bacteriological Warfare. 3rd Meeting (22 January 1937).
42. PRO WO188/648. CBW31. Committee of Imperial Defence Subcommittee on Bacteriological Warfare. Summary of Articles from the Romanian Press on Bacterial Warfare (21 April 1938). The article had also been published in Paris in the March edition of *L'Illustration*.
43. PRO WO188/650. Committee of Imperial Defence Subcommittee on Bacteriological Warfare. Note from Director of Naval Intelligence 2 November 1938 (21 November 1938).
44. PRO WO188/650. CBW42. Committee of Imperial Defence Subcommittee on Bacteriological Warfare. Practicality of Bacteriological Weapon in Future War (Translation) (12 December 1938).
45. PRO WO188/648. CBW29. Committee of Imperial Defence Subcommittee on Bacteriological Warfare. Second Report (29 April 1938).
46. PRO WO188/648. Committee of Imperial Defence Subcommittee on Bacteriological Warfare. 1st Meeting (17 November 1936).
47. Ibid.

48. PRO WO188/648. CBW29. Committee of Imperial Defence Subcommittee on Bacteriological Warfare. Second Report (29 April 1938).
49. Ibid.
50. Ibid.
51. PRO WO188/648. CBW34. Note by the Joint Secretary (19 May 1938).

3   Hankey's 'Step Further'

1. PRO, CAB104/234. Letter H.A. Sisson to Minister of Co-Ordination of Defence (11 September 1939). This may have been Henry Arnott Sisson who wrote *On Guard against Gas* (1938) (London: Hutchinson and Co).
2. PRO, CAB104/234. Letter Mellanby to Hankey (20 September 1939).
3. Ibid.
4. PRO, CAB104/234, Letter Hankey to Churchill (23 September 1939). Part of the joint Anglo-French Declaration on 3 September 1939 had noted that the Allies would abide by the 1925 Geneva Protocol.
5. PRO WO188/654. Letter Hankey to Churchill (6 December 1941).
6. Ibid.
7. PRO WO188/653. BW(40) 1st Meeting. War Cabinet. Bacteriological Warfare Committee (7 February 1940).
8. PRO WO188/653. WP(G)(39)111. War Cabinet Bacteriological Warfare. Note by the Lord President of the Council (21 November 1939).
9. PRO WO188/653. WP(G)(39)111. War Cabinet Bacteriological Warfare. Note by the Lord President of the Council (21 November 1939). Annex. Memo from MRC dated 24/10/39. Some Notes on Defence against Bacteriological Warfare.
10. Ibid.
11. PRO, WO188/653. WP(G)39112. War Cabinet. Bacteriological Warfare. Note by the Minister for Co-Ordination of Defence (21 November 1939); BW(40)1 Revise. War Cabinet. Bacteriological Warfare Subcommittee. Composition and Terms of Reference (7 March 1940). The initial membership was: Lord Hankey (Chair); Dr D.A.E. Cabot (Ministry of Agriculture and Fisheries); Dr T. Carnworth (Ministry of Health); Dr C.G. Douglas (Chemical Defence Research Dept. Porton); Captain W.H.D. Friedberger (Admiralty) (succeeded by Commander J.A.C. Hill on 28 February 1940); Mr J.C.F. Fryer (Director, Plant Pathology Laboratory, Harpenden); Dr P. Hartley (National Institute for Medical Research); Sir Patrick P. Laidlaw (National Institute for Medical Research); Sir John Ledingham (Lister Institute); Brigadier C.G. Ling (War Office); Sir Edward Mellanby (MRC); Air Vice-Marshal R.H. Peck (Air Ministry); Major-General H.M.J. Perry (War Office); Dr A. Landsborough Thomson (MRC); Prof. W.W.C. Topley (LSHTM); Mr K.B. Usher (Treasury); Mr R.S. Wood (Home Office and Ministry of Home Security).
12. PRO, WO188/653. BW(40)1 Revise. War Cabinet. Bacteriological Warfare Subcommittee. Composition and Terms of Reference (7 March 1940).
13. See Avery, Donald (1999) 'Canadian Biological and Toxin Warfare Research, Development and Planning, 1942–45' in Geissler, E. and van Courtland Moon, J.E. (eds) *Biological and Toxin Weapons: Research Development and Use from the Middle Ages to 1945* (Oxford: Oxford University Press). Avery describes Hankey's reaction as feigned in the light of the BW committee's reaction to Banting's report. However, Hankey's subsequent actions suggest that Banting genuinely caught his attention.

14. PRO WO188/653. BW(40)3. War Cabinet. Bacteriological Warfare Committee. Comments on Sir Frederick Banting's Memorandum (25 January 1940). Annex.
15. Ibid.
16. Ibid.
17. Ibid.
18. Ibid.
19. PRO WO188/653. BW(40) 1st Meeting. War Cabinet. Bacteriological Warfare Committee (7 February 1940).
20. Ibid.
21. Ibid.
22. Ibid.
23. The subcommittee consisted of: Prof. Sir J. Ledingham, Dr D.G. Douglas, Dr P. Hartley, Sir Patrick Laidlaw (who died suddenly after the subcommittee meetings but before their report was finalized), Major-General H.M. Perry, Prof. W.W.C. Topley.
24. PRO, WO188/653. BW(40)14. War Cabinet. Bacteriological Warfare Committee. Experiments on Methods of Spread of Bacteria. Report by Sir John Ledingham's Subcommittee (3 April 1940).
25. PRO, WO188/653. BW(40)21. War Cabinet. Bacteriological Warfare Committee. Experiments of Methods of Spread of Bacteria. Report by Dr C.H. Andrewes (3 June 1940).
26. PRO, WO188/653. BW(40) 3rd Meeting. War Cabinet. Bacteriological Warfare Committee (26 June 1940).
27. PRO, CAB104/234. Letter Hankey to Group-Captain Elliot (26 July 1940).
28. Ibid.
29. PRO, CAB104/234. Letter Fildes to Mellanby (26 July 1940).
30. PRO, CAB104/234. Letter Hankey to Elliot (9 August 1940).
31. PRO, WO188/653. BW(40)35. War Cabinet. Bacteriological Warfare Committee. Further Experiments on Methods of Spread of Bacteria. Note by the Chairman (23 September 1940).
32. Fildes, Sir Paul Gordon (1882–1971) had undertaken extensive research in bacteriology. His early work included a collaborative clinical trial of Salvarsan as a treatment for syphilis, a method for cultivating anaerobic bacteria and studies of bacterial nutrition. He was elected FRS in 1934, the same year that he moved to the newly founded MRC Bacterial Chemisty Unit. He returned to this unit, reconstituted at the Lister Institute, after the war and retired in 1949. After retiring he continued research in Howard Florey's Oxford laboratory until 1964.
33. Kohler, R.E. (1985) 'Bacterial Physiology: the Medical Context', *Bulletin of the History of Medicine*, 59, 54–74.
34. Henderson, David Willis Wilson (1903–68). Henderson was a microbiologist who had worked primarily on the immunology of *Salmonella* and *Clostridium* bacteria. He worked at the Lister Institute of Preventative Medicine from 1931 to 1940 when he moved to Porton Down. He soon became Fildes' deputy at Porton Down and then became the Superintendent of the Microbiology Research Department (MRD) after the war. He was president of the Society for General Microbiology from 1963 to 1965 and elected FRS in 1959. He retired from his directorship at Porton in 1964.
35. PRO, WO188/652. Porton Executive Committee. Meeting to Be Held at Porton (14 April 1942).
36. Barbary leaves can harbour spores of rust fungi which are a pathogen of cereals.

37. PRO, CAB104/234. Letter Jebb to Hankey (4 October 1940).
38. PRO, CAB104/234. Letter Hankey to Prime Minister (8 October 1940). An expert from Cambridge, Sir Edwin Butler, was consulted on the feasibility of the crop proposal and rejected the idea.
39. Unknown to the British, the Japanese had already produced a series of biological bombs with the earliest manufacture taking place in 1937. See Harris, S. (1999) 'The Japanese Biological Warfare Programme: an Overview' in Geissler, E. and van Courtland Moon, J.E. (eds) *Biological and Toxin Weapons: Research Development and Use from the Middle Ages to 1945* (Oxford: Oxford University Press).
40. PRO, WO188/653. BW(40)35. War Cabinet. Bacteriological Warfare Committee. Further Experiments on Methods of Spread of Bacteria. Note by the Chairman (23 September 1940).
41. PRO, WO188/654. Letter Fildes to Rt Hon. Mr Ernest Brown (8 January 1944).
42. PRO, WO188/654. Letter Fildes to Rickett (12 November 1940).
43. PRO, WO188/654. Letter Fildes to Thomson (20 January 1941).
44. PRO, WO188/654. Letter Rickett to Fildes (16 November 1940).
45. PRO, WO188/654. Fildes to Rickett (20 January 1941).
46. PRO, WO188/654. Letter Fildes to Rickett (25 November 1940).
47. PRO, WO188/654. Letter Fildes to Hankey (15 April 1941).
48. PRO, WO188/654. Letter Rickett to Fildes (14 May 1941).
49. PRO, WO188/654. Letter Fildes to Rickett (3 October 1941).
50. Carter, G.B. 'Biological Warfare and Biological Defence in the United Kingdom 1940–1979', *RUSI Journal* (December 1992), 67–74; Carter, G.B. and Pearson, G.S. (1999) 'British Biological Warfare and Biological Defence, 1925–45' in Geissler, E. and van Courtland Moon, J.E. (eds) *Biological and Toxin Weapons: Research Development and Use from the Middle Ages to 1945* (Oxford: Oxford University Press).
51. PRO, CAB104/234. Letter Hankey to Peck (29 September 1941).
52. PRO, CAB120/782. Hankey to Prime Minister (6 December 1942).
53. PRO, CAB121/103. Note (2 January 1942).
54. PRO, CAB121/103. Note by H.L. Ismay (3 January 1942).
55. PRO, WO188/654. Lansborough Thomson to Fildes (6 January 1942).
56. Carter, G.B. 'Biological Warfare and Biological Defence in the United Kingdom 1940–1979', *RUSI Journal* (December 1992), 67–74; Carter, G.B. and Pearson, G.S. (1999) 'British Biological Warfare and Biological Defence, 1925–45' in Geissler, E. and van Courtland Moon, J.E. (eds) *Biological and Toxin Weapons: Research Development and Use from the Middle Ages to 1945* (Oxford: Oxford University Press).
57. PRO, WO188/654. Letter Fildes to Topley (29 August 1941).
58. PRO, WO188/654. Item 118. Procedure for Work on Bacterial Warfare. Porton (19 January 1942).
59. PRO, WO188/656. BW(P)(42)3. Porton Experiments Subcommittee. Bacteriological Warfare: General Review (Dr P. Fildes) (31 March 1942). This was an idea which particularly appealed to the Admiralty as an offensive weapon, see CAB 127/18. Letter Vernon Donaldson to Everett (2 May 1942); Memorandum on NTD (Toxic Dust). Statement for Plans Division, Naval Staff (P. Fildes) (13 May 1942).
60. PRO WO188/652. Porton Executive Committee. Meeting to Be Held at Porton (14 April 1942). (Report on items for the agenda signed by Fildes).
61. Ibid.

62. Carter, G.B. 'Biological Warfare and Biological Defence in the United Kingdom 1940–1979', *RUSI Journal* (December 1992), 67–74.
63. PRO, WO188/653. BW Committee. Note of an informal meeting on 7 October 1942, in the Chancellor of the Duchy of Lancaster's Room.
64. A final series of trials took place on Gruinard in August 1943. See Carter, G.B. and Pearson, G.S. (1999) 'British Biological Warfare and Biological Defence, 1925–45', in Geissler, E. and van Courtland Moon, J.E. (eds) *Biological and Toxin Weapons: Research, Development and Use from the Middle Ages to 1945* (Oxford: Oxford University Press).
65. PRO, DEFE 55/124. (BDP 22) Cattle Disease in N.W. Scotland (1 April 1943). Almost all the deaths occurred at Mellon Udrigle and Opinan some $3\frac{1}{2}$ miles from the burial dump at Gruinard.
66. PRO, WO188/654. Letter Fildes to Duff Cooper (22 March 1943).
67. PRO, WO188/654. Letter Duff Cooper to Fildes (17 March 1943).
68. PRO, WO188/654. Letter Fildes to Duff Cooper (14 April 1943).
69. Ibid.
70. PRO, WO188/654. Letter Duff Cooper to Fildes (19 April 1943).
71. PRO, WO188/654. Letter Fildes to Duff Cooper (22 April 1943). One further case of an anthrax outbreak after Gruinard is mentioned briefly in the open literature – at Isle Martin in September 1943. See WO188/654. TAY9555. E.C. Lloyd. Ministry of Agriculture and Fisheries to Fildes (18 May 1945). No further experimental work was carried out on the island after August 1943.
72. PRO, WO188/654. Notes on a meeting held at Lord Hankey's office on Friday 30 January 1942.
73. Ibid.
74. PRO WO188/654. Letter Professor Newitt to Fildes (12 February 1942).
75. PRO WO188/652. Porton Executive Committee. Notes of 1st Meeting (14 April 1942).
76. Ibid.
77. PRO, WO188/654. B Research and SOE Operational Requirements (20 July 1942).
78. PRO, WO188/654. Porton (Fildes). Notes on Professor Newitt's Memorandum of July 20th 1942 (17 August 1942). Fildes did not volunteer any information on the identity of these suitable materials.
79. PRO, WO188/654. Letter Fildes to Duff Cooper (1 February 1943).
80. Ibid.
81. PRO, WO188/652. Porton Executive Committee. Minutes of the 2nd Meeting (5 October 1942); Porton Executive Committee. Meeting to be Held at Porton on 5.10.42. Statement on the items of the Agenda by Dr Fildes.
82. PRO, WO188/652. Porton Executive Committee. Minutes of the 2nd Meeting (5 October 1942).
83. PRO, WO188/652. Porton Executive Committee. Meeting to be Held at Porton on 5.10.42. Statement on the items of the Agenda by Dr Fildes.
84. PRO, WO188/653. Note of an informal meeting on the 7th October 1942, in the Chancellor of the Duchy of Lancaster's Room.
85. PRO, WO188/652. Porton Executive Committee. Minutes of the 2nd Meeting (5 October 1942).
86. PRO, WO188/657. BW(D)43 War Cabinet bacteriological warfare (Defence) Subcommittee. 1st Meeting (9 March 1943).
87. Ibid.

88. PRO, WO188/657. BW(D)(43)4. War Cabinet bacteriological warfare (Defence) Subcommittee. Report by Dr Fildes (2 July 1943).
89. Although Bernstein notes that work had commenced in 1941 and only became substantial in 1942. See Bernstein, B. (1990) 'Origins of the Biological Warfare Program' in Wright, S. (ed.) *Preventing a Biological Arms Race* (Cambridge, Mass.: MIT Press). See also van Courtland Moon, J.E. (1999) 'US Biological Warfare Planning and Preparedness: the Dilemmas of Policy', in Geissler, E. and van Courtland Moon, J.E. (eds) *Biological and Toxin Weapons: Research, Development and Use from the Middle Ages to 1945* (Oxford: Oxford University Press).
90. PRO, WO188/654. Report of a visit by Dr Fildes and Dr Henderson to the US and Canada in November–December 1942.
91. Bernstein, op. cit.
92. PRO, WO188/653. Note of an informal meeting on the 7th October 1942, in the Chancellor of the Duchy of Lancaster's Room.
93. PRO, WO188/654. Letter Fildes to Allen (27 November 1943).
94. PRO, CAB136/1. Letter Lord Rothschild to Philip Allen (23 December 1943).
95. PRO, CAB127/18. Letter Lord Rothschild to General Ismay (21 April 1944).
96. PRO, WO188/657. Letter Fildes to Brown (10 January 1944).
97. PRO, CAB136/1. BW(O)44 Bacteriological Warfare Committee. Operational Panel. 1st Meeting (7 January 1944).
98. PRO, CAB136/1. Letter Rothschild to Allen (10 January 1944).
99. PRO, CAB 136/1. Allen to Stone (14 January 1944).
100. PRO, CAB 136/1. Memo by R.G. Peck (13 January 1944).
101. PRO, CAB136/1. Minute by Philip Allen, secretary of the BW Committee (15 January 1944).
102. PRO, CAB136/1. Minute by Philip Allen, secretary of the BW Committee (15 January 1944).
103. PRO, WO188/654. Letter Fildes to Brown (28 January 1944). See also CAB 121/103 Memorandum on BW Intelligence up to 1 September 1944 for a specific link inferred between the V-1 rockets and biological warfare.
104. PRO, WO188/654. Letter Fildes to Brown (28 January 1944).
105. PREM 3/65. From Chairman of the War Cabinet Committee on bacteriological warfare to Prime Minister (27 January 1944).
106. PRO, WO188/654. Letter Allen to Fildes (21 February 1944).
107. PRO, WO188/654. Letter Fildes to Allen (10 February 1944).
108. PRO, CAB127/200. Note to Prime Minister (25 February 1944).
109. Ibid.
110. PRO, PREM 3/65. Prime Minister to Chancellor of Duchy of Lancaster (8 March 1944).
111. Ibid.
112. PRO, WO188/654. Failure of BW Policy in the European Theatre. P. Fildes (6 June 1944).
113. Ibid.
114. Ibid.
115. PRO, WO188/654. Review of BW. GS Comments. (No date 1944).
116. PRO, WO188/654. BIO/5293. Notes on Professor Murray's Memorandum (by Fildes) (7 September 1944). Goforth had also written his comments as a response to this memo outlining the state of biological warfare in Canada.
117. PRO, CAB120/782. Letter Ismay to Prime Minister (22 May 1944).
118. PRO, WO188/654. Letter Fildes to Oswald (17 June 1944).

119. Ibid.
120. PRO, WO188/654. Letter Fildes to Brown (30 June 1944). Initial membership: Air Vice-Marshal N.H. Bottomley (DGAS) (Chair); Major-General G. Brunskill (War Office); Surgeon Vice-Admiral Sir Sheldon Dudley (MDG, Admiralty); Air Commodore G.H. Mills (Air Ministry); Mr J. Davidson Pratt (MoS); Secretaries: Captain G.H. Oswald (Offices of the War Cabinet); Lieut.-Col. O.H. Wansbrough-Jones (War Office).
121. PRO, WO188/654. Letter Bottomley to Fildes (11 July 1944).
122. PRO, WO188/654. Letter Fildes to Air Marshal Bottomley (17 July 1944).
123. Ibid.
124. Deichmann, U. (1996) *Biologists under Hitler* (Cambridge, Mass.: Harvard University Press) pp. 277–419; Geissler, E. (1999) 'Biological Warfare Activities in Germany, 1923–45' in Geissler, E. and van Courtland Moon, J.E. (eds) *Biological and Toxin Weapons: Research, Development and Use from the Middle Ages to 1945* (Oxford: Oxford University Press).
125. CAB 121/103 BW(45)10. Inter-Services Subcommittee on Biological Warfare. German Biological Warfare Preparations. Note by the Biological Warfare Intelligence Committee (4 June 1945); Inter-Services Subcommittee on Biological Warfare. German Biological Warfare Intelligence. Note by the Chairman, Biological Warfare Intelligence Committee. BW(45)28 (n.d.).
126. Kohler notes how Fildes' research before the Second World War was becoming less concerned with the physiology of infection and almost entirely focused on pure biochemistry. Likewise, his research team was increasingly populated by chemists and biochemists throughout the 1930s. See Kohler, R.E. (1985) 'Bacterial Physiology: the Medical Context', *Bulletin of the History of Medicine*, 59, 54–74.
127. Anthrax was well characterized, having been the first disease specifically linked to one causative microbe, and its hardy spores meant that it was likely to survive a bomb blast. However, even these characteristics would not have rendered anthrax obvious in advance. Although they made sense once the goal of research was a bomb, Fildes had first entertained the notion of spraying aerosols of agents but was limited by the available dissemination devices for chemical warfare which produced too coarse a spray for respiration. See Carter, G.B. and Pearson, G.S. (1999) 'British Biological Warfare and Biological Defence, 1925–45', in Geissler, E. and van Courtland Moon, J.E. (eds) *Biological and Toxin Weapons: Research, Development and Use from the Middle Ages to 1945* (Oxford: Oxford University Press).

4   The Growth of Biological Warfare Research

1. PRO, WO188/654. BIO/5198. Post War Work on BW. P. Fildes (22 August 1944).
2. Ibid.
3. Ibid.
4. Ibid.
5. PRO, WO188/654. Draft. Post War BW Organisation. P. Fildes (3 October 1944).
6. PRO, WO188/654. Memorandum for MRC on BW, Biology Section, Porton (15 November 1944). Emphasis in original.
7. Fildes had been elected as a Fellow of the Royal Society in 1934.
8. PRO, WO188/654. The Future of BW. P. Fildes (30 January 1945).

9. PRO, WO188/654. Research Policy in BW. DW Henderson (3 January 1945). Handwritten across the top are the words: 'Not accepted by Fildes. Not forwarded'.
10. Ibid.
11. Ibid.
12. PRO, WO188/654. Letter Fildes to Oswald (3 November 1944).
13. PRO WO188/654. Letter Fildes to Oswald (22 May 1945).
14. PRO, WO188/654. BIO/7106. To Secretary ISSCBW from Biology Section, Porton (14 August 1945).
15. Harris, R. and Paxman, J. (1982) *A Higher Form of Killing: the Secret Story of Gas and Germ Warfare* (London: Chatto and Windus).
16. PRO, DEFE 2/1252. COS(45)402(0). Report by Sir Henry Tizard's 'Ad Hoc' Committee (16 June 1945).
17. PRO, DEFE 2/1252. Chiefs of Staff Joint Technical Warfare Committee. Future Development of Biological Warfare (6 December 1945). Annex by O.H. Wansbrough-Jones (3 December 1945). Wansbrough-Jones, Sir Owen Haddon (1905–82). Wansbrough-Jones trained in chemistry and then joined the Army in January 1940. By 1945 he had become Director of Special Weapons and Vehicles and attained the rank of brigadier. The following year he became the Scientific Advisor to the Army Council. In 1951 he moved to the Ministry of Supply and held the post of Chief Scientist from 1953 to 1959, when he moved into the private sector until his retirement in 1969.
18. PRO, DEFE 2/1252. Chiefs of Staff Joint Technical Warfare Committee. Future Development of Biological Warfare (6 December 1945).
19. Ibid.
20. PRO, CAB121/103. Report from Chiefs of Staff to the Defence Committee. Biological Warfare. Annex BW(45)22 (14 September 1945).
21. PRO, CAB 121/103. (DO(45)15) Defence Committee. Biological Warfare (5 October 1945).
22. PRO, DEFE 10/26. DRP(50)53. DRPC. BW Policy. Note by the chairman, BW Subcommittee (11 May 1950).
23. PRO, DEFE 10/26. DRP(50)53. DRPC. BW Policy. Note by the chairman, BW Subcommittee (11 May 1950). See below for discussion of the various committees involved in the governance of BW.
24. See Falk, Richard (1990) 'Inhibiting Reliance on Biological Weaponry: the Role and Relevance of International Law', in Wright, S. (ed.) *Preventing a Biological Arms Race* (Cambridge, Mass.: MIT Press) pp. 240–66; McElroy, R.J. (1991) 'The Geneva Protocol of 1925', in Krepon, M. and Caldwell, D. (eds) *The Politics of Arms Control Treaty Ratification* (New York: St Martin's Press – now Palgrave) pp. 125–66.
25. PRO, WO195/9087. AC9091/BRB1, BRAB Constitution and Terms of Reference (11 July 1946).
26. The Advisory Council on Scientific Research and Technical Development, later the Scientific Advisory Council, presided over a number of committees besides BRAB, including (in 1959) boards for advising on chemical defence, guided weapons, radar and signals, weapons and explosives and agricultural defence.
27. PRO, WO188/667. BW(47)32. Chiefs of Staff Committee, BW Subcommittee, Division of Responsibilities (3 November 1947). See also Johnson, F.A. (1980) *Defence by Ministry* (London: Duckworth) for a more general account of the organization of Government defence.

28. Edgerton, D. (1992) 'Whatever Happened to the British Warfare State? The Ministry of Supply 1945–1951' in Mercer, H., Rollings, N. and Tomlinson, J.D. (eds) *Labour Governments and Private Industry: the Experience 1945–1951* (Edinburgh: Edinburgh University Press).

29. PRO, WO188/667. BW(47)32. Chiefs of Staff Committee, BW Subcommittee, Division of Responsibilities (3 November 1947); PRO, WO 188/660. BW(47) 3rd Meeting (30 April 1947).

30. PRO, WO188/667. BW(47)32. Chiefs of Staff Committee, BW Subcommittee, Division of Responsibilities (3 November 1947).

31. PRO, WO188/667. BW(47)32. Chiefs of Staff Committee, BW Subcommittee, Division of Responsibilities (3 November 1947). See Agar, Jon and Balmer, Brian (1998) 'British Scientists and the Cold War: the Defence Policy Research Committee and Information Networks, 1947–1963', *Historical Studies in the Physical Sciences*, 28, 209–52.

32. Tizard, Sir Henry Thomas (1885–1959). Tizard trained as a chemist and spent the First World War undertaking research in the Royal Flying Corps. In 1920 he was appointed as assistant secretary to the Department of Scientific and Industrial Research until 1929 when he moved to Imperial College as Rector until 1942. He is widely known for his advocacy for the R&D of radar. He also backed Frank Whittle's work on jet propulsion and Barnes Wallis' development of the bouncing bomb. During the Second World War he spent his time in official and informal capacities advising Whitehall and the Services on defence research matters. In 1947 Tizard became chair of the Advisory Council on Scientific Policy and the Defence Research Policy Committee (DRPC) until his retirement in 1952.

33. For a general discussion of this theme see Jasanoff, J. (1987) 'Contested Boundaries in Policy-Relevant Science', *Social Studies of Science*, 17, 195–230; also Krige, J. (1990) 'Scientists as Policymakers: British Physicists "Advice" to Their Government on Membership of CERN (1951–1952)' in Frängsmyr, T. (ed.) *Solomon's House Revisited: the Organization and Institutionalization of Science* (Canton, Mass.: Science History Publications USA) pp. 270–91.

34. PRO, WO188/667. BW(46)17. ISSBW. Future development of biological warfare research (memorandum by Dr Henderson) (30 April 1946).

35. Ibid.

36. Ibid.

37. Ibid.

38. PRO, DEFE 10/19. DRPC. Final Version of Paper on Future of Defence Research Policy (30 July 1947).

39. Agar, J. and Balmer, B. (1998) 'British Scientists and the Cold War: the Defence Policy Research Committee and Information Networks, 1947–1963', *Historical Studies in the Physicial Sciences*, 28, 209–52.

40. PRO, DEFE 2/1252. Chiefs of Staff Joint Planning Staff. Control of Atomic Energy. Report by the Joint Planning Staff (27 February 1946).

41. The commission had been established on 24 January 1946 to deal with 'the elimination from national armaments of atomic weapons and all other major weapons adaptable to mass destruction'. See SPRI (1971) *The Problem of Chemical and Biological Warfare*. Vol. IV: *CB Disarmament Negotiations 1920–1970* (Stockholm: Almqvist and Wiksell).

42. PRO WO188/662. Annex to BW(48)9(0)Final or COS(48)108(0). BW Subcommittee Report to the Chiefs of Staff on the attitude to be adopted by representatives of the Atomic Energy Commission (10 May 1948).

43. Ibid.
44. Ibid.
45. Ibid.
46. PRO, WO188/662. BW(48)11(0) US Policy Document on BW (31 May 1948). It is not clear what the full title, remit or influence of this committee was.
47. PRO, WO188/662. BW(48)12(0). International Aspects of Biological Warfare (4 June 1948).
48. Ibid.
49. Ibid.
50. PRO, AIR20/11355. 1949 Report on BW. BW(49)40. 2nd Draft (27 January 1950). Note from W.F. Lamb.
51. PRO, DEFE 10/18. DRP (47) 53. DRPC. Future Defence Policy. 1 May 1947.
52. PRO, WO188/664. AC10911/BRB83. BRAB. Report on BW Policy (3 May 1950). Appendix. Extract from 1947 report on Biological Warfare BW (47) 20 Final.
53. PRO, DEFE 10/18. DRP (47) 53. DRPC. Future Defence Policy. 1 May 1947.
54. PRO, DEFE 10/19. DRPC. Final Version of Paper on Future of Defence Research Policy (30 July 1947).
55. PRO, WO 188/660. ISSBW. Shortage of Scientific Staff for Research in Biological Warfare (30 January 1947).
56. PRO, WO 188/704. Letter from Dr H.B. Hulme to Henderson (27 November 1946).
57. PRO, WO 188/660. Annex to BW(47)14. 1947 Statement by BRAB. Air Staff Requirement. Anti-personnel bomb for strategic use (24 April 1947). The causative agents of anthrax, brucellosis and botulism were considered for such a weapon by BRAB. More research was judged to be necessary in each case.
58. PRO, DEFE 10/18. DRP (47) 53. DRPC. Future Defence Policy. 1 May 1947.
59. PRO, WO188/660. BW(47)1st Meeting. 5 February 1947.
60. PRO. WO188/660. BW(47)12. Shortage of Scientific Staff and Equipment for Research on Biological Warfare (27 March 1947).
61. PRO, DEFE 10/19. DRPC. Final Version of Paper on Future of Defence Research Policy. 30 July 1947.
62. PRO, WO188/660. Chiefs of Staff Committee, BW Subcommittee. Note by Ministry of Supply (17 November 1947).
63. PRO, WO 188/660. BW(47)8. ISSBW. Shortage of Scientific Staff for Research in Biological Warfare (30 January 1947).
64. PRO, WO188/660. BW(47)3. ISSBW. BW Information for Service Personnel (12 February 1947).
65. Ibid.
66. PRO, WO188/662. BW(48)5(0). Technical Aspects of the International Control of BW. Report of the ad hoc panel convened by Dr F.J. Wilkins, DCRD (MoS) (23 February 1948).
67. PRO, WO188/661. Annex to BW(48)38 Final. 1948 Report on Biological Warfare (26 October 1948).
68. PRO, WO188/662. BW(48)9(0)Final or COS(48)108(0). BW Subcommittee Report to the Chiefs of Staff on the attitude to be adopted by representatives of the Atomic Energy Commission (10 May 1948).
69. PRO, WO188/662. BW(48)14(0). Report on Capabilities of Biological Warfare (2 September 1948).
70. Ibid.
71. Ibid.

72. PRO, WO188/662. BW(48)13(0). Technical Aspects of Biological Warfare (5 June 1948).
73. PRO, WO 188/704. Letter Wing Commander Lamb to Henderson (31 March 1947).
74. PRO, WO188/705. BW/4/35. Biological Warfare Meeting with Dr Haskins (20 April 1948).
75. PRO, DEFE 10/37. DRP(49). DRPC. 18th Meeting (6 December 1949).
76. PRO, WO188/663. BW(49)38. BW Subcommittee. Defence Research and Development Policy. Intelligence and Russian Development (14 October 1949).
77. Ibid.
78. PRO, WO188/663. BW(49)35. BW Subcommittee. Present State of Progress in Biological Warfare in Foreign Countries (10 August 1949). This contains a report from the JIC: 'Evidence of Soviet Interest in Saboteur Methods of BW' (4 August 1949).
79. Ibid.
80. PRO, WO188/663. BW(49)38. BW Subcommittee. Defence Research and Development Policy. Intelligence and Russian Development (14 October 1949).
81. PRO, WO188/663. BW(49) 5th Meeting. BW Subcommittee (31 October 1949). The statement is not clear considering that the US level of production of weapons in 1945 was zero.
82. PRO, WO188/663. BW(49) 5th Meeting. BW Subcommittee (31 October 1949).
83. BW(49)41 Final. Research and Development Policy in Relation to Intelligence and Russian Development. Report to the Defence Research Policy Committee (29 November 1949).
84. PRO, WO188/667. AC9554/BRB33. BRAB. Review of Work done by the Board during the Year 1947 (19 November 1947).
85. Ibid.
86. PRO, WO188/661. BW(48)22 BW Subcommittee. Mass Immunisation, Note by the Ministry of Health (31 May 1948).
87. Ibid.
88. PRO, WO188/661. BW(48)27(Final) BW Subcommittee. Biological Warfare – Civil Defence (29 June 1948).
89. PRO, WO 188/663. BW(49)8. BW Subcommittee. Civil Defence (3 March 1949).
90. PRO, WO188/663. BW(49)12. BW Subcommittee. Civil Defence (31 March 1949).
91. PRO, WO188/663. BW Subcommittee BW(49) 3rd Meeting (6 May 1949).
92. PRO, WO188/668. AC10875, BRAB 16th Meeting (16 March 1950).
93. PRO, WO188/668. AC11427/BRB88. BRAB. Memorandum on the Recruitment of Staff for Research in BW. Sir Paul Fildes (3 May 1951).
94. PRO, WO188/667. AC9554/BRB33. BRAB. Review of Work done by the Board during the Year 1947 (19 November 1947).
95. PRO, WO188/660. BW(47)8. ISSBW. Shortage of Scientific Staff for Research in Biological Warfare (30 January 1947). Annex II (dated 13 March 1947). Comments by DRPC.
96. PRO, WO188/667. AC9589/BRB38. The Requirements of the Biological Research Advisory Board of the Ministry of Supply in 'Microbiology', Sir Paul Fildes FRS (20 November 1947).
97. PRO, WO188/667. AC9523/25. University Facilities for Microbiology, Note by Sir Paul Fildes (9 October 1947).
98. Ibid.

99. PRO, WO188/667. Enclosure I to AC9464/BRB23. Microbiology Developments in Universities, 1947. Note by the Vice-Chairman of the University Grants Committee. 21 August 1947.
100. PRO, WO188/661. BW(48)4. BW Subcommittee. Research Programme for 1948 for the Micro-Biological Research Department, Porton (15 January 1948).
101. Florey, Howard Walter, Baron Florey (1898–1968). Nobel prize-winner, Florey is most celebrated for taking forward Fleming's studies of *Penicillium* mould and turning it into a working disease treatment. He was appointed head of the William Dunn School of Pathology at Oxford in 1935, elected FRS in 1941, knighted in 1944 and raised to the peerage in 1965.
102. PRO, WO188/661. BW(48)4. BW Subcommittee. Research Programme for 1948 for the Micro-Biological Research Department, Porton (15 January 1948).
103. Ibid.
104. PRO, WO188/661. BW(48)7 BW Subcommittee. New Laboratories at the MRD Porton (13 February 1948).
105. PRO, WO188/661BW(48)11(Final). BW Subcommittee. Recruitment of Scientific Staff and Construction of New Laboratories at the Microbiological Research Department, Porton. Report to the Chiefs of Staff (10 April 1948).
106. PRO, WO188/668. AC10911/BRB83, Report on BW Policy (4 May 1950).
107. PRO, WO188/668. AC11260/BRBM19, BRAB 19th Meeting (21 December 1950).
108. PRO, WO188/668. AC11427/BRB88. BRAB. Memorandum on the recruitment of staff for research in BW. Sir Paul Fildes (3 May 1951).
109. Ibid.
110. PRO, WO188/668. AC11472/BRBM20, BRAB 20th Meeting (3 May 1951).
111. Anon, 'Bacterial Warfare', *The Lancet*, 5 March 1949.
112. PRO, WO188/663. BW(49)16. BW Subcommittee. Discussion with US and Canadian Representatives (28 April 1949).
113. PRO, WO188/663. BW Subcommittee BW(49) 3rd Meeting. (6 May 1949).
114. PRO, WO188/663. BW(49)21. BW Subcommittee. Biological Warfare – Publicity (14 June 1949).
115. See Carter, G. (1992) *Porton Down: 75 Years of Chemical and Biological Research* (London: HMSO); PRO, WO 195/11643. AC11647/BRB91. BRAB. Report by the Chairman on the Work of the Board during 1951 (10 November 1951).
116. PRO, DEFE 10/25. DRPC (49) 134. Plant for Experiments in the Bulk Production of BW Agents. Report by the BW Subcommittee (15 November 1949); PRO, WO188/668. Amendments to AC10522/BRB70. Report on Plant for Experimentation on Bulk Production of Bacteria (28 September 1949); PRO, WO188/668. AC11260/BRBM19, BRAB 19th Meeting (21 December 1950).

5 Project Red Admiral

1. The term 'Red Admiral' appears rarely in the open literature. It is most directly attributed to the bomb project in a 1952 DRPC Review of R&D mentioned in PRO, AIR 20/8727. O.R. 1065. Minute from Dr O.H. Wansbrough-Jones, Ministry of Supply to 'W' (20 June 1952).
2. PRO, WO188/660. Chiefs of Staff Committee, BW Subcommittee. Note by Ministry of Supply (17 November 1947).
3. PRO, WO188/667. BW(46)17. ISSBW. Future development of biological warfare research (memo by Dr Henderson) (30 April 1946).

4. PRO, AIR 20/8727. OR/1006. Air Staff Requirement for a Biological Bomb (November 1946).
5. PRO, AIR 20/8733. An Assessment of the Potential Value of Biological Warfare (Draft) (19 January 1947).
6. Ibid.
7. Ibid.
8. Ibid.
9. Ibid.
10. Ibid.
11. PRO, WO 188/660. Annex to BW(47)14. 1947 Statement by BRAB. Air Staff Requirement. Anti-personnel bomb for strategic use (24 April 1947). It is curious that BRAB refer to botulism rather than botulinum toxin in this report.
12. PRO, WO 188/660. Annex to BW(47)14. 1947 Statement by BRAB. Air Staff Requirement. Anti-personnel bomb for strategic use (24 April 1947).
13. PRO, WO188/667. BW(46)17. ISSBW. Future development of biological warfare research (memo by Dr Henderson) (30 April 1946).
14. PRO, WO 188/660. Annex to BW(47)14. 1947 Statement by BRAB. Air Staff Requirement. Anti-personnel bomb for strategic use (24 April 1947).
15. PRO, AIR 20/8727. Air Staff Requirement for a Biological Bomb. Note from G. Combe (AVM) (D.G. Arm) (10 May 1947).
16. PRO, AIR 20/8727. Air Staff Requirement No. OR/ (Draft)(1947).
17. PRO, AIR 20/8727. O.R. 1065. Minute from Dr O.H. Wansbrough-Jones, Ministry of Supply to 'W' (20 June 1952).
18. PRO, AIR 20/8727. Minute. Air Ministry File No. CMS 865. D.G. Arm. (25 October 1947).
19. Probably the toxin ricin which was being researched at the the time.
20. PRO, AIR 20/8727. Air Staff Requirement No. OR/1065 (12 November 1947).
21. PRO, AIR 20/8727. Notes on DOR(A)'s Air Staff Requirement for a Strategic Toxic Weapon (27 October 1947).
22. PRO, AIR 20/8727. Air Staff Requirement No. OR/1065 (12 November 1947).
23. Ibid.
24. PRO, DEFE 10/22. DRP(48)116. DRPC. Timetable Forecast for Toxicological Warfare Development (9 August 1948).
25. PRO, AIR 20/8733. Paper on the Theoretical Effectiveness of BW Weapons against Potential Enemy Targets in Comparison with the Effect of Atomic Bombs on the Same Targets (no date. With 1948 papers).
26. Ibid.
27. Ibid.
28. Ibid.
29. See PRO, AIR 20/8733. Notes on Biological and Atomic Weapons – Comparative Cost and Ease of Production (March 1948 – date deleted).
30. PRO, AIR 20/11355. 1949 Report on Biological Warfare. Section V. The Practical Requirements for Offence and Defence. Air Ministry Draft Contribution (November 1949).
31. PRO, WO 189/261. Particulate Dispersion (B.W.). Porton Memorandum No. 40 (28 July 1950).
32. PRO, WO 188/665. BW(51)39. BW Subcommittee. BW Report 1950–1951 (7 December 1951); PRO, WO 189/261. Particulate Dispersion (B.W.). Porton Memorandum No. 40 (28 July 1950).

33. PRO, AIR 20/8727. O.R.1065. Minute from Dr O.H. Wansbrough-Jones, Ministry of Supply to 'W' (20 June 1952).
34. PRO, WO 188/663. BW(49) 4th Meeting. BW Subcommittee. (23 June 1949).
35. Ibid.
36. Ibid.
37. PRO, WO 188/705. Letter from Wansbrough-Jones to Henderson (19 March 1952).
38. PRO, WO 188/665. BW(51)1st Meeting. BW Subcommittee (19 January 1951).
39. PRO, WO 188/665. BW(51)39. BW Subcommittee. BW Report 1950–1951 (7 December 1951).
40. Ibid.
41. Ibid.
42. Ibid.
43. Ibid.
44. Ibid.
45. Ibid.
46. PRO, WO 188/666. BW(53)19 BW Subcommittee. Biological Warfare Report 1951–September 1953 (8 December 1953).
47. Ibid.
48. Ibid.
49. PRO, AIR 20/11355. From D.N. Roberts (Air Commodore. D. of Ops. to the Joint Secretaries BW Subcommittee (CMS.942/Ops.(B)3) (July 1953).
50. PRO, AIR 20/8727. Air Staff Target O.R. 1065. Biological Warfare Agents and Weapons, and the Associated Problems of their Storage and Handling under Storage Conditions. CMS.2484/54 (16 July 1954).
51. Ibid.
52. Ibid.
53. Ibid.
54. PRO, WO188/667. SAC373/BRB.AG1. BRAB 1st Meeting Agenda (25 July 1946).
55. PRO, WO188/667. AC9093/BRB3. BRAB. Facilities for the 'large scale' production of micro-organisms. Memo by Dr D.W. Henderson. Chief Superintendent MRD Porton (15 July 1946).
56. Ibid.
57. Ibid.
58. PRO, WO188/660. Chiefs of Staff Committee, BW Subcommittee. Note by Ministry of Supply (17 November 1947).
59. PRO, WO188/667. AC9554/BRB33. BRAB. Review of work done by the Board during the year 1947 (19 November 1947).
60. PRO, WO188/660. BW(47)42. Research Programme for 1948 of the Microbiological Research Department, Porton Memo by the Chief Superintendent (17 December 1947).
61. PRO, WO188/661. BW(48)4. BW Subcommittee. Research Programme for 1948 for the Micro-Biological Research Department, Porton (15 January 1948).
62. Ibid.
63. Ibid.
64. PRO, DEFE 10/25. DRPC (49) 134. Plant for Experiments in the Bulk Production of BW Agents. Report by the BW Subcommittee (15 November 1949). The plant capacity was six 112-litre batch fermentors. See Carter, G. and Balmer, B. (1999) 'Chemical and Biological Warfare and Defence, 1945–90' in Bud, R. and Gummett, P. (eds) *Cold War, Hot Science: Applied Research in*

Britain's Defence Laboratories 1945–1990 (Amsterdam: Harwood Academic Publishers).

65. PRO, WO188/668. AC11191/BRB84 (16 November 1950). Large-scale growth of bacteria could either be performed on a batch-by-batch basis or, more efficiently, on an ongoing continuous basis.
66. PRO, WO188/668. AC11641/BRB92. BW Annual Report 1950–51 (4 December 1951).
67. PRO, WO188/668. Amendments to AC10522/BRB70 (28 September 1948).
68. Ibid.
69. PRO, WO188/663. BW (49) 5th Meeting. BW Subcommittee. (31 October 1949).
70. Ibid.
71. PRO, DEFE 10/37. DRPC 17th Meeting (22 November 1949).
72. PRO, DEFE 10/25. DRPC (49) 134. Plant for Experiments in the Bulk Production of BW Agents. Report by the BW Subcommittee (15 November 1949).
73. PRO, DEFE 10/26. DRP (50) 14, Annex 2 (1st February 1950) (Annex dated 23rd January 1950).
74. Ibid.
75. Ibid.
76. Ibid.
77. Ibid.
78. Ibid.
79. PRO, DEFE 10/26. DRP (50) 14, Annex 1 (1st February 1950). (Annex dated 15th December 1949).
80. Ibid.
81. PRO, DEFE 10/26. DRP (50) 14, Annex 2 (1st February 1950). (Annex dated 23rd January 1950).
82. PRO, WO188/668. AC10875, BRAB 16th Meeting (16 March 1950).
83. PRO, WO188/668. AC10911/BRB83, Report on BW Policy (4 May 1950).
84. PRO, WO188/664. 100/BW/4/37. BW Subcommittee Meeting (8 May 1950).
85. PRO, WO188/664. 100/BW/4/37. BW Subcommittee Meeting (8 May 1950); WO188/668. AC10930/BRBM17, BRAB 17th Meeting (20 April 1950). Financial priorities fell outside of the ambit of BRAB, so it is likely that Crawford would not have consulted with them at all had economics been the only consideration.
86. Gowing, M. (1974) *Independence and Deterrence: Britain and Atomic Energy 1945–52*. Vol. 1 (London: Macmillan – now Palgrave).
87. PRO, WO188/668. AC10930/BRBM17, BRAB 17th Meeting (20 April 1950).
88. Ibid.
89. The argument was further strengthened by mentioning research cuts in the chemical weapons field prior to the Second World War.
90. PRO, WO188/668. AC10911/BRB83, Report on BW Policy (4 May 1950).
91. PRO, WO188/664. 100/BW/4/37. BW Subcommittee Meeting (8 May 1950).
92. PRO, DEFE 10/26. DRP(50)53. DRPC. BW Policy. Note by the chairman, BW Subcommittee (11 May 1950).
93. Ibid.
94. For a more detailed discussion of the uses of uncertainty in weapons research policy, see Mackenzie, D. (1993) *Inventing Accuracy: a Historical Sociology of Nuclear Missile Guidance* (London: The MIT Press) Ch. 7.
95. PRO, DEFE 10/26. DRP(50)53. DRPC. BW Policy. Note by the chairman, BW Subcommittee (11 May 1950).
96. Ibid.

97. Ibid.
98. Ibid.
99. Ibid.
100. PRO, WO188/. 117/BW/4/37. Biological Warfare Policy (9 June 1950). Attached extract from DRP(50) 11th Meeting of DRPC (16 May 1950).
101. Ibid.
102. Ibid.
103. Ibid.
104. PRO, WO188/664. 123/BW/4/37. Biological Warfare (24 June 1950). Annex B. Extract from COS(50) 87th Meeting (13 June 1950).
105. PRO, WO188/668. AC11260/BRBM19, BRAB 19th Meeting (21 December 1950).
106. PRO, WO188/664. BW(50) 3rd Meeting (21 August 1950).
107. PRO, WO188/664. BW(50) 3rd Meeting (21 August 1950); WO188/664. 123/BW/4/37. Biological Warfare (24 June 1950). Annex B. Extract from COS(50) 87th Meeting (13 June 1950).
108. PRO, WO188/668. AC11260/BRBM19, BRAB 19th Meeting (21 December 1950).
109. PRO, WO188/664. BW(50)38. BW Subcommittee. Experimental Plant No.2 – Microbiological Research Department, Porton (30 December 1950).
110. PRO, WO188/668. AC11872/BRBM25, BRAB 25th Meeting (14 May 1952).
111. PRO, WO195/12136. AC12140/BRB105. MRD Annual Report 1951–1952.
112. PRO, WO188/668. AC11950/BRBM26, BRAB 26th Meeting (12 July 1952).
113. PRO, WO188/666. BW(52)1st Meeting (19 June 1952).
114. PRO, WO188/666. BW(52)7. BW Subcommittee. Biological Warfare (1 May 1952).
115. PRO, WO188/666. BW(52) 1st Meeting (19 June 1952).
116. Ibid.
117. The delegation consisted of Dodds, Morgan, Spooner, Wilson Smith, McClurkin and Henderson.
118. PRO, WO188/668. AC 12127/BRBM27, BRAB 27th Meeting (6 December 1952).
119. BRAB record that $90m. had been spent on the plant.
120. PRO, WO188/668. AC12890/BRBM32, BRAB 32nd Meeting (15 June 1954).
121. Ibid.
122. Ibid.
123. PRO, WO195/12976. AC12980/BRB130. BRAB: Report of Work of Board for 1954.
124. PRO, WO195/13460. AC13646/BRB139. Report by the Chairman on the Work of the Board during the Year 1955 (7 November 1955).
125. PRO, WO188/670. AC13332/BRB.M34. BRAB 34th Meeting (4 June 1955).
126. Ibid.
127. PRO, WO188/670. AC13524/BRB.M35. BRAB 35th Meeting (5 December 1955).
128. PRO, WO195/13822. AC13826/BRB145. Report by the Chairman on the work of the Board during the year 1956 (5 November 1956).
129. See Bud, R. (1993) *The Uses of Life: a History of Biotechnology* (Cambridge: Cambridge University Press) pp. 111–16.
130. PRO, WO195/14357. MRE Annual Report 1956–1958.
131. PRO, WO195/14811. AC14820/BRB172. BRAB Report 1959.
132. Ibid.
133. PRO, WO195/15382. SAC457/BRB210. MRE Annual Report 1961–62.

6 Trials For Biological Warfare

1. PRO, WO188/657. BIO/6288. Proposal for Certain Trials at Sea (14 December 1944).
2. PRO, WO188/667. BW(46)17. ISSBW. Future development of biological warfare research (memo by Dr Henderson) (30 April 1946).
3. PRO, WO188/667. AC9554/BRB33. BRAB. Review of Work done by the Board during the Year 1947 (19 November 1947).
4. PRO, WO 188/663. BW/4/2. Naval Report on Operation 'Harness' by Captain G.S. Tuck (June 1949).
5. PRO, WO188/661. BW(48)4. BW Subcommittee. Research Programme for 1948 for the Microbiological Research Department, Porton (15 January 1948).
6. PRO, WO 188/660. BW(47)42. Research Programme for 1948 of the Microbiological Research Department, Porton. Memo by the Chief Superintendent (17 December 1947).
7. PRO, WO 188/661. BW(48)1. Security Policy and Cover Plan for Operation Harness (2 January 1948).
8. Ibid.
9. PRO, WO 188/661. BW(48)26 (Final) BW Subcommittee. Biological Warfare Trials. Security Policy and Cover Plan (22 June 1948).
10. PRO, WO 188/661. BW(48) 1st Meeting. BW Subcommittee (23 March 1948).
11. Ibid.
12. PRO, WO 188/661. BW(48)12. BW Subcommittee. Reconnaissance for Operation Harness (9 April 1948).
13. PRO, WO 188/663. BW/4/2. Naval Report on Operation 'Harness' by Captain G.S. Tuck (June 1949).
14. PRO, WO 188/661. Note of a Meeting held on Wednesday 14 April 1948 in the Ministry of Defence to discuss the Security Policy and Cover Plan for Operation Harness.
15. PRO, WO 188/661. BW(48)20. BW Subcommittee. Operation Harness – Medical Arrangements (28 May 1948).
16. PRO, WO 188/663. BW/4/2. Naval Report on Operation 'Harness' by Captain G.S. Tuck (June 1949).
17. PRO, WO 188/661. BW(48) 4th Meeting. BW Subcommittee (19 October 1948).
18. PRO, WO 188/661. BW(48)44. BW Subcommittee. Operation Harness. Note by the Medical Director-General, Admiralty (5 November 1948). The organisms listed are, respectively, plague (assuming that the '*B*' should read 'P' for *Pasteurella pestis*), *Actinobacillus mallei* responsible for glanders, and 'parrot fever' a form of pneumonia usually restricted to birds but capable of infecting humans; psittacosis is no longer considered to be a virus.
19. PRO, WO 188/661. BW(48)51. BW Subcommittee. Operation Harness – Security (23 December 1948).
20. PRO, WO 188/663. BW/4/2. Naval Report on Operation 'Harness' by Captain G.S. Tuck (June 1949).
21. The naval report records that 'Before this became a disciplinary matter the rating, who had a decidedly neurotic temperament, solved the problem by dropping a hatch on his foot and being removed to hospital.'
22. There are four species of *Brucella* capable of infecting humans, the specific one used is not identified.
23. PRO, WO 188/663. BW/4/2. Naval Report on Operation 'Harness' by Captain G.S. Tuck (June 1949).

24. Ibid.
25. PRO, DEFE10/263. BW(49)15. Operation Harness 1947–1949. Scientific Report (20 July 1949).
26. PRO, WO 188/663. BW/4/2. Naval Report on Operation 'Harness' by Captain G.S. Tuck (June 1949). Part II. Medical Report.
27. Ibid.
28. PRO, WO 188/663. BW(49) BW Subcommittee. 2nd Meeting (18 February 19). The common name for brucellosis is undulant fever. There is no written indication as to whether or not this was the name reported to the technician's family.
29. PRO, WO 188/663. Extract from a letter dated 30.12.48 from Mr R. Kingham.
30. PRO, DEFE10/263. BW(49)15. Operation Harness 1947–1949. Scientific Report (20 July 1949).
31. PRO, DEFE10/263. BW(49)15. Operation Harness 1947–1949. Scientific Report (20 July 1949); PRO, WO 188/663. BW(49)33 (Final) BW Subcommittee. BW Trials at Sea – Operation Harness. Report to the Chiefs of Staff and the Defence Research Policy Committee (18 August 1949).
32. PRO, WO 188/663. BW(49)28. BW Subcommittee. Operation Harness (20 June 1949).
33. PRO, WO 188/663. BW(49)30. BW Subcommittee. Operation Harness (21 June 1949).
34. PRO, WO188/663. BW(49)7. Chiefs of Staff Committee. BW Subcommittee. Biological Warfare Trials at Sea (28 February 1949).
35. PRO, WO188/663. BW Subcommittee BW(49) 3rd Meeting (6 May 1949).
36. Wright, S. (1990) 'Evolution of Biological Warfare Policy: 1945–1990', in Wright, S. (ed.) *Preventing a Biological Arms Race* (Cambridge, Mass.: MIT Press).
37. PRO, WO188/668. AC10875, BRAB 16th Meeting (16 March 1950).
38. The Canadians had concluded that the particles in the 4 lb bomb were 'far too large'. See PRO, WO188/665. BW(51)1st Meeting. BW Subcommittee (19 January 1951).
39. PRO, WO188/665. BW(51)7. BW Subcommittee. Field Trials with BW Agents. Report to the Chiefs of Staff (13 February 1951).
40. PRO, WO188/668. AC10875, BRAB 16th Meeting (16 March 1950).
41. PRO, WO188/668. BRB.SC.7, Report on Field Trials (28 March 1950).
42. PRO, WO188/668. AC11260/BRBM19, BRAB 19th Meeting (21 December 1950).
43. PRO, WO188/665. BW(51)7. BW Subcommittee. Field Trials with BW Agents. Report to the Chiefs of Staff (13 February 1951).
44. PRO, WO188/665. BW(51)1st Meeting. BW Subcommittee (19 January 1951).
45. PRO, WO188/665. BW(51)31. BW Subcommittee. BW Field Trials (1 October 1951).
46. PRO, WO188/668. AC11641/BRB92. BRAB. BW Annual Report 1950–51 (28 November 1951).
47. The pontoon contained 24 watertight compartments, some flooded and some used for tests. It was proposed that during live trials some men would remain in gas-tight compartments on the pontoon. The pontoon specified in one advance report on the tests would be 67 by 20 yards, and 10 feet deep, made of mulberry, and flooded in order to list it. A 25-yard arc of sampling points was fixed on deck and the source was to be placed at the end of a floating boom projecting from the pontoon. PRO, WO188/668. AC11641/BRB92. BRAB. BW Annual Report 1950–51 (28 November 1951).

48. PRO, WO188/665. BW(51)31. BW Subcommittee. BW Field Trials (1 October 1951). It is highly unlikely that this trial used pathogens as the proposals for 1952 mentioned that this new technique could not be proven until 'hot' trials were carried out. Whether the small trial in Shanklin Bay used simulant organisms or inert particles is not mentioned.
49. PRO, WO188/668. AC11560/BRBM22, BRAB 22nd Meeting (31 August 1951), Annex 2.
50. It was reported elsewhere that two seasons of pathogen trials at Suffield and Dugway with *B. suis* had shown that the observed versus theoretical dosage (dispersal efficiency) was 'poor', whereas the infectivity of the cloud was 'good'. See PRO, WO188/668. AC11641/BRB92. BRAB. BW Annual Report 1950–51 (28 November 1951). The 4 lb bomb was also reported at the end of 1951 to be one-fifth as good as predicted. See PRO, WO188/668. AC11714/BRBM23. BRAB 23rd Meeting (8 December 1951).
51. PRO, WO 195/10488. AC10492/BRB68. BRAB. Weapon Development and Testing. Memorandum by CS/MRD (20 July 1949).
52. PRO, WO188/668. AC11641/BRB92. BW Annual Report 1950–51 (4 December 1951).
53. PRO, WO188/668. AC11560/BRBM22, BRAB 22nd Meeting (31 August 1951).
54. Ibid.
55. Ibid. This and the other conclusions are paraphrased from Wansbrough-Jones' original memo, included as annex 1 to the minutes.
56. PRO, WO188/665. BW(51)4th Meeting. BW Subcommittee (2 November 1951).
57. PRO, WO188/665. BW(51)39. BW Subcommittee. BW Report 1950–1951 (7 December 1951).
58. PRO, WO188/668. AC11560/BRBM22, BRAB 22nd Meeting (31 August 1951). *Pasteurella pestis* has been designated *Yersinia pestis* since 1970.
59. PRO, WO188/668. AC11817/BRBM24, BRAB 24th Meeting (9 April 1952).
60. The possibility of using Venezuelan equine encephalitis (VEE) in the Cauldron tests was also raised in this discussion.
61. PRO, WO188/665. BW(51)1st Meeting. BW Subcommittee (19 January 1951).
62. PRO, WO188/666. BW(52)2. BW Subcommittee. Field Trials with BW Agents (12 February 1952). Appended extract from the COS (52) 23rd Meeting (8 February 1952).
63. PRO, WO188/666. BW(52)1 BW Subcommittee. Field Trials with BW Agents (29 January 1952).
64. Ibid.
65. PRO, WO188/666. BW(53)5 BW Subcommittee. Trials with BW Agents in the Bahamas. Memorandum by the Ministry of Supply (17 June 1953).
66. PRO, WO188/668. AC12059/BRB99 BW Field Trials at Sea. Comments by Sir Paul Fildes and Lord Stamp on PDSR(D)'s note BR./25b/82 (6 November 1952); AC12089/BRB103. Further Comments by Sir Paul Fildes and Lord Stamp on Operation Cauldron (25 November 1952).
67. Short-range trials involved distances of 25 yards: PRO, WO188/668. AC12166/BRB107. BRAB. Operation Hesperus 1953. Draft Programme (29 January 1953).
68. PRO, WO188/668, Appendix to AC12059/BRB99. BRAB. Trials at Sea – Future Policy (13 August 1952).
69. PRO, WO188/668, AC12089/BRB103 Further Comments by Sir Paul Fildes and Lord Stamp on Operation Cauldron (25 November 1952).
70. PRO, WO188/668, Appendix to AC12059/BRB99. BRAB. Trials at Sea – Future Policy (13 August 1952).

71. PRO, WO188/666. BW(52)2nd Meeting. BW Subcommittee (12 December 1952).
72. PRO, WO188/668. AC12128/BRB10. BRAB. Some Observations on the Planning of Future Trials, with particular reference to long distance trials and weapon development by Lord Stamp (30 December 1952).
73. Morton added that efficiency trials already formed part of the Hesperus plans.
74. PRO, WO188/668. MRD Report No.7 (8 May 1953).
75. PRO, WO188/668. AC12384/BRBM29, BRAB 29th Meeting (12 June 1953).
76. The comment about *Brucella suis* was echoed by Henderson who reported that the infecting dose in the field was a third that in the laboratory, although he blamed sampling equipment for this result. Poor recovery rates of *P. pestis* were eventually attributed to high humidity. However, similarly poor recovery rates with *Bacterium tularense* in the 1953 Hesperus trials suggested that humidity was not the factor responsible for the *P. pestis* results. Although *P. pestis* was still discounted on the grounds that it required large doses for infection. PRO, WO188/668. AC12459/BRB114. Operation Hesperus. Summary of Results (14 October 1953).
77. PRO, WO188/668. AC12166/BRB107. Operation Hesperus 1953 (19 January 1953). The long-range trials were to be performed mostly without animals.
78. *Bacterium tularense*, the causative agent of tularemia, is currently designated *Francisella tularensis*.
79. PRO, WO188/668. AC12227/BRBM28, BRAB 28th Meeting (10 February 1953).
80. Ibid.
81. PRO, WO188/668. AC12384/BRBM29, BRAB 29th Meeting (12 June 1953).
82. Ibid.
83. Hughes, S.S. (1977) *The Virus: a History of the Concept* (London: Heinemann). Hughes notes that between 1948 and 1959 the number of specifically human viruses known rose from 20 to 70.
84. PRO, WO188/665. BW(51)32. BW Subcommittee. Biological Warfare – Soviet Threat (4 October 1951).
85. PRO, WO188/668. AC11950/BRBM26. BRAB 26th Meeting (12 July 1952).
86. PRO, WO188/668. AC12127/BRBM27. BRAB 27th Meeting (6 December 1952).
87. Ibid.
88. PRO, WO188/668. AC12458/BRB113. BRAB. Viruses as BW Agents by Professor Wilson Smith (13 October 1953).
89. All of these were classified as viral in origin at this time.
90. PRO, WO188/668. AC12595/BRBM30, BRAB 30th Meeting (6–7 November 1953).
91. PRO, WO195/12976. AC12980/BRB130. BRAB Report on the Work of the Board during the Year 1954 (5 November 1954).
92. PRO, WO188/668. AC12384/BRBM29, BRAB 29th Meeting (12 June 1953).
93. PRO, WO188/668. MRD Report No. 7 (8 May 1953).
94. PRO, WO188/668. AC12384/BRBM29, BRAB 29th Meeting (12 June 1953).
95. PRO, ADM 1/24928. Report on Operation Hesperus (11 September 1953).
96. PRO, WO188/668. AC12459/BRB114. Operation Hesperus. Summary of Results (14 October 1953).
97. Ibid.
98. PRO, WO188/668. AC12526/BRB118. BRAB Report by the Chairman on the Work of the Board during the Year 1953 (27 October 1953).
99. PRO, WO188/668. AC12595/BRBM30, BRAB 30th Meeting (6–7 November 1953).

100. As mentioned earlier the causative agent of *Psittacosis* is no longer classified as a virus.
101. PRO, WO188/666. BW(53) 1st Meeting. BW Subcommittee (23 June 1953).
102. The costs had been estimated at £11 000 to the Ministry of Supply. The decision by the Air Ministry would add a further £15 000 to provide one flight a fortnight for the duration of the trials and an unspecified amount for Admiralty services. Crawford had estimated very roughly that £100 000 would be charged to R&D although he thought 'this might be on the high side'. PRO, WO188/666. BW(53) 1st Meeting. BW Subcommittee (23 June 1953).
103. PRO, ADM 1/27325. BW Trials in the Bahamas. C(53)224 (18 August 1953).
104. PRO, WO188/666. BW(53)11. Biological Warfare Field Trials (7 August 1953).
105. PRO, PREM 11/756. Article from *The Times* (12 March 1954).
106. PRO, WO188/668. AC12890/BRBM32, BRAB 32nd Meeting (15 June 1954).
107. PRO, WO188/666. BW(54)9. BW Subcommittee. Trials with BW Agents in the Bahamas (17 July 1954).
108. PRO, WO,188/666. BW(54)17. BW Subcommittee. Results of Trials with Biological Warfare Agents (23 December 1954).
109. PRO, WO188/666. BW(54)13. Trials with BW Agents in the Bahamas (11 August 1954).
110. PRO, WO188/668. AC12890/BRBM32, BRAB 32nd Meeting (15 June 1954).
111. Ibid.
112. PRO, WO188/670. AC13178/BRB.M33. BRAB 33rd Meeting (10 February 1955).
113. PRO, WO195/13460. AC13646/BRB139. BRAB. Report by the Chairman on the Work of the Board during the Year 1955 (7 November 1955).
114. PRO, WO188/670. AC13178/BRB.M33. BRAB 33rd Meeting (10 February 1955).
115. PRO, WO188/670. AC13332/BRB.M34. BRAB 34th Meeting (4 June 1955).
116. PRO, WO188/670. AC13178/BRB.M33. BRAB 33rd Meeting (10 February 1955).
117. PRO, WO188/670. AC13524/BRB.M35. BRAB 35th Meeting (5 December 1955). *B. globigii* is currently known as *Bacillus subtilis*. It was chosen as a simulant of anthrax primarily for its ability to form spores.
118. PRO, WO188/670. AC13700/BRB.M36. BRAB 36th Meeting (5 April 1956).
119. PRO, WO195/13780. AC13784/BRB144. SAC. Notes on a visit to the Microbiological Research Establishment Porton on Thursday 5th July 1956 (15 August 1956).
120. Cawood, Sir Walter (1907–67). Cawood, who trained in chemistry, had worked on chemical warfare and the design of proximity fuses just prior to the Second World War. He had been Deputy Director of the Royal Aircraft Establishment, Farnborough between 1947 and 1953, when he moved to the Ministry of Aviation. He became Chief Scientist in the War Office in 1959 until his return to the Ministry of Aviation in 1964.
121. PRO, WO195/13313. AC13317/M126. SAC Executive Officer's Report for the 126th Meeting of Council (14 June 1955).
122. PRO, WO188/670. AC13332/BRB.M34. BRAB 34th Meeting (4 June 1955).
123. Ibid.
124. PRO, WO195/13798. AC13802. SAC Executive Officer's Report for the 134th Meeting of Council to be held on 25th October 1956 (15 October 1956).
125. PRO, DEFE 10/281. DRPS/M(56)28. Defence Research Policy Staff. Meeting (2 November 1956).
126. Ibid.

127. PRO, WO195/13780. AC13784/BRB144. SAC. Notes on a visit to the Microbio-
     logical Research Establishment Porton on Thursday 5th July 1956 (15 August
     1956).

7 The Drift of Biological Weapons Policy

1. PRO, WO188/664. AC10911/BRB83. BRAB. Report on BW Policy (3 May 1950)
    Appendix. Extract from 1949 report on Biological Warfare BW(49)(40)(Final).
2. PRO, WO 188/664. BW(50)9 BW Subcommittee. Biological Warfare Policy.
    Memorandum by the Chairman, BW Subcommittee (30 May 1950).
3. PRO, WO 188/664. 98/BW/4/37. BW Subcommittee. BW Policy. Note by the
    Chairman (3 May 1950).
4. PRO, WO188/668. AC10930/BRBM17, BRAB 17th Meeting (20 April 1950).
5. Agar, J. and Balmer, B. (1998) 'British Scientists and the Cold War: the Defence
    Policy Research Committee and Information Networks, 1947–1963', *Historical
    Studies in the Physical Sciences*, 28, 209–52.
6. Their ability to influence atomic matters was further enhanced by the appoint-
    ment to the chair in 1952 of John Cockcroft, Director of the Atomic Energy
    Research Establishment, Harwell. Full responsibility for atomic weapon R&D
    policy was not granted to the committee until 1954.
7. PRO, WO 188/664. BW(50)9 BW Subcommittee. Biological Warfare Policy.
    Memorandum by the Chairman, BW Subcommittee (30 May 1950).
8. Ibid.
9. Ibid.
10. PRO, WO188/664. 100/BW/4/37. BW Subcommittee Meeting (8 May 1950).
11. PRO, WO188/664. 123/BW/4/37. Biological Warfare (24 June 1950).
12. PRO, WO188/663. BW(49) 4th Meeting. BW Subcommittee (23 June 1949).
13. PRO, WO188/664. 123/BW/4/37. Biological Warfare (24 June 1950). Annex
    B. Extract from COS(50)87th Meeting (13 June 1950).
14. PRO, WO188/664. 138/BW/4/21. BW Subcommittee. Biological Warfare.
    Informal Meeting (25 July 1950).
15. PRO, WO188/664. 123/BW/4/37. Biological Warfare (24 June 1950). Annex B.
    Extract from COS(50)87th Meeting (13 June 1950).
16. Ibid.
17. PRO, WO188/664. BW(50)3rd Meeting (21 August 1950).
18. See Wright, S. (1990) 'Evolution of Biological Warfare Policy: 1945–1990' in
    Wright, S. (ed.) *Preventing a Biological Arms Race* (Cambridge, Mass.: MIT Press).
19. PRO, WO188/884. 138/BW/4/21. BW Subcommittee. Biological Warfare.
    Informal Meeting (25 July 1950).
20. Ibid.
21. Ibid.
22. See PRO, AIR 20/11355. 1949 Report on Biological Warfare. Section V. The Prac-
    tical Requirements for Offence and Defence. Air Ministry Draft Contribution.
    (November 1949). This is the only open document where 'X-Toxin' or botuli-
    num is mentioned as a potential tactical weapon.
23. PRO, WO 188/703. Letter from Brigadier H.T. Findlay to Sir A. Crowe (3 August
    1950).
24. PRO, WO 188/705. C.S.(M). No Title (12 March 1952).
25. Ibid.
26. Ibid.

27. Ibid.
28. PRO, DEFE 4/53. COS(52)47th Meeting (1 April 1952).
29. To '(i) continue research and trials to determine the true risk of biological warfare (ii) establish the best defensive measures against biological warfare for the Services and for Civil Defence (iii) on the offensive side, concentrate mainly on the study of long range offensive possibilities.' See PRO, DEFE 4/53. COS(52) 47th Meeting (1 April 1952).
30. Ovendale, R. (ed.) (1994) *British Defence Policy since 1945* (Manchester: Manchester University Press).
31. PRO, PREM 11/49. COS(52)362. Report by the Chiefs of Staff on Defence Policy and Global Strategy to be communicated to the Governments of the old Commonwealth Countries, and to the United States Joint Chiefs of Staff (15 July 1952).
32. PRO, WO 188/705. Biological and Chemical Warfare Research and Development Policy. Report by the Chiefs of Staff. Draft. No date (1952).
33. Ibid.
34. Ibid.
35. Ibid.
36. PRO, WO188/668. AC11817/BRBM24, BRAB 24th Meeting (19 March 1952).
37. PRO, WO188/668. AC11872/BRBM25, BRAB 25th Meeting (14 May 1952).
38. PRO, ADM 1/27325. Private Office. Biological Warfare. C(52)208. Signed by Head of Cabinet Section (8 July 1952).
39. Ibid. Emphasis in original.
40. Ibid.
41. PRO, WO188/668. AC11950/BRBM26, BRAB 26th Meeting (12 July 1952).
42. PRO WO188/668. AC11872/BRBM25, BRAB 25th Meeting (25 April 1952).
43. Ibid.
44. PRO, WO188/668. AC11950/BRBM26, BRAB 26th Meeting (12 July 1952).
45. Ibid.
46. Carter, G. and Pearson, G. (1996) 'North Atlantic Chemical and Biological Research Collaboration: 1916–1995', *Journal of Strategic Studies*, 19(1), 74–103.
47. PRO, WO188/668. AC11950/BRBM26, BRAB 26th Meeting (12 July 1952).
48. PRO, WO188/666. BW(52)2nd Meeting. BW Subcommittee (12 December 1952); PRO, DEFE 10/38. DRP/M(52)5. DRPC Meeting (4 March 1952). Membership of the working party: Sir John Cockcroft (Chair), Dr Cockburn (Air Ministry), Sir Kenneth Crawford (MoS), Dr Wansbrough-Jones, Professor Dodds and Dr Henderson.
49. PRO, DEFE 10/38. DRP/M(52)5. DRPC Meeting (4 March 1952).
50. PRO, WO188/668. AC11950/BRBM26, BRAB 26th Meeting (12 July 1952); WO188/666. BW(52)2nd Meeting. BW Subcommittee (12 December 1952).
51. PRO, WO188/666. BW(53)19 BW Subcommittee. Biological Warfare Report 1951–September 1953 (8 December 1953).
52. PRO, DEFE 10/38. DRP/M(52)5. DRPC Meeting (4 March 1952).
53. PRO, WO188/668. AC11950/BRBM26, BRAB 26th Meeting (12 July 1952).
54. By which time the first British atomic bomb had been tested (October 1952) although this is not mentioned explicitly in any open discussions on biological warfare.
55. PRO, WO188/668. AC12127/BRBM27, BRAB 27th Meeting (6 December 1952).
56. The Principal Director of Scientific Research was the channel for advising BRAB on official policy (PRO, WO188/668. AC12127/BRBM27, BRAB 27th Meeting, 6 December 1952).

57. PRO, WO188/668. AC12127/BRBM27, BRAB 27th Meeting (6 December 1952).
58. PRO, WO188/668. AC12165/BRB106, Directive on Biological Warfare Policy (4 February 1953).
59. PRO, WO188/668. AC12227/BRBM28, BRAB 28th Meeting (10 February 1953).
60. Ibid.
61. PRO, WO188/668. AC11260/BRBM19, BRAB 19th Meeting (21 December 1950).
62. PRO, WO188/668. AC12227/BRBM27. BRAB 28th Meeting (10 February 1953).
63. PRO, WO188/668. AC12552/BRB120, Directive by the Minister of Supply, on Biological Warfare Research and Development (19 November 1953).
64. PRO, ADM 1/27325. Biological Warfare Research and Development Policy. Memorandum by the Minister of Defence. D (53) 44 (12 October 1953).
65. PRO, ADM 1/27325. (C(53)224). BW Trials in the Bahamas. From Deputy Chief of the Naval Staff (7 August 1953).
66. PRO, ADM 1/27325. Biological Warfare Research and Development Policy. Memorandum by the Minister of Defence. D (53) 44 (12 October 1953).
67. PRO, WO188/668. AC12595/BRBM30. BRAB 30th Meeting (6 November 1953).
68. PRO, WO188/668. AC12552/BRB120, Directive by the Minister of Supply, on Biological Warfare Research and Development (19 November 1953).
69. Ibid.
70. PRO, WO188/668. AC12745/BRBM31, BRAB 31st Meeting (19 February 1954).
71. Ibid.
72. PRO, WO188/666. BW Subcommittee. Ad hoc Meeting (30 March 1954).
73. PRO, WO188/668. AC12890/BRBM32. BRAB 32nd Meeting (15 June 1954).
74. The US research programme 'St Jo' aimed to develop anthrax cluster bombs. Testing took place using simulants over Minneapolis, St Louis and Winnipeg. See Meselson, M. (2000) 'Averting the Hostile Exploitation of Biotechnology', *The CBW Conventions Bulletin*, No. 48, pp. 16–19.
75. PRO, DEFE 10/33. DRPC. Review of Defence R&D (10 March 1954). The review was largely dismissed by the Chiefs of Staff for reasons which have little to do with chemical and biological warfare and which are more concerned with the 'long haul' – a long-term strategy which replaced the earlier concept of preparedness by 1957 – and the arrival of the hydrogen bomb. See PRO, AVIA 54/1749. MoD. DRPC Review (1954).
76. PRO, DEFE 10/33. DRPC. Review of Defence R&D (10 March 1954).
77. Ibid.
78. Ibid.
79. Ibid.
80. PRO, DEFE 10/33. DRPC. Review of Defence R&D. Report by Programmes Subcommittee (28 September 1954).
81. Ibid. Emphasis added. This policy statement clarifies the previous use of the term 'long range'.
82. PRO, DEFE 10/33. DRP/p(54)30. Review of Defence R&D Programmes – Chemical and Biological Warfare. Note by the Ministry of Supply (8 October 1954). It is not noted who in the Ministry was responsible for suggesting the changes. BRAB may well have been consulted but there is no record of this in the minutes which are in the public domain.
83. PRO, DEFE 10/33. DRP/p(54)30. Review of Defence R&D Programmes – Chemical and Biological Warfare. Note by the Ministry of Supply (8 October 1954).
84. PRO, DEFE 10/33. DRPC. Review of Defence R&D. Report by Programmes Subcommittee (28 September 1954).

85. Ibid.
86. Ibid.
87. PRO, DEFE 10/33. DRP/p(54)30. Review of Defence R&D Programmes – Chemical and Biological Warfare. Note by the Ministry of Supply (8 October 1954).
88. This is an instance of 'boundary work', the rhetorical struggle to define boundaries which later appear fixed by scientific authority. This authority can then be exploited by different groups to achieve their goals and interests. See Gieryn, T. (1983) 'Boundary Work and the Demarcation of Science from Non-Science: Strains and Interests in the Professional Ideologies of Scientists', *American Sociological Review*, 48, 781–95; Gieryn, T. (1995) 'Boundaries of Science' in Jasanoff, S. *et al.* (eds), *Handbook of Science and Technology Studies* (London: Sage) pp. 393–443; Jasanoff, S. (1987) 'Contested Boundaries in Policy-Relevant Science', *Social Studies of Science*, 17, 195–230.
89. PRO, DEFE 10/33. DRP/p(54)30. Review of Defence R&D Programmes – Chemical and Biological Warfare. Note by the Ministry of Supply (8 October 1954).
90. PRO, DEFE 10/33. DRP/P(54)40. DRPC. Report by the Committee on the Review of the R&D Programmes (18 November 1954).
91. PRO, DEFE 10/39. DRP/P(54)26,28,29,30,31. DRPC Meeting (12 October 1954).
92. PRO, DEFE 10/33. DRP/p(54)30. Review of Defence R&D Programmes – Chemical and Biological Warfare. Note by the Ministry of Supply (8 October 1954). Annex E. It is stated that these amendments had resulted from consultation with the Chief Scientist at the Ministry of Supply and the Controller of Munitions, reflecting discussions from a 12 October DRPC meeting.
93. PRO, DEFE 10/33. DRPC. Review of Defence R&D. Report by Programmes Subcommittee (28 September 1954).
94. PRO, DEFE 10/39. DRP/P(54)26,28,29,30,31. DRPC Meeting (12 October 1954).
95. Ibid.
96. PRO, DEFE 10/33. DRP/P(54)40. DRPC. Report by the Committee on the Review of the R&D Programmes (18 November 1954).
97. Ibid.
98. PRO, WO 188/670. AC1332/BRB.M34. BRAB. Minutes of 34th Meeting (3 June 1955).
99. PRO, DEFE 10/281. DRPS/P(56)49. Defence Research Policy Staff. Offensive Biological Weapons. Note by DRPS (Air) (24 October 1956).
100. Ibid.
101. PRO, WO188/664. BW(50)3 (Final) BW Subcommittee. Public Announcement on Biological Warfare. Report to the Chiefs of Staff (14 February 1950).
102. The figures for specific articles on BW and passing references (in brackets) were: 1946: 20 (9); 1947 5 (8); 1948: 8 (6); 1950: 33 (18).
103. PRO, WO188/664. BW(50)3 (Final) BW Subcommittee. Public Announcement on Biological Warfare. Report to the Chiefs of Staff (14 February 1950).
104. Ibid.
105. PRO, WO188/664. BW(50)8. BW Subcommittee. Public Announcement of Biological Warfare (22 March 1950).
106. PRO, WO188/665. BW(51)10. BW Subcommittee. Public Announcement on Biological Warfare (15 March 1951).
107. PRO, WO188/704. Letter Sir Kenneth Crawford (Ministry of Supply) to Henderson (14 June 1950).
108. PRO, WO188/665. BW(51) 4th Meeting. BW Subcommittee (2 November 1951).

109. PRO, WO188/665. BW(51) 5th Meeting. BW Subcommittee (29 November 1951).
110. Ibid. Emphasis in original.
111. PRO, WO188/665. BW(51) 5th Meeting. BW Subcommittee (29 November 1951).
112. Ibid.
113. Ibid.
114. PRO, WO188/665. BW(51)42. BW Subcommittee. Publicity on Biological Warfare (12 December 1951).
115. PRO, WO188/665. 294/BW/4/38. Publicity on Biological Warfare (21 December 1951).
116. PRO WO188/665. BW(51)6th Meeting. BW Subcommittee (19 December 1951).
117. PRO, PREM 11/756. Letter from Sir Norman Brook to Prime Minister (23 February 1952).
118. PRO, PREM 11/756. Letter to Brigadier Eubank (26 February 1952).
119. The discussion on 'educating' the public with the 'true facts' in order to enlighten them and solicit their sympathies should be construed as a classic example of what is frequently dubbed the 'deficit' approach to public relations in science. In this approach, which sociologists argue has historically been the dominant mode of science communication, the scientist's understanding of the public is marred. Their 'public' is a homogeneous, empty-headed mass waiting to be filled with science, rather than a differentiated audience ranging from the uninterested to the highly critical – and all capable of drawing on prior lay knowledge. See Gregory, J. and Miller, S. (1998) *Science in Public: Communication, Culture and Credibility* (New York: Plenum).
120. PRO, WO188/664. BW(50)5. BW Subcommittee. BW Sabotage of Water Supplies (21 February 1950).
121. PRO, WO 188/665. BW(51)1st Meeting. BW Subcommittee (19 January 1951).
122. PRO, WO 188/705. MRD/501/JFSS/NP. Letter from Stone to Wing Commander A.W. Howard, Ministry of Defence (26 January 1951).
123. PRO, WO188/665. BW(51)14. BW Subcommittee. Vulnerability of Water Reservoirs to BW Sabotage (1 May 1951).
124. PRO, WO188/665. BW(51)20. BW Subcommittee. Bacterial Sabotage (12 June 1951).
125. PRO, WO188/665. BW(51)4th Meeting. BW Subcommittee (2 November 1951).
126. PRO, WO188/665. BW Subcommittee. Biological Warfare – Soviet Threat (4 October 1951).
127. Ibid.
128. PRO, WO188/666. BW(53)19 BW Subcommittee. Biological Warfare Report 1951–September 1953 (8 December 1953).
129. PRO, WO195/13780. AC13784/BRB144. SAC. Notes on a visit to the Microbiological Research Establishment Porton on Thursday 5 July 1956 (15 August 1956).
130. Dockrill, M. (1988) *British Defence since 1945* (Oxford: Blackwell) pp. 41–64.
131. In 1955 Eden became the new Prime Minister and attempted to introduce further defence cuts. A year later the Suez crisis dominated military considerations. See Dockrill, op. cit., pp. 56–64.
132. PRO, DEFE 10/34. DRP/P(55)63. DRPC. Steps Necessary to Keep the Ministry of Supply Defence R&D Programme within a Ceiling of £170 m. Note by the Chairman (5 November 1955).

133. Ibid.
134. The DRP Staff formed the office of the DRPC.
135. PRO, DEFE 10/281. DRPS/P(56)49. Defence Research Policy Staff. Offensive Biological Weapons. Note by DRPS (Air) (24 October 1956).
136. PRO, WO 188/666. BW(55)10. BW Subcommittee. Disbandment of the BW and CW Subcommittees. Note by the Chairman (16 July 1955).
137. PRO, DEFE 10/34. DRP/P(55)50 (Final). DRPC. Review of Defence Research and Development (23 January 1956).

8   A New Threat

1. PRO, DEFE 10/34. DRP/P(55)50 (Final). DRPC. Review of Defence Research and Development (23 January 1956).
2. PRO, WO195/13460. AC13646/BRB139. Report by the Chairman on the Work of the Board during the Year 1955 (7 November 1955).
3. PRO, WO188/670. AC13524/BRB.M35. BRAB 35th Meeting (5 December 1955).
4. PRO, WO195/13822. AC13826/BRB145. Report by the Chairman on the Work of the Board during the Year 1956 (5 November 1956).
5. PRO, DEFE 10/281. DRPS/M(56)28. Defence Research Policy Staff. Meeting (2 November 1956).
6. PRO, CAB 131/17, DC(56)6. Defence Committee Minutes (10 July 1956). See Pearson, G., 'Farewell to Arms', *Chemistry in Britain*, 31/10 (Oct. 1995), 782–6; Carter, G. and Pearson, G. (1996) 'North Atlantic Chemical and Biological Research Collaboration: 1916–1995', *Journal of Strategic Studies*, 19, 74–103. The decision was, more specifically, to abandon the large-scale production of nerve gas and the development of nerve gas weapons and to destroy the residue of the Second World War stockpile of other chemical agents and weapons.
7. PRO, ADM 1/27325. DC(56)13. Brief for First Lord. From Head of Military Branch (June 1956).
8. Carter, G. and Pearson, G. (1996) 'North Atlantic Chemical and Biological Research Collaboration: 1916–1995', *Journal of Strategic Studies*, 19, 68.
9. PRO, ADM 1/27325. DC(56)13. Brief for First Lord. From Head of Military Branch (June 1956).
10. PRO, DEFE 10/281. DRPS/P(56)49. Defence Research Policy Staff. Offensive Biological Weapons. Note by DRPS (Air) (24 October 1956).
11. PRO, CAB 131/17, DC(56)6. Defence Committee Minutes (10 July 1956). See also PRO, CAB 131/17. DC(56)13 (Revise). Cabinet Defence Committee. Chemical Warfare Policy. Memorandum by the Minister of Defence (4 July 1956).
12. PRO, WO195/13822. AC13826/BRB145. Report by the Chairman on the Work of the Board during the Year 1956 (5 November 1956).
13. Wright, S. (1990) 'Evolution of Biological Warfare Policy: 1945–1990' in Wright, S. (ed.) *Preventing a Biological Arms Race* (Cambridge, Mass.: MIT Press).
14. PRO, WO188/670. AC13968/BRB.M37. BRAB. Minutes 37th Meeting (18 and 19 January 1957).
15. PRO, WO188/670. AC14088/BRB.M39. BRAB. Minutes 39th Meeting (8 and 9 May 1957).
16. Ibid.
17. Dodds, Sir Edward Charles, first baronet (1899–1973). Dodds was an eminent biochemist who was Professor of Biochemistry at the University of London and Director of the Courtauld Research Institute for Biochemistry. His most celebrated

research was on the synthetic oestrogen hormones. He was elected FRS in 1942 and served on the Royal Society Council, as well as on many other prominent committees. Dodds retired in 1965.

18. PRO, WO188/670. AC14088/BRB.M39. BRAB. Minutes 39th Meeting (8 and 9 May 1957).
19. Ibid.
20. Ibid.
21. PRO, WO195/14170. AC14176/CDB237. Chemical Defence Advisory Board. Annual Review of the Work of the Board for 1957(4 November 1957).
22. PRO, WO195/14146. Ptn/IT.4222/4141/57. Offensive Evaluation Committee – Conclusions and Recommendations of the Twelfth Tripartite Conference BW/CW Applications.
23. PRO, WO195/14822. AC14831A. BW Potential 1959 (26 November 1959) (revised 21 February 1960).
24. The tests involved naval vessels spraying clouds of *Bacillus globigii* and *Serratia marcescens* across the city in a number of simulated germ warfare attacks. See Cole, L.A. (1988) *Clouds of Secrecy: the Army's Germ Warfare Tests over Populated Areas* (Savage, Md: Rowman and Littlefield).
25. PRO, WO195/14822. AC14831A. BW Potential 1959 (26 November 1959) (revised 21 February 1960).
26. PRO, WO195/14064. AC14069.OEC.176. Ptn/Tu.1208/2129/57. Offensive Evaluation Committee. Study of the Possible Attack of Large Areas with BW Agents (no specific date, 1957).
27. Ibid.
28. A previous series of trials with zinc cadmium sulphide took place in various parts of southern England between 1953 and 1955. These sprayed material from a ground-based source for distances between 25 and 50 miles. The documents had not been made public at the time of writing and it is not clear how far these trials were connected with the LAC. The trials were carried out by CDEE and at this stage appear to have been linked more to chemical warfare. The term 'Large Area Concept' certainly does not enter advisory and policy discussion until 1957. See Evans, R. (1999) 'Germ Warfare Cloud Floated over Shire Counties', *The Guardian*, 2 November, 4.
29. PRO, WO195/14405. AC14413/BRBM41. BRAB 41st Meeting (18 July 1958).
30. National Research Council (1997) *Toxicologic Assessment of the Army's Zinc Cadmium Sulfide Dispersion Tests* (Washington, DC: National Academy Press) p. 117.
31. PRO, WO195/14405. AC14413/BRBM41. BRAB 41st Meeting (18 July 1958).
32. PRO, WO195/14593. PN68. Long Distance Travel of Particulate Clouds.
33. PRO, WO195/14334. AC134342/CDb249 OECM3. Offensive Evaluation Committee 3rd Meeting (17 April 1958).
34. Ibid.
35. PRO, WO195/14405. AC14413/BRBM41. BRAB 41st Meeting (18 July 1958).
36. Ibid.
37. Ibid.
38. Ibid.
39. PRO, DEFE 10/282. DRPS/P(57)19. Defence Research Policy Staff. Working Party on BW and CW. Note by the Secretary (6 February 1957). The membership of the committee was: Mr E.C. Williams (Chairman, Ministry of Defence); Captain R.I.A. Sarrell, Brigadier L.C.C. Harrison, Air Commodore J.N. Tomes, Mr W.H. Curtis (all DRPS, Ministry of Defence), Mr J.H.B. Macklen (Ministry of Defence),

Mr E.K.G. James (CDEE), Mr J.R. Morton (MRE) and Squadron Leader W.S.O. Randle (Secretary, Ministry of Defence).

40. PRO, DEFE 10/282. DRPS/P(57)59(Draft). Defence Research Policy Staff. Review of Defence Research and Development (31 May 1957). A month beforehand the Sandys White Paper on defence policy had called for increasing reliance on a nuclear deterrent, this preceded a range of severe cuts to the defence budget. See Dockrill, M. (1988) *British Defence since 1945* (Oxford: Blackwell) pp. 65–81.

41. The V agents are a range of nerve agents that were developed as chemical weapons after the Second World War.

42. PRO, AIR 8/1936. Brief for the Chief of Air Staff. Biological and Chemical Warfare (22 October 1957).

43. PRO, DEFE 10/283. DRPS/P(58)10. Report on BW & CW (28 February 1958).

44. Ibid.

45. Ibid.

46. Ibid.

47. Ibid.

48. Ibid.

49. Ibid.

50. Ibid.

51. Ibid.

52. Ibid.

53. PRO, DEFE 41/156. JP(58)65(Final). Chiefs of Staff Committee, Joint Planning Staff. Biological and Chemical Warfare. Report by the Joint Planning Staff (30 July 1958). The report is cited as DRP/P(58)29.

54. PRO, DEFE 41/156. JP(58)65(Final). Chiefs of Staff Committee, Joint Planning Staff. Biological and Chemical Warfare. Report by the Joint Planning Staff (30 July 1958).

55. Ibid.

56. Ibid.

57. Ibid.

58. Ibid.

59. Ibid.

60. PRO, WO188/665. 294/BW/4/38. Publicity on Biological Warfare (21 December 1951).

61. PRO, DEFE 41/156. JP(58)65(Final). Chiefs of Staff Committee, Joint Planning Staff. Biological and Chemical Warfare. Report by the Joint Planning Staff (30 July 1958).

62. Ibid.

63. Ibid.

64. Ibid.

65. Ibid.

66. Ibid.

67. PRO, DEFE 10/356. DRP/P(59)6. Ministry of Defence. DRPC. Biological and Chemical Warfare. Note by the DRP Staff (28 January 1959).

68. Ibid.

69. Ibid.

70. Ibid.

71. Ibid.

72. PRO, DEFE 10/355. 24159. DRP/M(59)2. DRPC Meeting (10 February 1959).

73. Ibid.

74. PRO, WO195/14745. AC14754/BRBM43. BRAB 43rd Meeting (28 July 1959). The letter is actually quoted in the minutes.
75. PRO, WO195/14204. AC14210/BRBM40. BRAB 40th Meeting (18 November 1957).
76. Ibid.
77. For a full discussion see Carter, G. and Balmer, B. (1999) 'Chemical and Biological Warfare and Defence, 1945–1990' in Bud, R. and Gummett, G. (eds) *Cold War, Hot Science: Applied Research in Britain's Defence Laboratories 1945–1990* (Amsterdam: Harwood Academic Publishers).
78. PRO, WO195/14847. AC14856/BRBM44. BRAB 45th Meeting (8 December 1959). The Ministry of Aviation was the successor to the Ministry of Supply.
79. PRO, WO195/14847. AC14856/BRBM44. BRAB 45th Meeting (8 December 1959).
80. Ibid.
81. Ibid.
82. PRO, WO195/14903. Future of MRE (1 March 1960).
83. PRO, WO195/14902. AC14911/BRBM46. BRAB 46th Meeting (1 March 1960).
84. Ibid.
85. PRO, WO195/14924. AC14933/BRBM47. BRAB 47th Meeting (24 March 1960).
86. PRO, WO195/15035. SAC110/BRB185. BRAB Report 1960.
87. PRO, WO195/14924. AC14933/BRBM47. BRAB 47th Meeting (24 March 1960).
88. PRO, WO195/15078. SAC153/M3. Advisory Council on Scientific Research and Technical Development 3rd Meeting (24 November 1960).
89. PRO, WO195/15168. SAC243/BRBM49. BRAB 49th Meeting (15 April 1961).
90. Ibid.
91. PRO, WO195/14405. AC14413/BRBM41. BRAB 41st Meeting (18 July 1958).
92. PRO, WO195/14905. AC14914/CDB271 OECM5. Offensive Evaluation Committee 5th Meeting (15 January 1960).
93. PRO, WO195/14745. AC14754/BRBM43. BRAB 43rd Meeting (28 July 1959).
94. PRO, WO195/14811. AC14820/BRB172. BRAB Report 1959.
95. Ibid.
96. PRO, WO195/14902. AC14911/BRBM46. BRAB 46th Meeting (1 March 1960).
97. PRO, WO195/14853. AC14862/M153. SAC 153rd Meeting (26 November 1959).
98. PRO, WO195/14902. AC14911/BRBM46. BRAB 46th Meeting (1 March 1960).
99. PRO, WO195/14876. AC14855. SAC Report for the Year 1959 (March 1960).
100. PRO, WO195/14813. AC14822/BRBM44. BRAB 44th Meeting (31 October 1959).
101. Ibid.
102. PRO, WO195/14995. SAC70/BRBM48. BRAB 48th Meeting (16 July 1960).
103. PRO, WO195/14905. AC14914/CDB271 OECM5. Offensive Evaluation Committee 5th Meeting (15 January 1960); WO195/15173. SAC248/CDB290. OECM8. Offensive Evaluation Committee 8th Meeting (13 April 1961).
104. WO, 195/15014. SAC89/CDB281 OECM6. Offensive Evaluation Committee 6th Meeting (15 July 1960).
105. PRO, WO195/15142. Porton Note 203. Large Area Coverage by Aerosol Clouds Generated at Sea (22 March 1961).
106. Ibid.
107. WO, 195/15014. SAC89/CDB281 OECM6. Offensive Evaluation Committee 6th Meeting (15 July 1960).

108. PRO, WO195/15813. Porton Field Trial Report No. 610. The Penetration of Built-Up Areas by Aerosols at Night (7 May 1964).
109. Ibid.
110. PRO, WO195/14745. AC14754/BRBM43. BRAB 43rd Meeting (28 July 1959).
111. Ibid.
112. Ibid.
113. PRO, WO195/14707. AC14716/BRB168. Field test requirements for determining airborne survival in relation to the large area concept. J.D. Morton (26 June 1959).
114. WO, 195/15014. SAC89/CDB281 OECM6. Offensive Evaluation Committee 6th Meeting (15 July 1960).
115. Ibid.
116. Ibid.
117. Ibid.
118. PRO, WO195/14636. AC14645/BRB162. Microbiological field trials at Porton. (29 April 1959).
119. Ibid.
120. WO, 195/15014. SAC89/CDB281 OECM6. Offensive Evaluation Committee 6th Meeting (15 July 1960).
121. PRO, WO195/14707. AC14716/BRB168. Field test requirements for determining airborne survival in relation to the large area concept. J.D. Morton (26 June 1959).
122. PRO, WO195/14813. AC14822/BRBM44. BRAB 44th Meeting (31 October 1959).
123. Ibid.
124. PRO, Wo195/15111. MRE Report No. 25. The Performance of Large Output Fine Sprays From Fast Moving Aircraft (16 January 1961).
125. PRO, WO195/14995. SAC70/BRBM48. BRAB 48th Meeting (16 July 1960). *Bacillus globigii* is currently named *Bacillus subtilis*.
126. PRO, WO195/14995. SAC70/BRBM48. BRAB 48th Meeting (16 July 1960).
127. PRO, WO195/15164. Early Warning Devices for BW Defence: the Situation in April 1961.
128. Ibid.
129. Ibid.
130. PRO, WO195/14853. AC14862/M153. SAC 153rd Meeting (26 November 1959).
131. PRO, WO195/15693. SAC768/M19. SAC 19th Meeting (5 November 1963).
132. PRO, WO195/15267. SAC342/BRB204. BRAB Report by the Chairman on the Work of the Board during the Year 1961 (7 November 1961).
133. PRO, DEFE 10/355. DRPC. Meeting (13 September 1960).
134. PRO, DEFE 13/440. Confidential Annex to COS(60) 59th Meeting (27 September 1960). Zuckerman, Solly, Baron created 1971 (Life Peer), of Burnham Thorpe, Norfolk (1904–93). Zuckerman was a zoologist and Professor of Anatomy at the University of Birmingham (1946–68). He had carried out research on the effects of bomb explosions during the Second World War. Zuckerman sat on and chaired a number of scientific advisory committees and was appointed as Chief Scientific Advisor to the Government between 1964 and 1971. He was a prolific writer, publishing in his field of primatology as well as on matters of science and defence policy.
135. PRO, WO195/15168. SAC243/BRBM49. BRAB 49th Meeting (15 April 1961). PRO, AIR 8/1936. COS.204/15/2/61. United Kingdom BW and CW Weapons Release of Information (20 February 1961).

136. PRO, WO195/14995. SAC70/BRBM48. BRAB 48th Meeting (16 July 1960).
137. Ibid.
138. Membership: Sir Harry Melville, Dr F.J. Wilkins, Professor E.R.H. Jones, Professor E.T.C. Spooner, Major-General J.R.C. Hamilton, Professor P.B. Medawar.
139. PRO, WO195/15287. SAC362/M51. BRAB 51st Meeting (6 December 1961).
140. Ibid. Membership: Dr W. Cawood (Chief Scientist, War Office) (Chairman), Sir John Carroll (Deputy Controller, R&D, Admiralty), Mr H. Constant (Scientific Advisor, Air Ministry), Mr E.C. Cornford (Chairman DRP Staff, Ministry of Defence), Dr W.B. Littler (Deputy Chief Scientist, War Office), Major-General H.J. Mogg (Director of Combat Development, War Office), Dr R.H. Purcell (Chief Scientific Advisor, Home Office). See PRO, DEFE10/490. 24144. DRP/P(62)33. DRPC. Chemical and Biological Warfare (10 May 1962).
141. PRO, DEFE 10/490. DRP/P(62)33. DRPC. Chemical and Biological Warfare. Note by the Joint Secretaries (10 May 1962).
142. Ibid.
143. Ibid.
144. PRO, DEFE 13/440. SZ/1177/62. Chemical and Biological Warfare Policy. Note to the Minister from G. Owen (signed on behalf of CSA) (20 December 1962).
145. Ibid.
146. PRO, AIR 8/1936. Chiefs of Staff Committee. Brief for Vice Chief of the Air Staff. Chemical and Biological Warfare (1 November 1962).
147. PRO, CAB 131/28. D(63)3. Cabinet Defence Committee Meeting (3 May 1963).
148. PRO, DEFE 24/31. d/Ds 6/8. Briefs for New Ministers. Chemical and Biological Warfare (7 October 1964).
149. PRO, CAB 131/28. D(63)3. Cabinet Defence Committee Meeting (3 May 1963).
150. PRO, DEFE 13/440. Cabinet Defence Committee. Biological and Chemical Warfare Policy (D.(63)14). Brief for the Minister of Defence (1 May 1963).
151. PRO, CAB 131/28. D(63)3. Cabinet Defence Committee Meeting (3 May 1963).
152. Ibid. It was pointed out to Cabinet by the Minister of Defence that 'we are generally believed in NATO to hold stocks of at least chemical weapons and we have never disclosed formally to NATO that we no such retaliatory capacity or modern defensive equipment'. See PRO, CAB 131/28. D(63)14. Cabinet Defence Committee. Biological and Chemical Warfare. Memorandum by the Minister of Defence (16 April 1963).
153. PRO, CAB 131/28. D(63)3. Cabinet Defence Committee Meeting (3 May 1963).
154. PRO, DEFE 24/31. d/Ds 6/8. Briefs for New Ministers. Chemical and Biological Warfare (7 October 1964).
155. PRO, WO195/15491. Appendix to SAC566. Technical Supplement to the Report for the Year 1962.
156. PRO, WO195/15608. MRE Report No. 29. MRE Annual Report 1962–63. The emergence of the field of aerobiology, the study of the behaviour of micro-organisms in an airborne state, can be attributed to the practical problems of biological warfare tackled at Porton Down. See Dando, M. (1999) 'The Impact of the Development of Modern Biology on the Evolution of Offensive Biological Warfare Programs in the Twentieth Century', *Defense Analysis*, 15(1), 43–62.
157. PRO, WO195/15608. MRE Report No. 29. MRE Annual Report 1962–63.
158. PRO, WO32/20457. Chemical and Biological Warfare Field Trials (28 May 1963).
159. Ibid.

160. PRO, WO195/15610. SAC685/BRBM54. BRAB 54th Meeting (13 May 1963).
161. PRO, WO32/20457. Chemical and Biological Warfare Field Trials (28 May 1963).
162. Ibid.
163. PRO, WO195/15749. SAC823/BRB231. BRAB. Field Trials Progress July, 1963–January 1964 (18 February 1964).
164. PRO, WO195/15693. SAC768/M19. SAC 19th Meeting (5 November 1963).
165. The number (162) denotes a particular strain of the bacteria used at Porton.
166. Harvard–Sussex Information Bank. MRE. Field Trial Report No. 4. The Viability, Concentration and Immunological Properties of Airborne Bacteria Released from a Massive Line Source. K.P. Norris, G.J. Harper, J.E.S. Greenstreet. September 1968.
167. A further four trials took place off Lyme Bay between 3 February and 26 April 1966.
168. Harvard–Sussex Information Bank. MRE Field Trial Report No. 5. Comparison of the Viability of *Escherichia coli* in airborne particles and on microthreads exposed in the field.
169. PRO, WO195/15819. SAC893/BRBM56. BRAB 56th Meeting (13 March 1964); PRO, WO195/15750. SAC824/BRB232. A Method for Studying the Viability of Micro-organisms of any Particle Size Held in the 'Airborne' State in any Environment for any Length of Time (14 February 1964).
170. Harvard–Sussex Information Bank. MRE Field Trial Report No. 5. Comparison of the Viability of *Escherichia coli* in airborne particles and on microthreads exposed in the field (no date).
171. PRO, WO195/14146. Ptn/IT.4222/4141/57.
172. PRO, WO195/14405. AC14413/BRBM41. BRAB 41st Meeting (18 July 1958).
173. Ibid.
174. PRO, WO195/15267. SAC342/BRB204. BRAB Report by the Chairman on the Work of the Board during the Year 1961 (7 November 1961).
175. PRO, WO195/15287. SAC362/M51. BRAB 51st Meeting (6 December 1961).
176. PRO, WO32/20457. Chemical and Biological Warfare Field Trials (28 May 1963).
177. PRO, WO195/15287. SAC362/M51. BRAB 51st Meeting (6 December 1961).
178. Ibid.
179. Ibid.
180. Ibid.
181. PRO, WO195/15491. Appendix to SAC566. Technical Supplement to the Report for the Year 1962.
182. PRO, WO195/15671. SAC746.BRB227. BRAB report by the Chairman on the Work of the Board during the Year 1963 (15 October 1963).
183. PRO, WO195/15506. SAC581/BRBM53. BRAB 53rd Meeting (24 November 1962); WO195/15610. SAC685/BRBM54. BRAB 54th Meeting (13 May 1963).
184. PRO, WO195/15610. SAC685/BRBM54. BRAB 54th Meeting (13 May 1963).
185. PRO, WO195/15751. MRE report No. VT1. Exploratory Ventilation Trial in the London Underground Railways. February 1964.
186. PRO, WO195/15709. SAC/784/BRBM55. BRAB 55th Meeting (12 October 1963).
187. Ibid.
188. PRO, WO195/15819. SAC893/BRBM56. BRAB 56th Meeting (13 March 1964).

9 Making Threats

1. Although this is a slightly arbitrary cut-off point for the narrative, at the time of writing it marks the point after which most of the literature in the UK archives remains closed.
2. It is clear that the US continued to research both bombs and large area sprays until the late 1960s, long after the UK had abandoned its research on bombs. See Meselson, M. (2000) 'Averting the Hostile Exploitation of Biotechnology', *The CBW Conventions Bulletin*, No. 48, pp. 16–19.
3. See discussion in Chapter 1. The links between knowledge and power have also been explored by Foucault who argues that the discourse of experts defines the limits of what it is possible and impossible to think and do – hence the link with power. See Foucault, M. (1980) *Power/Knowledge* (Brighton: Harvester); Rouse, J. (1987) *Knowledge and Power: Towards a Political Philosophy of Science* (Ithaca: Cornell University Press).
4. Carter and Pearson record that Fildes had objected to information about his wartime activities being revealed at an open day at Porton. See Carter, G.B. and Pearson, G.S. (1999) 'British Biological Warfare and Biological Defence, 1925–45' in Geissler, E. and van Courtland Moon, J.E. (eds) *Biological and Toxin Weapons: Research Development and Use from the Middle Ages to 1945* (Oxford: Oxford University Press).
5. Article I of the Treaty prohibits development, production, stockpiling and acquisition of weapons and of biological agents with 'no justification for prophylactic, protective and other peaceful purposes'. Use is not included but subsumed under the 1925 Geneva Protocol. Research is permitted to allow for defensive science. See Wright, S. (ed.) (1990) *Preventing a Biological Arms Race* (Cambridge, Mass.: MIT Press).
6. Carter, G. and Balmer, B. (1999) 'Chemical and Biological Warfare and Defence, 1945–1990' in Bud, R. and Gummett, G. (eds) *Cold War, Hot Science: Applied Research in Britain's Defence Laboratories 1945–1990* (Amsterdam: Harwood Academic Publishers).
7. In 1994, CAMR ceased to be the responsibility of the PHLS and became a separate Special Health Authority answerable to the Microbiological Research Authority and the Department of Health. See Carter, G. (2000) *Chemical and Biological Defence at Porton Down 1916–2000* (London: The Stationery Office).

Bibliography

Agar, J. and Balmer, B. (1998), 'British Scientists and the Cold War: the Defence Policy Research Committee and Information Networks, 1947–1963', *Historical Studies in the Physical Sciences*, 28, 209–52.

Avery, D. (1999), 'Canadian Biological and Toxin Warfare Research, Development and Planning, 1942–45' in Geissler, E. and van Courtland Moon, J.E. (eds) *Biological and Toxin Weapons: Research Development and Use from the Middle Ages to 1945* (Oxford: Oxford University Press) pp. 190–214.

Berger, P. and Luckman, T. (1966), *The Social Construction of Reality: a Treatise on the Sociology of Knowledge* (London: Penguin).

Bernstein, B. (1990), 'Origins of the Biological Warfare Program' in Wright, S. (ed.) *Preventing a Biological Arms Race* (Cambridge, Mass.: MIT Press) pp. 9–25.

Berridge, V. (1996), *AIDS in the UK: the Making of Policy, 1981–1994* (Oxford: Oxford University Press).

Boyer, P. (1985), *By the Bomb's Early Light: American Thought and Culture at the Dawn of the Atomic Age* (New York: Pantheon Books).

Brandt, A.M. and Gardner, M. (2000), 'The Golden Age of Medicine?' in Cooter, R. and Pickstone, J. (eds) *Medicine in the 20th Century* (Amsterdam: Harwood Academic Publishers) pp. 21–37.

Bryden, J. (1989), *Deadly Allies: Canada's Secret War 1937–1947* (Toronto: McClelland and Stewart).

Bud, R. (1993), *The Uses of Life: a History of Biotechnology* (Cambridge: Cambridge University Press).

Bud, R. and Gummett, P. (1999), 'Introduction: Don't You Know There's a War On?' in Bud, R. and Gummett, P. (eds) *Cold War, Hot Science: Applied Research in Britain's Defence Laboratories 1945–1990* (Amsterdam: Harwood Academic Publishers) pp. 1–28.

Camus, A. (1960), *The Plague* (London: Penguin), translated from the French by Gilbert, S. First published as *La Peste*, 1947.

Caplan, P. (ed.) (2000), *Risk Revisited* (London: Pluto Press).

Carter, G. (1992), 'Biological Warfare and Biological Defence in the United Kingdom 1940–1979', *RUSI Journal* (December), 67–74.

Carter, G. (1992), *Porton Down: 75 Years of Chemical and Biological Research* (London: HMSO).

Carter, G. (2000), *Chemical and Biological Defence at Porton Down 1916–2000* (London: The Stationery Office).

Carter, G. and Balmer, B. (1999), 'Chemical and Biological Warfare and Defence, 1945–1990' in Bud, R. and Gummett, P. (eds) *Cold War, Hot Science: Applied Research in Britain's Defence Laboratories 1945–1990* (Amsterdam: Harwood Academic Publishers) pp. 295–338.

Carter, G. and Pearson, G. (1996), 'North Atlantic Chemical and Biological Research Collaboration: 1916–1995', *Journal of Strategic Studies* 19, 74–103.

Carter, G. and Pearson, G. (1999), 'British Biological Warfare and Biological Defence, 1925–45' in Geissler, E. and van Courtland Moon, J.E. (eds) *Biological and Toxin Weapons: Research Development and Use from the Middle Ages to 1945* (Oxford: Oxford University Press) pp. 168–89.

Clarke, A.E. and Fujimura, J.H. (1992), *The Right Tools for the Job: At Work in Twentieth Century Life Sciences* (Princeton: Princeton University Press).

Cole, L. A. (1988), *Clouds of Secrecy: the Army's Germ Warfare Tests over Populated Areas* (Savage, Md: Rowman and Littlefield).

Collingridge, D. and Reeve, C. (1986), *Science Speaks to Power: the Role of Experts in Policymaking* (London: Pinter).

Dando, M. (1994), *Biological Warfare in the 21st Century* (London: Brasseys).

Dando, M. (1999), 'The Impact of the Development of Modern Biology on the Evolution of Offensive Biological Warfare Programs in the Twentieth Century', *Defense Analysis*, 15(1), 43–62.

Deichmann, U. (1996), *Biologists under Hitler* (Cambridge, Mass.: Harvard University Press).

Derbes, V.J. (1966), 'De Mussis and the Great Plague of 1348: a Forgotten Episode of Bacteriological War', *JAMA*, 169, 59–62.

Dockrill, M. (1988), *British Defence since 1945* (Oxford: Blackwell).

Doel, R.E. (1997), 'Scientists as Policymakers, Advisors and Intelligence Agents: Linking Contemporary Diplomatic History with the History of Contemporary Science' in Söderquist, T. (ed.) *The Historiography of Contemporary Science and Technology* (Amsterdam: Harwood).

Douglas, M. (1986), *Risk Acceptability according to the Social Sciences* (London: Routledge).

Douglas, M. (1992), *Risk and Blame: Essays in Cultural Theory* (London: Routledge).

Douglas, M. and Wildavsky, M. (1982), *Risk and Culture: an Essay on the Selection of Technical and Environmental Dangers* (Berkeley: University of California Press).

Edgerton, D. (1990), 'Science and War' in Olby, R.C., Cantor, G.N., Christie, J.J.R. and Hodge, M.J.S. (eds) *Companion to the History of Modern Science* (London: Routledge).

Edgerton, D. (1992), 'Whatever Happened to the British Warfare State? The Ministry of Supply 1945–1951' in Mercer, H. Rollings, N. and Tomlinson, J.D. (eds) *Labour Governments and Private Industry: the Experience 1945–1951* (Edinburgh: Edinburgh University Press).

Englehardt, T. Jr. and Caplan, A. (eds) (1987), *Scientific Controversies: Case Studies in the Resolution and Closure of Disputes in Science and Technology* (Cambridge: Cambridge University Press).

Evans, R. (1999), 'Germ Warfare Cloud Floated over Shire Counties', *The Guardian*, 2 November, 4.

Falk, R. (1990), 'Inhibiting Reliance on Biological Weaponry: the Role and Relevance of International Law', in Wright, S. (ed.) *Preventing a Biological Arms Race* (Cambridge, Mass.: MIT Press) pp. 241–66.

Foucault, M. (1980), *Power/Knowledge* (Brighton: Harvester).

Franz, D., Jahrling, P., Friedlander, A., McClain, D., Hoover, D., Bryne, R., Pavlin, J., Christopher, G. and Eitzen, E. (1997), 'Clinical Recognition and Management of Patients Exposed to Biological Warfare Agents', *JAMA*, 278(5), 399–411.

Geissler, E. (ed.) (1986), *Biological and Toxin Weapons Today* (Oxford: Oxford University Press).

Geissler, E. (1999), 'Biological Warfare Activities in Germany, 1923–45' in Geissler, E. and van Courtland Moon, J.E. (eds) *Biological and Toxin Weapons: Research, Development and Use from the Middle Ages to 1945* (Oxford: Oxford University Press) pp. 91–126.

Geissler, E. and van Courtland Moon, J.E. (eds) (1999), *Biological and Toxin Weapons: Research Development and Use from the Middle Ages to 1945* (Oxford: Oxford University Press).

Gieryn, T. (1983), 'Boundary Work and the Demarcation of Science from Non-Science: Strains and Interests in the Professional Ideologies of Scientists', *American Sociological Review*, 48, 781–95.

Gieryn, T. (1995), 'Boundaries of Science' in Jasanoff, S., Markle, G.E., Petersen, J.C. and Pinch, T. (eds) *Handbook of Science and Technology Studies* (London: Sage) pp. 393–443.

Gieryn, T. (1999), *Cultural Boundaries of Science: Credibility on the Line* (Chicago: University of Chicago Press).

Golinski, J. (1998), *Making Natural Knowledge: Constructivism and the History of Science* (Cambridge: Cambridge University Press).

Gowing, M. (1974), *Independence and Deterrence: Britain and Atomic Energy 1945–52* Vol. 1 (London: Macmillan – now Palgrave).

Gregory, J. and Miller, S. (1998), *Science in Public: Communication, Culture and Credibility* (New York: Plenum).

Guillemin, J. (1999), *Anthrax: the Investigation of a Deadly Outbreak* (Berkeley: University of California Press).

Gummett, P. (1980), *Scientists in Whitehall* (Manchester: Manchester University Press).

Haber, L.F. (1986), *The Poisonous Cloud: Chemical Warfare in the First World War* (Oxford: Clarendon Press).

Harris, R. and Paxman, J. (1982), *A Higher Form of Killing: the Secret Story of Gas and Germ Warfare* (London: Chatto and Windus).

Harris, S. (1994), *Factories of Death: Japanese Biological Warfare 1932–45 and the American Cover Up* (London: Routledge).

Harris, S. (1999), 'The Japanese Biological Warfare Programme: an Overview' in Geissler, E. and van Courtland Moon, J.E. (eds) *Biological and Toxin Weapons: Research Development and Use from the Middle Ages to 1945* (Oxford: Oxford University Press) pp. 127–52.

Hilgartner, S. (1992), 'The Social Construction of Risk Objects: Or How to Pry Open Networks of Risk', in Short J.F. Jnr and Clarke, L. (eds) *Organizations, Uncertainties and Risk* (Boulder, Colo.: Westview Press).

Hughes, S.S. (1977), *The Virus: a History of the Concept* (London: Heinemann).

Hugh-Jones, M. (1992), 'Wickham Steed and German Biological Warfare Research', *Intelligence and National Security*, 7(4), 379–402.

Irwin, A. (1995), *Citizen Science: a Study of People, Expertise and Sustainable Development* (London: Routledge).

Jasanoff, S. (1987), 'Contested Boundaries in Policy-Relevant Science', *Social Studies of Science*, 17, 195–230.

Jasanoff, S. (1990), *The Fifth Branch: Science Advisers as Policy-Makers* (Harvard: Harvard University Press).

Johnson, F.A. (1980), *Defence by Ministry* (London: Duckworth).

Johnson, R.H. (1994), *Improbable Dangers: U.S. Conceptions of Threat in the Cold War and After* (Basingstoke: Macmillan – now Palgrave).

Kohler, R.E. (1985), 'Bacterial Physiology: the Medical Context', *Bulletin of the History of Medicine*, 59, 54–74.

Krige, J. (1990), 'Scientists as Policymakers: British Physicists "Advice" to Their Government on Membership of CERN (1951–1952)' in Frängsmyr, T. (ed.) *Solomon's House Revisited: the Organization and Institutionalization of Science* (Canton, Mass.: Science History Publications USA) pp. 270–91.

Latour, B. (1987), *Science in Action* (Harvard: Harvard University Press).

Latour, B. (1988), *The Pasteurization of France* (Harvard: Harvard University Press).

Latour, B. (1999), *Pandora's Hope: Essays on the Reality of Science Studies* (Harvard: Harvard University Press).

Lederberg, J. (ed.) (1999), *Biological Weapons: Limiting the Threat* (Cambridge, Mass.: MIT Press).

Lupton, D. (1999), *Risk* (London: Routledge).

Lupton, D. (ed.) (1999), *Risk and Sociocultural Theory: New Directions and Perspectives* (Cambridge: Cambridge University Press).

McElroy, R.J. (1991), 'The Geneva Protocol of 1925', in Krepon, M. and Caldwell, D. (eds) *The Politics of Arms Control Treaty Ratification* (New York: St Martin's Press – now Palgrave) pp. 125–66.

MacKenzie, D. (1993), *Inventing Accuracy: a Historical Sociology of Nuclear Missile Guidance* (Cambridge, Mass.: MIT Press).

MacKenzie, D. (1999), 'Theories of Technology and the Abolition of Nuclear Weapons', in MacKenzie, D. and Wajcman, J. (eds) *The Social Shaping of Technology* (2nd edn) (Buckingham: Open University Press) pp. 419–42.

Mandell, G., Bennett, J. and Dolin, R. (eds) (1995), *Mandell, Douglas and Bennett's Principles and Practice of Infectious Diseases* (4th edn) (New York: Churchill Livingstone).

Mendelsohn, A.J. (1998), 'From Eradication to Equilibrium: How Epidemics Became Complex after World War I', in Lawrence, C. and Weisz, G. (eds), *Greater Than the Parts: Holism in Biomedicine, 1920–1950* (Oxford: Oxford University Press) pp. 303–31.

Mendelsohn, E. (1997), 'Science, Scientists and the Military', in Krige, J. and Pestre, D. (eds) *Science in the Twentieth Century* (Amsterdam: Harwood Academic Publishers) pp. 175–202.

Meselson, M. (2000), 'Averting the Hostile Exploitation of Biotechnology', *The CBW Conventions Bulletin*, No. 48, 16–19.

Mukerji, C. (1989), *A Fragile Power: Scientists and the State* (Princeton: Princeton University Press).

National Research Council (1997), *Toxicologic Assessment of the Army's Zinc Cadmium Sulfide Dispersion Tests* (Washington, DC: National Academy Press).

Nelkin, D. (1992), *Controversy: the Politics of Technical Decisions* (London: Sage).

Ovendale, R. (ed.) (1994), *British Defence Policy since 1945* (Manchester: Manchester University Press).

Pearson, G. (1995), 'Farewell to Arms', *Chemistry in Britain*, 31(10), 782–6.

Pile, J.C., Malone, J.D., Eitzen, E.M. and Freidlander, A.M. (1998), 'Anthrax as a Potential Biological Warfare Agent', *Arch. Intern. Med.*, 158, 429–34.

Porter, D. (1999), *Health, Civilization and the State: a History of Public Health from Ancient to Modern Times* (London: Routledge) p. 88.

Porter, R. (1997), *The Greatest Benefit to Mankind: a Medical History of Humanity from Antiquity to the Present* (London: HarperCollins).

Poupard, J.A., Miller, L.A. and Granshaw, L. (1989), 'The Use of Smallpox as a Weapon in the French and Indian War of 1763', *American Society of Microbiology News*, 55(3), 122–4.

Regis, E. (1999), *The Biology of Doom: the History of America's Secret Germ Warfare Project* (New York: Holt).

Rogers, P., Whitby, S. and Dando, M. (1999), 'Biological Warfare against Crops', *Scientific American*, 280(6), 61–7.

Roskill, S. (1970, 1972, 1974), *Hankey: Man of Secrets* (3 vols) (London: Collins).

Rouse, J. (1987), *Knowledge and Power: Towards a Political Philosophy of Science* (Ithaca: Cornell University Press).

Shanson, D.C. (1999), *Microbiology in Clinical Practice* (Oxford: Butterworth Heinemann).

Sismondo, S. (1993), 'Some Social Constructions', *Social Studies of Science*, 23, 515–53.

SIPRI (1971), *The Problem of Chemical and Biological Warfare*. Vol. II: *CB Weapons Today* (Stockholm: Almqvist & Wiksell).

SIPRI (1971), *The Problem of Chemical and Biological Warfare*. Vol. IV. *CB Disarmament Negotiations 1920–1970* (Stockholm: Almqvist & Wiksell).

Sisson, H.A. (1938), *On Guard against Gas* (London: Hutchinson and Co).

Sontag, S. (1989), *AIDS And Its Metaphors* (New York: Anchor).

Spinardi, G. (1997), 'Aldermaston and British Nuclear Weapons Development: Testing the "Zuckerman Thesis"', *Social Studies of Science*, 27(4), 547–82.

Sturdy, S. (1998), 'War as Experiment. Physiology, Innovation and Administration in Britain, 1914–1918: the Case of Chemical Warfare' in Cooter, R., Harrison, M. and Sturdy, S. (eds) *War, Medicine and Modernity* (Stroud: Sutton) pp. 65–84.

Tomes, N. (1998), *The Gospel of Germs: Men, Women and the Microbe in American Life* (Harvard: Harvard University Press).

Van Courtland Moon, J.E. (1999), 'US Biological Warfare Planning and Preparedness: the Dilemmas of Policy', in Geissler, E. and van Courtland Moon, J.E. (eds) *Biological and Toxin Weapons: Research, Development and Use from the Middle Ages to 1945* (Oxford: Oxford University Press) pp. 215–54.

Weart, S. (1988), *Nuclear Fear: a History of Images* (Harvard: Harvard University Press).

Wheelis, M. (1999), 'Biological Sabotage in World War I' in Geissler, E. and van Courtland Moon, J.E. (eds) *Biological and Toxin Weapons: Research Development and Use from the Middle Ages to 1945* (Oxford: Oxford University Press) pp. 35–62.

Whittemore, G.F. Jr (1975), 'World War I, Poison Gas, and the Ideals of American Chemists', *Social Studies of Science*, 5, 133–63.

Williams, R.E.O. (1985), *Microbiology for the Public Health: the Evolution of the Public Health Laboratory Service* (London: PHLS).

Wright, S. (1990), 'Evolution of Biological Warfare Policy: 1945–1990' in Wright, S. (ed.) *Preventing a Biological Arms Race* (Cambridge, Mass.: MIT Press) pp. 26–68.

Yearley, S. (1992), *The Green Case* (London: Routledge).

Zilinskas, R. (ed.) (2000), *Biological Warfare: Modern Offense and Defense* (Boulder, Colo.: Lynne Rienner).

Index

Actinobacillus mallei, see glanders
Admiralty, 20, 60, 164, 171, 203 (n. 59)
  and biological warfare policy, 141, 158
  and sea trials, 106, 111, 122–3, 126
Advisory Council on Scientific Policy, 168
Advisory Council on Scientific Research
    and Technical Development,
    see Scientific Advisory Council
aerobiology, 179, 231 (n. 156)
Air Ministry, 20, 133
  and biological bomb, 67, 79–91, 93,
    101, 124, 138, 154
  and biological warfare policy, 126, 158
  and Biological Warfare Subcommittee,
    60
  and field trials, 113, 122–3
  vulnerability, 125
  and weapons of mass destruction, 65
  see also Air Staff
Air Raids Precautions Department (Home
    Office), 19–20, 26–7
Air Staff, 12, 177–8
  biological bomb, 66, 79–91, 100–1
  see also Air Ministry
Allen, Philip, 47–9
anthrax, 19–20, 26, 29, 31–2,
    44, 49, 51, 117
anti-anthrax serum, 20, 26–7
Antigua, *see* Operation Harness
anti-livestock weapon (cattle cake), 11,
    39–41, 43, 45, 50, 53, 55, 185
  bomb, 39, 41–2, 45–52, 54, 56, 83,
    89, 121, 209 (n. 57)
  characteristics of, 3, 206 (n. 127)
  outbreak, 42, 195 (n. 12),
    204 (n. 65, n. 71)
  in sabotage, 14
  sea trials, 106–8
  sprayed, 71, 206 (n. 127)
  and US programme, 46, 142
Argentina, 14
atomic warfare, 1, 11, 55, 58, 113, 135,
    176, 221 (n. 6), 222 (n. 54)
  assessment, 68

biological warfare, comparison, 59,
    62–6, 80, 85–7, 96–7, 126, 129–30,
    133, 136, 154, 162–3, 185
  UK policy, 143, 147, 158, 228 (n. 40)
  and USSR, 71, 164
Australia, 173–4

Bacillus anthracis, see anthrax
Bacillus globigii, 36, 125, 194 (n. 7),
    220 (n. 117), 230 (n. 125)
  land trials, 175, 182, 227 (n. 24)
  sea trials, 107, 179–80
Bacillus prodigiosus, 15, 36, 118, 174,
    198 (n. 10), 227 (n. 24)
Bacillus subtilis, see Bacillus globigii
bacteria, *see under individual agents*
bacteriological warfare, *see* biological
    warfare
Bacterium tularense, see tularemia
Bahamas, *see* Operation Harness;
    Operation Ozone; Operation
    Negation
Banting, Frederick, 32–4, 201 (n. 13)
Ben Lomond, HMS, 106–7, 126, 157
biological bombs, 9, 15, 19–21, 26, 38,
    68, 128, 133, 151, 157, 159
  B/E1, 121
  cluster, 68, 82, 85, 88–9, 160
  E48, 87–9
  E61, 121
  M114, 89
  N-bomb, 11, 44–6, 54–5, 185: test,
    41–2; US order, 47–53, 56, 186
  plans for, 66–7, 72, 74, 79–91, 138, 144
  sea trials, 106, 108
  shells, 34–5
  see also Experimental Plant No. 2;
    Project Red Admiral
Biological Research Advisory Board
    (BRAB), 67, 142, 185
  assessment of biological warfare,
    128–30, 140
  and bomb, 66, 80–5
  and defensive measures, 72–4, 176

dissolution, 187
and dissolution of Ministry of Supply, 168–70
and experimental plants, 91–103
and London Underground, 180–2
and Operation Cauldron, 111–13, 117–18
and Operation Harness, 104–5, 109
and Operation Hesperus, 119–21
and Operation Negation, 124–5
and Operation Ozone, 124
research policy, 157, 167, 222 (n. 29, n. 56)
and sabotage, 152, 159
and staff, 74–6
terms of reference, 60
and US programme, 136–8, 142–3
and virology, 119–20
Biological and Toxin Weapons Convention, 187, 233 (n. 5)
biological warfare (BW)
anti-crop, 10, 17, 37–9, 53, 69, 80, 135, 163
anti-livestock, 10, 17, 31, 35, 43, 62, 80, 120, 154, 163
definition, 3, 21, 31
early use, 8–9
expenditure, 12, 66–8, 77–8, 130, 154–5, 162, 177–8, 220 (n. 102)
operational assessment, 176–7
research policy, 34, 40, 56–60, 62–3, 67–8, 72, 96–103, 112–14, 128–56, 174, 222 (n. 29)
UK policy, 2, 9–13, 19, 30, 34, 38, 40, 43, 47–54, 130–2, 135–8, 144–7, 156, 158, 162–7, 173, 176–8, 182–5, 223 (n. 75)
as untried warfare, 1–2, 16, 68–72, 85–7, 96, 128–9, 132–3, 136
see also under individual agents and biological weapons; civil research; defensive measures; ethics; sabotage
Biological Warfare Committee (Cabinet), 11, 42, 45, 48, 50, 52
Defence Panel, 47
Defence Subcommittee, 46–7
early discussion of BW, 32–6
exclusion from decision-making, 37, 39, 53–4, 186

Operational Panel, 47
Policy Panel, 47
and Special Operations Executive, 43–4
terms of reference, 32
Biological Warfare Subcommittee (Chiefs of Staff), 12, 87, 146
and biological bomb, 66, 83, 89
and defensive measures, 72–4
dissolution, 155–7
and experimental plants, 93–7, 101
and image of BW, 147–9
and Operation Cauldron, 111–14
and Operation Harness, 104–7, 110
and Operation Hesperus, 116
and Operation Ozone, 124
priority of BW, 66
and research policy, 72
and sabotage, 151–3
terms of reference, 60
threat assessment, 68–9, 129–30
and US programme, 132–4, 142
and weapons of mass destruction, 63
see also Inter-Services Subcommittee on Biological Warfare
biological weapons
aerosols, 9, 41, 53, 121
characteristics, 3–5
contaminated bullets, 26, 31, 33–6, 69
estimated effect, 16–19, 68–9, 82, 85–7, 89, 130, 133–4
glass containers, 15, 17, 26, 35
incapacitating, 3–4, 64, 77, 81, 84, 98, 114, 174, 177
limitations, 16, 31, 35, 39, 81–2, 89, 158, 164
recoil, 31, 40, 59, 114
sprayed, 15, 17, 25, 30, 33, 35, 39, 68–9, 82, 88, 121, 124, 174–5, 179–80
strategic use, 11, 68, 72, 80–5, 96, 132, 165, 177
tactical use, 80–1, 99, 134, 163–5, 177, 221 (n. 22)
as weapons of mass destruction, 62–5, 67
see also biological bombs; biological warfare
Biology Department Porton, 37–8, 42–3, 45, 53, 55, 74
future plans for, 56–8
see also Porton Down

bioterrorism, 2, 187
Birmingham University, 76
'Blitz', 38
Bottomley, Norman, 52, 56, 206 (n. 120)
botulinum toxin, 49, 80, 117
  characteristics, 4
  Second World War, research, 35, 40,
    43, 45
  tactical use, 134, 221 (n. 22)
  and US programme, 46
  see also botulism
botulism, 4, 19, 83, 209 (n. 57), 212 (n. 11)
Brook, Norman, 151
Brown, Ernest, 47–9
Brucella, species: *Brucella abortus*; *Brucella
    canis*; *Brucella melitensis, Brucella suis,
    see* brucellosis
brucellosis, 142, 217 (n. 28), 218
    (n. 50)
  bomb, suitability for, 83, 88–9,
    209 (n. 57)
  characteristics, 4, 216 (n. 22)
  sea trials, 107–25, 219 (n. 76)
Bufton, Sydney, 150
bursting chambers, *see* explosion
  chambers
Butler, Edwin, 203 (n. 38)

Cabinet
  decisions on CBW, 12–13, 157–8, 178
  Civil Defence Committee, 73
  Defence Committee, 59, 62, 123, 136,
    141, 147, 178
  see also Biological Warfare Committee;
    War Cabinet
Cambridge University, 76
Camp Detrick, 46, 88, 142–3
  and Operation Harness, 106, 109
Camus, Albert, 1, 187
Canada, 32, 42, 51, 57, 67
  BW research, 2, 69, 110–11, 172,
    217 (n. 38)
  collaboration with UK, 10, 43,
    87–9, 106, 130–1
  and Large Area Concept, 160
  Suffield, 88, 111, 116, 134,
    218 (n. 50)
  see also tripartite collaboration
Carroll, John, 171, 231 (n. 140)
cattle cake, *see* anthrax

Cawood, Walter, 125–6, 180–1,
    231 (n. 140)
  biography, 220 (n. 120)
  and BW policy, 147, 177
  and sea trials, 179
  and US programme, 142
Centre for Applied Microbiology and
    Research (CAMR), 187, 233 (n. 7)
Chamberlain, Neville, 30, 184
Chatfield, Lord, 29–30
Cherwell, Lord, 50
Chemical Defence Experimental
    Establishment (CDEE), 11, 19, 36, 92,
    187, 227 (n. 28)
  and biological bomb, 79, 87
  and Large Area Concept, 160, 175
  and sea trials, 179
  see also Porton Down
chemical warfare (CW), 14, 32, 98, 129,
    132, 154, 157, 160, 164–5, 167,
    197 (n. 38), 231 (n. 152)
  Air Staff requirement, 84
  biological warfare, comparison, 16, 18,
    20, 35, 41, 45, 50, 65, 105, 109
  definition, 194–5 (n. 8), 228 (n. 41)
  expenditure, 12, 162, 166, 177–8
  operational assessment, 176–7
  UK policy, 37, 135–8, 144–6, 158, 162,
    177–8, 226 (n. 6)
  as untried warfare, 1
cholera, 14, 17, 31, 120, 197 (n. 35)
Chiefs of Staff Planning Committee,
    164–6
Churchill, Winston, 36, 151
  and BW policy, 40
  and N-bomb, 48–50
civil research, 56–7, 74, 102–3, 168–70
Clostridium botulinum, *see* botulinum
    toxin; botulism
Cockburn, Robert, 138, 222 (n. 48)
Cockcroft, John, 138–9, 221 (n. 6),
    222 (n. 48)
Cold War, 2, 55, 187
Combe, Gerard, 83
Committee of Imperial Defence, 15, 19,
    22, 27
Committee of Imperial Defence
    Subcommittee on Bacteriological
    Warfare, 10, 24, 28, 32–3, 51, 74
  intelligence, 25–6

Subcommittee on Emergency
Bacteriological Services, 24
Subcommittee on Emergency Public
Health Laboratory Services, 24
terms of reference, 19
Cooper, Duff, 42, 46–7
cowpox, 124–5
Crawford, Kenneth, 222 (n. 48)
and priority of BW, 76, 96–100,
116, 129–30
and publicity, 149
and research policy, 135
and sabotage, 152–4
and US programme, 131–4

Davidson Pratt, J., 45, 101,
206 (n. 120)
Defence Microbiology Division, 187
Defence Research Policy Committee
(DRPC), 65, 67, 74, 77, 142, 158
assessment of BW, 88, 129, 138–9,
143–8, 164, 177
and biological bomb, 66–7, 84–5
and biological warfare policy, 164, 171
and chemical warfare policy, 158
and expenditure on BW, 167
and experimental plants, 91–103
and field trials, 111, 176
and Large Area Concept, 176
and priority of BW, 64, 66, 72, 75, 92,
154–7, 159, 170–1
and publicity, 150
terms of reference and responsibilities,
60–2, 129, 221 (n. 6)
see also Defence Research
Policy Staff
Defence Research Policy Staff (DRPS)
and BW policy, 158, 162–7
and expenditure on BW,
155, 162, 166–7
responsibilities, 226 (n. 134)
and sea trials, 126–7
see also Defence Research Policy
Committee
defensive measures, 11, 62, 72–4, 140,
143–4, 178
antibiotics, 62
antitoxins, 19–20, 27–8
gas masks, 26, 73, 176
sera, 20, 26, 28–9

vaccination, 17, 29, 68, 72–3,
107, 140, 163
Department of Scientific and Industrial
Research, 102, 168
detection, 179
and defence, 73, 140
and research policy, 68, 72, 140, 162,
175–6, 183
Dodds, Charles, 159, 168, 181,
215 (n. 117), 222 (n. 48)
biography, 226–7 (n. 17)
Douglas, Captain Stewart Ranken, 15–20
biography, 198 (n. 8)
Dugway, 46, 88, 111, 218 (n. 50)
dysentery, 23

early warning, *see* detection
eastern equine encephalitis, 124
Eden, Anthony, 225 (n. 131)
Edgewood Arsenal, 142
Emergency Public Health Laboratory
Service, 10, 22–4, 27–9, 184
epidemics, 3, 15–18, 21–4, 29, 31, 33, 35,
39, 43, 45, 53–4, 59, 61–2, 64
Escherichia coli, 179–80
ethics, 18, 51, 64, 76, 82, 145, 163
Exercise St Jo(e), 143, 223 (n. 74)
Experimental Plant No. 1, 11, 75, 91–3
Experimental Plant No. 2, 12, 78,
91–103, 126, 128–31, 139–40,
142, 157
expertise, 6–8, 184–6
explosion (bursting) chambers, 61, 83,
111, 113, 126, 130

field trials, 34, 83, 97, 130, 157
land, 12–13, 46, 87–9, 111, 118,
120, 154
Norwich, 172
pathogen, 12, 61, 79
Salisbury, 112
sea, 12–13, 78–9, 103, 127–8, 157,
179–80, 218 (n. 48)
simulant, 13, 61, 116–17, 172–5,
179–82
Whitehall, 125
see also Gruinard Island; London
Underground; Operation
Cauldron; Operation Harness;
Operation Hesperus; Operation

field trials – *continued*
Ozone; Operation Negation; zinc cadmium sulphide
Fildes, Paul Gordon, 11, 41, 53–4, 74, 169, 186, 206 (n. 127)
arrival at Porton, 38–9
biography, 202 (n. 32), 206 (n. 126)
and experimental plants, 96, 100–2
and future of Biology Department, 55–9
and influence of BRAB, 139, 169–70
and Large Area Concept, 170, 182
and N-bomb, 41–2, 45–53, 113, 186
and sabotage, 152–3
and sea trials, 104, 114–16, 124–5
and Special Operations Executive, 43–5
and US programme, 46, 142
and virology, 119–20
Findlay, H.T., 134, 152
First World War, 9, 14, 23, 197 (n. 38)
Fisher, Reginald, 173–4
flies, 40, 45
Florey, Howard Walter, 75, 120
biography, 211 (n. 101)
and experimental plants, 92–3, 100
foot and mouth, 31, 120, 154
France, 30, 32, 38, 148, 197 (n. 35)
BW research programme, 2, 34–5, 41
Paris Metro, 15
Francisella tularensis, see tularemia
Fraser, Lord, 131
Fred, Edwin B., 46

gas gangrene, 20, 27
Geneva Protocol (1925), 14, 30, 60, 86, 98, 136–7, 154, 163, 165, 233 (n. 5)
Germany, 10–11, 19, 29–30, 33, 39, 44, 58, 184–5
BW research programme, 53, 55, 148, 200 (n. 40)
intelligence on, 25–6, 49, 71
germ theory, 9, 53
germ warfare, *see* biological warfare
Gladstone, Gareth, 37
glanders, 14, 44, 107, 216 (n. 18)
Global Strategy Review (Chiefs of Staff), 135–8, 141

Griffith, F., 21, 199 (n. 17)
Gruinard Island, 41–2, 44–5, 104, 113, 204 (n. 64)
Gulf War, 187

Hankey, Maurice Pascal Alers, 11, 15–16, 29–30, 48, 139
biography, 198 (n. 6)
and BW Committee (Cabinet), 32–3, 53, 184, 186, 201 (n. 11)
and BW Subcommittee (Chiefs of Staff), 73
and BW Subcommittee (Committee of Imperial Defence), 19–20, 25, 28
and early plans for Porton, 36–41
and field trials, 114, 119
and secrecy, 27
and Special Operations Executive, 43
Haskins, Caryl, 70, 110–11
Henderson, David Willis Wilson, 37, 55, 138–9, 186, 222 (n. 48)
biography, 202 (n. 34)
and BW assessment, 140
and BW bomb, 83, 87–8, 90
and experimental plants, 91–2, 96–7, 102
and field trials, 126, 219 (n. 76)
and future of Biology Department, 57–9, 61–2
and Large Area Concept, 161–2, 171, 173, 175
and London Underground, 181
and Operation Cauldron, 111
and Operation Harness, 104–5, 107, 109–10
and Operation Hesperus, 116, 118
and publicity, 150
and sabotage, 126–7, 153–4, 156, 159
and staff, 75
and US programme, 46, 87–8, 133, 136–7, 142–3, 215 (n. 117)
high explosive, 35, 51
Hitler, Adolf, 53
Hoare, Samuel, 24
Home Defence Committee, 60, 72
Home Office, 60, 164
Horn Island, 46
Hulme, Henry, 66

influenza, 120
intelligence reports, 11, 14, 25–8, 34,
    49, 97, 164
    see under individual countries
Inter-Services Subcommittee on
    Biological Warfare (ISSBW),
    52–3, 74
    and defensive measures, 72
    and experimental plants, 91
    planning for BW, 55–8, 60
    see also Biological Warfare
        Subcommittee
Ismay, Hastings, 52
Italy, 148

Japan, 2, 148, 203 (n. 39)
Jarman, Lance, 126
Joint Intelligence Committee (JIC),
    60, 70–2, 130, 155
    and publicity, 149–51
Joint Technical Warfare Committee
    (Chiefs of Staff), 59, 61

Kaffa, siege of, 8
Koch, Robert, 9
Korean War, 113, 136–7, 154

Laidlaw, Patrick, 30, 33, 201 (n. 11),
    202 (n. 23)
Lamb, George, 70
Landsborough Thomson, A., 199 (n. 17),
    201 (n. 11)
Large Area Concept (LAC), 12, 163,
    180, 182–3, 185
    definition, 160
    and early warning, 175–6
    and sabotage, 181–2
    trials, 161–2, 170–5
League of Nations, 16–17, 199 (n. 14)
Ledingham, John Charles Grant,
    21, 27, 199 (n. 17), 201 (n. 11),
    202 (n. 23)
    biography, 198 (n. 8)
    early plans for BW research, 34–7
    initial memo on BW, 15–20
Littler, William, 176, 231 (n. 140)
London School of Hygiene and Tropical
    Medicine, 15, 119
London Underground, 15, 125, 180–2
Lister Institute, 15, 37, 58, 169

McAuliffe, A.C., 132–4
Macmillan, Harold, 178
mass destruction, weapons of, 12, 143,
    176, 208 (n. 41)
    biological weapons as, 62–5, 67, 129,
        136, 185
    policy, 62, 79
mass production, 11–12, 62, 68, 79,
    214 (n. 65)
    and N-bomb, 47–53
    and USSR, 70–2, 153–4
    see also Experimental Plant No. 1;
        Experimental Plant No. 2
Medical Research Council (MRC), 10, 19,
    26, 36, 43, 55, 58, 133, 169, 198 (n. 7)
    assessment of BW potential, 29–33
    Bacterial Chemistry Unit, 37
    and civilian bacteriological service,
        21, 24
    defensive measures, 72–4, 152–3
    and experimental plants, 91–2, 102
    staff, 74
    and Wickham Steed affair, 15
Mellanby, Edward, 19, 23, 34, 199 (n. 17),
    201 (n. 11)
    assessment of BW potential, 29–32
    biography, 199 (n. 18)
    and defensive measures, 73
    and early plans for Porton, 36–7
Merck, George W., 46
MI5, 125
Microbiological Research Department
    (MRD), 59, 78, 117, 122, 125–6, 156
    and biological bomb, 79–80, 83–4
    and defensive measures, 73, 140
    expenditure, 154–5
    and experimental plants, 92, 94–5, 102
    and Ministry of Supply, 60
    recruitment, 66–7, 74–7, 98–9, 120,
        129, 168
    and research policy, 157
    and sabotage, 152
    and virology, 119–20
    visit to, 149–51
    see also Porton Down
Microbiological Research Establishment
    (MRE), 159, 161, 183, 186–7
    and civil work, 167–8
    and dissolution of Ministry of Supply,
        168–70

Microbiological Research Establishment
(MRE) – *continued*
   and Large Area Concept, 172, 175, 180
   see also Porton Down
microthread technique, 180
Middlesex Hospital, 37
Miles, Arnold Ashley, 169, 172, 181
Ministry of Agriculture and Fisheries,
   26, 42
Ministry of Aviation, 125, 168–9, 171
Ministry of Defence, 92, 126, 138, 153, 169
Ministry of Economic Warfare, *see* Special
   Operations Executive
Ministry of Health, 23–4, 32, 60, 102
   and defensive measures, 72–4, 153
Ministry of Supply, 45, 74, 143
   and biological bomb, 83–4, 138
   and BRAB, 60
   and BW policy, 139–41, 144–6
   and defence research budget,
      154–5, 162, 166–7
   dissolution, 168–70
   and experimental plants, 91, 100
   and field trials, 105, 113, 123,
      126, 171–2, 181
   and Large Area Concept, 160, 171–2
   and sabotage, 153
Morrison, Herbert, 37
Morton, John, 116–17, 160, 172–3,
   219 (n. 73), 227–8 (n. 39)

N, *see* anthrax
Narvik, HMS, 106–7
National Gas Turbine Establishment, 175
National Institute for Medical Research,
   15, 30, 153
Newcastle disease, 120
Newitt, Dudley Maurice, 43–5, 53
Nixon, Richard M., 187
North Atlantic Treaty Organisation
   (NATO), 178, 231 (n. 152)
Norway, 14

Offensive Evaluation Committee
   (Ministry of Supply), 160–1, 172–4
Operation Aladdin, *see* Operation
   Vegetarian
Operation Cauldron, 110–19, 122,
   149–50, 218 (n. 60)
Operation Harness, 78, 88, 104–10

Operation Hesperus, 116–21, 122,
   219 (n. 73, n. 76)
Operation Negation, 124–5, 127
Operation Ozone, 120–4
Operation Vegetarian, 40–1, 48
Oxford University, 75

paratyphoid, 19, 23
Parnham Sound, *see* Operation Harness
Pasteur, Louis, 9
Pasteurella pestis, *see* plague
pathogens, 3, 194 (n. 7)
   see under individual diseases
Peck, Richard, 48, 52, 201 (n. 11)
penicillin, 70
Pidcock, Geoffrey, 87–8
Pike, Thomas, 146, 155
Pine Bluff, 101, 142
Pittman, R.W., 162, 174
plague, 1, 8, 31, 71, 89, 118
   characteristics, 4, 218 (n. 58)
   plans to use, 80, 82
   sea trials, 107, 114–15, 117,
      216 (n. 18), 219 (n. 76)
Porton Down, 10–12, 14, 33, 48,
   182, 185
   establishment of BW programme at,
      36–41
   see also Biology Department Porton;
      Chemical Defence Experimental
      Station; Microbiological Research
      Department; Microbiological
      Research Establishment
Porton Executive Committee, 43, 45
   terms of reference, 41
Porton Experiments Committee,
   37–9, 41, 48
Postgraduate Medical School, University
   of London, 76
Project Red Admiral, 79, 90, 93, 101,
   211 (n. 1)
   see also biological bombs
Psittacosis, 31, 107, 120, 122, 124,
   216 (n. 18), 220 (n. 100)
public health, 9–11, 17–24, 26–9,
   38, 55, 71–2, 74, 184
Public Health Laboratory Service, *see*
   Emergency Public Health Laboratory
   Service
Public Record Office (PRO), 5

publicity, 58, 137, 178
  newspapers, 15, 20, 26, 77, 123,
    147–51, 224 (n. 102)
  Parliamentary questions, 27
  compare secrecy

Q fever, 120, 161

rabies, 31, 80
ricin, 212 (n. 19)
rickettsiae, 194 (n. 6)
Rideal, Eric, 167
rinderpest, 120, 154
risk, sociology of, 7–8
Romania, 14, 26
Rothschild, Lord, 47–8, 52
Royal Air Force (RAF), 12, 42, 175
  and biological bomb, 79–91
  see also Air Staff; Air Ministry
Royal Society, 57
Russia, 197 (n. 35)
  see also Soviet Union
rust, wheat, 135, 202 (n. 36)

sabotage, 19–22, 31, 33–5, 44, 69–70,
    99, 136, 156, 185, 187
  anti-livestock, 62, 136, 154
  First World War, 14
  and Large Area Concept, 181–2
  London Underground, 180–2
  and other BW, 125–7, 159, 177
  reservoirs, 17, 68, 151–4
  US, 132
  USSR, 71
Scientific Advisory Council (Ministry of
    Supply), 60, 169, 207 (n. 26)
  and Large Area Concept, 170, 175
  and sea trials, 125–6
Scotland, 12
  see Gruinard Island; Operation
      Cauldron; Operation Hesperus
Second World War, 2, 9, 11, 55, 60, 93,
    113, 115, 146, 148, 153
  UK BW programme, 36–53, 55–9, 186
secrecy, 2, 5–6, 27, 36–7, 40, 52, 168,
    185–6
  and anthrax, 42
  and BRAB, 139
  and field trials, 105–7, 114–15,
    123, 181

and newspapers, 147–51
  compare publicity
Serratia marcescens, *see Bacillus prodigiosus*
simulants, *see* field trials; zinc cadmium
    sulphide
Sisson, H.A., 29–30, 201 (n. 1)
smallpox, 8, 120, 124
Smith, Wilson, 120, 122, 124, 168–9,
    176, 181, 215 (n. 117)
Soviet Union, 10, 26, 55, 150, 187,
    195 (n. 12)
  atomic weapons, 62, 96, 129, 157
  BW research programme, 2
  as BW target, 81–2, 85–7, 135, 163, 177
  intelligence on, 63, 70–2, 98, 119,
    130, 153–4
  as potential BW users, 136–7, 152,
    163–5
Spain, 14, 23, 26
Special Operations Executive (SOE),
    37, 42–5
Spooner, Edward, 119, 122, 181,
    215 (n. 117), 231 (n. 138)
Stamp, Trevor, 93, 114–16, 118
  and field trials, 116–17
  and sabotage, 152–3
Stevenson Committee, 132
Stimson, Henry L., 46
Stolzenberg, Hugo, 26
Stone, J.F.S., 153
streptomycin, 93
Suez crisis, 166–7, 225 (n. 131)

tetanus, 20, 31, 44
  antitoxin, 19–20, 27
Thorneycroft, Peter, 181
Tizard, Henry Thomas, 61, 138
  biography, 208 (n. 32)
  and experimental plants, 95, 99
  and publicity, 77, 148–9
Todd, Alexander, 177
Topley, William Whiteman Carlton,
    15, 25, 28, 39, 41, 199 (n. 17),
    201 (n. 11), 202 (n. 23)
  biography, 198 (n. 8)
  and Emergency Public Health
      Laboratory Service, 21–4
  initial memo on BW, 16–20
  response to Banting, 33
  and secrecy, 27

toxic dust, 41
toxins, 84
  definition, 3
  see also botulinum toxin; ricin
Treasury, 19, 76, 104, 120
trials, *see* field trials
tripartite collaboration, 87–9, 109–10,
    136, 138, 164, 166
  division of labour, 130–1
  and Large Area Concept, 160, 162
  and sabotage, 159, 180
  see also United States; Canada
tularemia, 31, 121, 161
  characteristics, 4
  sea trials, 107–8, 118–19, 124–5,
    219 (n. 76)
  suitability for BW, 88
typhoid, 10, 17, 19–20, 23, 31, 82, 120

Union of Soviet Socialist Republics
    (USSR), *see* Soviet Union
United Nations Atomic Energy
    Commission, 63
United States (US), 42, 57, 185
  BW policy, 64, 110–11, 132–4, 158–9
  BW research programme, 2, 46,
    50, 59, 101–2, 111, 134–7,
    142–3, 172, 174
  collaboration with UK, 10, 43, 45,
    87–9, 93–6, 99–101, 106, 118,
    130–4, 139, 141, 144, 147, 159,
    166–7, 178
  Committee on Biological Warfare,
    64, 69
  and detection of BW agents, 175
  and Large Area Concept, 160–1
  and N-bomb, 47–52, 56
  and sabotage, 14, 154, 181
  weapons, 63, 88–9, 118, 131–2, 135,
    233 (n. 2)
  see also Camp Detrick; Dugway;
    Edgewood Arsenal; Horn Island;
    Pine Bluff; Vigo Plant

University College Hospital, 120
University College London, 58

vaccinia virus, *see* cowpox
variola virus, *see* smallpox
Venezuelan equine encephalitis,
    118–19, 122, 124, 218 (n. 60)
Vigo Plant, 50
viruses, 21, 33, 46, 74, 89, 119–20,
    216, 219 (n. 83)
  see also under individual agents

Wales, 42
Wansborough-Jones, Owen Haddon,
    59, 120, 168, 206 (n. 120), 222 (n. 48)
  biography, 207 (n. 17)
  and biological bomb, 88
  and BW policy, 138–9
  and experimental plants, 102, 138
  and field trials, 113–14, 118
  and Large Area Concept, 171
  and publicity, 77, 150
  and US programme, 133, 142, 159, 167
War Cabinet, 11, 29–30, 32–3, 40, 43
  exclusion from decision-making,
    36–7, 53
  and N-bomb, 47–50
War Office, 60, 123, 153, 158, 168–9
White, Bruce, 153
Wickham Steed, Henry, 15–16, 19, 25
Woods, Donald, 37, 181

X-base, *see* Gruinard Island
X toxin, *see* botulinum toxin

yellow fever, 31
Yersinia pestis, *see* plague

zinc cadmium sulphide, 161–2,
    170–2, 227 (n. 28)
  see also field trials; Large Area Concept
Zuckerman, Solly, 176–7
  biography, 230 (n. 134)